Climate Change Law and Practice

Climate Change Law and Practice

Dr Louise Smail

Bloomsbury Professional
LONDON • DUBLIN • EDINBURGH • NEW YORK • NEW DELHI • SYDNEY

BLOOMSBURY PROFESSIONAL
Bloomsbury Publishing Plc
50 Bedford Square, London, WC1B 3DP, UK
1385 Broadway, New York, 10018, USA
Bloomsbury Publishing Ireland Ltd
29 Earlsfort Terrace, Dublin 2, D02 AY28, Ireland

BLOOMSBURY and the Diana logo are trademarks of Bloomsbury Publishing Plc

First published in Great Britain 2025

1

British Library Cataloguing-in-Publication Data

A catalogue record for this book is available from the British Library.

ISBN:	PB:	978 1 52653 145 2
	Epdf:	978 1 52653 147 6
	Epub:	978 1 52653 146 9

Typeset by Evolution Design and Digital Ltd (Kent)

For product safety related questions contact productsafety@bloomsbury.com

To find out more about our authors and books visit www.bloomsburyprofessional.com. Here you will find extracts, author information, details of forthcoming events and the option to sign up for our newsletters

Preface

Climate change is one of the most pressing issues of our time and is affecting many parts of the world. As the impacts of climate change become increasingly evident, there is a critical need for robust legal frameworks to address these challenges. This book, *Climate Change Law and Practice*, aims to provide a comprehensive overview of the legal mechanisms and practices that have been developed to combat climate change, particularly focusing on key cases from around the world.

The field of climate change law is relatively new, but it has rapidly evolved over the past few decades. It encompasses a wide range of legal disciplines, including environmental law, human rights law, international law, and corporate law. This interdisciplinary nature makes climate change law a complex and dynamic field, requiring a deep understanding of various legal principles and their application to climate-related issues.

One of the most significant developments in climate change law has been the increase in the number of climate litigation cases. As governments and corporations have been slow to take meaningful action to reduce greenhouse gas (GHG) emissions, individuals and organisations have increasingly turned to the courts to seek justice and accountability. Climate litigation has become a powerful tool for driving climate action and holding those responsible for climate change accountable.

KEY CASES IN CLIMATE CHANGE LAW

Urgenda Foundation v State of the Netherlands is a landmark case in climate change litigation. In 2015, the Dutch court ordered the government to reduce its GHG emissions by at least 25 per cent by 2020 compared to 1990 levels. The court's decision was based on the government's duty of care to protect its citizens from the dangers of climate change, making it one of the first cases to establish a legal obligation for governments to take climate action. Urgenda argued that the Dutch state was legally obliged to take action to reduce emissions to avert catastrophic harm, while the state acknowledged the facts of climate change but rejected the idea that it could be legally obliged to act.

The case went through several appeals, with the Hague Court of Appeal upholding the 2015 court decision in 2018. The Dutch Government continued to challenge the ruling, arguing against the Court of Appeal's findings, including the human rights-based obligation to reduce emissions. However, in December 2019, the Supreme Court of the Netherlands confirmed the lower courts' decisions, stating that the Dutch Government must reduce emissions immediately in line with its human rights obligations. This case set a significant precedent for future climate litigation, emphasising the importance of integrating human rights considerations into climate policies.

Verein KlimaSeniorinnen Schweiz v Switzerland is a landmark case in climate change litigation. The case was brought by an association of senior women, known as Senior Women for Climate Protection Switzerland, against the Swiss Government. The plaintiffs argued that Switzerland's inadequate climate policies violated their rights to life and health under Articles 2 and 8 of the European Convention on Human Rights (ECHR). They claimed that the government's failure to take sufficient action to reduce GHG emissions exposed them to increased health risks from heatwaves exacerbated by climate change.

After exhausting all national remedies, the plaintiffs took their case to the European Court of Human Rights (ECtHR) in 2020. They argued that the Swiss Federal Supreme Court's rejection of their case was arbitrary and violated their right to a fair trial under Article 6 of the ECHR. They also claimed that the Swiss authorities and courts failed to address the content of their complaints, violating their right to an effective remedy under Article 13.

The ECtHR accepted the case and communicated it to the Swiss Government in March 2021. The case was given priority status, and the Swiss Government was required to submit a response. The International Commission of Jurists (ICJ) and the European Network of National Human Rights Institutions (ENNHR) submitted third-party interventions, highlighting the effects of climate change on the right to life and the right to respect for private and family life.

In April 2022, the Chamber of the ECtHR relinquished jurisdiction in favour of the Grand Chamber of the Court, recognising the case's significance in interpreting the Convention. The Grand Chamber examined the case, and on 9 April 2024, it ruled that Switzerland had violated the ECHR by failing to adequately address climate change. The court found that Switzerland's climate policies were insufficient and that the government had failed to protect the plaintiffs' rights to life and private life under Articles 2 and 8 of the ECHR.

This case is significant as it is the first time an international court has ruled that state inaction on climate change violates human rights. It sets a precedent for future climate litigation and underscores the importance of robust climate policies to protect human rights in the face of climate change.

These cases represent just a few examples of the growing body of climate litigation around the world. They demonstrate the diverse legal strategies being employed to address climate change, from constitutional and human rights arguments to corporate accountability and environmental protection. As climate litigation continues to evolve, it will play an increasingly important role in shaping climate policy and driving action to mitigate the impacts of climate change.

Milieudefensie and Others v Royal Dutch Shell plc is an historic ruling in which a Dutch court ordered Royal Dutch Shell to reduce its carbon emissions by 45 per cent by 2030 compared to 2019 levels. The court found that Shell's climate policies were insufficient and that the company had a duty of care to reduce its emissions in line with the Paris Agreement. This case is a landmark in holding corporations accountable for their contributions to climate change.

Held v Montana is a case brought by 16 youth plaintiffs, marking the first case in the US to be based on a constitutional right to a healthy environment. The plaintiffs argued that Montana's energy policies, which promote and permit the extraction of fossil fuels, significantly contribute to climate change and violate their constitutional rights. They also challenged a provision within the Montana Environmental Policy Act (MEPA) that prevents state agencies from considering GHG emissions or their potential impacts on the climate during environmental reviews. This case underscores the plaintiffs' contention that the state's failure to address GHG emissions directly harms them and infringes upon their right to a clean and healthful environment.

The court, after reviewing scientific evidence on the impact of GHG emissions on climate change, concluded that the plaintiffs were indeed being harmed by climate change and that these harms could be attributed to Montana's energy policies and the state's failure to consider GHG emissions in its environmental reviews.

INTERNATIONAL TREATIES AND OPINIONS

The International Tribunal for the Law of the Sea (ITLOS) has been the first international body to issue an advisory opinion on states' obligations under the United Nations Convention on the Law of the Sea (UNCLOS) to preserve and protect oceans form the adverse effects of climate change caused by man-made GHG emissions.

Two other international courts, the Inter-American Court of Human Rights (IACtHR) and the International Court of Justice (ICJ) are expected to issue advisory opinions in 2025. Climate change law has seen a growing increase in cases against government and organisations within countries and outside. These opinions are now bringing into question what obligations states do owe each other. This seems to be happening through a series of advisory opinions which are trying to clarify the scope of state obligations concerning climate change under international law.

These are statements or interpretations of law provide by a court or tribunal in response to legal questions submitted by authorised states, agencies, international organisations or other bodies such as the UN Security Council and UN General Assembly (UNGA). An advisory opinion is not legally binding on states; however, it can be influential on the definitive interpretation of state obligations under international law.

CONCLUSION

The field of climate change law is rapidly evolving, and the cases highlighted in this book illustrate the critical role that legal mechanisms play in addressing the climate crisis. By examining these key cases, it is possible to gain a deeper understanding of the legal principles and strategies that are being used to combat climate change and hold governments and corporations accountable. As the impacts of climate change become more severe, the need for robust legal frameworks and effective climate litigation will only continue to grow. This book aims to provide a comprehensive overview of these developments and to inspire further action and innovation in the field of climate change law and practice.

Dr Louise Smail
April 2025

About the Author

Louise Smail is a specialist risk and safety consultant with extensive experience in corporate governance. Previously, Louise has worked as principal consultant and director of two international consulting groups. Louise offers clients assistance with the preparation and validation of risk management plans with the aim of ensuring clients have the highest standards in public safety. Louise has extensive experience in the fields of risk management, organisational resilience, and health, safety and environment law with a wide range of organisations, including local government, emergency services, the Cabinet Office, process and chemical industries, utilities, waste and construction. Louise gave expert evidence to the Ladbroke Grove Rail Public Inquiry.

Louise provides advice on environmental risk management including: contaminated land; writing reports; and negotiating with land owners and lease holders. Louise writes extensively and lectures on risk management and health, safety and environmental issues.

Louise is a member of the British Computer Society – Chartered Information Technology Practitioner – and is a chartered member of the Institute of Occupational Safety and Health (CMIOSH).

Louise is the editor and contributor to the book *Corporate Liability: Work related Deaths and Criminal Prosecutions* (3rd edn, February 2014). Louise is also author of *Waste Regulation Law* (2016), *Law of Renewable Energy* (2020), and *Water and Waste Regulation Law* (2024).

> 'The spring, the summer, the childing autumn, angry winter, change their wonted liveries; and the mazèd world, by their increase, now knows not which is which' (Titania, Midsommer Night's Dream)

Contents

Table of Statutes

[All references are to paragraph numbers]

Table of Statutory Instruments

[All references are to paragraph numbers]

Table of EU Legislation

[All references are to paragraph numbers]

PROPOSALS

RECOMMENDATIONS

REGULATIONS

Table of International Legislation

[All references are to paragraph numbers]

Table of International Conventions and Other Materials

[All references are to paragraph numbers]

Table of Cases

[All references are to paragraph numbers]

N

O

P

R

Chapter 1

Can Legislation Save the Planet?

1.01 Climate change law and related litigation has increased and governments and organisations are being held to account (see **Chapter 13**). Although political and change and political will is a factor in both the speed and use of climate law there is no doubt that countries not making efforts to change are now the outliers (see **Chapter 3**). This book looks at how climate change law is working and the areas where cases have been brought and their success or otherwise.

The Paris Agreement (see **3.05**) has caused many governments to review their strategy and carbon reduction aspirations in order to meet their own legally binding requirements.

THE STRINGENCY OF CLIMATE LAW

1.02 As the global community deals with the challenges posed by climate change, the evolution and implementation of climate laws have become a vital part of climate change strategy. The strictness and rigour with which these laws are designed and enforced, aiming to mitigate greenhouse gas emissions, promote sustainability, and uphold environmental integrity, is a vital part of how they will work effectively.

Defining stringent climate law

1.03 Stringent climate laws typically encompass legally binding targets for emission reductions, robust mechanisms for compliance, and comprehensive frameworks for accountability and reporting. The laws themselves can take many forms, including national regulations, regional agreements, and international treaties (see **Chapter 14**).

Some of the most notable examples include:

- **The Paris Agreement:** This agreement, adopted in 2015, aims to limit global warming to 2°C with the aim of restricting it to 1.5°C. The agreement establishes national commitments, Nationally Determined Contributions (NDCs), that countries must regularly evaluate and improve to reflect their highest level of ambition to limit global warming (see **3.05**).
- **The European Green Deal:** The European Union (EU) has set a clear pathway to becoming the world's first climate-neutral continent by 2050. This plan includes legislation aimed at reducing emissions across various sectors, promoting renewable energy, and fostering circular economies (see **7.07**).
- **National laws and regulations:** Countries such as the United Kingdom (UK) have enacted laws (see **5.02**) (the Climate Change Act 2008), which commits to legally binding carbon budgets and sets interim emission reduction targets for 2030 and beyond.

Impacts of stringent climate laws

1.04 The stringency of climate laws affects various stakeholders, including governments, corporations, and individuals:

- **Environmental impact:** Climate laws can lead to significant reductions in emissions, improved air (see **13.10**) and water quality (see **13.11**), and enhanced biodiversity protection. This can be achieved by setting clear targets and accountability mechanisms (see **13.26**) and can encourage innovation and investment in green technologies (see **13.21**).
- **Economic considerations:** While it may be argued that climate laws can impose economic burdens on industries, many studies suggest that the long-term benefits, such as job creation in renewable energy sectors and reduced healthcare costs associated with pollution outweigh the economic burdens. Transitioning to a sustainable economy does require up-front investment but can also open doors to new markets and opportunities.

- **Social implications:** Climate laws can promote social equity by ensuring that vulnerable communities are included in the transition to a low-carbon economy. Initiatives such as just transition frameworks (see **13.12**) aim to protect those affected by the shift away from fossil fuels, ensuring that no one is left behind.

Challenges to stringent climate law

1.05 Despite their importance there are several challenges to the effectiveness of stringent climate laws:

- **Political will:** The level of commitment from political leaders can vary significantly, influenced by public opinion, economic interests, and lobbying efforts. In some regions, political resistance can hinder the implementation of strict climate measures (see **13.61**).
- **Enforcement and compliance:** The efficacy of climate laws is only as good as their enforcement. A lack of resources, inadequate monitoring systems, and weak penalties for non-compliance can undermine the effectiveness of even the most robust legal frameworks (see **13.22**).
- **Global cooperation:** Climate change is a global issue and requires coordinated action across nations. The disparities in economic capacity and political priorities can create tensions in international agreements which make it challenging to uphold stringent commitments (see **Chapter 14**).

The stringency of climate law plays an important role in addressing the climate crisis and shaping the global efforts to combat environmental degradation. As countries and organisations move towards more rigorous legislation, it is essential to create comprehensive, enforceable, and equitable laws that reflect the urgency of the situation (see **7.42**). The transition toward a sustainable future will depend not only on the strictness of climate laws but on the working together of stakeholders, governments, businesses, and citizens. Only through a shared commitment to climate action and the use of effective climate change laws can we hope to safeguard our planet for future generations (see **Chapter 14**).

POLITICAL WILL AND LEADERSHIP

1.06 As the urgency of addressing climate change increases, the significance of political will and leadership in driving effective climate law becomes important. The commitment of political leaders to prioritise environmental issues and implement changes that support climate action is important. This isn't just about the relevant governments but also influential figures from the private sector, civil society, and international organisations; together, these elements play a crucial role in determining the effectiveness and enforcement of climate legislation.

- **Defining priorities:** Political will is vital for prioritising climate action on national and international agendas. Where leaders make commitments to addressing climate change, it results in the establishment of ambitious goals and the allocation of the resources necessary for implementing effective climate policies. For instance, countries that have demonstrated strong political will have made significant strides in implementing renewable energy projects and reducing greenhouse gas emissions (see **7.14**).

- **Legislative action:** Strong political will helps the passage of climate laws and leaders who prioritise climate action can mobilise legislative bodies to enact policies, set legally binding emission reduction targets, and create frameworks for accountability and enforcement. Countries like the UK and Germany have enacted ambitious climate laws driven by dedicated political leadership (see **Chapter 5** and see **Chapter 7**).
- **Public engagement and support:** Political will is reflected not only in policy decisions but also in efforts to engage the public. Leaders who communicate the importance of climate action effectively can mobilise public support and foster a culture of environmental stewardship. A well-informed electorate is more likely to advocate for and support robust climate policies, creating a feedback loop that further influences legislative action (see **Chapter 4**).

As mentioned above, however, there is also a type of leadership beyond politics:

- **Cross-sectoral leadership:** Effective climate action often requires collaboration across multiple sectors, this includes government, business, academia, and civil society. Leaders in the private sector can complement political will by investing in sustainable technologies, adopting climate-friendly practices, and holding governments accountable for climate commitments (see **Chapter 14**).
- **International cooperation:** Climate change is a global challenge that means there needs to be collaboration between countries and political leaders play a central role in fostering international cooperation through treaties and agreements, such as the Paris Agreement (see **Chapter 14**). Leadership at international climate summits can steer discussions, build coalitions, and create frameworks for collective action. Strong leadership from influential nations can set an example that drives global commitments toward stringent climate measures.
- **Innovative solutions:** Leaders can inspire innovative approaches to climate challenges, encouraging the adoption of new technologies and practices. By championing research and development in renewable energy, carbon capture, and sustainable agriculture, these leaders can catalyse advancements that align with stringent climate laws and promote long-term sustainability (see **13.44**).

Challenges to political will and leadership

1.07

- **Political polarisation:** In many countries, climate change has become a polarising issue and a divided political landscapes can hinder consensus-building and derail climate initiatives. These issues need to be navigated while fostering bipartisanship to create effective climate legislation (see **10.02**).
- **Economic pressures:** Economic interests may conflict with climate goals, particularly in fossil fuel-dependent regions. Political leaders may face resistance from industry lobbyists and this can undermine their commitment

to stringent climate action (see **3.61**). Balancing economic growth with environmental sustainability is a challenge that requires strong leadership and innovative solutions.

- **Public opinion and misinformation:** Misinformation about climate change can sway public sentiment against climate action (see **13.25**). Leaders must be proactive in educating the public and overcoming doubt to build support for climate initiatives. Transparency and clear communication about the impacts of climate change and the benefits of proposed solutions are essential for cultivating public will (see **Chapter 4**).

In summary, political will and leadership are essential elements in the formulation, implementation, and enforcement of climate law. Strong political commitment can drive legislative action, garner public support, and facilitate international cooperation. Effective leadership also extends beyond politics, covering cross-sector engagement and innovative collaboration, this bridges the gap between policy, industry, and society (see **13.07**). While there are still challenges, the resolve of leaders to prioritise climate action can significantly influence global efforts to combat climate change and shape a sustainable for future generations.

INTERNATIONAL COOPERATION AND CLIMATE CHANGE LAW

1.08 International cooperation is fundamental to addressing the global challenge of climate change (see **13.07**). Environmental issues transcend national borders, making multilateral frameworks and agreements essential for effective climate action (see **14.02**). Climate change law, therefore, is not just a domestic concern but a collective issue that requires countries to work in towards shared goals (see **Chapter 14**).

The imperative of international cooperation

1.09

- **Global nature of climate change:** Climate change caused by greenhouse gas emissions does not respect national boundaries and actions taken by one country can significantly affect others which makes it imperative for nations to collaborate on solutions (see **Chapter 14**). For example, emissions from industrial activities in one country can contribute to rising sea levels and extreme weather events that affect communities worldwide (see **11.25**).
- **Shared responsibility:** The principle of 'common but differentiated responsibilities' underscores the notion that while all countries are responsible for addressing climate change, their obligations may differ based on their historical contributions to the problem and their varying capacities to respond (see **14.41**). This principle encourages equity in climate action and promotes cooperation among nations at different levels of economic development.

Key mechanisms of international cooperation

1.10

- **Treaties and agreements:** Various international treaties and agreements facilitate cooperation on climate change. The most prominent of these is the United Nations Framework Convention on Climate Change (UNFCCC) (see **2.16**), established in 1992, which serves as a foundation for subsequent agreements and negotiations. The Paris Agreement (see **2.37**), adopted in 2015 under the UNFCCC, represents a landmark commitment where countries set their own NDCs to limit global warming and undertake periodic reviews and updates of these commitments.
- **Intergovernmental organisations:** Organisations such as the Intergovernmental Panel on Climate Change (IPCC) (see **2.14**) play a crucial role in the international climate regime. The IPCC provides scientific assessments of climate change, offering policymakers the information needed to make informed decisions (see **2.16**). These organisations facilitate dialogue, build capacity, and foster a community of practice among countries.
- **Financial mechanisms:** International cooperation often includes financial support for climate action (see **2.20**), especially for developing countries. Mechanisms like the Green Climate Fund (GCF) (see **2.61**) are designed to assist nations in implementing climate strategies, improving resilience, and transitioning to low-emission economies. This financial support is crucial for enabling vulnerable nations to participate meaningfully in global climate efforts.
- **Technology transfer and capacity building:** Cooperation also encompasses the sharing of technology and expertise to enhance climate resilience and mitigation efforts. Initiatives aimed at technology transfer help developing countries access cleaner technologies and practices, while capacity-building programs provide training and resources to improve local responses to climate challenges (see **2.62**).

Challenges to international cooperation

1.11

- **Political will and commitment:** Variations in political will among countries can hinder international cooperation. Along with national interests, economic pressures, and domestic politics can influence a country's commitment to international agreements which can lead to inconsistency in efforts to combat climate change (see **13.06**).
- **Compliance and accountability:** Ensuring that countries adhere to their commitments poses a significant challenge (see **2.60**). The effectiveness of international climate law hinges on the mechanisms in place to monitor and verify compliance (see **13.22**). There is often a lack of binding enforcement measures, which can undermine accountability (see **13.61**).
- **Disparities in capacity:** Differences in economic and technological capacities among countries can complicate cooperative efforts. The developing nations are often the hardest hit by climate change and may struggle to meet their commitments without external support. Addressing

these disparities calls for fair distribution of resources and technology, balancing the needs of all nations.

- **Geopolitical tensions:** Geopolitical rivalries and conflicts can obstruct international cooperation on climate change (see **2.62**) and distrust among countries can hinder collective action and affect negotiations, particularly in forums such as the UNFCCC Conference of the Parties (COP) meetings (see **Appendix III**).

International cooperation is essential for effective climate change law and action. The intricate global nature of climate change necessitates collaborative frameworks that bring together nations, organisations, and other stakeholders to share knowledge, resources, and responsibilities. While significant progress has been made through treaties, financial mechanisms, and technological exchanges, challenges remain in achieving consistent and equitable cooperation. To overcome these obstacles requires a sustained political will, commitment to accountability and a shared vision for a sustainable future (see **13.61**). Working together, the global community can strengthen the legal frameworks needed to protect the planet and ensure the well-being of future generations.

TECHNICAL ADVANCES AND CLIMATE CHANGE LAW

1.12 The relationship between technical advances and climate change law is key to the fight against global warming and environmental degradation (see **13.49**). Innovations in technology play a crucial role in enabling countries to meet their climate goals, while climate change laws create a framework that encourages and regulates the use of these technologies.

Key technical advances

1.13

- **Renewable energy technologies:**
  - Technological advancements in solar, wind, and other renewable energy sources have made clean energy more accessible and cost-effective. For instance, the cost of solar photovoltaic (PV) systems has fallen dramatically over the past decade, making solar energy a viable option for both developed and developing nations.
  - Energy storage solutions, such as batteries, enhance the reliability of renewable energy by allowing excess energy to be stored and used during periods of high demand or low production.
- **Energy efficiency improvements:**
  - Innovations in energy efficiency, such as smart grids, LED lighting, and energy-efficient appliances, have reduced energy consumption across various sectors. These advances help meet sustainability targets and lower greenhouse gas emissions.
  - Building technologies, such as advanced insulation materials and smart thermostats, contribute to reducing energy usage in residential and commercial buildings.

- **Carbon Capture and Storage (CCS):**
  - CCS technology allows for the capture of carbon dioxide (CO_2) emitted from industrial processes and its subsequent storage underground. This technology can play a vital role in reducing emissions from sectors that are hard to decarbonise (see **13.51**).
  - Developments in direct air capture technologies are also emerging, aiming to remove CO_2 directly from the atmosphere.
- **Sustainable agriculture:**
  - Innovations in precision agriculture (see **13.54**), including drones, sensors, and data analytics, help optimise resource use and reduce emissions in farming. Techniques such as agroforestry and regenerative agriculture promote soil health and biodiversity while sequestering carbon.
  - Biotechnology is also advancing sustainable practices through genetically modified crops that require fewer inputs and are more resilient to climate stressors.
- **Electric and hybrid vehicles:** The rise of electric vehicles (EVs) and hybrid technologies represents a significant move towards reducing emissions from the transportation sector. Advances in battery technology enhance the range and affordability of EVs, contributing tomore sustainable mobility solutions (see **13.21**).

Impacts on climate change law

1.14

- **Regulatory frameworks:**
  - Technological advances necessitate the development of new regulatory frameworks (see **Chapter 3**) that address emerging issues, such as data privacy in smart grids, liability in carbon capture projects, and incentive structures for renewable energy deployment.
  - Climate change laws increasingly integrate provisions to promote innovation, such as tax incentives and subsidies for green technologies.
- **Setting standards and targets:**
  - Governments can establish ambitious emission reduction targets (see **1.17**) that are informed by technical advances, ensuring laws are aligned with achievable technological capabilities.
  - For instance, emissions standards for vehicles and industries can be updated to reflect advancements in energy efficiency and alternative fuel technologies.
- **Incentivising research and development:**
  - Climate change laws often include incentives for research and development (R&D) in clean technologies by fostering innovation, these laws can accelerate the adoption of new solutions that contribute to climate change mitigation.
  - International agreements may encourage collaborative R&D efforts, promoting technology transfer between developed and developing nations.
- **Monitoring and reporting:**
  - Advances in data collection and analysis technologies enable better monitoring of emissions and compliance with climate laws. For

example, satellite imagery and machine learning can track deforestation and land-use changes more effectively.
- Enhanced monitoring capabilities support transparent reporting and accountability mechanisms, essential for assessing the effectiveness of climate policies (see **13.26**).

Challenges at the intersection of technology and law

1.15

- **Rapid technological change:**
  - The pace of technological advancement can outstrip the ability of legal frameworks to adapt. As new technologies emerge, existing laws may become outdated, creating gaps in governance and regulation (see **11.09**).
  - Policymakers must remain agile, adjusting regulatory frameworks to accommodate new developments while ensuring public safety and environmental protection (see **Chapter 2**).
- **Equity and access:**
  - The benefits of technological advances may not be equitably distributed, particularly affecting vulnerable populations in developing countries (see **3.21**). Climate change law must address issues of access to technology and include provisions for capacity building.
  - Ensuring that all nations, regardless of economic status, benefit from technological advancements is crucial for achieving global climate goals.
- **Incentivising the right solutions:**
  - The legal mechanisms put in place must intentionally promote technologies that genuinely reduce emissions rather than merely shifting the environmental burden. For instance, biofuels should be regulated to prevent negative impacts on food security and land use (see **12.19**).
  - Policymakers need to conduct thorough assessments to identify and incentivise the most effective and sustainable technologies.

Technical advances play a fundamental role in shaping climate change law by providing the tools and solutions necessary for effective climate action. Conversely, robust climate legislation is vital for encouraging innovation and ensuring that technological developments align with sustainability goals. While significant progress has been made, ongoing collaboration between lawmakers, scientists, and the private sector is essential to navigate the challenges and harness the full potential of technology in the fight against climate change.

SOCIETAL AWARENESS AND ENGAGEMENT

1.16 Climate change law plays a critical role in shaping societal awareness and engagement regarding environmental issues and, by providing a legal framework for addressing climate change, these laws not only establish responsibilities and obligations for governments and corporations but also influence public perception and participation in climate action.

Establishing a framework for awareness

1.17

- **Setting emission reduction targets:** Climate change laws often include specific, legally binding targets for greenhouse gas emissions reductions (see **8.07**). These targets serve as benchmarks for progress and can elevate public consciousness about the urgency of addressing climate change. When communities understand their local, national, or global targets, they are more likely to recognise the importance of collective and individual action.
- **Promoting transparency:** Many climate change laws require governments and corporations to report on their emissions, energy use, and sustainability practices (see **Chapter 4**). This transparency fosters accountability and provides the public with crucial information about environmental impacts. Accessible reporting mechanisms can enable communities to track progress toward climate goals, generate public dialogue, and engage citizens in climate action initiatives.
- **Educating the public:** Legal frameworks often encourage educational programmes and public awareness campaigns aimed at informing citizens about climate change and its impacts. By fostering public understanding of climate issues, laws can empower individuals to make informed choices and advocate for more sustainable practices in their daily lives.

Facilitating public engagement

1.18

- **Encouraging participation:** Climate change laws frequently include provisions for public participation in decision-making processes (see **4.02**). For example, laws may require public consultations on proposed projects or policies, enabling citizens to voice their concerns and contribute to discussions about climate action. This participatory approach empowers communities and enhances democratic engagement, ensuring that diverse perspectives are considered in policy development.
- **Incentives for local initiatives:** Many climate laws offer incentives for local governments and communities to implement their own climate action plans (see **4.41**). These incentives can encourage grassroots initiatives, such as renewable energy projects, sustainable transportation programmes, and community resilience strategies. By promoting local engagement, laws can strengthen community ties and foster a sense of ownership over climate action (see **4.43**).
- **Supporting advocacy and activism:** Climate change laws can provide a legal basis for environmental advocacy and activism (see **4.46**). Legal frameworks that protect the rights of communities to challenge harmful practices or hold corporations accountable can empower citizens to act.

Activism inspired by legal protections can raise societal awareness by highlighting the importance of climate justice and environmental equity (see **4.71**).

Influencing behavioural change

1.19

- **Creating norms and expectations:** Climate change laws can help shape social norms around sustainability and, by establishing regulations that prioritise reducing emissions, conserving resources, and promoting renewable energy, these laws can influence public attitudes and expectations regarding environmental responsibility. When sustainable practices are legally mandated or incentivised, they become more socially accepted and encouraged (see **4.67**).
- **Driving corporate responsibility:** Climate laws oblige businesses to comply with regulations and adopt sustainable practices. As corporate responsibility grows in importance because of legal pressure, consumers become more aware of businesses' environmental impacts (see **4.57**). This awareness can lead to shifts in consumer behaviour, with individuals seeking out environmentally-friendly products and services and supporting companies that prioritise sustainability.
- **Educating future generations:** By integrating climate change education into formal and informal education systems, laws can cultivate a generation that is more aware of environmental issues and engaged in finding solutions (see **4.31**). Education initiatives that stem from climate law can inspire young people to think critically about sustainability and encourage them to become climate advocates.

Challenges to societal engagement

1.20

- **Public apathy and misinformation:** Despite legal frameworks promoting awareness, societal engagement can be hindered by apathy or misinformation (see **4.93**). In some cases, individuals may feel overwhelmed or powerless in the face of climate change, leading to disengagement. Legal efforts must work alongside robust communication strategies that counter misinformation and inspire action.
- **Inequity in access:** Climate change laws must ensure equitable access to information and participation opportunities, as marginalised communities may face barriers to engagement. Ensuring that all voices are heard and valued in decision-making processes is crucial for fostering broad societal awareness and collective action (see **4.31**).
- **Complexity of regulation:** The complexity of climate change laws can sometimes create confusion among the public. Simplifying legal language and providing clear explanations can help demystify these laws and enhance understanding, thereby encouraging greater participation and support from society.

Climate change law plays a pivotal role in enhancing societal awareness and engagement through the establishment of frameworks that promote transparency, education, and public participation. By encouraging collective action and influencing individual behaviours, these laws empower communities to take ownership of climate challenges (see **3.100**). While there are numerous challenges in fostering engagement, effective climate legislation complemented by strategic communications and equitable practices can drive meaningful societal involvement in mitigating climate change (see **3.101**). Ultimately, as public consciousness grows, so too does the potential for transformative action towards a sustainable future (see **3.108**).

ADAPTATION AND RESILIENCE

1.21 Climate change law plays a crucial role in promoting adaptation and building resilience within communities, economies, and ecosystems facing the impacts of a changing climate. As the frequency and severity of climate-related events such as floods, droughts, heatwaves, and rising sea levels continue to increase, the need for effective legal frameworks that facilitate adaptation strategies becomes more pressing.

Facilitating adaptation through legal frameworks

1.22

- **Establishing adaptation policies:** Climate change laws often mandate the development of adaptation strategies at local, regional, and national levels (see **3.115**). These policies can identify vulnerable sectors and populations, prioritise actions, and allocate resources effectively and, by providing a structured approach, these policies enable governments to systematically address the risks posed by climate change and enhance adaptive capacity.
- **Integrating science and research:** Climate change law often mandates the use of scientific research and data to inform adaptation policies. This integration of evidence-based practices helps ensure that adaptation strategies are responsive to changing climate conditions (see **7.17**). Legal frameworks can support collaboration between scientists, policymakers, and communities to gather and disseminate relevant information regarding climate risks and potential solutions.
- **Promoting ecosystem-based approaches:** Climate change laws can promote ecosystem-based adaptation (EbA) strategies, which enhance resilience by utilising natural systems and processes (see **13.08**). Legal provisions may protect wetlands, forests, and other ecosystems that provide essential services such as flood protection, climate regulation, and habitat for biodiversity. By preserving and restoring natural systems, these laws can reduce vulnerability and enhance community resilience.
- **Incentivising private sector investment:** Legal frameworks that prioritise adaptation can create incentives for private sector investment in resilient infrastructure and technologies. For instance, laws that encourage green building practices, renewable energy adoption, and sustainable land use can promote climate-resilient development (see **13.06**). Financial mechanisms, such as grants or tax credits, can further stimulate investment in adaptation measures (see **8.14**).

Enhancing resilience through legal mechanisms

1.23

- **Public participation and inclusion:** Climate change laws often emphasise the importance of stakeholder engagement and public participation in planning and implementation processes. Involving communities, particularly those most vulnerable to climate impacts, ensures that adaptation strategies are locally relevant and culturally appropriate (see **4.33**). Engaging diverse voices fosters a sense of ownership and commitment to resilience efforts.

- **Disaster risk reduction:** Many climate change laws incorporate disaster risk reduction (DRR) strategies within their frameworks (see **3.99**). By integrating climate adaptation with disaster management, these laws promote preparedness, response, and recovery measures that enhance community resilience (see **3.102**). This can include building infrastructure that can withstand extreme weather events, implementing early warning systems, and developing community emergency plans.
- **Financial mechanisms and support:** Climate change laws can establish financial instruments to support adaptation efforts (see **3.114**). These may include dedicated funds for climate resilience initiatives, insurance schemes for vulnerable communities, and mechanisms for accessing international climate finance (see **9.24**). By providing financial resources, these laws enable local governments and communities to implement necessary adaptation measures.
- **Monitoring and evaluation:** Effective climate change law often incorporates mechanisms for monitoring and evaluating adaptation efforts. By tracking progress and assessing the effectiveness of implemented strategies, policymakers can adjust approaches as needed and ensure continuous improvement in building resilience. These mechanisms also help communicate successes and challenges, making the case for sustained investment and action.

Challenges and considerations

1.24

- **Policy coherence and integration:** While climate change laws aim to promote adaptation and resilience, it is essential that these frameworks are coherent with other policies, such as land use, development, and environmental regulations (see **13.22**). Disparate policies can create confusion and hinder effective implementation. Ensuring that adaptation measures are integrated across various sectors is crucial for maximising effectiveness.
- **Funding and resources:** Inadequate funding can be a significant barrier to effective adaptation (see **13.08**). While laws can create provisions for financial support, securing adequate resources and ensuring equitable distribution remains a challenge. Governments must prioritise adaptation initiatives in budget allocations and seek innovative funding sources.
- **Capacity building:** The successful implementation of climate adaptation measures requires adequate knowledge, skills, and capacity at various levels of governance. Climate change laws need to incorporate provisions for building capacity within communities, local governments, and institutions to effectively respond to climate impacts (see **3.96**).
- **Monitoring and data collection:** Effective adaptation strategies require robust data collection and monitoring mechanisms. However, many regions, particularly developing countries, lack the necessary infrastructure for reliable data collection (see **13.06**). Laws need to facilitate investment

in data systems that inform adaptation planning and decision-making processes.

Climate change law plays a vital role in facilitating adaptation and resilience in the face of the growing challenges posed by climate change and, by establishing legal frameworks that prioritise adaptation strategies, promote stakeholder engagement, and incentivise private sector involvement, these laws contribute to building communities that can effectively withstand and respond to climate impacts (see **8.04**). While challenges remain, a well-designed legal landscape that integrates adaptation within broader environmental and development policies can significantly enhance societal resilience, ensuring that vulnerable populations and ecosystems are better equipped to navigate the uncertainties of a changing climate (see **8.07**). As the complexity of climate-related risks escalates, continued investment in adaptive legal frameworks will be essential to safeguard the future of communities and ecosystems worldwide.

LONG-TERM PERSPECTIVES FOR CLIMATE CHANGE LAW

1.25 As the challenges posed by climate change become increasingly urgent, the importance of robust climate change law cannot be overstated. Moving forward, the long-term perspectives for climate change law will be shaped by evolving scientific understanding, technological advancements, political dynamics, social movements, and the global response to climate impacts.

Integration of climate change across legal frameworks

1.26 One of the most critical perspectives for climate change law is its integration across a broader range of legal frameworks (see **Chapter 14**). In the future, legal systems are likely to:

- **Incorporate climate considerations into all sectors:** Climate change considerations will increasingly permeate various areas of law, including land use, transportation, public health, and economic development. Legal frameworks will require environmental impact assessments that account for climate risks, ensuring that policies and projects at all levels are aligned with climate goals.
- **Establish climate-resilient governance structures:** More jurisdictions may adopt governance structures that prioritise climate resilience. This could involve creating specialised agencies or taskforces to coordinate responses to climate change across different sectors and levels of government (see **13.06**).

Strengthening international cooperation

1.27 Given the global nature of climate change, international cooperation will remain vital in shaping the long-term outlook for climate change law. Key developments may include:

- **Enhancing global agreements:** Future international agreements are likely to evolve to reflect increasingly ambitious emission reduction targets and adaptation strategies. Mechanisms such as carbon markets, technology transfer, and climate finance will be critical in fostering compliance and cooperation among countries (see **13.06**).
- **Accountability mechanisms:** As reliance on international agreements grows, so too will the need for robust accountability frameworks. Enhanced monitoring, verification, and enforcement mechanisms may be developed to ensure that countries meet their commitments and adhere to established climate standards (see **13.26**).

Climate justice and equity

1.28 Long-term perspectives for climate change law must encompass equity and justice considerations. This includes:

- **Addressing historical injustices:** Future legal frameworks are expected to emphasise reparative justice for communities disproportionately affected by climate change, particularly marginalised and Indigenous populations (see **13.57**). This may involve recognition of historical responsibilities and financial restitution.
- **Promoting inclusive participation:** Ensuring that diverse voices and perspectives, particularly from vulnerable communities, are included in decision-making processes will be essential in shaping equitable climate action (see **7.31**). Laws may evolve to institutionalise mechanisms for inclusive participation, ensuring that adaptation and mitigation strategies reflect the needs of all stakeholders.

Taxation and economic instruments

1.29 Economic policies and instruments will increasingly play a role in climate change law:

- **Carbon pricing mechanisms:** More jurisdictions are likely to embrace carbon pricing mechanisms, such as carbon taxes or cap-and-trade systems, as a way to reduce greenhouse gas emissions. These mechanisms can incentivise lower emissions while generating revenue that can be reinvested in sustainable initiatives (see **3.11**).
- **Sustainable finance:** Legal frameworks may evolve to facilitate sustainable finance practices, encouraging investments that support climate resilience and mitigation. This could involve the development of criteria for green investments and the regulation of financial institutions to promote environmental sustainability (see **13.08**).

Technological adaptation and innovation

1.30 Advancements in technology will significantly influence the future of climate change law:

- **Regulating emerging technologies:** Legal frameworks will need to adapt to new technologies that impact climate change, such as artificial intelligence, geoengineering, and renewable energy innovations. Regulation will be necessary to address potential risks and benefits associated with these technologies, ensuring they contribute positively to climate goals (see **3.93**).
- **Promoting R&D through law:** Laws may increasingly incentivise R&D in clean technologies, fostering innovation that can lead to breakthrough solutions for mitigating and adapting to climate change.

Resilience and adaptation focus

1.31 Long-term climate change law will likely place greater emphasis on resilience and adaptation strategies:

- **Legally mandated adaptation plans:** Future legal frameworks may require governments at all levels to develop and implement legally mandated adaptation plans that address specific vulnerabilities within communities and ecosystems. These plans could involve stakeholder engagement and multi-sectoral collaboration (see **1.22**).
- **Integration of disaster risk reduction:** Climate change laws may increasingly integrate disaster risk reduction strategies, ensuring that preparedness, response, and recovery measures are aligned with long-term climate goals. This integration will enhance community resilience to climate impacts (see **3.102**).

The long-term perspectives for climate change law point toward a more integrated, adaptive, and justice-oriented approach to governance in the context of climate change. As the world faces escalating climate impacts, the evolution of climate law will be crucial in facilitating effective response strategies that are equitable, resilient, and sustainable. Ongoing engagement, innovation, and collaboration will be vital in creating a legal landscape that not only addresses current challenges but also anticipates future needs, ensuring a liveable planet for generations to come. Emphasising climate justice, international cooperation, and the integration of climate considerations into all sectors will be central to a successful long-term climate strategy.

Chapter 2

History of the Recognition of Climate Change

INTRODUCTION

2.01 Understanding the history of climate change recognition provides context for current climate science and policy efforts. This history highlights the gradual but profound evolution in our understanding of the Earth's climate system and the impact of human activities on global climate patterns.

EARLY WORK

2.02 The recognition of how climate change has occurred is not new. Work over the centuries, through scientific discovery, environmental observation and political action, has added to the body of knowledge concerning climate change.

1824 – Joseph Fourier

2.03 Jean-Baptiste Joseph Fourier was a French mathematician and physicist born in 1768, in Auxerre in France and is probably best known for initiating the Fourier series investigation, which was eventually developed into Fourier analysis, and harmonic analysis and its application to heat transfer and vibrations. Fourier's mathematical theory of heat conduction was based on Newton's law of cooling, with the flow of heat between two adjacent particles being proportional to the difference in temperature:

> 'Heat, like gravity, penetrates every substance of the universe, its rays occupy all parts of space. The object of our work is to set forth the mathematical laws which this element obeys. The theory of heat will hereafter form one of the most important branches of general physics.'[1]

Fourier established the fundamental equation that governs the transfusion or spreading out of heat and solved it by using the infinite series of trigonometric function now called the Fourier series.

$$f(x) = a_0 + \sum_{n=1}^{\infty} \left(a_n \cos\frac{n\pi x}{L} + b_n \sin\frac{n\pi x}{L}\right)$$

Fourier compared variations in temperature between day and night and between summer and winter and concluded that the planet was much warmer than a simple analysis might suggest. He calculated that the planet would be much colder if the incoming radiation was the only warming effect. He had the idea that the Earth's atmosphere acts like an insulator and this was the first formulation of what is now called the Greenhouse Gas effect, but he didn't use that term, that came later from the work of a Swedish metrologist called Nils Gustaf Ekholm in 1901.

1856 – Eunice Foote

2.04 Eunice Foote presented her research in 1856 and described how tubes of gas heated when exposed to sunlight. Her work was discovered in 2011 by Raymond Sorenson who unearthed a presentation of Foote's work at the 10th annual meeting of the American Association for the Advancement of Science in 1956, two years before Tyndall's experiments started. She didn't present her work herself, it was presented by a friend, Joseph Henry, as Foote, as an amateur scientist and a woman, might not have been taken seriously if she

1 Fourier, Jean-Joseph Baptiste, *Théorie Analtique de la Chaleur* (*The Analytical Theory of Heat*) (1822).

had presented her own research. It seems at the time no one appreciated the importance of her findings.

1859 – John Tyndall

2.05 The greenhouse gas effect is often attributed to John Tyndall who conducted experiments demonstrating that carbon dioxide (CO_2) and water vapour trap heat, highlighting the warming potential of these gases. In 1859 he began studying the radiative properties of various gases and part of his experimentation included the construction of the first ratio spectrometer which was used to measure the absorptive powers of gases such as water vapour, 'carbonic acid' (now known as CO_2) ozone and hydrocarbons. Amongst his discoveries was the ability of odourless gases and vapours to absorb and transmit radiant heat. Tyndall's experiments also showed that water vapour, CO_2 and ozone are the best absorbers of heat radiation and that even small quantities of these gases absorb more effectively than the atmosphere itself. He concluded that, among the constituents of the atmosphere, water vapour is the strongest absorber of radiant heat and is therefore the most important gas controlling Earth's surface temperature. He said, that without water vapour, the Earth's surface would be 'held fast in the iron grip of frost'. He later speculated on how fluctuations in water vapour and CO_2could be related to climate change. Therefore a significant alteration in the quantity of water vapour or CO_2 would produce changes in the climate and this had probably happened in the past. As John Tyndall said:

> 'This aqueous vapour is a blanket more necessary to the vegetable life of England than clothing is to man. Remove for a single summer-night the aqueous vapour from the air which overspreads this country, and you would assuredly destroy every plant capable of being destroyed by a freezing temperature. The warmth of our fields and gardens would pour itself unrequited into space, and the sun would rise upon an island held fast in the iron grip of frost.'

On the memorial stone to John Tyndall in Belap, Valais, Switzerland, it says:

> '... the aqueous vapour of the atmosphere must act powerfully in intercepting terrestrial radiation; its changes in quantity would produce corresponding changes of climate. Subsequent researches must decide whether this vera causa is competent to account for the climatal changes which geologic research reveal.'[2]

Although Tyndall did many of his experiments in the Royal Institution's laboratory, the initial idea for his research came from his time in the fields and glaciers on the Alps. Many of these glaciers are now retreating due to the increasing climate temperatures.

1896 – Svante Arrhenius

2.06 Svante Arrhenius was a Swedish scientist, originally a physicist but referred to as a chemist. He is one of the founders of physical chemistry.

2 Tyndall, John, 'The Bakerian lecture—On the absorption and radiation of heat by gases and vapours, and on the physical connexion of radiation, absorption, and conduction' (1862) 11 Proceedings of the Royal Society of London, 1860 – 1862 100 – 104.

Arrhenius was the first person to use the principles of physical chemistry to estimate the extent to which increases in atmospheric CO_2 are responsible for the Earth's increasing surface temperature. A problem frequently studied in his time was that of the different glaciations that the planet had gone through throughout its history. He wanted to find out if the determining factor for these climatic events could be the concentration of CO_2 in the Earth's atmosphere. John Tyndall had already focused on this by identifying methane, water vapour and CO_2 as atmospheric gases that cause the greenhouse effect.

In 1895 Arrhenius wanted to quantify the influence of CO_2 on the greenhouse gas effect. He did many calculations by hand and published his findings in an article in 1896. In this, Arrhenius concluded that the reduction in atmospheric CO_2 levels to half the existing ones would drop the temperature of the planet between 4 and 5°C and could lead to a massive cooling like the ones during glaciation.

Arrhenius developed the first quantitative model of how increases in atmospheric CO_2 could raise global temperatures, predicting that doubling CO_2 could lead to a significant temperature rise. Arrhenius did not see this as a significant problem. He said that if industry continued to burn fuel at the current (1896) rate then he estimated it would take three thousand years for the CO_2 levels to rise so high. One thing that was considered was the effect that the oceans had on absorbing any extra gas.

At the time of Arrhenius's book of 1908, where he again raised the possibility of future warming of the Earth, the rate of coal burning was already significantly higher than in 1896 and he then suggested that warming could appear within a few centuries rather than millennia.

MID-20TH-CENTURY ADVANCEMENTS

1938 – Guy Stewart Callendar

2.07 Callendar was an amateur scientist and gathered records form 147 weather stations across the world. He then did calculations and discovered that global temperatures had risen 0.3°C over the previous 50 years. Callendar argued that CO_2 emissions from industry were responsible for global warming, but this was largely ignored by scientists, who didn't believe that humans could have such an impact on the climate system. He worked from home in West Sussex and his research first appeared in the quarterly Journal of the Meteorological Society in April 1938. For a time this became known as the Callendar effect. Callendar's calculations were simple but proved to be accurate when compared to modern analysis.

1950s – Charles David Keeling

2.08 Keeling was known for making extremely precise measurements of CO_2 that indicated that atmospheric concentrations were increasing. This led to the recognition that human activity could have a significant impact on the Earth's climate system. He was the first to confirm the accumulations of atmospheric CO_2 and he produced a dataset, now widely known as the Keeling curve. Before this it was assumed that the oceans would be able to absorb the excess carbon dioxide produced due to the burning of fossil fuels and other industrial activities.

Keeling also constructed one of the first models of the carbon cycle into which future man-made CO_2 can be introduced in order to predict concentration levels in air and water into the next century. Keeling's few years of measurements demonstrated the now well-known seasonal cycle in atmospheric CO_2 due to the 'breathing' of the biosphere.

INCREASING AWARENESS (1960S–1980S)

1965 – President's Science Advisory Committee Report on atmospheric carbon dioxide[3]

2.09 President Lyndon B Johnson's science advisory committee warned of the impact of pollution on humanity's role in addressing the future. The committee suggested 'economic incentives to discourage pollution' in which 'special taxes would be levied against polluters'.

In Appendix Y4, the authors linked the 'measurable' effects of fossil fuel production to the increase in atmospheric CO_2. The report states that 'fossil fuel combustion is the only new major producer of carbon dioxide, having increased the quantity of CO_2 in the atmosphere and ocean from 1860 to 1960 by roughly 7%'.

The authors then posed two open questions:

> 'What will the total quantity of CO_2 injected into the atmosphere (but only partly retained there) be at different future times?'
>
> 'What would be the total amount of CO_2 injected into the air if all recoverable reserves of fossil fuels were consumed?'

Their answer follows:

> 'At present rates of expansion in fossil fuel consumption, this condition could be approached within the next 150 years.'

1970S

1970 – Earth Day[4]

2.10 This was first celebrated in 1970 when the US senator from Wisconsin organised a national demonstration to raise awareness about environmental

3 PSAC, *Restoring the Quality of our Environment* (The White House, 1965).

4 See 'Earth Day', https://www.loc.gov/item/today-in-history/april-22/#:~:text=Earth%20Day%20was%20first%20observed,sites%20across%20the%20United%20States

issues. Rallies took place across the country and, by the end of the year, the US Government had created the Environmental Protection Agency. By 1990, Earth Day was celebrated by more than 140 countries around the globe.

1972 – First international Summit, Stockholm

2.11 On 5–16 June 1972 the United Nations Conference on the Human Environment took place. It was the first world conference to make the environment a major issue. The participants adopted a series of principles for the management of the environment, including the Stockholm Declaration and Action Plan for the Human Environment.[5] The UN-convened conference marked a turning point in the development of international environmental politics. It led to both the creation of the United Nations Environment Programme (UNEP)[6] and commitments to coordinate global efforts to promote sustainability and safeguard the natural environment.

United Nations Environment Programme

2.12 Climate change, however, was just a footnote at the Stockholm Conference. The issue was viewed largely as a scientific concern, and not a pressing political 'problem', but between this conference in 1972 and the latter half of the 1980s, some politicians took note as scientists increasingly warned of the risks posed by increased greenhouse gas (GHG) emissions. This was recognised at the First World Climate Conference in 1979, and the Toronto Conference on the Changing Climate in 1988.

1979 – First World Climate Conference

2.13 Climate change was recognised as a serious problem at the World Climate Conference, held in Geneva in 1979. The meeting was sponsored by the World Meteorological Organisation (WMO). The gathering explored how climate change might affect human activities. After two weeks of deliberation the organisers issued a World Climate Change Declaration:

> 'Having regard to the all-pervading influence of climate on human society and on many fields of human activities and endeavour, the Conference finds that it is now urgently necessary for the nations of the world: (a) To take full advantage of man's present knowledge of climate; (b) To take steps to improve significantly that knowledge; (c) To foresee and prevent potential man-made changes in climate that might be adverse to the well-being of humanity.'[7]

5 *Report of the United Nations Conference on the Human Environment Stockholm, 5–16 June 1972*, A/CONF.48/14/Rev.1 (UN, 1973), adoption of the action plan for the human environment, p 67.

6 United Nations Environment Programme, https://www.unep.org

7 World Meteorological Organisation declaration of the World Climate Conference.

1980S

1988 – Intergovernmental Panel on Climate Change (IPCC)

2.14 The IPCC was established by the UN to assess scientific information related to climate change, its impacts, and potential mitigation strategies. The initial task was outlined in the in the UN General Assembly Resolution 43/53 of 6 December 1988[8] and was to prepare a comprehensive review and recommendations with respect to the:

- state of knowledge of the science of climate change;
- social and economic impact of climate change;
- potential response strategies; and the
- elements for inclusion in a possible future international convention on climate.

Since 1988 the IPPC has had six assessment cycles and delivered six assessment reports and produces a range of Methodology Reports, Special Reports and Technical Papers in response to request for information on specific scientific and technical matters from the United Nations Framework Convention on Climate Change (UNFCCC), governments and international organisations.

1988 – James Hansen

2.15 Hansen was formerly a Director of the NASA Goddard Institute for Apec studies and adjunct professor at Columbia University's Earth Institute where he directed the programme on Climate Science, Awareness and Solutions.

He is probably best known for the testimony[9] he gave on climate change to congressional committees in the 1980s that helped to broaden the awareness of global warming issues. On 23 June 1988, Hansen testified to the US Senate that greenhouse effects had been detected, indicating that the climate was, in fact, changing:

> 'Climate change is a long-term issue. Strategies will need to be adjusted as we go along. However, it is important to start now with common-sense economically sound steps that slow emissions of greenhouse gases, including CO_2, and air pollution. Early emphasis on air pollution has multiple immediate benefits, including the potential to unite interests of developed and developing countries. Barriers to energy efficiency need to be removed. Research and development of alternative energies should be supported, including a hard look at next generation nuclear power. Ultimately strategic decisions rest with the public and their representatives, but for that reason we need to make the science and alternative scenarios clearer.'

8 UN General Assembly Resolution 43/53 of 6 December 1988, Protection of global climate for present and future generations of mankind: resolution / adopted by the General Assembly. A/RES/43/53.

9 Statement of Dr James E Hansen. Head of Nasa Goddard Institute for Space Studies before the Committee on Governmental Affairs, US Senate.

INTERNATIONAL AGREEMENTS (1990S–PRESENT)

1990 First Assessment Report (FAR), IPCC

2.16 This first report served as the basis of the United Nations Framework Convention on Climate Change (UNFCCC) and not only effects the establishment of the UNFCCC but also the First session of the conference of the Parties (COP) held in Berlin in 1995. The executive summary of the Working Group (WG) I Summary for Policymakers report that said they were certain that emissions resulting from human activities were substantially increasing the atmospheric concentrations of GHGs, resulting, on average, in an additional warming of the Earth's surface. They calculated with confidence that CO_2 had been responsible for over half the enhanced greenhouse effect.

The 1990 Second World Climate Conference called for a framework treaty on climate change

2.17 Sponsored by the WMO, UNEP and other international organisations, this conference featured negotiations and ministerial-level discussions among 137 states plus the European Community. The final declaration, adopted after tough bargaining, did not specify any international targets for reducing emissions. However, it did support several principles later included in the Climate Change Convention. These were climate change as a 'common concern of humankind', the importance of equity, common but differentiated responsibilities for countries at different levels of development, sustainable development, and the precautionary principle.

In December 1990, the UN General Assembly approved the start of treaty negotiations

2.18 The Intergovernmental Negotiating Committee for a Framework Convention on Climate Change (INC/FCCC) met for five sessions between February 1991 and May 1992. Facing a strict deadline – the June 1992 Rio 'Earth Summit' – negotiators from 150 countries finalised the Convention in just 15 months. It was adopted in New York on 9 May 1992.

1992 – UN Framework Convention on Climate Change (UNFCCC)

2.19 At the Earth Summit in Rio de Janeiro, the UNFCCC was established to coordinate global efforts to address climate change.

The Convention entered into force on 21 March 1994

2.20 This was 90 days after the receipt of the 50th instrument of ratification (after signing a convention a state must also ratify it). The next critical date was 21 September when developed country Parties started submitting national communications describing their climate change strategies. Meanwhile, the INC continued preparatory work, meeting for another six sessions to discuss matters relating to commitments and arrangements for the financial mechanism, technical and financial support to developing countries, and procedural and institutional matters. The INC was dissolved after its 11th and final session in February 1995, and the Conference of the Parties (COP) became the Convention's ultimate authority.

1995 – IPCC Second Assessment Report (SAR) published

2.21 The IPCC completed its Second Assessment Report in December 1995. The major conclusions were that GHG concentrations were increasing, the global climate had been changing, and would likely continue to change, probably due to human influence.

1995 – The first meeting of the UNFCCC Conference of Parties (COP 1) took place in Berlin, Germany[10]

2.22 Every year, countries who are party to the UNFCCC meet to measure progress and negotiate multilateral responses to climate change. Today there are 198 Parties to the Convention.

1997 – Kyoto Protocol

2.23 In short, the Kyoto Protocol operationalises the UNFCCC by committing industrialised countries and economies in transition to limit and reduce GHG emissions in accordance with agreed individual targets. The Convention itself asks those countries to adopt policies and measures on mitigation and to report periodically. The Kyoto Protocol is based on the principles and provisions of the Convention and follows its annex-based structure. It only binds developed countries and places a greater burden on them under the principle of 'common but differentiated responsibility and respective capabilities', because it recognises that they are largely responsible for the current high levels of GHG emissions in the atmosphere.

In its Annex B, the Kyoto Protocol sets binding emission reduction targets for 37 industrialised countries and economies in transition and the European Union (EU). Overall, these targets added up to an average 5 per cent emission reduction compared to 1990 levels over the five-year period 2008–12 (the first commitment period).

10 See United Nations Climate Change, 'History of the Convention', https://unfccc.int/process/the-convention/history-of-the-convention

2000S

2001 – IPCC Third Assessment Report (TAR) published

2.24 This report built on past assessments and incorporated new results for the previous five years of research. Since the SAR, additional data from new studies of current paleoclimates,[11] improved analysis for datasets, more rigorous evaluation of their quality and comparisons of different sources had led to a greater understanding of climate change. It also included information for policymakers. In the second edition of the TAR this was:

- global average surface temperature had increased over the 20th century by 0.6°C;
- temperatures had risen during the past four decades in the lowest eight kilometres of the atmosphere;
- snow cover and ice extent had decreased;
- global average sea level had risen and ocean heat had increased;
- changes had also occurred in other important aspects of climate:
  - precipitation had likely increased by 0.5 to 1 per cent per decade in the 20th century over most mid- and high latitudes of the Northern Hemisphere continents, and it was likely that rainfall had increased by 0.2 to 0.3 per cent per decade over the tropical (10°N to 10°S) land areas;
  - in the mid- and high latitudes of the Northern Hemisphere, over the latter half of the 20th century, it was likely that there had been a 2 to 4 per cent increase in the frequency of heavy precipitation events;
  - since 1950 it was very likely that there had been a reduction in the frequency of extreme low temperatures, with a smaller increase in the frequency of extreme high temperatures;
  - warm episodes of the El Niño – Southern Oscillation (ENSO) phenomenon (which consistently affects regional variations of precipitation and temperature over much of the tropics, sub-tropics and some mid-latitude areas) had been more frequent, persistent and intense since the mid-1970s, compared with the previous 100 years;
  - over the 20th century (1900 to 1995), there were relatively small increases in global land areas experiencing severe drought or severe wetness;
  - in some regions, such as parts of Asia and Africa, the frequency and intensity of droughts had been observed to increase in recent decades;
- some important aspects of climate appeared not to have changed:
  - a few areas of the globe had not warmed in recent decades, mainly some parts of the Southern Hemisphere oceans and parts of Antarctica;
  - no significant trends of Antarctic sea-ice extent were apparent since 1978, the period of reliable satellite measurements;
  - changes globally in tropical and extra-tropical storm intensity and frequency were dominated by inter-decadal to multi-decadal variations, with no significant trends evident over the 20th century;
  - no systematic changes in the frequency of tornadoes, thunder days, or hail events were evident in the limited areas analysed;

11 Paleoclimates – relating to, or being a climate distinctive to a past geologic age.

- emissions of GHGs and aerosols due to human activities continued to alter the atmosphere in ways that are expected to affect the climate;
- concentrations of atmospheric GHGs and their radiative forcing had continued to increase because of human activity;
- anthropogenic aerosols were short-lived and mostly produce negative radiative forcing;
- natural factors had made small contributions to radiative forcing over the past century;
- confidence in the ability of models to project future climate had increased;
- there was new and stronger evidence that most of the warming observed over the last 50 years was attributable to human activity;
- human influence would continue to change atmospheric composition throughout the 21st century regarding:
  - — GHG emissions;
  - — aerosols;
  - — radiative forcing;
- global average temperature and sea level were projected to rise under all IPCC Special Report Emissions Scenarios (SRES) with the following all being of concern:
  - — temperature;
  - — precipitation;
  - — extreme events;
  - — El Niño;
  - — monsoons;
  - — thermohaline circulations;
  - — snow and ice sea level;
- anthropogenic[12] climate change would persist for many centuries.

Further action was required to address remaining gaps in information and understanding.

2005 – Kyoto Protocol enters into force

2.25 The Kyoto Protocol was adopted on 11 December 1997, but, owing to the ratification process, only entered into force on 16 February 2005.

2006 – 'An Inconvenient Truth'

2.26 Former US Vice President Al Gore's documentary[13] brought mainstream attention to climate change. Called 'The Inconvenient Truth', filmmaker Davis Guggenheim followed Al Gore on a lecture circuit, as the former presidential candidate campaigned to raise public awareness of the dangers of global warming and called for immediate action to curb its destructive effect.

In a research paper in 2006,[14] an analysis of the impact of the film was made. It concluded that, in the US, the debate was largely about the scientific proof

12 Anthropogenic – referring to environmental change caused or influenced by people, either directly or indirectly.

13 *An Inconvenient Truth.*

14 L W George, 'How "An Inconvenient Truth" Expanded the Climate Change Dialogue and Reignited and Ethical Purpose in the United States', thesis, George Town University (2013).

and partisan politics of the issue, only afterwards had it had evolved into an issue of ethical concern. While the response is attributable to many factors, research and data show that, unlike any work or event before it, the film was a turning point in shifting the US to thinking and acting more consciously about the warming climate.

2007 – IPPC Fourth Assessment Report: AR4 Climate Change 2007: The Physical Science Basis[15]

2.27 This built upon past IPCC assessments and incorporated new findings from the past six years of research. Scientific progress since the TAR was based upon large amounts of new and more comprehensive data, more sophisticated analyses of data, improvements in understanding of processes and their simulation in models and more extensive exploration of uncertainty ranges.

'Human and natural drivers for climate change'

2.28

> 'Global atmospheric concentrations of carbon dioxide, methane and nitrous oxide have increased markedly as a result of human activities since 1750 and now far exceed pre-industrial values determined from ice cores spanning many thousands of years. The global increases in carbon dioxide concentration are due primarily to fossil fuel use and land use change, while those of methane and nitrous oxide are primarily due to agriculture:
>
> - ... The global atmospheric concentration of carbon dioxide has increased from a pre-industrial value of about 280 ppm to 379 ppm in 2005. The atmospheric concentration of carbon dioxide in 2005 exceeds by far the natural range over the last 650,000 years (180 to 300 ppm) as determined from ice cores...
> - The primary source of the increased atmospheric concentration of carbon dioxide since the pre-industrial period results from fossil fuel use, with land-use change providing another significant but smaller contribution...
> - The global atmospheric concentration of methane has increased from a pre-industrial value of about 715 ppb to 1732 ppb in the early 1990s and was 1774 ppb in 2005. The atmospheric concentration of methane in 2005 exceeds by far the natural range of the last 650,000 years (320 to 790 ppb) as determined from ice cores...
> - The global atmospheric nitrous oxide concentration increased from a pre-industrial value of about 270 ppb to 319 ppb in 2005. ...'[16]

15 IPPC, *Fourth Assessment Report: AR4 Climate Change 2007: The Physical Science Basis* (CUP, 2007).

16 IPPC, *Fourth Assessment Report: AR4 Climate Change 2007: The Physical Science Basis* (CUP, 2007). CEOS EO Handbook Case Studies Satellite Observations in Support of Climate Challenges, https://eohandbook.com/eohb2011/casestudy_carbon.html

'Direct observations of recent climate change'

2.29

'Warming of the climate system is unequivocal, as is now evident from observations of increases in global average air and ocean temperatures, widespread melting of snow and ice, and rising global average sea level....

- Eleven of the last twelve years (1995–2006) rank among the 12 warmest years in the instrumental record of global surface temperature (since 1850)...
- ...
- The average atmospheric water vapour content has increased since at least the 1980s over land and ocean as well as in the upper troposphere. ...
- Observations since 1961 show that the average temperature of the global ocean has increased to depths of at least 3000 m and that the ocean has been absorbing more than 80% of the heat added to the climate system. Such warming causes seawater to expand, contributing to sea level rise....
- Mountain glaciers and snow cover have declined on average in both hemispheres. Widespread decreases in glaciers and ice caps have contributed to sea level rise (ice caps do not include contributions from the Greenland and Antarctic Ice Sheets). ...
- New data since the TAR now show that losses from the ice sheets of Greenland and Antarctica have *very likely* contributed to sea level rise over 1993 to 2003...
- Global average sea level rose at an average rate of 1.8 [1.3 to 2.3] mm per year over 1961 to 2003. The rate was faster over 1993 to 2003: about 3.1 [2.4 to 3.8] mm per year....
- ...

At continental, regional and ocean basin scales, numerous long-term changes in climate have been observed. These include changes in arctic temperatures and ice, widespread changes in precipitation amounts, ocean salinity, wind patterns and aspects of extreme weather including droughts, heavy precipitation, heat waves and the intensity of tropical cyclones ...

- Average arctic temperatures increased at almost twice the global average rate in the past 100 years. Arctic temperatures have high decadal variability, and a warm period was also observed from 1925 to 1945.
- Satellite data since 1978 show that annual average arctic sea ice extent has shrunk by 2.7 [2.1 to 3.3]% per decade, with larger decreases in summer of 7.4 [5.0 to 9.8]% per decade. ...
- Temperatures at the top of the permafrost layer have generally increased since the 1980s in the Arctic (by up to 3°C). ...

...'[17]

Some climate aspects were observed not to have changed

2.30 Antarctic sea ice extent continued to show interannual variability and localised change but no statistically significant average trend, consistent with

17 IPPC, *Fourth Assessment Report: AR4 Climate Change 2007: The Physical Science Basis* (CUP, 2007). Zhang, 'Warming of the Climate System Is Unequivocal: Highlights of the Fourth IPCC Assessment Report' (2007) 44(2) United Nations Chronicle 8, https://www.un.org/en/chronicle/article/warming-climate-system-unequivocal-highlights-fourth-ipcc-assessment-report

the lack of warming reflected in atmospheric temperatures averaged across the region.

There was insufficient evidence to determine whether trends existed in the meridional overturning circulation (MOC) of the global ocean or in small-scale phenomena such as tornadoes, hail, lightning and dust-storms

A paleoclimate perspective

2.31

- Paleoclimatic information supported the interpretation that the warmth of the last half-century was unusual in at least the previous 1,300 years. The last time the polar regions had been significantly warmer than present for an extended period (about 125,000 years previously), reductions in polar ice volume led to 4 to 6 m of sea level rise.
- Average Northern Hemisphere temperatures during the second half of the 20th century were very likely higher than during any other 50-year period in the previous 500 years and likely the highest in at least the past 1,300 years.
- Global average sea level in the last interglacial period (about 125,000 years previously) was likely 4 to 6 m higher than during the 20th century, mainly due to the retreat of polar ice.

Projections for future changes of climate

2.32 For the next two decades, a warming of about 0.2°C per decade was projected for a range of SRES. Even if the concentrations of all GHGs and aerosols were kept constant at year 2000 levels, a further warming of about 0.1°C per decade would be expected:

- Continued greenhouse gas emissions at or above 2007 current rates would cause further warming and induce many changes in the global climate system during the 21st century that would *very likely* be larger than those observed during the 20th century.
- There was now higher confidence in projected patterns of warming and other regional-scale features, including changes in wind patterns, precipitation and some aspects of extremes and of ice.
- Anthropogenic warming and sea level rise would continue for centuries due to the time scales associated with climate processes and feedback, even if GHG concentrations were to be stabilised.

The report concluded that warming of the climate system was unequivocal and that human influence was clear.

2009 – Parties fail to reach agreement on a successor to the Kyoto Protocol at COP 15, Copenhagen, Denmark

2.33 In 1995, COP 1 negotiations began with proposals to strengthen the UNFCCC's commitments which resulted in the adoption of the Kyoto Protocol.

In subsequent years, 192 of the UNFCCC parties ratified the Protocol but this was derailed when the US did not ratify it in 2001. The Doha Amendment[18] extended the Kyoto commitments until 2020.

Negotiations on what would follow the Kyoto Protocol from 2020 onwards began at COP 13 in 2007.

This failure to reach agreement in Copenhagen at COP 15 in 2009 meant the next major attempt didn't take place until Paris in 2015 at COP 21.

2014–15 – IPCC Fifth Assessment Report (AR5) published

2.34 Compared to past WGII reports, the WGII AR5[19] assessed a substantially larger knowledge base of relevant scientific, technical, and socioeconomic literature. Increased literature facilitated comprehensive assessment across a broader set of topics and sectors, with expanded coverage of human systems, adaptation, and the ocean.

'Observed Impacts, Vulnerability, and Exposure'

2.35

> 'In recent decades, changes in climate have caused impacts on natural and human systems on all continents and across the oceans. Evidence of climate-change impacts is strongest and most comprehensive for natural systems. Some impacts on human systems have also been attributed to climate change, with a major or minor contribution of climate change distinguishable from other influences. ... Attribution of observed impacts in the WGII AR5 generally links responses of natural and human systems to observed climate change, regardless of its cause.
>
> In many regions, changing precipitation or melting snow and ice are altering hydrological systems, affecting water resources in terms of quantity and quality (*medium confidence*). Glaciers continue to shrink almost worldwide due to climate change (*high confidence*), affecting runoff and water resources downstream (*medium confidence*). Climate change is causing permafrost warming and thawing in high- latitude regions and in high-elevation regions (*high confidence*).
>
> Many terrestrial, freshwater, and marine species have shifted their geographic ranges, seasonal activities, migration patterns, abundances, and species interactions in response to ongoing climate change (*high confidence*). ... While only a few recent species extinctions have been attributed as yet to climate change (*high confidence*), natural global climate change at rates slower than current anthropogenic climate change caused significant ecosystem shifts and species extinctions during the past millions of years (*high confidence*).
>
> ...
>
> Adaptation is becoming embedded in some planning processes, with more limited implementation of responses (*high confidence*). Engineered and technological options are commonly implemented adaptive responses, often integrated within

18 Doha Amendment to the Kyoto Protocol.

19 IPPC, *Fifth Assessment Report: AR5 Climate Change 2014: Impacts, Adaptation and Vulnerability* (CUP, 2014).

existing programs such as disaster risk management and water management. There is increasing recognition of the value of social, institutional, and ecosystem-based measures and of the extent of constraints to adaptation. Adaptation options adopted to date continue to emphasise incremental adjustments and co- benefits and are starting to emphasise flexibility and learning (*medium evidence, medium agreement*). Most assessments of adaptation have been restricted to impacts, vulnerability, and adaptation planning, with very few assessing the processes of implementation or the effects of adaptation actions (*medium evidence, high agreement*).'

'Future Risks and Opportunities for Adaptation'

2.36

'Key risks are potentially severe impacts relevant to Article 2 of the United Nations Framework Convention on Climate Change, which refers to "dangerous anthropogenic interference with the climate system." Risks are considered key due to high hazard or high vulnerability of societies and systems exposed, or both. Identification of key risks was based on expert judgment using the following specific criteria: large magnitude, high probability, or irreversibility of impacts; timing of impacts; persistent vulnerability or exposure contributing to risks; or limited potential to reduce risks through adaptation or mitigation. ...

...

Increasing magnitudes of warming increase the likelihood of severe, pervasive, and irreversible impacts. Some risks of climate change are considerable at 1 or 2°C above preindustrial levels .... Global climate change risks are high to very high with global mean temperature increase of 4°C or more above preindustrial levels in all reasons for concern ..., and include severe and widespread impacts on unique and threatened systems, substantial species extinction, large risks to global and regional food security, and the combination of high temperature and humidity compromising normal human activities, including growing food or working outdoors in some areas for parts of the year (*high confidence*). The precise levels of climate change sufficient to trigger tipping points (thresholds for abrupt and irreversible change) remain uncertain, but the risk associated with crossing multiple tipping points in the earth system or in interlinked human and natural systems increases with rising temperature (*medium confidence*).

... Risks are reduced substantially under the assessed scenario with the lowest temperature projections ... compared to the highest temperature projections ... particularly in the second half of the 21st century (*very high confidence*). Reducing climate change can also reduce the scale of adaptation that might be required. Under all assessed scenarios for adaptation and mitigation, some risk from adverse impacts remains (*very high confidence*).'

2015 – Paris Agreement (COP 21)

2.37 This landmark agreement aimed to limit global warming to well below 2°C above pre-industrial levels, with efforts to limit the temperature increase to 1.5°C. Nearly all nations committed to reducing their carbon emissions. The overarching goal is to hold 'the increase in the global average temperature to well below 2°C above pre-industrial levels' and pursue efforts 'to limit the temperature increase to 1.5°C above pre-industrial levels'.

Implementation of the Paris Agreement requires economic and social transformation, based on the best available science. The Paris Agreement works on a five-year cycle of increasingly ambitious climate action or, ratcheting up, carried out by countries. Since 2020, countries have been submitting their national climate action plans, known as nationally determined contributions (NDCs). Each successive NDC is meant to reflect an increasingly higher degree of ambition compared to the previous version.

2018 – IPCC Special Report on Global Warming of 1.5°C[20]

2.38 This special report highlighted the urgent need for rapid and far-reaching 'transitions' in land, energy, industry, buildings, transport, and cities to limit the impact of global warming to 1.5°C above pre-industrial levels and related global GHG emission pathways contained in the Decision of COP 21 of the UNFCCC to adopt the Paris Agreement.

'Understanding Global Warming of 1.5°C'

2.39

> 'A.1 Human activities are estimated to have caused approximately 1.0°C of global warming above pre-industrial levels, with a *likely* range of 0.8°C to 1.2°C. Global warming is *likely* to reach 1.5°C between 2030 and 2052 if it continues to increase at the current rate. (*high confidence*)...
>
> ...
>
> A.2 Warming from anthropogenic emissions from the pre-industrial period to the present will persist for centuries to millennia and will continue to cause further long-term changes in the climate system, such as sea level rise, with associated impacts (*high confidence*), but these emissions alone are *unlikely* to cause global warming of 1.5°C (*medium confidence*). ...
>
> ...
>
> A.3 Climate-related risks for natural and human systems are higher for global warming of 1.5°C than at present, but lower than at 2°C (*high confidence*). These risks depend on the magnitude and rate of warming, geographic location, levels of development and vulnerability, and on the choices and implementation of adaptation and mitigation options (*high confidence*). ...'[21]

'Projected Climate Change, Potential Impacts and Associated Risks'

2.40

> 'B.1 Climate models project robust differences in regional climate characteristics between present-day and global warming of 1.5°C, and between 1.5°C and 2°C. These differences include increases in mean temperature in most

20 IPCC Special Report, *Global Warming of 1.5°C* (2018), https://www.ipcc.ch/sr15/

21 IPCC Special Report, *Global Warming of 1.5°C* (2018), *Summary for Policymakers*, https://www.ipcc.ch/sr15/

land and ocean regions (*high confidence*), hot extremes in most inhabited regions (*high confidence*), heavy precipitation in several regions (*medium confidence*), and the probability of drought and precipitation deficits in some regions (*medium confidence*). ...

...

B.2 By 2100, global mean sea level rise is projected to be around 0.1 metre lower with global warming of 1.5°C compared to 2°C (*medium confidence*). Sea levels will continue to rise well beyond 2100 (*high confidence*), and the magnitude and rate of this rise depend on future emission pathways. A slower rate of sea level rise enables greater opportunities for adaptation in the human and ecological systems of small islands, low-lying coastal areas and deltas (*medium confidence*). ...

...

B.3 On land, impacts on biodiversity and ecosystems, including species loss and extinction, are projected to be lower at 1.5°C of global warming compared to 2°C. Limiting global warming to 1.5°C compared to 2°C is projected to lower the impacts on terrestrial, freshwater and coastal ecosystems and to retain more of their services to humans (*high confidence*). ...

...

B.4 Limiting global warming to 1.5°C compared to 2°C is projected to reduce increases in ocean temperature as well as associated increases in ocean acidity and decreases in ocean oxygen levels (*high confidence*). Consequently, limiting global warming to 1.5°C is projected to reduce risks to marine biodiversity, fisheries, and ecosystems, and their functions and services to humans, as illustrated by recent changes to Arctic sea ice and warm-water coral reef ecosystems (*high confidence*). ...

...

B.5 Climate-related risks to health, livelihoods, food security, water supply, human security, and economic growth are projected to increase with global warming of 1.5°C and increase further with 2°C. ...

...

B.6 Most adaptation needs will be lower for global warming of 1.5°C compared to 2°C (*high confidence*). There are a wide range of adaptation options that can reduce the risks of climate change (*high confidence*). There are limits to adaptation and adaptive capacity for some human and natural systems at global warming of 1.5°C, with associated losses (*medium confidence*). The number and availability of adaptation options vary by sector (*medium confidence*). ...'[22]

'Emission Pathways and System Transitions Consistent with 1.5°C Global Warming'

2.41

'C.1 In model pathways with no or limited overshoot of 1.5°C, global net anthropogenic CO_2 emissions decline by about 45% from 2010 levels

22 IPCC Special Report, *Global Warming of 1.5°C* (2018), *Summary for Policymakers*, https://www.ipcc.ch/sr15/

by 2030 (40–60% interquartile range), reaching net zero around 2050 (2045–2055 interquartile range). For limiting global warming to below 2°C CO_2 emissions are projected to decline by about 25% by 2030 in most pathways (10–30% interquartile range) and reach net zero around 2070 (2065–2080 interquartile range). Non-CO_2 emissions in pathways that limit global warming to 1.5°C show deep reductions that are similar to those in pathways limiting warming to 2°C. (*high confidence*) ...

...

C.2 Pathways limiting global warming to 1.5°C with no or limited overshoot would require rapid and far-reaching transitions in energy, land, urban and infrastructure (including transport and buildings), and industrial systems (*high confidence*). These systems transitions are unprecedented in terms of scale, but not necessarily in terms of speed, and imply deep emissions reductions in all sectors, a wide portfolio of mitigation options and a significant upscaling of investments in those options (*medium confidence*). ...

...

C.3 All pathways that limit global warming to 1.5°C with limited or no overshoot project the use of carbon dioxide removal (CDR) on the order of 100–1000 $GtCO_2$ over the 21st century. CDR would be used to compensate for residual emissions and, in most cases, achieve net negative emissions to return global warming to 1.5°C following a peak (*high confidence*). CDR deployment of several hundreds of $GtCO_2$ is subject to multiple feasibility and sustainability constraints (*high confidence*). Significant near-term emissions reductions and measures to lower energy and land demand can limit CDR deployment to a few hundred $GtCO_2$ without reliance on bioenergy with carbon capture and storage (BECCS) (*high confidence*). ...'[23]

'Strengthening the Global Response in the Context of Sustainable Development and Efforts to Eradicate Poverty'

2.42

'D.1 Estimates of the global emissions outcome of current nationally stated mitigation ambitions as submitted under the Paris Agreement would lead to global greenhouse gas emissions in 2030 of 52–58 $GtCO_2eq\ yr^{-1}$ (*medium confidence*). Pathways reflecting these ambitions would not limit global warming to 1.5°C, even if supplemented by very challenging increases in the scale and ambition of emissions reductions after 2030 (*high confidence*). Avoiding overshoot and reliance on future large-scale deployment of carbon dioxide removal (CDR) can only be achieved if global CO_2 emissions start to decline well before 2030 (*high confidence*). ...

...

D.2 The avoided climate change impacts on sustainable development, eradication of poverty and reducing inequalities would be greater if global warming were limited to 1.5°C rather than 2°C, if mitigation and adaptation synergies are maximised while trade-offs are minimised (*high confidence*). ...

23 IPCC Special Report, *Global Warming of 1.5°C* (2018), *Summary for Policymakers*, https://www.ipcc.ch/sr15/

...

D.3 Adaptation options specific to national contexts, if carefully selected together with enabling conditions, will have benefits for sustainable development and poverty reduction with global warming of 1.5°C, although trade-offs are possible (*high confidence*). ...

...

D.4 Mitigation options consistent with 1.5°C pathways are associated with multiple synergies and trade-offs across the Sustainable Development Goals (SDGs). While the total number of possible synergies exceeds the number of trade-offs, their net effect will depend on the pace and magnitude of changes, the composition of the mitigation portfolio and the management of the transition. (*high confidence*) ...

...

D.5 Limiting the risks from global warming of 1.5°C in the context of sustainable development and poverty eradication implies system transitions that can be enabled by an increase of adaptation and mitigation investments, policy instruments, the acceleration of technological innovation and behaviour changes (*high confidence*). ...

...

D.6 Sustainable development supports, and often enables, the fundamental societal and systems transitions and transformations that help limit global warming to 1.5°C. Such changes facilitate the pursuit of climate-resilient development pathways that achieve ambitious mitigation and adaptation in conjunction with poverty eradication and efforts to reduce inequalities (*high confidence*). ...

...

D.7 Strengthening the capacities for climate action of national and sub-national authorities, civil society, the private sector, indigenous peoples and local communities can support the implementation of ambitious actions implied by limiting global warming to 1.5°C (*high confidence*). International cooperation can provide an enabling environment for this to be achieved in all countries and for all people, in the context of sustainable development. International cooperation is a critical enabler for developing countries and vulnerable regions (*high confidence*). ...'[24]

RECENT DEVELOPMENTS

2020 – Paris Agreement takes legal effect

2.43 On 4 November 2016, the Paris Agreement entered into force.

24 IPCC Special Report, *Global Warming of 1.5°C* (2018), *Summary for Policymakers*, https://www.ipcc.ch/sr15/

2021 – COP 26 in Glasgow: Together for our Planet

2.44 The UN Climate Change Conference in Glasgow (COP 26) brought together 120 world leaders and over 40,000 registered participants, including 22,274 party delegates, 14,124 observers and 3,886 media representatives.

The outcome of COP 26 was the Glasgow Climate Pact.

Recognising the emergency

2.45 Countries reaffirmed the Paris Agreement goal of limiting the increase in the global average temperature to well below 2°C above pre-industrial levels and pursuing efforts to limit it to 1.5°C. And they went further, expressing 'alarm and utmost concern that human activities have caused around 1.1°C of warming to date, that impacts are already being felt in every region, and that carbon budgets consistent with achieving the Paris Agreement temperature goal are now small and being rapidly depleted.' They recognised that the impacts of climate change would be much lower at a temperature increase of 1.5°C compared with 2°C.

Accelerating action

2.46 Countries stressed the urgency of action 'in this critical decade', when CO_2 emissions must be reduced by 45 per cent to reach net zero around mid-century, but with present climate plans – the NDCs – falling far short on ambition, the Glasgow Climate Pact called on all countries to present stronger national action plans the following year, instead of in 2025, which was the original timeline. Countries also called on the UNFCCC to do an annual NDC Synthesis Report to gauge the present level of ambition.

Moving away from fossil fuels

2.47 In perhaps the most contested decision in Glasgow, countries ultimately agreed to a provision calling for a phase-down of coal power and a phase-out of 'inefficient' fossil fuel subsidies – two key issues that had never been explicitly mentioned in decisions of UN climate talks before, despite coal, oil and gas being the main drivers of global warming. Many countries, and non-governmental organisations (NGOs), expressed dissatisfaction that the language on coal was significantly weakened (from phase-out to phase-down) and, consequently, was not as ambitious as it needed to be.

Delivering on climate finance

2.48 Developed countries came to Glasgow falling short on their promise to deliver US$100 billion a year for developing countries. Voicing 'regret', the Glasgow outcome reaffirmed the pledge and urged developed countries to fully deliver on the US$100 billion goal urgently. Developed countries, in a report, expressed confidence that the target would be met in 2023.

Stepping up support for adaptation

2.49 The Glasgow Pact called for a doubling of finance to support developing countries in adapting to the impacts of climate change and building resilience. This may not provide all the funding that poorer countries need, but it would significantly increase finance for protecting lives and livelihoods, which so far made up only about 25 per cent of all climate finance (with 75 per cent going towards green technologies to mitigate GHG emissions). Glasgow also established a work programme to define a global goal on adaptation, which would identify collective needs and solutions to the climate crisis already affecting many countries.

Completing the Paris rulebook

2.50 Countries reached agreement on the remaining issues of the so-called Paris rulebook, the operational details for the practical implementation of the Paris Agreement. Among them are the norms related to carbon markets, which will allow countries struggling to meet their emissions targets to purchase emissions reductions from other nations that have already exceeded their targets. Negotiations were also concluded on an Enhanced Transparency Framework, providing for common timeframes and agreed formats for countries to regularly report on progress, designed to build trust and confidence that all countries are contributing their share to the global effort.

Focusing on loss and damage

2.51 Acknowledging that climate change is having increasing impacts on people especially in the developing world, countries agreed to strengthen a network – known as the Santiago Network – that connects vulnerable countries with providers of technical assistance, knowledge and resources to address climate risks. They also launched a new 'Glasgow dialogue' to discuss arrangements for the funding of activities to avert, minimise and address loss and damage associated with the adverse effects of climate change.

New deals and announcements

2.52 There were many other significant deals and announcements, outside of the Glasgow Climate Pact, which could have major positive impacts if they are indeed implemented. These include the below.

Forests

2.53 137 countries took a landmark step forward by committing to halt and reverse forest loss and land degradation by 2030. The pledge is backed by $12 billion in public and $7.2 billion in private funding. In addition, CEOs from more than 30 financial institutions with over $8.7 trillion of global assets committed to eliminate investment in activities linked to deforestation.

Methane

2.54 103 countries, including 15 major emitters, signed up to the Global Methane Pledge, which aims to limit methane emissions by 30 per cent by 2030, compared to 2020 levels. Methane, one of the most potent GHGs, is responsible for a third of current warming from human activities.

Cars

2.55 Over 30 countries, six major vehicle manufacturers and other actors, like cities, set out their determination for all new car and van sales to be zero-emission vehicles by 2040 globally and 2035 in leading markets, accelerating the decarbonisation of road transport, which currently accounts for about 10 per cent of global GHG emissions.

Coal

2.56 Leaders from South Africa, the UK, the US, France, Germany, and the EU announced a ground-breaking partnership to support South Africa – the world's most carbon-intensive electricity producer – with $8.5 billion over the next 3–5 years to make a just transition away from coal to a low-carbon economy.

2022 – COP 27 Sharm El Sheikh

Private finance

2.57 Decisions taken in Sharm El Sheikh require countries to make an extra effort to address the climate crisis, emphasising the need for multilateral development banks and international financial institutions to leverage private financing for developing countries.

Establishing a dedicated fund for loss and damage

2.58 COP 27 had an agreement to provide loss and damage funding for vulnerable countries hit hard by floods, droughts and other climate disasters. This was the first time that countries recognised the need for finance to respond to loss and damage associated with the catastrophic effects of climate change and agreed to the establishing of a fund and the necessary funding arrangements. A 'transitional committee' will be asked to make recommendations on how to operationalise both the new funding arrangements and the fund for consideration and adoption at COP28.

Maintaining a clear intention to keep 1.5°C within reach

2.59 The IPCC says limiting warming to around 1.5°C requires global GHG emissions to peak before 2025 at the latest, and be reduced by 43 per cent by 2030. A press release from UN Climate Change[25] shows implementation of current pledges by national governments puts the world on track for a 2.5°C warmer world by the end of the century.

Holding business and institutions to account

2.60 The transparency of commitments from businesses and institutions would be a priority of UN Climate Change in 2023. The UN Secretary-General asked UN Climate Change to come up with a plan for early 2023 on how to ensure transparency and accountability with non-state actors.

Mobilising more financial support for developing countries

2.61 The COP 27 cover decision, known as the Sharm el-Sheikh Implementation Plan, highlights that a global transformation to a low-carbon economy is expected to require investments of at least US $4–6 trillion a year and much funding will require rapid and comprehensive transformation of the financial system and its structures and processes, engaging governments, central banks, commercial banks, institutional investors and other financial actors.

One of the key outcomes of the decisions on climate finance is a call for developed country Parties to provide resources for the second replenishment of the Green Climate Fund. All countries welcomed the recent pledges made to the Adaptation Fund (totalling US $211.58 million), the Least Developed Countries Fund (totalling US $70.6 million), and the Special Climate Change Fund (totalling US $35 million).

Making the pivot towards implementation

2.62 The decisions adopted at COP 27 have a strong focus on implementation and aim to strengthen action by countries to cut GHG emissions and adapt to the impacts of climate change, as well as boost the support of finance, technology and capacity building needed by developing countries.

Nations resolved to make the transition to low-emission and climate-resilient development ambitious, just and equitable. At COP 27 it was decided to establish a work programme on 'just transition', which is expected to build on and complement the work to urgently scale up mitigation ambition and implementation.

The Paris Agreement calls on signatories to consider 'the imperatives of a just transition of the workforce and the creation of decent work and quality jobs in accordance with nationally defined development priorities'.[26] That means a

25 Press Release, 'Climate Plans Remain Insufficient: More Ambitious Action Needed Now', UN Climate Change (26 October 2022).

26 Paris Agreement to the United Nations Framework Convention on Climate Change, 12 December, 2015

just transition is not a fixed set of rules, 'but a vision and a process based on dialogue and an agenda shared by workers, industry, and governments that need to be negotiated and implemented in their geographical, political, cultural, and social contexts,' according to the International Institute for Sustainable Development.[27]

2023 – COP 28 Dubai

2.63 The COP 28 UN Climate Change Conference in Dubai, the United Arab Emirates, was the biggest of its kind. Some 85,000 participants, including more than 150 Heads of State and Government, were among the representatives of national delegations, civil society, business, Indigenous Peoples, youth, philanthropy, and international organisations in attendance at the Conference from 30 November to 13 December 2023.

COP 28 Decisions

2.64 COP 28 was particularly momentous as it marked the conclusion of the first 'global stocktake' of the world's efforts to address climate change under the Paris Agreement. Having shown that progress was too slow across all areas of climate action – from reducing GHG emissions, to strengthening resilience to a changing climate, to getting the financial and technological support to vulnerable nations – countries responded with a decision on how to accelerate action across all areas by 2030. This includes a call on governments to speed up the transition away from fossil fuels to renewables such as wind and solar power in their next round of climate commitments.

27 International Institute for sustainable development, 'Just Transition', https://www.iisd.org/topics/just-transition

Chapter 3

Climate Change Laws and Policies

3.01 Climate change law and policies are designed to mitigate and adapt to the impacts of climate change. These frameworks operate at various levels, from international agreements to national laws and local regulations.

INTERNATIONAL AGREEMENTS

3.02 International agreements on climate change are the frameworks for global cooperation to mitigate and adapt to the impacts of climate change. These agreements establish targets, mechanisms, and strategies for countries to collectively address climate change.

United Nations Framework Convention on Climate Change (UNFCCC)

3.03 **Adoption:** 1992 at the Earth Summit in Rio de Janeiro.

Objective: Stabilise greenhouse gas (GHG) concentrations in the atmosphere at a level that would prevent dangerous anthropogenic interference with the climate system.

Significance: Provides a framework for negotiating specific international treaties (protocols) that may set binding limits on GHGs.

Key Provisions: Common but differentiated responsibilities, periodic conferences (COPs).

Kyoto Protocol

3.04 **Adoption:** 1997, entered into force in 2005.

Objective: Legally binding emissions reduction targets for 37 industrialised countries and the European Community to reduce GHG emissions by an average of 5 per cent compared to 1990 levels during the first commitment period (2008–12).

Mechanisms:

- Emissions trading: allow countries that have emission units to spare to sell excess capacity to countries that are over their targets.
- Clean Development Mechanism (CDM): Enables developed countries to invest in emission reduction projects in developing countries and earn certified emission reduction (CER) credits.
- Joint Implementation (JI): Allows developed countries to earn emission reduction units (ERUs) from projects in other developed countries.

Paris Agreement

3.05 **Adoption:** 2015, entered into force in 2016.

Objective: Limit global warming to well below 2°C above pre-industrial levels, and pursue efforts to limit the temperature increase to 1.5°C.

Nationally Determined Contributions (NDCs): Each country sets its own emission reduction targets, which are reviewed and updated every five years.

Key Features:

- **Global Stocktake:** Every five years, a global assessment of progress towards the agreement's long-term goals.
- **Financial Support:** Developed countries committed to mobilising $100 billion per year by 2020 to support climate action in developing countries.
- **Transparency Framework:** A system for tracking progress and ensuring accountability through reporting and review.

Doha Amendment to the Kyoto Protocol

3.06 **Adoption:** 2012, entered into force in 2020.

Second Commitment Period: 2013–20, with new emission reduction targets for participating countries.

Significance: Extended the Kyoto Protocol until the implementation of the Paris Agreement.

The Glasgow Climate Pact

3.07 **Adoption:** 2021 at the COP 26 in Glasgow.

Key Outcomes:

- **Mitigation Efforts:** Encourages countries to strengthen their 2030 emissions targets by the end of 2022.
- **Adaptation and Finance:** The Glasgow Climate pact called for a doubling of adaptation finance from 2019 levels by 2025.
- **Coal and Fossil Fuels:** Includes a call to accelerate efforts towards the phase-down of unabated coal power and phase-out of inefficient fossil fuel subsidies.

Montreal Protocol and Kigali Amendment

3.08

- **Montreal Protocol (1987):** Initially aimed at phasing out ozone-depleting substances, it indirectly contributes to climate change mitigation.
- **Kigali Amendment (2016):** Aims to phase down hydrofluorocarbons (HFCs), potent GHGs, with the potential to avoid up to 0.5°C of global warming by 2100.

EUROPEAN UNION (EU)

3.09 Regional agreements and initiatives play a critical role in addressing climate change by facilitating cooperation amongst countries within a specific region. These initiatives often complement global efforts and address region-specific climate challenges. In contrast to sectors in the EU Emissions Trading System (ETS), which are regulated at EU level, Member States are responsible for national policies and measures to limit emissions from the sectors covered by the Effort Sharing legislation. Member States have to adopt their national energy and climate action plans (NECPs), covering the period from 2021 to 2030, in which they set out national objectives and corresponding policies and measures.

Policies and measures could include:

- reducing transport needs
- promoting public transport
- a shift away from transport based on fossil fuels
- support schemes for retrofitting buildings
- more efficient heating and cooling systems
- renewable energy for heating and cooling
- more climate-friendly farming practices
- conversion of livestock manure to biogas.

How EU action helps reduce national emissions

3.10 Measures taken at EU level also help Member States to reduce emissions in sectors covered by the Effort Sharing Regulation (ESR).[1] For instance:

- all new cars and vans in the EU must be zero-emission vehicles as from 2035;
- emission reductions from buildings will be aided by measures to improve their energy performance, eco-design requirements for energy-related products, and energy labelling systems to inform consumers;
- restrictions on fluorinated industrial gases (F-gases) and implementation of other EU environmental policies, eg on soil protection and waste, will also contribute to reaching the national targets.

European Green Deal

3.11 **Objective:** Make Europe the first climate-neutral continent by 2050.

Key Actions: Emission reductions, investment in green technologies, the circular economy, and biodiversity protection.

The European Green Deal[2] aims to make Europe the first climate-neutral continent. The aim of the green deal is to transform the EU into a modern, resource-efficient and competitive economy, ensuring:

1 Effort Sharing Regulation. Regulation (EU) 2023/857 of the European Parliament and of the Council of 19 April 2023 amending Regulation (EU) 2018/842 on binding annual greenhouse gas emission reductions by Member States from 2021 to 2030 contributing to climate action to meet commitments under the Paris Agreement, and Regulation (EU) 2018/1999 [2023] OJ L111/1.

2 European Commission, 'The European Green Deal – Striving to be the first climate-neutral continent', https://ec.europa.eu/newsroom/know4pol/items/664852

- no net emissions of GHGs by 2050;
- economic growth decoupled from resource use;
- no person and no place left behind.

The European Commission has adopted a set of proposals to make the EU's climate, energy, transport and taxation policies fit for reducing net GHG emissions by at least 55 per cent by 2030, compared to 1990 levels.

Delivering the path to climate-neutral Europe by 2050

3.12 The EU set out proposals in July 2021 to make all sectors of the EU economy fit to meet the challenge starting by reducing emissions to at least 55 per cent by the end of the decade. It produced the 'Fit for 55' legislation

Fit for 55: Delivering on proposals

3.13 The Fit for 55 package of legislation makes all sectors of the EU's economy fit to meet this target. It sets the EU on a path to reach its climate targets in a cost-effective and competitive way.

EU Emissions Trading System (ETS) reform[3]

3.14 **Mechanism:** Cap-and-trade system – sets a cap on the total amount of certain GHGs that can be emitted by installations covered by the system.

Impact: Encourages companies to reduce emissions and invest in clean technologies.

The ETS is designed to:

- make polluters pay for their GHG emissions, help bring emissions down and generate revenues to finance the EU's green transition,
- operate in all EU countries, plus Iceland, Liechtenstein and Norway (EEA-EFTA states),
- cover emissions from around 10,000 installations in the energy sector and manufacturing industry, as well as aircraft operators flying within the EU and departing to Switzerland and the UK – or around 40 per cent of the EU's emissions,
- and also cover emissions from maritime transport from 2024.

3 Directive (EU) 2023/959 of the European Parliament and of the Council of 10 May 2023 amending Directive 2003/87/EC establishing a system for greenhouse gas emission allowance trading within the Union and Decision (EU) 2015/1814 concerning the establishment and operation of a market stability reserve for the Union greenhouse gas emission trading system [2023] OJ L130/134.

Cap-and-trade system

3.15 A cap is a set limit on the total amount of GHGs that can be emitted by the installations and aircraft operators covered by the system. The cap is reduced annually in line with the EU's climate target, ensuring that emissions decrease overtime. Since 2005, the EU ETS has helped bring down emissions from power and industry plants by 37 per cent. The cap is expressed in emission allowances, where one allowance gives the right to emit one ton of CO_2eq (carbon dioxide equivalent). For each year, companies must surrender enough allowances to fully account for their emissions, otherwise fines are imposed.

Within the cap, companies primarily buy allowances on the EU carbon market, but they also receive some allowances for free. Companies can also trade allowances with each other. If an installation or operator reduce their emissions, they can either keep the spare allowances to use in the future or sell them.

The declining cap offers companies some certainty about the scarcity of allowances long term and ensures that allowances have market value. Allowance price provides an incentive for companies to reduce emissions. It also determines the revenues that the EU ETS generates from the sale of allowances. Since 2013, the EU ETS has generated over €152 billion in revenue.

The revenue from the EU ETS feeds mostly into national budgets. Member States use these revenues to support investments in renewable energy, energy efficiency improvements and low-carbon technologies that help reduce emissions further. The sale of allowances also supplies the EU ETS with funds for low-carbon innovation and energy transition, the Innovation Fund and the Modernisation Fund.

ETS EU legislative framework

3.16 Launched in 2005, the EU ETS operates in trading phases. The system is now in its fourth trading phase (2021–30). Its legislative framework is spelled out in the ETS Directive. Over the years there have been several revisions, aligning the system with the overarching EU climate targets.

The ETS Directive for phase 4 was first revised in 2018 in line with the EU's 2030 climate and energy framework.[4] In light of the European Green Deal and the EU's more ambitious climate targets another revision of the Directive for phase 4 was launched in 2021.

On 14 July 2021, the European Commission presented 'Fit for 55' – a package of proposals to reform EU climate and energy policy, including the EU ETS. The European Parliament and Member States in the Council of the EU had adopted the ETS-related proposals by June 2023.

4 EU Climate Energy Framework, https://www.consilium.europa.eu/en/policies/climate-change/2030-climate-and-energy-framework/#:~:text=The%202030%20framework%20aims%20to,especially%20for%20oil%20and%20gas

Auctioning

3.17 On 14 July 2021, the European Commission adopted a series of legislative proposals setting out how it intends to achieve climate neutrality in the EU by 2050, including the intermediate target of an at least 55 per cent net reduction in GHG emissions by 2030. The package revised several pieces of EU climate legislation, including the EU ETS, the Effort Sharing Regulation, transport and land use legislation, and set out the ways in which the Commission intends to reach EU climate targets under the European Green Deal.

Auctioning is a transparent method for allocating emission allowances and puts into practice the principle that the polluter should pay. Businesses covered by the EU ETS have to buy an increasing proportion of allowances through auctions.

Auctioning is the default method of allocating allowances as of phase 3 of the EU ETS (2013–20).

ETS 2

3.18 The ETS2 is to be fully operational in 2027 and its first step is to monitor and report on emissions will begin in 2025.

Climate Law

3.19 **Binding Target:** Legally binding target to cut emissions by at least 55 per cent by 2030 compared to 1990 levels.

The European Climate Law[5] writes into law the goal set out in the European Green Deal for Europe's economy and society to become climate-neutral by 2050. The law also sets the intermediate target of reducing net GHG emissions by at least 55 per cent by 2030, compared to 1990 levels.

Climate neutrality by 2050 means achieving net-zero GHG emissions for EU countries as a whole, mainly by cutting emissions, investing in green technologies and protecting the natural environment.

The law aims to ensure that all EU policies contribute to this goal and that all sectors of the economy and society play their part. It:

- sets the long-term direction of travel for meeting the 2050 climate neutrality objective through all policies, in a socially fair and cost-efficient manner;
- sets a more ambitious EU 2030 target, to set Europe on a responsible path to becoming climate-neutral by 2050;
- creates a system for monitoring progress and taking further action if needed;
- provides predictability for investors and other economic actors;
- ensures that the transition to climate neutrality is irreversible.

5 Regulation (EU) 2021/1119 of the European Parliament and of the Council of 30 June 2021 establishing the framework for achieving climate neutrality and amending Regulations (EC) No 401/2009 and (EU) 2018/1999 ('European Climate Law') [2021] OJ L243/1.

The European Climate Law sets a legally binding target of net-zero GHG emissions by 2050. The EU Institutions and the Member States are bound to take the necessary measures at EU and national level to meet the target, considering the importance of promoting fairness and solidarity among Member States.

The Climate Law includes measures to keep track of progress and adjust our actions, accordingly, based on existing systems such as the governance process for Member States' NECPs, regular reports by the European Environment Agency, and the latest scientific evidence on climate change and its impacts.

Progress will be reviewed every five years, in line with the global stocktake exercise under the Paris Agreement.

The Climate Law also addresses the necessary steps to get to the 2050 target:

- Based on a comprehensive impact assessment, the EU has set a new target for 2030 of reducing net GHG emissions by at least 55 per cent compared to levels in 1990. The new EU 2030 target is included in the law.
- In July 2021, the Commission adopted a series of proposals to revise all relevant policy instruments to deliver the additional emissions reductions for 2030.
- The law also includes a process for setting a 2040 climate target.

The Climate Law includes:

- a legal objective for the EU to reach climate neutrality by 2050;
- an ambitious 2030 climate target of at least 55 per cent reduction of net emissions of GHGs as compared to 1990, with clarity on the contribution of emission reductions and removals;
- recognition of the need to enhance the EU's carbon sink through a more ambitious land use, land use change, and forestry (LULUCF) regulation, for which the Commission made a proposal in July 2021 which entered into force in May 2023;
- a process for setting a 2040 climate target, considering an indicative GHG budget for 2030–50 to be published by the Commission;
- a commitment to negative emissions after 2050;
- the establishment of a European Scientific Advisory Board on Climate Change, that will provide independent scientific advice;
- stronger provisions on adaptation to climate change;
- strong coherence across EU policies with the climate neutrality objective;
- a commitment to engage with sectors to prepare sector-specific roadmaps charting the path to climate neutrality in different areas of the economy.

The European Climate Law was published in the *Official Journal* on 9 July 2021 and entered into force on 29 July 2021.

New EU Emissions Trading System for building and road transport fuels

3.20 As part of the 2023 revisions of the ETS Directive, a new emissions trading system, named ETS2, was created, separate from the existing EU ETS.

This new system will cover and address the CO_2 emissions from fuel combustion in buildings, road transport and additional sectors (mainly small industry not covered by the existing EU ETS).

The ETS2 will complement other policies of the European Green Deal in the covered sectors, helping Member States to achieve their emission reduction targets under the ESR. So far, emission reductions in those sectors have been insufficient to put the EU on a firm path towards its 2050 climate neutrality goal. The carbon price set by the ETS2 will provide a market incentive for investments in building renovations and low-emissions mobility.

The ETS2 will become fully operational in 2027. Although it will be a 'cap and trade' system like the existing EU ETS, the ETS2 will cover emissions upstream. It will be fuel suppliers, rather than end consumers such as households or car users, that will be required to monitor and report their emissions.

Social Climate Fund (SCF)

3.21 The SCF[6] was created alongside the ETS2 for emissions from fuel combustion in buildings, road transport and additional sectors. It provides Member States with dedicated funding so that the most affected vulnerable groups, such as households in energy or transport poverty, are directly supported. Member States may use the SCF to support structural measures and investments:

- in energy efficiency and renovation of buildings;
- clean heating and cooling;
- integration of renewable energy; and
- zero- and low-emission mobility solutions.

Member States will have the option of spending part of the resources on temporary direct income support. All these measures and investments will be compiled into national Social Climate Plans following a country-wide consultation. Member States will submit these plans to the European Commission by June 2025. The Commission will assess the plans and disburse payments to the Member States only if the milestones and targets set in the plans are achieved.

To finance these measures the SCF will pool revenues from the auctioning of allowances from the ETS2 as well as 50 million allowances from the existing EU ETS. Together with a mandatory 25 per cent contribution by the Member States to their Social Climate Plans, the SCF should mobilise at least €86.7 billion over the 2026–32 period.

To facilitate the implementation of the SCF, the Commission launched a dedicated initiative to help Member States develop their Social Climate Plans under the Technical Support Instrument. The Commission is also enabling an exchange of good practices among Member States through dedicated formation of the Commission Expert Group on Climate Change Policy (CCEG).

6 Social Climate Fund: Regulation (EU) 2023/955 of the European Parliament and of the Council of 10 May 2023 establishing a Social Climate Fund and amending Regulation (EU) 2021/1060 [2023] OJ L130/1.

Effort Sharing Regulation (ESR)

3.22 The ESR[7] establishes binding annual GHG emission targets for Member States from 2021 to 2030. These national targets concern emissions from the following sectors:

- domestic transport (excluding aviation)
- buildings
- agriculture
- small industry
- waste.

These sectors account for almost 60 per cent of emissions in the EU. The ESR is part of a set of policies and measures to help reduce the EU's emissions by at least 55 per cent by 2030, compared to 1990 levels. This is a milestone to deliver the European Green Deal and achieve climate neutrality by 2050. The ESR is also part of the Energy Union strategy and the EU's implementation of the Paris Agreement.

Reducing emissions by 10 per cent by 2020

3.23 The ESR was preceded by the Effort Sharing Decision establishing the emission reduction targets from 2013 to 2020. The objective was to reduce emissions in the EU by 10 per cent compared to 2005 levels. In 2020, the EU27's emissions covered by the Effort Sharing Decision were 16.3 per cent lower than in 2005, meaning the EU overachieved its target by six percentage points.

Reducing emissions by 40 per cent by 2030

3.24 The ESR was adopted on 14 May 2018, with the aim to reduce emissions from key sectors by 30 per cent by 2030 (compared to 2005 levels). On 19 April 2023, following a package of proposals from the European Commission to implement the Green Deal, the ESR was amended. Among other changes, the 2030 emission reduction target was set to -40 per cent compared to 2005 levels.

The ESR assigns each Member State with an emission reduction target for 2030, a set of annual emission allocations for each year from 2021 to 2030, and flexibility to deal with annual fluctuations in GHG emissions due to weather or economic conditions.

7 Effort Sharing Regulation. Regulation (EU) 2023/857 of the European Parliament and of the Council of 19 April 2023 amending Regulation (EU) 2018/842 on binding annual greenhouse gas emission reductions by Member States from 2021 to 2030 contributing to climate action to meet commitments under the Paris Agreement, and Regulation (EU) 2018/1999 [2023] OJ L111/1.

Gases and sources

3.25 The ESR covers the seven GHGs:

- carbon dioxide (CO_2)
- methane (CH_4)
- nitrous oxide (N_2O)
- hydrofluorocarbons (HFCs)
- perfluorocarbons (PFCs)
- sulphur hexafluoride (SF_6)
- nitrogen trifluoride (NF_3)

The targets apply to domestic GHG emissions from IPCC source categories of energy, industrial processes and product use, agriculture and waste.

Regulation and land use, land-use change and forestry (LULUCF)[8]

3.26 The rate of build-up of CO_2 in the atmosphere can be reduced by using the fact that atmospheric CO_2 can accumulate as carbon in vegetation and soils in terrestrial ecosystems. Under the UNFCCC any process, activity or mechanism which removes a GHG from the atmosphere is referred to as a 'sink'. Human activities impact terrestrial sinks, through land use, land use change and forestry (LULUCF), consequently, the exchange of CO_2 (carbon cycle) between the terrestrial biosphere and the atmosphere is altered.

The IPCC Sixth Assessment Report found that the 'Agriculture, Forestry and Other Land Use (AFOLU)' sector, on average, accounted for 13–21 per cent of global total anthropogenic GHG emissions in the period 2010–19. Estimated anthropogenic net CO_2 emissions from AFOLU (based on bookkeeping models) result in a net source of +5.9±4.1 $GtCO_2eq/yr$ between 2010 and 2019 with an unclear trend. Land-use change drivers net AFOLU CO_2 emission fluxes, with deforestation being responsible for 45 per cent of total AFOLU emissions. In addition there is a net carbon sink and source of GHG emissions, land plays an important role in climate through albedo[9] effects, evapotranspiration, and aerosol loading through emissions of volatile organic compounds.

The IPCC report found that the LULUCF sector provided significant near-term mitigation potential while providing food, wood and other renewable resources as well as biodiversity conservation. Mitigation measures in forests and other natural ecosystems provide the largest share of the LULUCF mitigation potential between 2020 and 2050. Among LULUCF activities, reducing deforestation has the largest potential to reduce anthropogenic GHG emissions, followed by carbon sequestration in agriculture and ecosystem restoration, including afforestation and reforestation.

8 LULUCF: Regulation (EU) 2023/839 of the European Parliament and of the Council of 19 April 2023 amending Regulation (EU) 2018/841 as regards the scope, simplifying the reporting and compliance rules, and setting out the targets of the Member States for 2030, and Regulation (EU) 2018/1999 as regards improvement in monitoring, reporting, tracking of progress and review [2023] OJ L107/1.

9 'Albedo' – fraction of light that a surface reflects.

Mitigation activities in the LULUCF sector can have multiple synergies with the Sustainable Development Goals (SDGs), such as enhancing biodiversity and ecosystem functions, employment and local livelihoods. In another light, the IPCC report recognises that some activities, such as deployment of afforestation of naturally unforested land, can compound climate-related risks to biodiversity, water and food security, and livelihoods, especially if not implemented with due consideration of the local conditions, including current use of the land. Such risks can best be managed if LULUCF mitigation is pursued in response to the needs and perspectives of multiple stakeholders to achieve outcomes that maximise synergies while limiting trade-offs.

However, the main challenges of LULUCF activities are their potential reversibility and the non-permanence of carbon stocks. The storage of CO_2 through vegetation and soil management can be reversed by human activities, natural disturbances or a combination of the two, and it is also prone to climate change impacts. Such severe impacts include wildfires, mass mortality of trees and weakening natural land carbon sinks, and are already observed and projected to increase with every additional increment of global warming. Concerted, rapid and sustained actions that limit global warming to close to 1.5°C would substantially reduce projected losses and damages related to climate change in ecosystems, according to the IPCC.

CO_2 emissions and standards for cars and vans[10]

3.27 Passenger cars and light commercial vehicles (vans) are respectively responsible for around 16 per cent, and 3 per cent of total, EU emissions of CO_2, the main GHG driving climate change.

To reduce emissions, the EU has a Regulation that sets CO_2 emission performance standards for new passenger cars and vans.[11]

With tighter CO_2 emission targets in place since 2020, the average CO_2 emissions from all new passenger cars registered in Europe fell by 27 per cent between 2019 and 2022, while the average emissions from new vans dropped by 10 per cent. The main driver of this decrease in emissions is the increase in zero-emission vehicles, which respectively amounted to 13.4 per cent and 6 per cent of the 2022 EU (and Norway and Iceland) new car and van fleet.

On 19 April 2023, the European Parliament and the Council amended the Regulation to strengthen the CO_2 emission performance standards for new passenger cars and vans and bring them in line with the EU's ambition to reach climate neutrality by 2050. This amendment strengthened the emission targets applying from 2030 and set a 100 per cent emission reduction target for both cars and vans from 2035 onwards.

10 Regulation (EU) 2023/851 of the European Parliament and of the Council of 19 April 2023 amending Regulation (EU) 2019/631 as regards strengthening the CO2 emission performance standards for new passenger cars and new light commercial vehicles in line with the Union's increased climate ambition [2023] OJ L110/5.

11 Emission Performance Standards: Regulation (EU) 2019/631 of the European Parliament and of the Council of 17 April 2019 setting CO2 emission performance standards for new passenger cars and for new light commercial vehicles, and repealing Regulations (EC) No 443/2009 and (EU) No 510/2011 (Type Approval Regulation) [2019] OJ L111/13.

Benefits

3.28 The amended Regulation (EU) 2019/631 will:

- contribute to reaching at least 55 per cent net GHG emission reductions by 2030 compared to 1990 as well as achieving climate neutrality by 2050, in line with the European Climate Law;
- provide benefits to EU citizens and vehicle users as a result of the wider deployment of clean and affordable zero-emission vehicles; and
- spur innovation in zero-emission technologies, strengthening the EU's technological leadership of the automotive value chain and stimulating employment in the EU.

Target levels

3.29 Below are the EU fleet-wide CO_2 emission targets set in the Regulation:

For 2020–24

- Cars: 95 g CO_2/km
- Vans: 147 g CO_2/km

These target levels refer to the New European Driving Cycle (NEDC) emission test procedure.

For 2025–34

The targets that will apply from 2025 onwards are based on the Worldwide Harmonized Light Vehicles Test Procedure (WLTP) and were set out in Commission Implementing Decision (EU) 2023/1623:[12]

- Cars: 93,6 g CO_2/km (2025–29) and 49,5 g CO_2/km (2030–34)
- Vans: 153,9 g CO_2/km (2025–9) and 90,6 g CO_2/km (2030–34)

From 2035 onwards, the EU fleet-wide CO_2 emission target for both cars and vans is 0 g CO_2/km, corresponding to a 100 per cent reduction.

The annual specific emission targets of each manufacturer are based on these EU fleet-wide targets, considering the average mass of its registered new vehicles. Since 2021, those specific emission targets are based on the WLTP.

Incentive mechanism for zero- and low-emission vehicles (ZLEV)

3.30 From 2025 to 2029, a ZLEV crediting system will apply both for car and van manufacturers. The system will alleviate a manufacturer's specific emission target if its share of new ZLEV (vehicles with emissions between 0 and 50 g CO_2/km) registered in a given year exceeds the following benchmarks:

12 Commission Implementing Decision (EU) 2023/1623 of 3 August 2023 specifying the values relating to the performance of manufacturers and pools of manufacturers of new passenger cars and new light commercial vehicles for the calendar year 2021 and the values to be used for the calculation of the specific emission targets from 2025 onwards, pursuant to Regulation (EU) 2019/631 of the European Parliament and of the Council and correcting Implementing Decision (EU) 2022/2087 (notified under document C(2023) 5068) [2023] OJ L200/5.

- Cars: 25 per cent ZLEV
- Vans: 17 per cent ZLEV

Exceeding the ZLEV benchmark by one percentage point will increase the manufacturer's CO_2 target (in g CO_2/km) by 1 per cent. The alleviation of the emission target will be capped at a maximum of 5 per cent to safeguard the environmental integrity of the Regulation.

To calculate the ZLEV share in a manufacturer's fleet, an accounting rule gives a greater weight to ZLEVs with lower CO_2 emissions. An additional multiplier may apply for cars registered in Member States with a low share and number of ZLEVs registered in 2017.

Penalties for excess emissions

3.31 If the average CO_2 emissions of a manufacturer's fleet exceed its specific emission target in a given year, the manufacturer must pay for each of its new vehicles registered in that year, an excess emissions premium of €95 per g/km over target.

Pooling

3.32 Different manufacturers can act jointly to meet their emissions target. When forming a pool, manufacturers must respect the rules of competition law. Pooling between car and van manufacturers is not possible.

Exemptions and derogations

3.33 Manufacturers responsible for fewer than 1,000 new cars or fewer than 1,000 new vans registered in the EU per year are exempt from meeting a specific emission target in the following year, unless they voluntarily apply for a derogation.

Manufacturers can apply for a derogation from their specific emission target subject to the following conditions:

- A 'small volume' manufacturer (responsible for less than 10,000 new cars or less than 22,000 new vans registered per year) can propose its own derogation target, based on the criteria set in Article 10 of the Regulation.
- A 'niche' car manufacturer (responsible for between 10,000 and 300,000 new cars registered per year) can apply for a derogation for the years until 2028, included. The derogation targets are calculated as set out in Article 10(4) of the Regulation and in point 5 of Part A of its Annex I. Feel free to access the values used to calculate the 'niche' derogation target from 2025 onwards.

Eco-innovations

3.34 To promote the development of new and advanced technologies reducing CO_2 emissions from vehicles, manufacturers can obtain emission credits for cars and vans which are equipped with innovative technologies (eco-innovations) whose full CO_2 savings are impossible to demonstrate during their type-approval.

However, the manufacturer must demonstrate these savings based on independently verified data. The maximum emission credits for these eco-innovations per manufacturer are 7 g CO_2/km per year until 2024, 6 g CO_2/km from 2025 to 2029, and 4 g CO_2/km from 2030 to 2034. From 2025, the efficiency improvements for air conditioning systems will become eligible as eco-innovations.

In-service verification

3.35 Manufacturers must ensure that the CO_2 emissions recorded on the certificates of conformity of their vehicles and the in-service CO_2 emissions of such vehicles correspond. Type-approval authorities must verify this correspondence in selected vehicles, as well as the presence of any strategies to artificially improve the vehicle's performance during type-approval tests.

In the case where deviations or artificial strategies are detected, type-approval authorities must report those to the Commission, who will take them into account when calculating the average specific emissions of a manufacturer. Authorities must also ensure the correction of the certificates of conformity and may take additional measures as set out in the Type Approval Regulation.[13]

Real-world emissions

3.36 To assess the real-world representativeness of the CO_2 emissions and the fuel or energy consumption values determined during type-approval, as well as to prevent the growing of the gap between emissions tested in the laboratory and real-world emissions, the Commission is collecting real-world data from cars and vans using on-board fuel consumption monitoring (OBFCM) devices, starting with vehicles first registered in 2021.

Carbon Border Adjustment Mechanism (CBAM)

3.37 The CBAM[14] aims to ensure that equal treatment of domestic and imported goods, it does this by applying a charge to carbon emitted during the production of imported carbon-intensive goods, such as aluminium, iron and steel. It has the aim of preventing carbon leakage.

13 European Commission, 'CO_2 emission performance standards for cars and vans', https://climate.ec.europa.eu/eu-action/transport/road-transport-reducing-co2-emissions-vehicles/co2-emission-performance-standards-cars-and-vans_en

14 Regulation (EU) 2023/956 of the European Parliament and of the Council of 10 May 2023 establishing a carbon border adjustment mechanism [2023] OJ L130/52.

Renewable Energy Directive

3.38 The Renewable Energy Directive[15] is the legal framework for the development of clean energy across all sectors of the EU economy. This supports cooperation between EU countries towards this goal.

Energy Efficiency Directive

3.39 The Energy Efficiency Directive[16] is about using energy more efficiently to contribute to reducing the EU's overall energy consumption. The Energy Efficiency Directive is therefore a key driver of Europe's energy transition.

The revised directive

3.40 The revised Energy Efficiency Directive (Directive EU/2023/1791) significantly raises the EU's ambition concerning energy efficiency. It establishes 'energy efficiency first' as a fundamental principle of EU energy policy, giving it legal standing for the first time. This means that energy efficiency must be considered by EU countries in all relevant policy and major investment decisions taken in the energy and non-energy sectors.

The 2023 revision of the directive follows a proposal for a recast directive on energy efficiency put forward by the Commission in July 2021, as part of the EU Green Deal package. The 2021 proposal was further enhanced as part of the REPowerEU plan, presented by the Commission in May 2022, aiming to decrease the EU's dependency on fossil fuel imports from Russia.

Full implementation of the Energy Efficiency Directive will be key for the EU to comply with the commitment of the Global Pledge to double the global rate of energy efficiency improvements from about 2 per cent to over 4 per cent by 2030.

REPowerEU Plan

3.41 This was put in place:

> 'In response to the hardships and global energy market disruption caused by Russia's invasion of Ukraine, the European Commission is implementing its REPowerEU Plan to phase out Russian fossil fuel imports.
>
> Launched in May 2022, REPowerEU is helping the EU to
>
> - save energy
> - diversify energy supplies
> - produce clean energy

15 Directive (EU) 2023/2413 of the European Parliament and of the Council of 18 October 2023 amending Directive (EU) 2018/2001, Regulation (EU) 2018/1999 and Directive 98/70/EC as regards the promotion of energy from renewable sources, and repealing Council Directive (EU) 2015/652 [2023] OJ L2023/2413.

16 Directive (EU) 2023/1791 of the European Parliament and of the Council of 13 September 2023 on energy efficiency and amending Regulation (EU) 2023/955 [2023] OJ L231/1.

Thanks to REPowerEU, we've safeguarded EU citizens and businesses from energy shortages, supported Ukraine by weakening Russia's war chest, accelerated the transition to clean energy and stabilised prices.

Putin's attempt to divide Europe by weaponizing energy supplies has failed. Our joint efforts continue and Europe is now better prepared and more united than ever.

Key Achievements

By acting together over the past two years, we have

- Reduced gas consumption by 18%
- Overcome our dependency on Russian fossil fuels
- Ensured access to secure and affordable energy
- Produced more electricity from wind and solar than from gas for the first time ever
- Rapidly increased renewable energy installation.'[17]

Energy consumption targets

3.42 The 2023 revised directive raises the EU energy efficiency target, and it is therefore binding for EU countries to collectively ensure an additional 11.7 per cent reduction in energy consumption by 2030, compared to the projections of the EU reference scenario 2020. As a result, overall EU energy consumption by 2030 should not exceed 992.5 million tons of oil equivalent (Mtoe) for primary energy and 763 Mtoe for final energy.

EU countries have agreed to help achieve the EU target by setting indicative national contributions using a combination of objective criteria which reflect national circumstances (energy intensity, GDP per capita, energy savings potential and earlier efforts for energy efficiency by EU countries).

The directive also includes an enhanced 'gap-filling mechanism' that will be triggered if countries fall behind in delivering their national contributions. EU countries can use either the projections of the EU reference scenario 2020 or its updated version (communicated to them in December 2023). In March 2024, the Commission communicated on corrected indicative national contributions (covering also the update of the reference scenario) to be used in the EU countries' updated integrated NECPs in June 2024.

Annual energy savings obligation

3.43 The revised directive more than doubles the annual energy savings obligation (Article 8) by 2028. This is one of the key policy instruments of the directive to meet the headline target and to drive energy savings in end-use sectors, such as buildings, industry and transport:

17 European Commission, 'REPowerEU Affordable, secure and sustainable energy for Europe', https://commission.europa.eu/strategy-and-policy/priorities-2019-2024/european-green-deal/repowereu-affordable-secure-and-sustainable-energy-europe_en

EU countries are required to achieve cumulative end-use energy savings for the entire obligation period (running from 2021 to 2030), equivalent to new annual savings of at least (for relevant years):

- 1.3 per cent 2024–25
- 1.5 per cent 2026–27
- 1.9 per cent 2028–30

Energy and poverty consumers

3.44 The revised directive puts a stronger focus on alleviating energy poverty. It aims at empowering consumers through stronger requirements for EU countries to raise awareness and provide information on energy efficiency. It also emphasises the creation of one-stop shops, technical and financial advice and consumer protection via out-of-court mechanisms for the settlement of disputes.

Furthermore, it includes improved regulations to identify and remove barriers related to split incentives for energy efficiency renovations between tenants and owners or among multiple owners.

The changes introduced require EU countries to prioritise energy efficiency improvements for vulnerable customers, individuals affected by energy poverty and those living in social housing. To address any potential negative impacts, the revenue generated from the extension of the EU ETS to buildings and transport will be used through the Social Climate Fund.

Under the energy savings obligation, each EU country is responsible for achieving a share of its energy savings among vulnerable customers and those affected by energy poverty. The criteria for determining these targets will be defined by each country, allowing flexibility for tailored solutions based on country-specific circumstances.

Audit obligations, technical competence requirements and investments reporting

3.45 To optimise energy savings in the industrial sector, the directive expands the scope of energy audit obligations to include all those companies, regardless of their size, which are consuming energy above a certain threshold. Small and medium-sized enterprises (SMEs) would also have to carry out an energy audit, where there is significant energy saving potential. Meanwhile, the directive makes energy management systems a mandatory requirement for large industrial energy consumers to monitor and optimise their energy efficiency.

Additionally, under the revised directive, EU countries will need to ensure an appropriate level of competence for energy efficiency-related professionals, aligning them with market needs and enforcing clearer and stricter requirements for the necessary competencies. This includes energy service providers, energy auditors, energy managers and installers.

The directive mandates EU countries to report on energy efficiency investments, including energy performance contracts, as part of the Governance

Regulation,[18] ensuring transparency and accountability. It also establishes project development assistance mechanisms at national, regional, and local levels to support energy efficiency investments and facilitate the attainment of the EU's ambitious energy efficiency targets.

Heating and cooling supply

3.46 To ensure a fully decarbonised district heating and cooling supply by 2050, the definition of efficient district heating and cooling was also modified in the revised directive. Minimum requirements will be gradually changed to allow for a progressive integration of renewable energy and waste heat and cold in the system.

Support for new high-efficiency cogeneration units using natural gas and connected to district heating in efficient district heating and cooling systems will only be possible until 2030, whereas any other fossil fuel use will be banned for new heat generation capacities in such systems. EU countries will also have to promote local heating and cooling plans in large municipalities having populations above 45,000.

Energy performance of data centres

3.47 The revised directive introduces an obligation for the monitoring and reporting of the energy performance of data centres. A European database will collect and publish data, which is relevant for the energy performance and water footprint of data centres with a significant energy consumption.

The Delegated Regulation (EU/2024/1364)[19] setting out the information and key performance indicators for the reporting obligation was published on 17 May 2024.

For the preparation of the delegated regulation, the Commission ordered a study that was completed at the end of 2023 on the energy performance and sustainability of data centres.

Alternative Fuels Infrastructure Regulations (AFIR)

3.48 The specific objectives of the AFIR[20] are:

18 Regulation (EU) 2018/1999 of the European Parliament and of the Council of 11 December 2018 on the Governance of the Energy Union and Climate Action, amending Regulations (EC) No 663/2009 and (EC) No 715/2009 of the European Parliament and of the Council, Directives 94/22/EC, 98/70/EC, 2009/31/EC, 2009/73/EC, 2010/31/EU, 2012/27/EU and 2013/30/EU of the European Parliament and of the Council, Council Directives 2009/119/EC and (EU) 2015/652 and repealing Regulation (EU) No 525/2013 of the European Parliament and of the Council [2018] OJ L328/1. See European Commission, 'Governance of the Energy Union and Climate Action', https://climate.ec.europa.eu/eu-action/climate-strategies-targets/governance-energy-union-and-climate-action_en

19 Commission Delegated Regulation (EU) 2024/1364 of 14 March 2024 on the first phase of the establishment of a common Union rating scheme for data centres [2024] OJ L2024/1364.

20 Regulation (EU) 2023/1804 of the European Parliament and of the Council of 13 September 2023 on the deployment of alternative fuels infrastructure, and repealing Directive 2014/94/EU [2023] OJ L234/1.

- to ensure minimum infrastructure to support the required uptake of alternative fuel vehicles across all transport modes and in all EU Member States to meet the EU's climate objectives;
- to ensure full interoperability of the infrastructure; and
- to ensure comprehensive user information and adequate payment options at alternative fuels infrastructure.

The regulation sets a number of mandatory national targets for the deployment of alternative fuels infrastructure in the EU, for road vehicles, vessels and stationary aircraft.

For publicly available electric recharging infrastructure for light duty road vehicles (cars and vans), the regulation sets out mandatory national fleet-based targets (eg for every battery electric light duty vehicle a total power output of at least 1.3 kW must be provided through publicly accessible recharging stations while for every plug-in hybrid light-duty vehicle, a total power output of at least 0.8 kW must be provided). It also sets out distance-based targets for light duty and heavy-duty road vehicles on the Trans-European Transport Network (TEN-T) core and comprehensive network. It also requires EU Member States to ensure a number of recharging stations are in place for heavy-duty vehicles in urban nodes and in safe and secure parking.

The regulation also includes provisions for ensuring the user-friendliness of recharging infrastructure (eg payment options, price transparency and consumer information, non-discriminatory practices, smart recharging).

For hydrogen, publicly accessible hydrogen refuelling stations must be deployed with a maximum distance of 200 km in between them along the TEN-T core and the TEN-T comprehensive network and at least one must be available in every urban node.

For electricity supply to vessels and stationary aircraft, the regulation sets targets for the deployment of shore-side electricity supply for larger seagoing container and passenger ships in maritime ports and for inland waterway vessels, and for electricity supply to stationary aircraft at TEN-T core and comprehensive network airports.

It also contains provisions for EU Member States to ensure minimum coverage of publicly accessible refuelling points for liquefied methane dedicated to heavy-duty vehicles on the TEN-T core and comprehensive network and to ensure an appropriate number of liquified methane refuelling points in maritime TEN-T ports.

The regulation reformulates provisions concerning Member States' national policy frameworks for the deployment of alternative fuels infrastructure, including provisions for areas where no mandatory EU-wide targets are set and the reporting on the deployment of such infrastructure.

ReFuelEU Aviation Regulation

3.49 The ReFuelEU Aviation Directive[21] is part of the EU's Fit for 55 package. It aims to reduce the EU's net GHG emissions by at least 55 per cent

21 Regulation (EU) 2023/2405 of the European Parliament and of the Council of 18 October 2023 on ensuring a level playing field for sustainable air transport (ReFuelEU Aviation) [2023] OJ L2023/2405.

by 2030 compared to 1990 levels by increasing both demand for and supply of sustainable aviation fuels.

FuelEU Maritime Regulation

3.50 The EU has adopted the FuelEU Maritime Regulation[22] to increase the share of renewable and low-carbon fuels in the fuel mix of international maritime transport in the EU. The FuelEU Maritime Regulation sets well-to-wake GHG emission intensity requirements on energy used onboard ships over 5,000 GT trading in the EU and came into force 1 January 2025.

The regulation also requires passenger and container ships to connect to onshore power supplies at major EU ports from 2030, when at berth for more than two hours. This will be extended to all ports with onshore power supply from 2035.

The FuelEU Maritime Regulation sets requirements on annual average GHG intensity of energy used by ships trading in the EU or European Economic Area (EEA), measured as GHG emissions per energy unit (gCO_2e/MJ).

GHG emissions are calculated in a well-to-wake perspective, including emissions related to extraction, cultivation, production and transportation of the fuel, in addition to emissions from energy used onboard the ship.

Calculations will be set relative to the average well-to-wake fuel GHG intensity of the fleet in 2020 of 91.16 gCO_2e per megajoule (MJ). This will start at a 2 per cent reduction in 2025, increasing to 6 per cent in 2030, and accelerating from 2035 to reach an 80 per cent reduction by 2050.

Ship owners:

- Needed to submit a FuelEU Monitoring Plan to an accredited verifier, such as Det Norske Veritas (DNV). This plan should have outlined how the ship owner intended to monitor and report emissions for each ship in the fleet. This should have been completed by 31 August 2024.
- Needed to start reporting key data related to FuelEU Maritime from 1 January 2025. This data includes fuel consumption, CO_2 emissions, and distance travelled.
- Need to have an individual ship's FuelEU partial report verified, a maximum one month after change of company.
- Need to submit the individual ships' FuelEU reports by 31 January 2026.
- By 30 April 2026, need to have the compliance balance approved in the FuelEU database.
- By 30 June 2026, need to have the FuelEU Document of Compliance onboard. This is also the penalty payment deadline.

22 Regulation (EU) 2023/1805 of the European Parliament and of the Council of 13 September 2023 on the use of renewable and low-carbon fuels in maritime transport, and amending Directive 2009/16/EC [2023] OJ L234/48.

Energy Performance Buildings Directive

3.51 Aiming to achieve a fully decarbonised building stock by 2050, the Energy Performance of Buildings Directive[23] contributes directly to the EU's energy and climate goals.

Buildings are the single largest energy consumer in Europe. The building sector is therefore crucial to achieving the EU's energy and climate goals.

Key facts on energy and EU buildings

3.52 Eighty-five per cent of EU buildings were built before 2000 and, amongst those, 75 per cent have a poor energy performance. Acting on the energy efficiency of buildings is therefore key to saving energy, reducing bills for citizens and small enterprises and achieving a zero-emission and fully decarbonised building stock by 2050. These facts, and those below, come from the Eurostat energy balances and EEA Greenhouse Gas Inventory, 2023:

- around 40 per cent of energy consumed in the EU is used in buildings;
- over one-third of the EU's energy-related GHG emissions come from buildings;
- +/- 80 per cent of energy used in EU homes is for heating, cooling and hot water.

To boost the energy performance of buildings, the EU has established a legislative framework that includes the revised Energy Performance of Buildings Directive (Directive (EU) 2024/1275) and the revised Energy Efficiency Directive (Directive (EU) 2023/1791).

Together, the directives promote policies that will help:

- achieve a highly energy efficient and decarbonised building stock by 2050;
- create a stable environment for investment decisions;
- enable consumers and businesses to make more informed choices to save energy and money.

Revised Energy Performance of Buildings Directive

3.53 The revised Energy Performance of Buildings Directive (Directive (EU) 2024/1275) helps increase the rate of renovation in the EU, particularly for the worst-performing buildings in each country. It also supports better air quality, the digitalisation of energy systems for buildings and the roll-out of infrastructure for sustainable mobility.

Recognising the differences across EU countries in factors such as the existing building stock, geography and climate, the directive allows governments to decide on the renovation measures best suited to their specific national context.

23 Directive (EU) 2024/1275 of the European Parliament and of the Council of 24 April 2024 on the energy performance of buildings [2024] OJ L2024/1275.

Countries can also exempt various categories of buildings from the rules including historical buildings and holiday homes.

Crucially, the revised directive facilitates targeted financing of investments in the building sector, complementing other EU instruments and fighting energy poverty by supporting vulnerable consumers. EU countries also must ensure that there are safeguards for tenants, such as through rent support or caps on rent increases.

To ensure that buildings are fit for the EU's enhanced climate ambition under the European Green Deal, the revised directive contributes to the objective of reaching emission reductions of at least 60 per cent in the building sector by 2030 compared to 2015, and achieving a decarbonised, zero-emission building stock by 2050.

It works hand in hand with other policies of the Green Deal package, in particular with the emissions trading system for fuels used in buildings, the revised Energy Efficiency Directive (Directive (EU) 2023/1791), the revised Renewable Energy Directive (Directive (EU) 2023/2413), as well as the Alternative Fuels Infrastructure Regulation (Regulation (EU) 2023/1804).

3.54 Other measures in the revised Energy Performance of Buildings Directive (EPBD) include:

- the gradual introduction of minimum energy performance standards for non-residential buildings based on national thresholds to trigger the renovation of buildings with the lowest energy performance;
- a binding target to decrease the average energy performance of the national residential building stock by 16 per cent by 2030 in comparison to 2020, and by 20–22 per cent by 2035, based on national trajectories;
- an enhanced standard for new buildings to be zero-emission and the calculation of whole life-cycle carbon for new buildings;
- enhanced long-term renovation strategies, to be renamed national Building Renovation Plans;
- increased reliability, quality and digitalisation of Energy Performance Certificates with energy performance classes to be based on common criteria;
- the introduction of building renovation passports to guide building owners in their staged and deep energy renovations;
- increased deployment of solar technologies for all new buildings and certain existing non-residential buildings where technically and economically feasible, and ensuring that new buildings are solar-ready (fit to host solar installations);
- a gradual phase-out of boilers powered by fossil fuels, starting with the end of subsidies for stand-alone boilers powered by fossil fuels from 1 January 2025;
- one-stop shops for the energy renovations of buildings for homeowners, small and medium-sized enterprises and other stakeholders;
- further roll-out of recharging points for electric vehicles in buildings, removing barriers to their installation, enabling smart charging and introducing measures for bike parking in buildings;
- data collection and sharing, to improve knowledge on the building stock and awareness of energy consumption in buildings.

Updated EU rules to decarbonise gas markets and promote hydrogen

3.55 The Commission has a provisional agreement between the European Parliament and Council on updated EU rules to decarbonise the gas market and create a hydrogen market. The new rules are to facilitate the uptake of renewable and low-carbon gases, including hydrogen, while ensuring security of supply and affordability of energy for all citizens in the EU. The decarbonisation of the gas sector and the creation of a hydrogen market will make a key contribution to the EU's efforts to reach climate neutrality by 2050. Renewable and low-carbon gases will help cut emissions in heavy-emitting sectors and support the competitiveness of European industry. This agreement will help the EU reinforce its energy independence and further reduce imports of fossil fuels from Russia, as set out in the REPowerEU Plan.

EU methane regulation for the energy sector

3.56 The adoption of this regulation[24] marks another step in the implementation of the European Green Deal and REPowerEU. With Europe importing a large part of the fossil energy it consumes, the regulation will also help to reduce methane emissions from imported fossil fuels. The regulation will progressively introduce more stringent requirements to ensure that exporters gradually apply the same monitoring, reporting and verification obligations as EU operators.

Transforming economies and societies

3.57 The European Green Deal set the blueprint for this change which should bring many benefits, from the creation of new opportunities for innovation, investment and green jobs, to improving our health and well-being.

All 27 EU Member States committed to turning the EU into the first climate neutral continent by 2050 and pledged to reduce emissions by at least 55 per cent by 2030, compared to 1990 levels.

The EU now has legally binding climate targets covering all key sectors of the economy. The overall package includes:

- emissions reduction targets across a broad range of sectors;
- a target to boost natural carbon sinks;
- an updated ETS to cap emissions, put a price on pollution and generate investments in the green transition; and
- social support for citizens and small businesses.

24 Regulation (EU) 2024/1787 of the European Parliament and of the Council of 13 June 2024 on the reduction of methane emissions in the energy sector and amending Regulation (EU) 2019/942 [2024] OJ L2024/1787.

Member States will now spend 100 per cent of their emissions trading revenues on climate and energy-related projects and the social dimension of the transition.

The new Social Climate Fund will dedicate €65 billion from the EU budget, and over €86 billion in total to support the most vulnerable citizens and small businesses with the green transition. This will ensure there are opportunities for everyone, by tackling inequality and energy poverty, and strengthening the competitiveness of European companies, leaving no one behind.

To ensure a level playing field, the European CBAM will ensure that imported products companies, the new will also pay a carbon price at the border in the sectors covered. This is a valuable tool for promoting global emissions reductions and leveraging the EU market to pursue global climate goals.

As a further step on the path towards climate neutrality, the Commission presented its assessment for a 2040 climate target for the EU in February 2024. It recommended reducing net GHG emissions in the EU by 90 per cent by 2040 compared to 1990 levels, which is in line with recent scientific advice and the EU's commitments under the Paris Agreement. The European Parliament and Member States will discuss this target, and the next Commission will put forward legislative proposals on that basis.

Making transport sustainable for all

3.58 With the new CO_2 standards, all new cars and vans registered in Europe will be zero-emission by 2035. As an intermediary step towards zero emissions, average emissions of new cars will have to come down by 55 per cent by 2030, and new vans by 50 per cent by 2030. This will put road transport on a firm path to zero-emission mobility in 2050.

The EU is working to create the infrastructure citizens will need to charge zero-emission vehicles for short and long journeys. Targets will be mandatory to deploy electric recharging and hydrogen refuelling infrastructure along European roads. Sufficient public charging capacity will be in place to meet the demands of the bigger fleet of zero-emission cars that will come onto the market as well as further supply of private chargers at home or at work.

In addition, from 2027, road transport will be covered by emissions trading, putting a price on pollution, stimulating cleaner fuel use, and reinvesting in clean technologies.

Carbon pricing also applies to the aviation sector. Until recently, it applied to flights within the EEA and departing flights to Switzerland and the UK. From 2024, non-domestic flights to and from outermost regions were covered too.

To promote sustainable aviation fuels (SAF), the minimum share of SAF required to be blended with kerosene by aviation fuel suppliers and supplied to EU airports has been increased.

Carbon pricing has also been extended to the maritime sector. A target for gradual reductions for the annual average GHG intensity of the energy used onboard by ships has been established to promote the uptake of renewable and low-carbon fuels.

Leading Green industrial revolution

3.59 With the Green Deal Industrial Plan, presented in February 2023, the aim is to enhance the competitiveness of Europe's net-zero industry, and accelerate the transition to climate neutrality.

In 2021 the value of the EU's net-zero start-ups ecosystem was €100 billion, doubling since 2020. There was more than 400 GW of wind and solar renewable energy production capacity in the EU in 2022, an increase of over 25 per cent compared to 2020. There were also 4.5 million green jobs in the European economy in 2019, up from 3.2 million in 2000.

The aim of the Green Deal Industrial Plan is to secure Europe's place as the home of industrial innovation and clean tech. To achieve this, the plan covers four key pillars:

- Predictable and simplified regulatory environment
- Faster access to funding
- Enhancing skills
- Facilitating open and fair trade for resilient supply chains

The Net-Zero Industry Act, presented in March 2023, is part of the Green Deal Industrial Plan to scale up manufacturing of clean technologies in the EU, create green jobs and make sure the Union is well-equipped for the clean-energy transition. It will create better conditions to set up net-zero projects in Europe and attract investments.

Cleaning the EU energy system

3.60 The Russian aggression in Ukraine and subsequent disruption of the energy market and prices, only reinforced the idea that the EU needs to end its dependence on Russian fossil fuels and accelerate the green transition.

With the REPowerEU Plan, presented in May 2022, the Commission unveiled its plans to help the EU:

- deploy more renewable energy;
- save energy; and
- diversify energy supplies.

In March 2023, the EU agreed on stronger legislation to increase its renewables capacity, by raising its binding target for 2030 to a minimum of 42.5 per cent, up from the current 32 per cent target, with the ambition to reach 45 per cent. This would almost double the existing share of renewable energy in the EU.

In addition, reducing energy consumption is essential to bring down both emissions and energy costs for consumers and industry.

A new binding EU-level target is established to improve energy efficiency by 11.7 per cent by 2030. Member States will have to make annual savings of an average of 1.49 per cent from 2024 to 2030. Member States will now have to also implement energy efficiency improvements as a priority among people affected by energy poverty.

The tax system for energy products must also support the green transition by giving the right incentives. Still under negotiation, the Commission proposed to align the minimum tax rates for heating and transport with climate objectives, while mitigating the social impact and supporting vulnerable citizens.

Renovating buildings for greener lifestyles

3.61 The Commission aims to at least double renovation rates in the next ten years and make sure renovations lead to higher energy and resource efficiency. This will enhance the quality of life for people living in and using the buildings, reduce Europe's GHG emissions, foster digitalisation and improve the reuse and recycling of materials.

To spur the necessary renovations, a revision of the EU's Energy Performance of Buildings Directive was proposed in 2021 to gradually improve the energy performance of buildings across Europe, taking carefully into account national circumstances.

The necessary improvements can be achieved through a number of individual measures, such as installing insulation, replacing old windows or doors, upgrading heating systems, or installing solar panels.

The newly created Social Climate Fund will support EU citizens most affected or at risk of energy or mobility poverty. It will provide over €86 billion in total to support the most vulnerable citizens and small businesses with the green transition.

The Fund will support these vulnerable groups through structural measures and investments in energy efficiency, the renovation of buildings (eg insulation), clean heating and cooling (eg heat pumps), and integration of renewable energy (eg solar panels) as well as in zero- and low-emission mobility and transport, including public transport.

To complement new EU rules on buildings and guide Member States' efforts, there is a new indicative national benchmark of 49 per cent renewable energy in the buildings sector.

The public sector will also be subject to a new annual energy consumption reduction target of 1.9 per cent. The obligation of Member States to renovate each year at least 3 per cent of total floor area of buildings owned by the public administration is extended from the central government to all levels of public administration.

In addition, from 2027, building and transport fuels will be covered by emissions trading, putting a price on pollution, stimulating cleaner fuel use, and reinvesting in clean technologies.

Working with nature to protect the planet

3.62 Restoring nature and enabling biodiversity to thrive again offers a quick and cheap solution to absorb and store carbon. The EU's biodiversity strategy for 2030 is a comprehensive long-term plan to protect nature and put Europe's biodiversity on the path to recovery, for the benefit of people, the climate and the planet.

The strategy contains specific commitments and actions:

- enlarging the existing Natura 2000 areas, the EU-wide network of protected land and sea areas;
- launching an EU nature restoration plan, including the first ever Nature Restoration Law, currently under negotiation;[25]
- unlocking funding for biodiversity, to enable the necessary transformative change; and
- introducing measures to tackle the global biodiversity challenge.

In particular, nature restoration plays an important role in limiting the progress of global warming by capturing and storing carbon, and in adapting to climate change, as well as in mitigating the impact of increasingly violent natural disasters such as floods, droughts and heatwaves.

Additionally, the unsustainable use of natural resources, in particular the degradation and pollution of soils, is a major driver of the climate and biodiversity crises. To tackle this, the Commission proposed a Soil Monitoring Law, which will put the EU on a pathway to healthy soils by 2050, by gathering data on soil health and making it available to farmers and other soil managers.[26]

Enhancing net carbon removals and boosting carbon sinks in the EU is paramount. The EU target for net carbon removals by natural sinks will increase to 310 million tons of CO_2e by 2030. Member States share responsibility for removing carbon from the atmosphere, they are responsible for caring for and expanding their carbon sinks to meet the new EU target.

Bioenergy contributes to the phase-out of fossil fuels and the decarbonisation of the EU economy. But it must be used sustainably. A strict, new criterion to avoid unsustainable forest harvesting and to protect areas of high-biodiversity value will be applied in line with the increased climate and biodiversity ambition.

Boosting global climate action

3.63 The European Green Deal has already set a positive example and led major international partners to set their own target dates for climate neutrality.

With investment in renewable energy technologies, the EU is developing expertise and products that will also benefit the rest of the world.

With the shift to green transport, the EU is creating world leading companies which can serve a growing global market. By working with international

25 Proposal for a Directive of the European Parliament and of the Council on Soil Monitoring and Resilience (Soil Monitoring Law) COM/2023/416 final; European Parliament, 'Soil monitoring: deal with Council on new EU law with better support for farmers', press release, 10 April 2025, https://www.europarl.europa.eu/news/en/press-room/20250407IPR27692/soil-monitoring-deal-with-council-on-new-eu-law-with-better-support-for-farmers#:~:text=Monitoring%20and%20assessing%20EU%20soils,EU%20methodology%20for%20sampling%20points.

26 Proposal for a Directive of the European Parliament and of the Council on Soil Monitoring and Resilience (Soil Monitoring Law) COM/2023/416 final; Communication from the Commission to the European Parliament, the Council, the European Economic and Social Committee and the Committee of the Regions EU Soil Strategy for 2030 Reaping the benefits of healthy soils for people, food, nature and climate COM/2021/699 final.

partners, emissions reductions in maritime transport and aviation around the world can be achieved.

At the UN's COP 28 Summit in Dubai in 2023, the EU pushed for substantially scaling up global climate ambition to keep the 1.5°C objective within reach, in line with the Paris Agreement. The EU also secured agreement to accelerate the global transition away from fossil fuels and triple renewables and double energy efficiency this decade.

NATIONAL/REGIONAL LEGISLATION/POLICY

UK law

3.64 The UK has implemented a comprehensive set of climate laws and policies aimed at reducing GHG emissions, promoting sustainable development, and transitioning to a low-carbon economy. Here are some key elements of the UK's climate framework:

Climate Change Act 2008

3.65 This landmark legislation established a legally binding framework for the UK to reduce its GHG emissions.

- **Carbon budgets:** The Act sets five-yearly carbon budgets, which cap the total amount of GHGs the UK can emit during each period. These budgets are designed to ensure a steady path towards meeting the long-term target.
- **2050 target:** Originally, the Act mandated at least an 80 per cent reduction in GHG emissions by 2050 (compared to 1990 levels). This target was updated in 2019 to net-zero.

Net Zero Strategy

3.66 In 2021, the UK Government published 'Net Zero Strategy: Build Back Greener', outlining how the UK intends to meet its net-zero emissions target by 2050.

- **Clean energy:** Expanding renewable energy sources, such as wind and solar power, and phasing out coal.
- **Electric vehicles:** Promoting electric vehicles (EVs) with a plan to end the sale of new petrol and diesel cars by 2030.
- **Building efficiency:** Improving the energy efficiency of homes and buildings through retrofitting and new building standards.

The Ten Point Plan for a Green Industrial Revolution

3.67 Announced in 2020, this plan focuses on ten key areas to drive the UK's green transition, create jobs, and reach net-zero emissions:

1. Advancing offshore wind
2. Driving the growth of low carbon hydrogen
3. Delivering new and advanced nuclear power
4. Accelerating the shift to zero-emission vehicles
5. Green public transport, cycling, and walking
6. Jet zero and greener maritime
7. Homes and public buildings
8. Carbon capture, usage, and storage (CCUS)
9. Protecting and restoring the natural environment
10. Green finance and innovation

Renewable energy incentives

3.68 The UK has various schemes to encourage the development of renewable energy, such as the below.

Contracts for Difference (CfD)

3.69 A mechanism to support low-carbon electricity generation by providing stability and predictability to renewable energy projects.

Renewable Heat Incentive (RHI)

3.70 Supports the use of renewable heat technologies among households, communities, and businesses.

Energy White Paper 2020

3.71 This document outlines the UK's plan for the transformation of the energy system to reach net-zero emissions by 2050. It focuses on:

- decarbonising electricity generation;
- increasing energy efficiency; and
- ensuring the energy system is resilient and secure.

Environment Act 2021

3.72 The Environment Act 2021 aims to ensure that environmental standards are maintained and improved post-Brexit. It includes:

- legally binding targets for air quality, water resources, biodiversity, and waste reduction; and
- provision for the establishment of the Office for Environmental Protection (OEP) to hold the government accountable.

Climate adaptation

3.73 The UK also has policies aimed at adapting to the impacts of climate change:

- **National Adaptation Programme (NAP):** Sets out actions to address the risks identified in the UK Climate Change Risk Assessment (CCRA), focusing on infrastructure, health, and the natural environment.
- **Flood and Coastal Erosion Risk Management Strategy:** Strategies to manage and mitigate flood and coastal erosion risks.

Carbon pricing

3.74 The UK has implemented mechanisms to price carbon emissions to incentivise reduction: the UK Emissions Trading Scheme (UK ETS) was launched in 2021, replacing the EU ETS for the UK post-Brexit, to cap and reduce emissions from power and heavy industry.

Local and regional initiatives

3.75 Local government in the UK also plays a crucial role in implementing climate policies through various initiatives:

- **Local Climate Action Plans:** Many local authorities have declared climate emergencies and developed detailed plans to reduce emissions and enhance sustainability at the local level.
- **City Deals and Regional Partnerships:** Collaborative efforts to promote green growth and innovation across regions.

These laws and policies collectively aim to guide the UK towards a sustainable, low-carbon future, balancing economic growth with environmental stewardship.

US

Regional Greenhouse Gas Initiative (RGGI): Cap-and-trade programme in the northeastern US

3.76 **Participants:** 11 US states in the Northeast and Mid-Atlantic regions.

Mechanism: Cap-and-trade programme aimed at reducing GHG emissions from the power sector.

Results: Significant reductions in CO_2 emissions and substantial investment in energy efficiency and renewable energy.

The Regional Greenhouse Gas Initiative (RGGI) is a cooperative effort among the states of Connecticut, Delaware, Maine, Maryland, Massachusetts, New Hampshire, New Jersey, New York, Pennsylvania, Rhode Island, and Vermont to cap and reduce power sector CO_2 emissions.

The RGGI is composed of individual CO_2 Budget Trading Programs in each participating state. Through independent regulations, based on the RGGI Model Rule, each state's CO_2 Budget Trading Program limits emissions of CO_2 from electric power plants, issues CO_2 allowances and establishes participation in regional CO_2 allowance auctions.

The RGGI is the first market-based, cap-and-invest regional initiative in the US. Within the RGGI states, fossil-fuel-fired electric power generators with a capacity of 25 megawatts or greater ('regulated sources') are required to hold allowances equal to their CO_2 emissions over a three-year control period.

A CO_2 allowance represents a limited authorisation to emit one short ton of CO_2 from a regulated source, as issued by a participating state. Regulated sources can use a CO_2 allowance issued by any participating state to demonstrate compliance in any state. They may acquire allowances by purchasing them at regional auctions, or through secondary markets.

The RGGI cap

3.77 The RGGI CO_2 cap represents a regional budget for CO_2 emissions from the power sector. For 2024, the RGGI cap for the 11 participating states was 157,184,044 CO_2 allowances and the adjusted cap is 142,422,869 CO_2 allowances. Because Pennsylvania's RGGI regulation is currently under a court injunction, Pennsylvania will not be releasing any allowances until further notice. The RGGI cap for the other ten participating states is 84,162,784 CO_2 allowances and the adjusted cap is 69,401,609 CO_2 allowances.

Post-2020 cap levels have been established through programme review and are detailed in the Principles to Accompany Model Rule Amendments. On 15 March 2021, the RGGI states announced the Third Adjustment for Banked Allowances which is applied to the RGGI cap to account for banked CO_2 allowances accumulated through the fourth control period. The adjustment is made over a five-year period (2021–25), as specified in the 2017 Model Rule.

Historical cap levels

3.78 For 2012–19, the regional cap refers to a nine-state region (Connecticut, Delaware, Maine, Maryland, Massachusetts, New Hampshire, New York, Rhode Island, and Vermont). For 2009–11 and 2020, the regional cap refers to a ten-state region (Connecticut, Delaware, Maine, Maryland, Massachusetts, New Hampshire, New Jersey, New York, Rhode Island, and Vermont). For 2021, 2022, and 2023 the regional cap refers to the eleven participating RGGI states (Connecticut, Delaware, Maine, Maryland, Massachusetts, New Hampshire, New Jersey, New York, Rhode Island, Vermont, and Virginia).

Cost Containment Reserve

3.79 The RGGI states have established a Cost Containment Reserve (CCR), consisting of a quantity of allowances in addition to the cap which are held in reserve. These are sold if allowance prices exceed predefined price levels, so that the CCR will only trigger if emission reduction costs are higher than projected. The CCR is replenished at the start of each calendar year.

The CCR trigger price is $15.92 in 2024 and will increase by 7 per cent per year thereafter. The size of the CCR is 10 per cent of the regional cap each year.

Emissions Containment Reserve

3.80 Beginning in 2021, states implementing the Emissions Containment Reserve (ECR) will withhold allowances from circulation to secure additional emissions reductions if prices fall below an established trigger price. The ECR will trigger only if emission reduction costs are lower than projected.

Auctioning and reinvestment

3.81 Allowances are offered through quarterly, regional CO_2 allowance auctions. These auctions are sealed-bid, uniform price auctions that are open to all qualified participants. They result in a single quarterly clearing price.

States are able to reinvest the proceeds from these CO_2 allowance auctions in consumer benefit programmes to improve energy efficiency and accelerate the deployment of renewable energy technologies. See the Auction Results page for an overview of the proceeds generated by each auction, and the Reinvestment page for more detail on how states have reinvested the auction proceeds to benefit consumers and further reduce pollution.

In addition to purchasing allowances at auction, entities are also able to trade allowances on secondary markets, either directly via over-the-counter trades, or indirectly through futures contracts on exchanges such as ICE and Nodal Exchange.

Potomac Economics provides independent expert monitoring of the competitive performance and efficiency of the RGGI allowance market. This includes:

- Identifying attempts to exercise market power, collude, or otherwise manipulate prices in the auction and/or the secondary market;
- Making recommendations regarding proposed market rule changes to improve the efficiency of the market for RGGI Allowances;
- Assessing whether the auctions are administered in accordance with the noticed auction rules and procedures.

Tracking and compliance

3.82 RGGI CO_2 budget sources are required to possess CO_2 allowances equal to their CO_2 emissions over a three-year control period. Sources must also hold allowances equal to 50 per cent of their emissions during each interim control period (the first two calendar years of each three-year control period). For more materials on compliance and interim compliance, see the Compliance page.

The RGGI COATS platform enables tracking of RGGI emissions, allowance, and other market data, including CO_2 emissions from regulated power plants and CO_2 allowance transactions among market participants.

California's cap-and-trade program: state-level emissions trading scheme – state regulation

3.83 The cap-and-trade program is a key element of California's strategy to reduce greenhouse gas (GHG) emissions. It complements other measures to ensure that California cost-effectively meets its goals for GHG emissions reductions.

The Cap-and-Trade Regulation establishes a declining limit on major sources of GHG emissions throughout California, and it creates a powerful economic incentive for significant investment in cleaner, more efficient technologies. The program applies to emissions that cover approximately 80 per cent of the state's GHG emissions. The California Air Resources Board creates allowances equal to the total amount of permissible emissions (ie, the 'cap'). One allowance equals one metric ton of CO_2 equivalent emissions (using the 100-year global warming potential). Each year, fewer allowances are created and the annual cap declines. An increasing annual auction reserve (or floor) price for allowances and the reduction in annual allowances creates a steady and sustained carbon price signal to prompt action to reduce GHG emissions. All covered entities in the cap-and-trade program are still subject to existing air quality permit limits for criteria and toxic air pollutants.

ARB Emissions Trading Program

3.84 Assembly Bill 32 requires California to return to 1990 levels of GHG emissions by 2020. All programmes developed under AB 32 contribute to the reductions needed to achieve this goal and will deliver an overall 15 per cent reduction in GHG emissions compared to the 'business-as-usual' scenario in 2020 if nothing at all was done.

The Cap-and-Trade Program is a key element of California's climate plan. It sets a state-wide limit on sources responsible for 85 per cent of California's GHG emissions and establishes a price signal needed to drive long-term investment in cleaner fuels and more efficient use of energy. The program is designed to provide covered entities with the flexibility to seek out and implement the lowest-cost options to reduce emissions.

Program covers about 450 entities

3.85

- It started in 2013 for electricity generators and large industrial facilities emitting 25,000 $MTCO_2e$ or more annually.
- It started in 2015 for distributors of transportation, natural gas, and other fuels.
- In 2014, California's programme linked with the Canadian province of Québec.
- It was designed to link with similar trading programmes in other states and regions.

The cap

3.86

- It was set in 2013 at about 2 per cent below the emissions level forecast for 2012.
- It declined about 2 per cent in 2014.
- From 2015 to 2020, it declined about 3 per cent annually.

Free allocation of allowances

3.87

- Applies to large industrial facilities.
- Focus on free allocation early in the programme, transitioning to a more auction-based system later in programme.
- Allocation of allowances for most industrial sectors is set at about 90 per cent of average emissions, based on benchmarks that reward efficient facilities.
- For most industrial sectors, distribution of allowances is updated annually according to the production at each facility.

Electrical distribution and natural gas utilities

3.88

- There is free distribution of allowances, with the requirement that the value of allowances must be used to benefit ratepayers and achieve GHG emissions reductions.
- For electrical distribution utilities, free allocation is set at about 90 per cent of average emissions.
- For natural gas utilities, free allocation is based on natural gas supplied in 2011 to non-covered entities.

Cost containment and market flexibility mechanisms

3.89

- Trading of allowances is allowed to minimise the cost of pollution controls.
- Banking of allowances is allowed to guard against shortages and price swings.
- 4 per cent of allowances are held in a strategic reserve to contain costs.
- Multi-year compliance periods to buffer annual variations in product output.

Offsets

3.90

- Allowed for up to 8 per cent of a facility's compliance obligation.
- Limited to emissions-reduction projects in the US.
- Restricted to projects in five areas: forestry, urban forestry, dairy digesters, destruction of ozone- depleting substances, and mine methane capture.
- Offsets must be independently verified.
- Currently analysing rice cultivation protocol.
- Emissions Reporting and Verification through the Mandatory Reporting Regulation.[27]

27 California Air Resources Board, Mandatory Greenhouse Gas Reporting Regulation, https://ww2.arb.ca.gov/mrr-regulation

- Covered entities must report emissions and additional data annually (as required since 2008).

Independent third-party verification

3.91

- Every year, covered entities turn in allowances and offsets for 30 per cent of the previous year's emissions.
- Each compliance period, covered entities turn in allowances and a limited number of offsets covering the remainder of emissions in that compliance period.
- If the compliance deadline is missed or there is a shortfall, four allowances must be provided for every ton of emissions that was not covered in time.
- The programme includes mechanisms to prevent market manipulation.
- ARB has a market monitoring group that coordinates with state and federal agencies on market oversight.

US and Canada – Western Climate Initiative (WCI)

3.92 **Participants:** US states and Canadian provinces.

Objective: Develop and implement a joint strategy to reduce GHG emissions.

Key Feature: Market-based cap-and-trade programme.

The Western Climate Initiative (WCI) is a collaboration between western states, Canadian provinces, and Mexican states to reduce GHGs in their region. The Initiative was originally signed on 26 February 2007, by the governors of Washington, Oregon, California, Arizona and New Mexico. It invited other states, provinces, Mexican states and Indian tribes to join as partners or observers. The provinces of British Columbia and Manitoba and the states of Utah and Montana have formally joined as partners. Kansas, Wyoming, Nevada, Colorado, Alaska, Idaho, the provinces of Quebec, Saskatchewan and Ontario and the Mexican states of Sonora, Tamaulipas, Baja and Chihuahua are all observers.

The Initiative directs the staff of the partners (signatories) to accomplish three tasks:

- set a regional GHG reduction goal that is consistent with each partner's individual reduction goal;
- join a multi-state registry to track, manage and credit entities that report their GHG emissions and the reductions they make; and
- develop a design for a regional multi-sector market-based mechanism, such as a load-based cap-and-trade programme, to help achieve the emission reductions. This design was to be completed by 26 August 2008, 18 months after the Initiative was signed by the five founding partners.

The partners have accomplished two of the three tasks: a regional reduction goal has been established and all partners (and observers) have joined The Climate Registry, the only multi-state registry in the US.

Regional Reduction Goal: Working with the emissions inventory and projection for each of the partner jurisdictions, the WCI determined that a 15 per cent reduction from 2005 levels by 2020 was consistent with all of the partners' individual goals. With each partner reaching its own goal, the region was assured of achieving this level of reduction. For Washington, the regional goal was consistent with the goals set out in Executive Order 07-02 and Senate Bill 6001. The Quebec legislators and government officials reaffirmed their support for the province's cap-and-trade programme on the 9 April 2025. This resolution came a day after US President Donald Trump issued an executive order saying that climate change policies were an 'overreach' of their authority, especially citing California's cap-and-trade programme

The Climate Registry: The Climate Registry is developing standard protocols to ensure consistent, accurate and verifiable reporting of GHGs. These protocols will ensure that a ton of carbon, wherever emitted or reduced, is counted in the same way, giving assurance to any carbon trading markets that have formed or will form.

The Climate Registry is a non-profit corporation whose Board of Directors is made up of each of the governments that are its members. Currently, there are 39 states, the District of Columbia, three Canadian provinces and four Mexican states that are members. (All 13 Canadian provinces have committed to join.)

Latin America and the Caribbean

Regional Climate Change Strategy of Central America (ERCC)

3.93 **Objective:** Enhance regional coordination and integration to address climate change impacts.

Key Areas: Adaptation, mitigation, technology transfer and capacity building.

This project developed an integrated Regional Programme on Air Quality, Climate Change and Health for Central America to strengthen governance mechanisms, foster high-level political commitment and maximise the benefits of related regional and national strategies in the region. It built upon the roadmap for integrated climate change mitigation and clean air action developed in a previous Climate and Clean Air Coalition (CCAC)-funded workshop with the Central American Integration System (SICA).

This project also assessed how short-lived climate pollutants (SLCPs) and the health benefits of SLCP mitigation can be integrated into the updated NDCs currently under development in SICA member states, Belize, Costa Rica, El Salvador, Guatemala, Honduras, Nicaragua, Panama, and the Dominican Republic.

Amazon Cooperation Treaty Organization (ACTO)

3.94 **Objective:** Promote sustainable development and environmental protection in the Amazon Basin.

Key Actions: Forest conservation, biodiversity protection and climate change mitigation.

ACTO is an intergovernmental organisation formed by the eight Amazonian countries: Bolivia, Brazil, Colombia, Ecuador, Guyana, Peru, Suriname, and Venezuela, which signed the Amazon Cooperation Treaty (ACT), becoming the only socioenvironmental block in Latin America. ACTO, with a broad vision of the South-South cooperation process, works in different dimensions within the framework of the implementation of the ACT: political-diplomatic, strategic and technical, building synergies among governments, multilateral organisations, cooperation agencies, organised civil society, social movements, scientific community, productive sectors and society as a whole.

Asia-Pacific

Asia-Pacific Partnership on Clean Development and Climate (APP)

3.95 **Participants:** Australia, Canada, India, Japan, South Korea, and the US.

Objective: Accelerate the development and deployment of clean energy technologies.

Key Areas: Energy efficiency, renewable energy, and cleaner fossil energy.

The APP represents around half of the world's emissions, energy use, GDP and population, and is an important initiative that engages, for the first time, the key GHG-emitting countries in the Asia-Pacific region. Its focus is on the development, deployment and transfer of cleaner, more efficient technologies, the APP is also the way business, government and researchers have agreed to work together. The partnership established eight public-private sector task forces covering:

- cleaner fossil energy;
- renewable energy and distributed generation;
- power generation and transmission;
- steel;
- aluminium;
- cement;
- coal mining; and
- buildings and appliances.

Association of Southeast Asian Nations (ASEAN)

3.96 **ASEAN Climate Change Initiative (ACCI):** Framework for regional cooperation on climate change.

Key Actions: Mitigation and adaptation strategies, capacity building, and policy integration.

China

National carbon market

3.97 On 4 February 2024, the State Council of China published a new regulation that establishes a legal foundation for the national ETS, to take effect on 1 May 2024.

The initial draft of the 'Interim Regulations for the Management of Carbon Emissions Trading' underwent consultation in 2016 under the National Development and Reform Commission (NDRC). In 2018, the Ministry of Ecology and Environment (MEE) took over climate change policy responsibility and published a second draft in 2019, which was open for consultation. The final draft, subject to additional public input in 2021, was officially adopted in 2024.

The key modifications of the new regulation are:

- **ETS governance framework:** new authorities become national-level regulators.
- **Enhanced enforcement measures and penalties for covered entities:** the regulation introduces a comprehensive liability framework for covered entities, combining financial and non-financial enforcement measures.
- **New enforcement measures and penalties for technical services and market participants:** consultant firms, third-party verifiers and testing organisations involved in measurement, reporting and verification (MRV) data fraud may face penalties up to 10 times their illegal gains, as well as business disqualification
- **Allowance auctioning:** auctioning, one of the two allocation methods alongside free allocation, is to be introduced and gradually expanded, though no timeline has been specified.
- **Trading:** China Emission Allowances are indicated as eligible trading products, but other spot products may be approved by the State Council going forward.
- **Offsets:** offset credits are allowed in the national ETS, but the Interim Regulations do not specify qualitative or quantitative limits.
- **Information disclosure:** covered entities are required to disclose their annual emissions information, which provincial authorities will publish along with the verification result and possible irregularities.
- **Regional market integration:** Existing regional emissions trading systems shall improve relevant market management rules according to this regulation.

Launched in July 2021, the China national ETS is the largest carbon market in the world, covering five billion tons of CO_2 from more than 2,200 fossil-fuel power plants. The new regulation signals an increased focus on emissions trading as part of China's long-term climate change strategy.

Africa

African Union (AU)

3.98 **African Strategy on Climate Change (ASCC):** Framework for coordinated response to climate change across the continent.

Key Actions: Enhancing adaptive capacity, promoting renewable energy, and improving resilience.

Africa Adaptation Initiative (AAI)

3.99 **Objective:** Strengthen collaboration and mobilise resources for climate adaptation in Africa.

Focus Areas: Agriculture, water resources, and disaster risk reduction.

Middle East and North Africa (MENA)

Regional Climate Change Strategy for the MENA Region

3.100 **Objective:** Address shared climate challenges like water scarcity, desertification, and extreme temperatures.

Key Actions: Renewable energy deployment, water resource management, and cross-border cooperation.

Pacific Islands

Secretariat of the Pacific Regional Environment Programme (SPREP)

3.101 A regional organisation established by the governments and administrations of the Pacific charged with protecting and managing the environment and natural resources of the Pacific.

The headquarters is based in Apia, Samoa with other SPREP offices in Fiji, the Republic of the Marshalls Islands and Vanuatu. SPREP has around 150 staff recruited from around the Pacific region and the world and has an annual budget of approximately US $35 million (in 2022).

The establishment of SPREP in 1993 sent a clear signal to the global community of the deep commitment of Pacific island governments and administrations to better management of the environment within the context of sustainable development.

The strategic direction for SPREP is clearly set out in the 2017–2026 SPREP Strategic Plan. The Plan outlines the mandate, vision and programmes for the organisation, and places strong emphasis on effective delivery of services to SPREP member countries and territories.

There are four regional goals:

- Pacific people benefit from strengthened resilience to climate change.
- Pacific people benefit from healthy and resilient island and ocean ecosystems.
- Pacific people benefit from improved waste management and pollution control.
- Pacific people and their environment benefit from commitment to and best practice of environmental governance.

Pacific Islands Framework for Action on Climate Change (PIFACC)

3.102 **Objective:** Build resilience to climate change and manage risks.

Key Areas: Disaster risk management, climate change adaptation, and sustainable development.

Pacific Adaptation to Climate Change (PACC)

3.103 Objective: Implement adaptation measures in key sectors like agriculture, water, and coastal management.

Arctic Region

Arctic Council

3.104 Objective: Promote cooperation among Arctic states and indigenous communities on sustainable development and environmental protection.

Key Actions: Climate monitoring, ecosystem protection, and addressing black carbon and methane emissions.

Arctic Council Strategic Plan

3.105 This Strategic Plan[28] was adopted in recognition of the Arctic Council's 25th anniversary at the Council's 12th Ministerial Meeting. It reflects the shared values and joint aspirations of the Arctic States and the Permanent Participants, to advance sustainable development, environmental protection, and good governance in the Arctic.

The plan has a number of goals listed below.

Arctic climate

3.106 Monitor, assess and highlight the impacts of climate change in the Arctic to encourage compliance with the Paris Agreement and support stronger global measures to reduce GHGs and SLCPs, while strengthening circumpolar cooperation on:

- climate science and observations;
- reduction of emissions;
- climate change mitigation, adaptation and resilience; and
- exchange of knowledge and innovative technologies in support of these efforts.

Healthy and resilient Arctic ecosystems

3.107 Promote pollution prevention, monitoring, assessment, conservation and protection of Arctic biodiversity, ecosystems and species habitats, based on best available science, and respecting the importance of sustainable development for all current and future generations of Arctic inhabitants.

28 Arctic Council Strategic Plan 2021, https://arctic-council.org/about/#:~:text=The%20Council's%20Strategic%20Plan%202021,rights%20and%20wellbeing%20are%20respected

Healthy Arctic marine environment

3.108 Promote conservation and sustainable use of the Arctic marine environment for the benefit of all current and future generations of Arctic inhabitants, encourage safety at sea, prevention of marine pollution and cooperate to improve knowledge of the Arctic marine environment, monitor and assess current and future impacts on Arctic marine ecosystems, work together to enhance cooperation on marine issues and promote respect for the rule of law and existing legal frameworks applicable to Arctic waters.

Sustainable social development

3.109 Enhance work aimed at social and cultural inclusion and at improving health, safety, resilience and well-being of all Arctic inhabitants with a particular focus on Indigenous Peoples.

Sustainable economic development

3.110 Advance cooperation on sustainable and diverse economic development in the Arctic, promote economic cooperation, knowledge and information sharing on innovative, sustainable and low-emission technologies, for the benefit and increased resilience of all Arctic inhabitants with a particular focus on Indigenous Peoples.

Knowledge and communications

3.111 Generate, collect, analyse and communicate science, and traditional knowledge and local knowledge, as appropriate, and enhance understanding of the Arctic within and beyond the region to inform policy shaping and decision-making.

Stronger Arctic Council

3.112 Strengthen the Arctic Council as the pre-eminent high-level circumpolar forum for effective coordination and cooperation and enhance its ability to efficiently respond to emerging challenges and opportunities in the Arctic.

India

National Action Plan on Climate Change (NAPCC)

3.113 Climate change policies in India[29] have primarily focused on supporting synergies between development and outcomes for the climate. India was one of the few countries that passed the Energy Conservation Act in 2001 which

29 Indian School of Public Policy, 'India's Climate Change Policy: Challenges and Recommendations', https://www.ispp.org.in/indias-climate-change-policy-challenges-and-recommendations/

underwent an amendment in August 2022. Some changes include consumers meeting their energy needs from non-fossil sources, application of the Energy Conservation Building Code (ECBC) to office and residential buildings for loads equal to or more than 100 KW, and specification of energy consumption standards for ships and vehicles.

India has developed its policy response through missions and programmes to reduce its climate vulnerability. On 30 June 2008, the National Action Plan on Climate Change (NAPCC) was released. It is a national strategy of eight sub-missions to help adapt and magnify ecological sustainability in India's development path. These are the National Solar Mission (NSM), the National Mission for Enhanced Energy Efficiency (NMEEE), the National Mission on Sustainable Habitat (NMSH), the National Water Mission (NWM), the National Mission for Sustaining the Himalayan Ecosystem (NMSHE), the National Mission on Strategic Knowledge for Climate Change (NMSKCC), the National Mission for a Green India (GIM), and the National Mission for Sustainable Agriculture (NMSA).

On 3 August 2022, the Union Cabinet, under the Chairmanship of the Prime Minister, passed the updated NDC for consideration by the United Nations Framework Convention on Climate Change (UNFCCC) under the Paris Agreement, to reach India's goal of net-zero emissions by 2070. This was a translation of the Panchamrit (five nectar elements) – India's action plan against climate change, announced at COP 26 in Glasgow, UK.

Quantified goals

3.114

- To reduce the emissions intensity of its GDP by 45 per cent by 2030, from the 2005 level.
- To achieve about 50 per cent cumulative electric power installed capacity from non-fossil fuel-based energy resources by 2030, with the help of the transfer of technology and low-cost international finance including from the Green Climate Fund (GCF).
- To create an additional carbon sink of 2.5 to 3 billion tons of CO_2 equivalent through additional forest and tree cover by 2030.

Non-quantified goals

3.115

- To put forward and further propagate a healthy and sustainable way of living based on traditions and values of conservation and moderation, including through a mass movement for 'LIFE'– 'Lifestyle for Environment' as a key to combating climate change.
- To adopt a climate-friendly and cleaner path than the one followed hitherto by others at the corresponding level of economic development.
- To better adapt to climate change by enhancing investments in development programmes in sectors vulnerable to climate change, particularly agriculture, water resources, the Himalayan region, coastal regions, and health and disaster management.

- To mobilise domestic and new and additional funds from developed countries to implement the above mitigation and adaptation actions in view of the resource required and the resource gap.
- To build capacities, create a domestic framework and international architecture for quick diffusion of cutting-edge climate technology in India and joint collaborative R&D for such future technologies.

LOCAL AND MUNICIPAL POLICIES

Urban climate action plans

New York City

3.116 Adapt NYC is New York City's plan to adapt to climate change.

Adaptation means preparing New York City's communities, infrastructure, buildings, land, critical infrastructure, and natural systems for climate change impacts now and in the future. This requires close coordination across city agencies, partnership across all levels of government, and active engagement with New Yorkers. Adaptation is one component of New York City's integrated strategy to prepare for a changing climate, along with working toward a more sustainable, equitable and just city.

Climate change hazards

3.117 Climate change is impacting New York City and its residents, and causing more extreme heat, extreme rainfall, coastal storm surge, and chronic tidal flooding.

Adaptation measures

3.118 Since its colonial founding over 400 years ago, New York City has developed and shaped its built environment to a regional climate of moderate seasonal weather patterns and stable sea levels. Marshes were drained, shorelines were extended, forests were cleared and open land was paved over, leading to New York City's explosive growth. In the present day, those development patterns have left New Yorkers more vulnerable to climate change, with the onset of more frequent and intense rainstorms, ocean surge and tidal flooding, and longer and extreme heatwaves. Now, the City must adapt its built and natural environment to be more resilient and sustainable as a way of protecting New Yorkers from climate change. The City of New York employs a variety of measures to adapt the city's buildings, infrastructure and land use to climate change.

Citywide plans are available, including:

- Climate Adaptation Plan for Public Housing (NYCHA)
- Comprehensive Waterfront Plan
- Cool Neighbourhoods NYC

- Rainfall Ready NYC
- Wastewater Resiliency Plan
- Special Initiative for Recovery and Resiliency (SIRR)
- Progressive Design Build
- Zoning for Carbon Neutrality
- NYC Climate Resiliency Design Guidelines
- Transportation Resiliency
- Design and Planning for Flood Resiliency
- Neighbourhood Coastal Flood Protection Guidance
- FEMA's Hazard Mitigation grants

Extreme heat adaptation measures include:

- expanding the tree canopy;
- cooling streets and roofs;
- cooling centres; and
- cooling homes.

Coastal flood adaptation measures include:

- protecting and expanding natural coasts;
- building coastal protection;
- NYCHA recovery and resiliency;
- the Build It Back program;
- the Building Code; and
- zoning regulations.

Extreme rainfall adaptation measures include:

- cloudburst management;
- sewer upgrades;
- stormwater capture;
- Green Infrastructure stormwater management;
- the Bluebelt Program;
- the Southeast Queens Project;
- Resilient NYC Partners;
- building level stormwater management; and
- stormwater playgrounds.

Social resiliency measures include:

- focusing on the most at-risk communities; and
- climate-training communities.

Environmental justice

3.119 The Mayor's Office, the Environmental Justice Interagency Working Group, and the Environmental Justice Advisory Board are working on the City's first comprehensive study of the present state of environmental justice in NYC. The Environmental Justice Report will identify the city's environmental justice areas, analyse environmental and climate issues, and identify which communities are disproportionately impacted by environmental burdens and not seeing the benefits of green investments made by the City. The report will study issues city-wide but also include a focus on how these issues impact the city's environmental justice areas.

Legislation

3.120 Creation of the CityWide Climate Adaptation Plan.

London

3.121 London has a 1.5°C Compatible Climate Action Plan that looks at the different scenarios London can take to reduce its emissions and to reach the zero carbon target.

Building Energy Efficiency – Arup built a model to help understand how energy efficiency can be achieved.

Zero Carbon Energy Systems – Element Energy modelled four scenarios to zero carbon energy by 2050, based on electrification, decarbonisation of gas, decentralisation of energy or a patchwork solution.

Adaptation – Mott McDonald have reviewed London's existing activity on climate adaptation and identified where there is need for more to avoid the impacts of increasingly hot, dry summers and unpredictable weather.

Tokyo

3.122 The Japanese Government aims to achieve carbon neutrality by 2050. In order to achieve this goal, on 12 May 2023, the government passed the GX Promotion Act (Act on Promotion of Smooth Transition to a Decarbonized Growth-Oriented Economic Structure). GX is an abbreviation for 'green transformation', and refers to, in Japan, 'a transformation to utilize renewable energy sources with less dependency on fossil fuels, as well as activities to realize such transformation'. The GX Promotion Act took effect on 30 June 2023, and its main points are:

- the government shall formulate a strategy to promote GX in a comprehensive and systematic manner (GX Promotion Strategy);
- the government will issue approximately 20 trillion yen in GX Economy Transition Bonds over ten years starting in FY2023 to support investments to realize the GX Promotion Strategy. The government will repay the GX Economy Transition Bonds with funds collected from operators through the carbon pricing scheme described below;
- the government will introduce a scheme for carbon pricing. Specifically, (i) from FY2028 onwards, the government will collect contributions from fossil fuel importers in proportion to the amount of CO_2 emitted from imported fossil fuels, and (ii) the government will allocate CO_2 emission allowances to power generators using a bidding system from FY2033 and collect contributions in proportion to the amount of emissions; and
- the government has established the GX Promotion Organization (official name: Organization for the Promotion of Transition to a Decarbonized Pro-Growth Economic Structure) to support private sector investment in GX.

Green Transformation (GX) University of Tokyo

3.123 Tokyo has UTokyo Climate Action as the University of Tokyo's Commitment to Climate Change. The guiding principles of UTokyo in the

'UTokyo Compass', which was made public on 30 September 2021, stated that UTokyo has positioned Green Transformation (GX) as one of the pillars of its action plan, which includes leading international GX. In the future, UTokyo is set to accelerate specific initiatives, such as the formulation of a roadmap for UTokyo as a business entity to attempt to achieve virtually zero GHG emissions and collaborate with the local communities where its campuses are located.

UTokyo will lead an international green transformation informed by scientific expertise that mobilises the knowledge generated at UTokyo. Specifically, it will strengthen and steadily implement the Global Commons

The Stewardship Initiative is an international collaborative project that aims to develop mechanisms for the better management of stable global systems as the shared property of all humankind (global commons). It aims to convene the Energy Transitions Initiative – Center for Global Commons (ETI-CGC) as an industry-academia collaborative platform to discuss pathways and policies for Japan to decarbonise (effectively achieve zero GHG emissions) by the middle of this century and contribute to the transformation of Japanese society from a scholarly perspective.

It aims to decarbonise the activities of the entire UTokyo organisation. Specifically, a roadmap toward the goal of halving the university's effective GHG emissions in Scopes 1 and 2 by 2030 as against the 2013 figure will be formulated, and the systems and policy measures required to achieve this goal will be clarified. UTokyo will also collaborate with international society and participate in the international Race to Zero campaign as an institution that promotes action to reach effectively zero GHG emissions by 2050.

Chapter 4

Information to Raise Awareness

INTRODUCTION

4.01 Raising awareness about climate change is important as it can drive both individual and collective action. This chapter covers various strategies and initiatives which have been used to try and increase public understanding of climate change issues and incentivise action.

GLOBAL AWARENESS CAMPAIGNS

Earth Hour

4.02 Earth Hour came from a think tank initiated by Earth Hour Co-Founder, Andy Ridley, resulting in the formation of a partnership between

World Wide Fund for Nature (WWF)-Australia, Leo Burnett and Fairfax Media to address the climate change issue. In 2007, there was still a degree of scepticism and denial on the issue of climate change. Earth Hour came as an inspiration to rally people to the reality of climate change and start a dialogue about what individuals could do to help address the planet's environmental challenges. Leo Burnett partnered with WWF to promote the idea and help make the campaign happen in Sydney. This campaign has now gone beyond Australia and climate change to symbolise the growing global pursuit of a better, sustainable future for all.

Earth Hour was started as a lights-out event in Sydney, Australia in 2007. WWF-Australia inspired Sydney-siders to show their support for climate action and more than 2.2 million individuals and 2,000 businesses turned their lights out for one hour in the first Earth Hour event. Since 2007 it has grown and now has millions of supporters in 185 countries and territories.

The annual lights-out event is held towards the end of March to encourage businesses, individual households and communities and businesses to turn off their non-essential lights for one hour as a symbol of their commitment to the planet. The second-to-last and last weekend of March is around the time of the Spring and Autumn equinoxes in the northern and southern hemispheres respectively, which allows for near coincidental sunset times in both hemispheres, thereby ensuring the greatest visual impact for a global 'lights-out' event.

Since the event began:

- WWF-Uganda has created the world's first Earth Hour Forest;
- more than 250,000 Russians voiced support for better protection of their country's seas and forests;
- Argentina has used its 2013 Earth Hour campaign to help pass a Senate bill for a 3.4 million hectares of Marine Protected Areas in the country;
- thousands of wood-saving stoves have been distributed to families in Madagascar;
- solar-powered lights have been installed in three villages without electricity in India;
- the WWF in Paraguay used the Earth Hour platform to build public support to gain an extension of the logging moratorium, helping to reduce deforestation;
- education programmes for schools have been launched in Thailand and Taiwan;
- hundreds of thousands of LED lights have been installed by girl scouts in the US; and
- more than 2,123 mitigation actions have been submitted by Earth Hour City Challenge 2014 participating cities.

Climate strikes

4.03 In November 2006, the Australian Youth Climate Coalition was formed to organise climate change actions involving youths and school children. In England in 2010 there were school walk-outs over climate change aligned to Climate Camp.[1]

1 Climate Camp was an annual camp which ran for five years and was disbanded in 2011.

In late November 2015, an independent group of students invited other students from around the world to miss school on the first day of the 2015 United Nations Climate Change Conference in Paris. On 30 November, the first day of the conference, a 'climate strike' was organised in over 100 countries and over 50,000 people participated. The movement focused on three areas: 100 per cent clean energy, keeping fossil fuels in the ground and helping climate refugees.

Fridays for Future movement

4.04 In 2018, the school strike for climate movement was initiated by Greta Thunberg outside the Swedish Parliament. This movement was participated in on a global scale. Greta decided not to attend school until the 9 September after heatwaves and wildfires in Sweden. She has said she was inspired by the teen activists at Marjory Stoneman Douglas High School in Parkland, Florida, who organised the March for Our Lives.

Among her demands were that the Swedish Government reduce carbon emissions as per the Paris Agreement. On 7 September, just before the general elections, she announced that she would continue to strike every Friday until Sweden aligned with the Paris Agreement. She coined the slogan *Fridays for Future*, which gained worldwide attention, and inspired school students across the globe to take part in student strikes.

Between 2019 and 2020 Greta took a year out of school to concentrate on activism and became well known for her impassioned speeches to world leaders.

In April 2019, aged 16, Ms Thunberg told members of the European Parliament: 'Our house is falling apart and our leaders need to start acting accordingly, because at the moment they are not.'

Five months later, she sailed by yacht across the Atlantic to address a UN climate action summit in New York:

> 'I should be back in school on the other side of the ocean,' she told delegates. 'Yet you all come to us young people for hope. How dare you! You have stolen my dreams and my childhood with your empty words.'

Although Greta Thunberg has not devised any specific environmental strategies, she has been credited with raising public awareness of climate change across the world, especially amongst young people.

Further climate strikes

4.05

- **Global Climate Strike for Future of 15 March 2019**
  On 15 March 2019, a series of school strikes urging adults to take responsibility and stop climate change took place. More than a million people demonstrated in about 2,200 events worldwide across 125 countries.
- **Second Global Climate Strike on 24 May 2019**
  A second wave of global climate strikes began with actions in New Zealand and Australia on 24 May 2019. Hundreds of thousands of school students

around the world went on strike in more than 1,600 towns in at least 125 countries.
(On 15 June 2021, the Auckland chapter of New Zealand's School Strike 4 Climate movement formally disbanded on the grounds that it had been racist towards BIPOC (Black, Indigenous and people of colour).)

- **International climate strike in Aachen on 21 June 2019**
  Fridays for Future Deutschland called for a major climate strike under the motto 'Climate justice without borders – United for a future' also inviting people from 17 countries to come to Aachen on 21 June 2019.
- **International conference in Lausanne on 5–9 August 2019**
  From 5–9 August 2019, the University of Lausanne hosted 450 young Europeans from the climate strike movement for the 'SMILE for Future ' conference ('Summer Meeting in Lausanne Europe').
- **Global Week of Climate Action on 20–27 September 2019**
  The September Global Week for Climate Action was a series of strikes and events from 20 to 27 September 2019, primarily focused on the two Fridays 20 and 27 September.
- **Fourth Global Climate Strike on 29 November 2019**
  On 29 November 2019, three days before the start of the United Nations Climate Change Conference (COP 25) in Madrid, demonstrations took place in 2,400 cities across 157 countries to protest government inaction on the climate crisis.
- **Global Climate Strike on 25 September 2020**
  On 25 September 2020, a global climate strike took place. Strikes were scheduled in thousands of locations around the globe.
- **Global Climate Strike on 19 March 2021**
  On Friday 19 March 2021, another global climate strike saw protests in hundreds of places around the planet; due to the ongoing Covid-19 pandemic, the scale of in-person gatherings was much reduced compared to previous years.
- **Global Climate Strike on 24 September 2021**
  On 24 September 2021 strikes were scheduled in more than 1,400 locations around the globe. Strikes were held in more than 90 countries with big events in Europe, the Americas and Africa.
- **Global Climate Strike on 25 March 2022**
  On 25 March 2022, a global climate strike took place. Protesters marched across Brooklyn Bridge as part of the Global Climate Strike movement in Manhattan.
- **Global Climate Strike on 23 September 2022**
  On 23 September 2022, a global climate strike took place. More than 30,000 people took part in Berlin.
- **Global Climate Strike on 3 March 2023**
  On 3 March 2023, a global climate strike took place. In Germany strikes were scheduled in more than 240 locations, including in Berlin where more than 18,000 people took part.

- **Digital climate strike**
  The climate strike online movement, sometimes referred to as 'digital strike', was started by two Asian-American climate activists in April 2019: Iris Zhan, from Howard County, Maryland, US; and George Zhang, from Los Angeles, California, US. This branch of climate striking was created in order to make climate activism accessible to those unable to strike physically.

United Nations Campaigns

UN Environment Programme (UNEP): Towards a pollution free planet[2]

4.06 With the end goal to eradicate all forms of pollution by 2030, the UN Environment Programme was tasked by the UN Environment Assembly to coordinate the implementation of a global plan 'Towards a pollution-free planet'.

Beat Plastic Pollution

4.07

> 'Governments, industry, and individuals must embrace a circular approach that considers the full life cycle of plastics, from production, to consumption, to waste management. This means that when plastic is introduced into the economy, it remains there, while harmful, avoidable, and unnecessary plastics are eliminated and substituted with sustainable options and practices.'[3]

#BeatPlasticPollution calls for a stronger, more agile, innovative, and forward-looking presence to engage governments, industry, and individuals in making deliberate changes and choices across the plastic value chain to eliminate the use of unnecessary, avoidable, and problematic plastic products.

It calls on governments, industry, and individuals to:

- reduce the size of the plastics problem by eliminating problematic or unnecessary plastics, including hazardous chemicals;
- design for circularity by ensuring all plastics are reusable, recyclable, or compostable;
- close the loop by collecting and recycling plastics; and
- improve waste collection across the globe and responsibly dispose of plastics that cannot be recycled.

New Plastics Economy Commitment

4.08 In 2018 the UNEP's Plastics Global Commitment joined forces with the Ellen McArthur Foundation on Global Commitment to form the New Plastics Economy Commitment. The agreement unites private and public sector leaders to pursue circular economies around plastics.

2 UN Environment Assembly, 'Implementation plan " Towards a Pollution-Free Planet"', UNEP/EA.4/Res.21, https://www.unep.org/environmentassembly/implementation-plan-towards-pollution-free-planet

3 UNEP, 'Beat Plastic Pollution', https://www.unep.org/beatpollution/beat-plastic-pollution

Global Tourism Plastics Initiative

4.09 The Initiative unites the tourism sector behind a common vision to address the root causes of plastic pollution. It enables businesses, governments, and other stakeholders to act and lead by example in the shift towards the reuse of plastics. It was developed within the framework of the Sustainable Tourism Programme of the One Planet network, and is led by UNEP and the World Tourism Organization (UNWTO), in collaboration with the Ellen MacArthur Foundation

Beat Air Pollution

4.10

> 'Governments, development organizations, the private sector, civil society organizations and individuals must reduce unsustainable behaviour and leverage finance and investments towards air quality measures and solutions.'[4]

#BeatAirPollution calls for a stronger, more agile, innovative, and forward-looking presence to engage governments, industry, and individuals in making deliberate changes and choices to reduce air pollution by:

- improving access to and the use of renewable energy;
- making lifestyle changes to minimise pollution and waste;
- implementing decisive policies to safeguard clean air and tackle emissions; and
- investing in air quality monitoring and technology to reduce air pollution.

Clean Air Day #CleanAirNow

4.11 This national day of clean air for the skies is calling on everyone from governments to corporations and individuals to invest in #Clean Air Now.

Climate and Clean Air Coalition (CACC)

4.12 A coalition to reduce short-lived climate pollutants (SLCPs) – methane, black carbon, hydrofluorocarbons (HFCs) and tropospheric ozone – that drive both climate change and air pollution.

Beat Nitrogen Pollution

4.13

> 'Governments, industry, and individuals must advocate for sustainable nitrogen management. This means tackling excess nitrogen and balancing its efficient production and consumption to avoid inefficient usage. Solutions exist, and more are in development. But they are widely unknown. Stronger communication and advocacy can help set the agenda to combat nitrogen pollution.'[5]

4 UNEP, 'Beat Air Pollution', https://www.unep.org/beatpollution/air
5 UNEP, 'Beat Nitrogen Pollution', https://www.unep.org/beatpollution/nitrogen

#BeatNitrogenPollution calls for a stronger, more agile, innovative, and forward-looking presence to engage governments, industry, and individuals to adopt an integrated approach towards improving the management of the nitrogen cycle to avoid inefficiencies and waste.

Political momentum for collective action on nitrogen is increasing. In 2019, the UN Environment Assembly – the world's foremost environmental decision-making body – adopted a resolution calling for sustainable nitrogen management and, in 2022, a second resolution was adopted.

Global Partnership on Nutrition Management

4.14 The Global Partnership on Nutrient Management (GPNM) is a response to the 'nutrient challenge' of how to reduce the amount of excess nutrients in the global environment consistent with global development. The GPNM reflects a need for strategic, global advocacy to move governments and stakeholders towards lowering nitrogen and phosphorus inputs to human activities. It provides a platform for governments, UN agencies, scientists and the private sector to create a common agenda, mainstream best practices and integrate assessments, so that policy making and investments are effectively 'nutrient proofed'. The GPNM also provides a space where countries and other stakeholders can create more cooperative work across the variety of international and regional fora and agencies dealing with nutrients, including the importance of assessment work.

Global Partnership on Plastic Pollution and Marine Litter

4.15 Creating an informed global community working together to achieve an ocean that is not harmed by marine litter and plastic pollution – by eliminating discharges and carrying out targeted removal.

Global Wastewater Initiative

4.16 The Global Wastewater Initiative (GWWI) has been working over the past ten years to implement and scale-up efforts to tackle wastewater pollution worldwide. It was formed in 2013 and is anchored to the Global Programme of Action for the Protection of the Marine Environment from Land-Based Activities (GPA).

Beat Chemical Pollution

4.17

> 'Governments, industry, and individuals must advocate for and adopt integrated lifecycle approaches to ensure the sound management of chemicals and waste.'[6]

6 UNEP, *Study on Industry Involvement in the Integrated Approach to Financing the Sound Management of Chemicals and Waste* (2022), https://www.unep.org/resources/report/study-industry-involvement-integrated-approach-financing-sound-management

#BeatChemicalPollution calls for a stronger, more agile, innovative, and forward-looking presence to engage governments, industry, and individuals to implement a specific, inclusive, and financially backed framework that ensures sound chemical management.

Largely led by the Strategic Approach to International Chemicals Management, a multi-sector policy framework, political momentum for collective action on sound chemical management is increasing. In September 2023, a Global Framework on Chemicals was adopted providing a new vision for a planet that is free of harm from chemicals and waste. Based on 28 targets, the framework outlines a roadmap for governments and industries to implement policies to reduce chemical pollution, promote safer alternatives, and address the lifecycle of chemicals, including in products and waste.

Beat Waste Pollution

4.18

> 'It is critical that integrated solid waste management strategies that include a rights-based approach are implemented at national, regional, and city levels to envision a zero-waste future.'[7]

#BeatWastePollution calls for sustainable actions towards zero waste by mainstreaming the reduce, reuse, and recycling practices where waste is viewed as a valuable resource that can have a second life and secondary raw materials are safely recovered.

The UNEP's International Environmental Technology Centre (IETC) provides developing countries with technical and advisory support through in-country demonstration projects and innovative waste prevention and management methods and technologies to improve human well-being, reduce the impact of climate change, increase resilience, and create job opportunities to envision a zero-waste future.

In December 2022, the UN General Assembly adopted Resolution 77/161, promoting zero-waste initiatives and environmentally sound waste management practices that advance sustainable development.

Breathe Life

4.19 Air pollution in our cities and in our homes is killing 6.5 million people each year and is driving climate change. The #BreatheLife global campaign aims to reduce air pollution, improve health and preserve our climate.

Champions of the Earth

4.20 The UNEP's Champions of the Earth award is the world's flagship environmental honour. Since 2005, the UNEP has recognised heroes who inspire, encourage others to join them, and defend a cleaner future.

7 UNEP, 'Beat Waste Pollution', https://www.unep.org/beatpollution/waste

Clean Seas

4.21 UNEP launched #CleanSeas in February 2017, with the aim of engaging governments, the general public, civil society and the private sector in the fight against marine plastic litter. The campaign aims to address the root-cause of marine litter by targeting the production and consumption of non-recoverable and single-use plastic.

Glowing Glowing Gone

4.22 A global campaign using creativity to accelerate climate and ocean action. In the last 30 years, 50 per cent of the world's corals have died and the situation is getting worse.

International Day of Clean Air for Blue Skies

4.23 Ninety-two per cent of our world is exposed to polluted air causing an estimated seven million premature deaths every year. Air pollution is an environmental risk to human health and an avoidable cause of death and disease worldwide.

Lead paint

4.24 The Global Alliance to Eliminate Lead Paint is a voluntary partnership formed by the UNEP and the World Health Organization (WHO) to prevent exposure to lead, while promoting the phase-out of paints containing lead. The Alliance is guided by an Advisory Council chaired by the US Environmental Protection Agency (US EPA) and consisting of government representatives from Colombia, the Republic of Moldova, Kenya, Thailand, the International Pollutants Elimination Network (IPEN), the Health and Environmental Alliance (HEAL), the American Bar Association Rule of Law Initiative (ABA ROLI), the World Coating Council (WCC) (formerly the International Paint and Printing Ink Council (IPPIC)), AkzoNobel and Pacific Paint (Boysen) Philippines (paint companies).

Stop Food Loss and Waste

4.25 Between 691 and 783 million people faced hunger in 2022, with a mid-range of 735 million. This represents an increase of 122 million people compared to 2019, before the Covid-19 pandemic.

Think.Eat.Save

4.26 People were asked to join the Reduce Your Foodprint campaign in support of the SAVE FOOD Initiative to reduce food loss and waste along the entire chain of food production and consumption – run by the Food and Agriculture Organization (FAO) and trade fair organiser Messe Düsseldorf – and the UN Secretary General's Zero Hunger Challenge. The campaign specifically targets food wasted by consumers, retailers and the hospitality industry.

World Environment Day

4.27 This event has been led by the UNEP since it started in 1973. Its aim is to put a spotlight on the environmental challenges that are being faced by the world and is now one of the largest environmental platforms for environmental outreach.

- **2023 Côte d'Ivoire – #BeatPlasticPollution**
  This was held on the Côte d'Ivoire and focused on showcasing solutions to plastic pollution. The unanimous passing of the resolution established an intergovernmental negotiating committee (INC) to develop a legally binding global instrument to end plastic pollution.
- **2022 Sweden – #OnlyOneEArth**
  This was to remember the world's first environmental summit 50 years prior in 1972 (the United Nations Conference on Human Environment). At the 2022 event the host nation, Sweden, pledged to stop issuing licences for new coal, oil and natural gas extraction. Over 65 million people celebrated World Environment Day online.
- **2021 Pakistan – #Generation Restoration**
  The focus was on ecosystem restoration and the theme was 'Reimagine. Recreate. Restore'. It looked at how humanity has been exploiting the planet's ecosystems and called for a concerted global effort to repair the damage that has been done. Every three seconds, the world loses enough forest to cover a football pitch and, over the last century, half of all wetlands have been destroyed.
- **2020 Columbia – #Time For Nature**
  World Environment Day 2020 focused on biodiversity which is a concern both urgent and existential. Fourteen world leaders, including those from Colombia, Costa Rica, Finland, France and the Seychelles released a statement calling on governments to support a new global goal to protect at least 30 per cent of the planet's land and ocean by 2030.
- **2019 People's Republic of China – #Beat Air Pollution**
  The theme in 2019 was air pollution. Hosted by China, President Xi Jinping stressed his country's willingness to share its experience combating air pollution with other nations. China also launched its Air Quality Improvement Report (2013–18) to show successful policies and reflect on lessons learned.
- **2018 India – #Beat Plastic Pollution**
  The 45th World Environment Day had the theme 'Beat Plastic Pollution'. Over 6,000 people gathered at Versova Beach in Mumbai to join UN Environment Champion of the Earth, Afroz Shah, in a beach clean-up. Here they collected over 90,000 kg of plastic. The Indian Government made a commitment to ban all single-use plastics, which is 70 per cent of marine litter, by 2022 and European Union (EU) lawmakers agreed on a ban by 2025.
- **2017 Canada – #ImWithNature**
  'I'm with nature' was the theme in 2017. It inspired more than 1,800 events, from tree-planting in Mumbai to ivory burning in Angola to a running race through Brazil's Iguaçu National Park. Prime Minister Justin

Trudeau joined UNEP's Erik Solheim to connect with nature by paddling kayaks along the Niagara River.

- **2016 Angola – #WildForLife**
  This was the start of #WildforLife, at the time the UNEP's biggest ever digital campaign and a move to counter international wildlife crime. Angola promised to curb the trading of elephant ivory. China, a key destination for illegal wildlife products, subsequently pledged to close down its domestic ivory market.
- **2015 Italy – #ConsumeWithCare**
  World Environment Day in 2015 was celebrated under the theme 'Seven Billion People. One Planet. Consume with Care': it was the most popular subject on Twitter (now X) in more than 20 countries.
- **2014 Barbados – #ClimateChange**
  The theme 'Raise Your Voice Not the Sea Level!' was to raise awareness of the dangers facing island nations from climate change. The next year, small island states secured an agreement at the Paris climate talks to pursue the ambitious goal of limiting the increase in average global temperature to 1.5°C.
- **2013 Mongolia – #ThinkEatSave**
  The year's theme was 'Think.Eat.Save'. The campaign highlighted the environmental toll of food waste, getting people to make informed choices so as to reduce the ecological impact of food production.
- **2012 Brazil – #DoesItIncludeYou?**
  World Environment Day returned to Rio de Janeiro, Brazil. The theme 'Green Economy: Does it Include You?' amplified the UNEP's efforts to create a more sustainable global financial order. The World Environment Day website posted more than 4.25 million visits, a new record at the time.
- **2011 India – Forests: Nature at Your Service**
  World Environment Day 2011 featured a contest between actor Don Cheadle and entrepreneur Gisele Bündchen to see who could attract more social media followers. Bündchen planted the first of 50,000 trees in Rio de Janeiro's Grumari Municipal Park. People around the world registered more than 4,000 activities related to World Environment Day.
- **2010 Rwanda – Many Species. One Planet. One Future**
  World Environment Day's Legacy Initiative raised more than US $85,000 for gorilla conservation and solar lighting in villages across Rwanda. Voters in a global online competition chose names for several baby gorillas, highlighting their threatened status during the International Year of Biodiversity.
- **2009 Mexico – Your Planet Needs You: Unite to Combat Climate Change**
  The 2009 World Environment Day reflected the urgency that nations agree on a new deal at the crucial climate convention meeting in Copenhagen some 180 days later in the year, and the links with overcoming poverty and improved management of forests.
- **2008 New Zealand – Kick the Habit Towards a Low Carbon Economy**
  The focus of the global 2008 celebrations hosted in New Zealand was solutions and the opportunities for countries, companies and communities

to 'Kick the habit' and de-carbonise their economies and lifestyles. Measures included greater energy efficiency in buildings and appliances, including light bulbs, up to a switch towards cleaner and renewable forms of electricity generation and transport systems.

- **2007 Norway – Melting Ice – a Hot Topic?**
  The theme 'Melting Ice? – A Hot Topic', marked the first of three consecutive years in which the day drew attention to climate change. It came just as the Intergovernmental Panel on Climate Change's (IPCC's) Fourth Assessment Report stated that warming of the climate was unequivocal.
- **2006 Algeria – Deserts and Desertification – Don't Desert Drylands!**
  A decade after the UN Convention to Combat Desertification entered into force, World Environment Day reminded people about the pressures on drylands when Algeria hosted the celebrations under the slogan 'Deserts and Desertification – Don't Desert Drylands!'
- **2005 US – Green Cities: Plan for the Planet!**
  Held in North America for the first time, with San Francisco hosting hundreds of events around the theme 'Green Cities: Plan for the Planet'. This was the year the Kyoto Protocol came into force and the event included the participation of former US Vice-President Al Gore and former Mayor of San Francisco Gavin Newsom.
- **2004 Spain – Wanted! Seas and Oceans – Dead or Alive?**
  'Wanted! Seas and Oceans -- Dead or Alive?' reflected not only the activities in Barcelona, where several activities related to seas and oceans were being held, but also the UNEP's important activities in the field of marine environment and sustainable coastal livelihoods.
- **2003 Lebanon – Water – Two Billion People Are Dying for It!**
  The celebrations took place in Beirut, Lebanon, a first for West Asia. The theme of 'Water – Two Billion People are Dying for It!' was chosen in support of the International Year of Fresh Water.
- **2002 People's Republic of China – Give Earth a Chance**
  The southern Chinese city of Shenzhen hosted a series of events to not only raise environmental awareness but also promote continued environmental action.
- **2001 Italy and Cuba – Connect with the World Wide Web of Life**
  UN Secretary-General Kofi Annan chose World Environment Day to launch the Millennium Ecosystem Assessment, an effort to map the health of the planet. Reflecting the theme 'Connect with the World Wide Web of Life', the festivities took place across several cities: Torino, Italy; Havana, Cuba; Hue, Viet Nam; and Nairobi, Kenya.
- **2000 Australia – The Environment Millennium – Time to Act**
  UNEP launched a World Environment Day website, making it easier for people around the world to register their activities and build a sense of global community. The main events took place in Adelaide, Australia under the theme 'The Environment Millennium – Time to Act', ahead of the international summit that set the Millennium Development Goals.
- **1999 Japan – Our Earth – Our Future – Just Save It!**
  1999 World Environment Day involved calls:

— on every sector of society to work together to establish solutions to the environmental ills facing our planet;
— to give a human face to environmental issues;
— to empower people to become active agents of sustainable and equitable development;
— to promote an understanding that communities are pivotal to changing attitudes toward environmental issues; and
— to advocate partnerships which will ensure all nations and peoples to enjoy a safer and more prosperous future.

- **1998 Russian Federation – For Life on Earth – Save Our Seas**
  World Environment Day 1998 highlighted threats to marine using the theme of 'For Life on Earth – Save our Seas' in support of the International Year of the Ocean.

- **1997 Republic of Korea – For Life on Earth**
  The theme was 'For Life on Earth' and also honoured the 25th anniversary of the UNEP. The world had celebrated a number of significant milestones since the creation of the UNEP 25 years prior at the Stockholm Conference on the Human Environment and World Environment Day 1998 also marked the 10th anniversary of the negotiation of the Montreal Protocol on the preservation of the ozone layer, ten years since the Brundtland Report and five years since world leaders had gathered in Rio de Janeiro for the Earth Summit.

- **1996 Türkiye – Our Earth, Our Habitat, Our Home**
  Nigerian activist Ken Saro-Wiwa received a posthumous Global 500 award during World Environment Day 1996 celebrations in Ankara, Türkiye. With the award, World Environment Day highlighted the link between human and environmental rights.

- **1995 South Africa – We the Peoples: United for the Global Environment**
  South Africa hosted a year after Nelson Mandela became president. Mandela attended the celebrations, drawing international attention to environmental themes. A year earlier, the anti-Apartheid leader used the day to declare Cape Town's Table Mountain a 'gift to the Earth' and proof of South Africa's commitment to protect biodiversity.

- **1994 UK – One Earth One Family**
  The theme for 1994 was to remind everyone that there is only one Earth. That this is the point in history where the Earth is experiencing significant stress.

- **1993 People's Republic of China – Poverty and the Environment – Breaking the Vicious Circle**
  China hosted World Environment Day 1993 in Beijing, to raise environmental awareness in the world's most populous nation, under the theme 'Poverty and the Environment – Breaking the Vicious Circle'. The event returned to China in 2002, hosted by the city of Shenzhen.

- **1992 Brazil – Only One Earth, Care and Share**
  Held in Rio de Janeiro, Brazil, during the UN Conference on Environment and Development, better known as the Earth Summit, nations negotiated landmark treaties on climate change, desertification and biodiversity, and set the course for contemporary sustainable development.

- **1991 Sweden – Climate Change. Need for Global Partnership**
A speech was given by the President of Brazil, Fernando Collor:

> 'Unbridled, disorderly growth — achieved at any cost — waste, and an excessively consumeristic approach, have clearly aggravated the problems which Man has sought to solve as much as the tragic poverty that is perpetuated in the "developing" world.
>
> Today it is clear that growth, divested of concern for its effects on the environment, results in an undermining of the objectives which it aims to fulfil, placing the target of development coupled with social welfare at an ever-greater distance.
>
> It is not a matter of spurning the objectives of well-being propitiated by material advancement, laudable though they are in themselves; rather, it is a matter of rethinking the very notion of progress — a progress that is not reduced to the mere enumeration of growth statistics but that implies, besides improvement of social indicators, real and effective concern for environmental protection.'

- **1990 Mexico – Children and the Environment**
The Mexican Government hosted World Environment Day, to send forth a clear message: LET US BUILD A BETTER PLANET FOR CHILDREN. A NEW CRUSADE

- **1989 Belgium – Global Warming; Global Warning**
A year after the establishment of the IPCC, World Environment Day was hosted in Brussels, Belgium and reiterated the mounting concern about global warming. The theme was revisited more than any other in subsequent World Environment Day campaigns.

- **1988 Thailand –When People Put the Environment First, Development Will Last**
The main celebrations rotated around the globe, starting in Bangkok, Thailand. The theme of 'When People Put the Environment First, Development Will Last' came a year after the Brundtland Report laid out its blueprint for sustainability.

- **1987 Kenya – Environment and Shelter: More Than A Roof**
The UNEP hosted the day at its headquarters in Nairobi, Kenya, presenting the first of its Global 500 awards to environmental champions awarding Wangari Maathai. The awards became a feature of World Environment Day celebrations through to 2003.

- **1986 Canada – A Tree for Peace**
The theme 'A Tree for Peace' coincided with the International Year of Peace. Reflecting World Environment Day's growing profile, political and religious leaders, including French President François Mitterrand, Indian Prime Minister Rajiv Gandhi and Uganda's President Yoweri Museveni, took part in a global ceremony by planting a tree and stressing the links between conflict and environmental destruction.

- **Preceding year themes.**
  - 1985 Pakistan – Youth: Population and the Environment
  - 1984 Bangladesh – Desertification
  - 1983 Bangladesh – Managing and Disposing Hazardous Waste: Acid Rain and Energy
  - 1982 Bangladesh – Ten Years After Stockholm (Renewal of Environmental Concerns)

- — 1981 Bangladesh – Ground Water; Toxic Chemicals in Human Food Chains
- — 1980 Bangladesh – A New Challenge for the New Decade: Development Without Destruction
- — 1979 Bangladesh – Only One Future for Our Children – Development Without Destruction
- — 1978 Bangladesh – Development Without Destruction
- — 1977 Bangladesh – Ozone Layer Environmental Concern; Lands Loss and Soil Degradation
- — 1976 Canada – Water: Vital Resource for Life
- — 1975 Bangladesh – Human Settlements
- — 1974 US – Only One Earth
- — 1973 Switzerland – Only One Earth

UN Decade on Ecosystem Restoration[8]

4.28 The world depends on healthy ecosystems for food and energy security and water supplies and their continued degradation contributes to climate change and enhances the risk of an ecological collapse. The UN says the loss would be catastrophic for our planet and a huge setback in achieving the United Nations Sustainable Development Goal, now is the time to rebuild what has been lost.

Global Climate Action Summit

4.29 The Global Climate Action Summit in 2018 marked the midpoint between the historic signing of the Paris Agreement in 2015, which aimed to limit global temperature rise to no more than 2°C and its next scheduled step to 2020 when countries would bolster their commitments. Hoping to recapture the same ambitious spirit of the Paris Agreement, the summit allowed leaders to share their successes so far and then announce new initiatives that raise the bar. Organisers expected the Global Climate Action Summit to be the biggest climate event ever held in the US.

EDUCATIONAL INITIATIVES

UK Sustainability and Climate Change Strategy: a strategy for the education and children's services systems[9]

4.30 This was an initiative of the UK Conservative Party launched in 2022 and updated in 2023. Its aim is for the UK to be the world-leading education sector in sustainability and climate change by 2030.

8 UN Environment Assembly Resolution 5/14 End plastic pollution: towards an international legally binding instrument.

9 Sustainability and Climate Change Strategy: a strategy for the education and children's services systems, Department for Education.

The document lists five steps that are aimed at making education more sustainable and preparing young people for a world impacted by climate change:

- Appointing youth focal points
- Attending COP 28
- Developing climate action plans
- Expanding the climate ambassador scheme
- Launching the National Education Nature Park

EU Green Education initiatives

4.31 The EU is encouraging and supporting the education and training sector to act for a greener, more sustainable future and to build the sustainability competences of learners. Support for green and digital transitions is a priority area for EU policy cooperation in education.

- **Education for Climate Coalition**
  The Education for Climate Coalition is a growing community of pupils, students, teachers and organisations active on climate change and sustainability.
- **Council Recommendation on learning for the green transition and sustainable development**
  A Council Recommendation on learning for the green transition and sustainable development supports Member States in embedding sustainability in education and training.[10]
- **European Sustainability Competence Framework**
  The European Sustainability Competence Framework sets out the knowledge, skills and attitudes learners of all ages need to acquire for the green transition.
- **Working Group on Sustainability in School Education**
  A dedicated working group on sustainability in school education regularly produces input papers and key messages. The working groups on Vocational Education and Training, and Adult Learning and Higher Education also deal with the green transition and sustainability.
- **Erasmus+ and European Solidarity Corps**
  Erasmus+ and European Solidarity Corps support a variety of initiatives related to sustainability in education and training, including student and staff exchanges, research and volunteering
- **Dedicated call on climate change and sustainability education**
  The Horizon Europe Programme has a dedicated call on climate change and sustainability education. Horizon Europe is the EU's key funding programme for research and innovation.
- **InvestEU programme**

10 Council Recommendation of 16 June 2022 on learning for the green transition and sustainable development 2022/C243/01 ST/9795/2022/INIT [2022] OJ C243.

The InvestEU programme enables Member States to access funding for sustainable education infrastructure and the development of skills.

- **Researchers at Schools initiative**
  The Researchers at Schools initiative connects young researchers with teachers and pupils on climate change and sustainable development.
- **Erasmus+ DiscoverEU Green route**
  The Erasmus+ DiscoverEU Green route inspires young people to plan and discover Europe in a sustainable way.
- **Teaching Award**
  The 2022 European Innovative Teaching Award selected 50 outstanding projects focused on sustainability and was themed 'learning together, promoting creativity and sustainability'.
- **EU Learning Corner**
  The EU Learning Corner includes teaching and learning materials on sustainability and the climate and environmental crisis for primary and secondary schools

Public workshops and seminars

Climate Fresk

4.32 Cédric Ringenbach founded the Climate Fresk non-governmental organisation (NGO) in 2018. Its goal is to raise awareness of and participation in workshops and to train and upskill Climate Fresk facilitators.

It proposes a collaborative serious game based on 42 cards where the participants draw a fresco, hence 'fresk', which summarises the work of the IPCC. As of 2023, over a million people have participated.

MEDIA AND COMMUNICATION STRATEGIES

Documentaries and films

'An Inconvenient Truth'

4.33 'An Inconvenient Truth' is a documentary film released in 2006, directed by Davis Guggenheim and featuring former US Vice-President Al Gore. The film focuses on raising awareness about climate change and the urgent need for action to address it. Here is an overview of the film, its impact, and its significance.

The film is structured around a multimedia presentation that Al Gore had been giving around the world on the subject of climate change. Gore presented scientific data and research that demonstrate the reality of global warming. The film uses charts, graphs, and visual animations to illustrate the increase in carbon dioxide levels, rising global temperatures, and melting glaciers.

Interspersed with the presentation are personal anecdotes and reflections from Gore about his own life and his commitment to the climate cause. The film emphasises the need for immediate action to reduce greenhouse gas emissions, the potential catastrophic consequences of inaction, and the role of individuals and governments in combating climate change.

The film won two Oscars, including Best Documentary Feature and Best Original Song ('I Need to Wake Up' by Melissa Etheridge) and received positive reviews for its compelling and accessible presentation of climate science.

The film influenced public opinion and policymakers and contributed to the momentum for environmental legislation and international agreements. Al Gore continued his advocacy with the establishment of The Climate Reality Project and the release of a follow-up film, 'An Inconvenient Sequel: Truth to Power' (2017), which focuses on the progress made since the first film and ongoing challenges.

Some critics and climate change sceptics questioned the accuracy of the predictions and the scientific consensus presented in the film. Whilst the film raised awareness, it started debates about the best approaches to address climate change, including the roles of renewable energy, carbon pricing, and technological innovation. The presentation of scientific evidence, combined with Al Gore's advocacy, helped motivate public awareness and action.

'Before the Flood'

4.34 This documentary from 2016, which was narrated and produced by Leonardo DiCaprio, presents a riveting account of the changes which are occurring around the world due to climate change, as well as the actions of individuals. It looks at how individuals and society can make changes to prevent a catastrophic disruption to the life of the planet.[11]

'Our Planet'

4.35 This was an original Netflix documentary series and a collaboration between the WWF, Netflix and Silverback films. It showcases the world's natural wonders, species and wildlife spectacle.

'Our Planet' was influenced by the dissatisfaction with existing science and environment programming. It was going to focus on environmental issues but needed to secure a large audience and then show them the environmental crisis that was looming. Keith Scholey joined the BBC Natural History Unit which he later became the head of. In 2012 he and Alistair Fothergill founded Silverback Films. Scholey saw climate change as a crisis in communication. The WWF carried out an impact report which showed that, as a result of watching the show, viewers had a higher recall of facts relating to the interconnectedness of nature and the extent of wildlife loss in recent decades. Surveyed viewers also showed 'a more sophisticated understanding' of climate change and its complexity.

11 United Nations Creative Community Outreach (CCOI), 'Before the Flood'.

CORPORATE AND INSTITUTIONAL INITIATIVES

4.36 Raising climate change awareness is crucial for mobilising action at all levels. The following are some examples of corporate and institutional activities dedicated to increasing awareness about climate change.

These activities show how both corporations and institutions are actively working to raise awareness about climate change through education, transparency, public engagement and collaborative efforts.

Corporate activities

Public campaigns and education

Nike

4.37 Nike runs campaigns like 'Move to Zero,' which not only focus on sustainability in products but also educate consumers on the importance of reducing waste and carbon emissions.

Patagonia

4.38 Patagonia actively campaigns for environmental causes, using its platforms to raise awareness about climate change and encourage activism among its customers.

Sustainability reports and transparency

Starbucks

4.39 Starbucks releases 'Global Environmental and Social Impact Reports' that highlight efforts and progress in sustainability and climate change mitigation.

Tesla

4.40 Tesla publishes detailed impact reports outlining the company's environmental footprint, sustainability initiatives, and progress towards its goals.

Collaborative initiatives

RE100

4.41 This is a global initiative where companies commit to 100 per cent renewable energy. Members like IKEA, Google, and Apple not only commit to clean energy but also advocate for wider adoption of renewable energy.

We Mean Business Coalition

4.42 Companies like Unilever and Microsoft collaborate to advocate for stronger climate policies and share best practices on reducing emissions and increasing sustainability.

Employee engagement programmes

Google

4.43 Google engages employees through its 'Green Team', which focuses on sustainability initiatives within the company and educates employees on environmental issues.

Microsoft

4.44 Microsoft runs internal programmes like 'Hack for Sustainability', where employees work on projects aimed at reducing the company's environmental impact and promoting sustainable practices.

Sponsorship and partnerships

Amazon

4.45 Partners with The Nature Conservancy for the 'Right Now Climate Fund' to support initiatives aimed at reducing emissions and preserving natural habitats.

Ben & Jerry's

4.46 Partners with climate advocacy groups like 350.org to raise awareness and drive action on climate change, often through campaigns and sponsored events.

Institutional activities

Climate education programmes

Harvard University

4.47 Harvard University integrates climate change into its curriculum across multiple disciplines and offers dedicated programmes such as the 'Harvard Climate Leadership Program'.

Yale University

4.48 Yale's 'Program on Climate Change Communication' works to improve public understanding and engagement with climate change through research and education.

Public lectures and workshops

Stanford University

4.49 Stanford hosts public lectures and seminars through the Stanford Woods Institute for the Environment, focusing on various aspects of climate science and policy.

University of California, Berkeley

4.50 Berkeley organises events and workshops through its Berkeley Center for Green Chemistry, aimed at educating students and the public about sustainable practices.

Collaborative research initiatives

Massachusetts Institute of Technology (MIT)

4.51 MIT collaborates with other institutions and organisations through initiatives like the Climate CoLab, which crowdsources climate change solutions from the public.

Oxford University

4.52 Oxford runs the Oxford Climate Society, which organises events, discussions, and campaigns to raise awareness and understanding of climate issues among students and the broader community.

Community outreach and advocacy

London School of Economics (LSE)

4.53 The Grantham Research Institute on Climate Change and the Environment engages in extensive outreach to inform policymakers and the public about climate risks and policies.

University of British Columbia (UBC)

4.54 UBC engages with local communities through its Social Ecological Economic Development Studies (SEEDS) Sustainability Program, which involves students and staff in projects that address local environmental issues and raise awareness.

Media and publications

Columbia University

4.55 Through its Earth Institute, Columbia publishes extensive research and reports on climate change that are accessible to the public, helping to disseminate important findings and raise awareness.

Princeton University

4.56 The Princeton Environmental Institute produces the *Princeton Environmental News* which highlights climate change research and initiatives to a broader audience.

CORPORATE RESPONSIBILITY CAMPAIGNS

4.57 Corporate responsibility campaigns to raise awareness about climate change are used for educating the public, influencing behaviour and inspiring group action. The following are some examples of such campaigns.

These campaigns illustrate how corporations can leverage their influence, resources, and platforms to raise awareness about climate change, encourage sustainable practices and inspire action among consumers and other stakeholders.

Apple – 'Better' campaign

4.58 Apple launched the 'Better' campaign to highlight its commitment to environmental sustainability. The campaign includes a series of videos and reports that detail Apple's efforts to use 100 per cent recycled aluminium in its products, achieve carbon neutrality, and power its facilities with renewable energy. It raises awareness about the importance of sustainable practices in technology manufacturing and encourages consumers to consider the environmental impact of their purchases.

Ben & Jerry's – 'Save Our Swirled'

4.59 Ben & Jerry's campaign focuses on raising awareness about climate change and advocating for policy action. The campaign includes limited-edition flavours, educational content, and partnerships with climate advocacy groups. It engages consumers in climate activism, encourages political action, and highlights the urgency of addressing climate change.

Google – 'Environmental Insights Explorer'

4.60 Google's tool provides cities with data to help them reduce carbon emissions and become more sustainable. The tool uses Google's data and analytics capabilities to track emissions, energy use, and solar potential in urban areas. It raises awareness about the role of data and technology in combating climate change and supports cities in making informed decisions to reduce their carbon footprint.

IKEA – 'People & Planet Positive'

4.61 IKEA's sustainability strategy focuses on becoming a circular and climate-positive business by 2030. The campaign includes using renewable and recycled materials, increasing energy efficiency, and promoting sustainable living among customers. It raises awareness about the importance of a circular economy and sustainable home furnishings.

Microsoft – 'AI for Earth'

4.62 Microsoft's programme leverages artificial intelligence (AI) to tackle environmental challenges. The campaign includes grants for projects that use AI to address issues like climate change, water conservation, and biodiversity. It highlights the role of technology in environmental sustainability and promotes innovative solutions to combat climate change.

Nike – 'Move to Zero'

4.63 Nike's initiative to achieve zero carbon and zero waste. The campaign includes using recycled materials in products, reducing carbon emissions across its supply chain, and educating consumers about sustainable practices. It engages a broad audience in the conversation about sustainability in fashion and sportswear, promoting eco-friendly products and practices.

Patagonia – 'Don't Buy This Jacket'

4.64 Patagonia's iconic advertisement encourages consumers to think twice before buying new products. The campaign promotes the repair and reuse of existing products and highlights Patagonia's commitment to environmental responsibility. It challenges consumer culture and promotes a message of sustainability and minimalism, raising awareness about the environmental costs of consumerism.

Starbucks – 'Starbucks Greener Stores'

4.65 This is Starbucks' initiative to design, build, and operate 10,000 Greener Stores globally by 2025. The campaign focuses on reducing environmental impact through energy efficiency, water conservation, and waste reduction. It raises awareness about sustainable practices in the retail and food service industry and encourages other businesses to adopt greener operations.

Tesla – 'Tesla Impact Report'

4.66 Tesla's annual report details the company's sustainability efforts and environmental impact. The report covers Tesla's advancements in electric vehicles, renewable energy and battery storage solutions. It raises awareness of the benefits of electric vehicles and renewable energy and demonstrates Tesla's commitment to sustainability.

Unilever – 'Sustainable Living Plan'

4.67 Unilever's comprehensive plan aims to decouple its growth from its environmental impact while increasing positive social impact. The campaign includes public commitments to reduce greenhouse gas emissions, improve water usage and achieve sustainable sourcing of raw materials. It increases awareness about corporate responsibility in consumer goods and encourages other companies to adopt similar sustainability practices.

ART AND CULTURE

4.68 Climate change art is a medium through which to communicate the urgency and impact of global warming. Many artists use various forms of art to raise awareness, provoke thought, and inspire action. There are some examples below.

Visual art

'Ice Watch' by Olafur Eliasson and Minik Rosing

4.69 Large blocks of glacial ice were transported from Greenland and installed in public spaces in cities like Copenhagen, Paris and London. The melting ice serves as a visual and tactile representation of climate change. The artwork aims to make the distant phenomenon of melting glaciers more immediate and tangible for urban audiences.

The first installation was in Copenhagen, at City Hall Square, from 26 to 29 October 2014, to mark the publication of the UN IPCC's Fifth Assessment Report on Climate Change. The second installation took place in Paris, at Place du Panthéon, from 3 to 13 December 2015, on the occasion of the UN Climate Conference COP 21, and the third version of Ice Watch was on view from 11 December 2018 to 2 January 2019 at two locations in London – outside Bloomberg's European headquarters and in front of the Tate Modern.

'The Drowned World' by Isaac Cordal

4.70 This series of small sculptures features miniature figures partially submerged in water, often in urban settings. The figures appear to be in meetings or daily activities, oblivious to their environment. The work critiques societal inaction on climate change and highlights the consequences of rising sea levels.

'Climate Signals' by Justin Brice Guariglia

4.71 Electronic highway signs were repurposed to display climate change-related messages like 'Climate Change At Work' and 'Warning: Rising Sea

Levels'. The installation uses familiar public signage to communicate urgent environmental messages in a way that is hard to ignore. Signs were located across all five boroughs of New York City, to celebrate the diversity of the city with their placement. Each sign featured languages commonly spoken in its neighbourhood.

Eighteen programmatic partners, including social justice organisations, scientific research consortia, local environmental advocacy groups, established museums and more co-presented events at or near the exhibition sites to build understanding of, and engagement with, climate change. This programming ensured that the work had a meaningful impact on civic culture and community life. 'Climate Signals' was designed to break the climate silence and encourage thought, dialogue, and action to address the greatest challenge of our time.

Installations and sculptures

'Falling Tide' by Jason deCaires Taylor

4.72 'Falling Tide' is underwater sculptures placed off the coast of the Canary Islands, designed to encourage coral reef regeneration. The sculptures depict human figures and animals, merging art with marine conservation. The work aims to raise awareness about coral reef degradation and promote marine biodiversity.

Taylor creates underwater museums and sculpture parks beneath the water, having submerged over 1,200 living artworks throughout the world's oceans and seas. Themes explored by these artistic installations include, among others, the climate emergency, environmental activism, and the regenerative attributes of nature. The sculptures create a habitat for marine life whilst illustrating humanity's fragility and its relationship with the marine world. Taylor's subjects mainly feature members of the local community, focusing on their connections with their own coastal environments.

'The Blue Trees' by Konstantin Dimopoulos

4.73 Trees in various cities are painted blue with environmentally safe pigments to draw attention to deforestation and the importance of trees in combating climate change. The striking blue colour transforms public spaces and provokes conversations about environmental stewardship. This change highlights ecological issues, such as the ecocide of our forests and climate change, and effects a transformation in the psyche of people by raising our social consciousness referencing how individually and collectively we shape the world we inhabit.

'Pollution Pods' by Michael Pinsky

4.74 A series of interconnected geodesic domes simulating the air quality of various cities around the world, from clean air to highly polluted environments.

Visitors experience the stark contrast in air quality, raising awareness about the health impacts of pollution and the need for cleaner air policies.

The five interconnected geodesic domes contain carefully mixed recipes emulating the relative presence of ozone, particulate matter, nitrogen dioxide, sulphur dioxide and carbon monoxide which pollute London, New Delhi, San Paolo and Beijing. Starting from a coastal location in Norway, the visitor passes through increasingly polluted cells, from dry and cold locations to hot and humid.

Pollution Pods has been commissioned by the Norwegian University of Science and Technology as part of Climart, a four-year research project that examines the underlying psychological mechanisms involved in both the production and reception of visual art, using these findings in an attempt to unite the natural sciences and the visual arts.

Photography

'The End of Nature' by Daniel Beltrá

4.75 Aerial photographs depicting the impact of human activities on natural landscapes, such as deforestation, melting ice caps, and oil spills. The dramatic images highlight the scale of environmental destruction and encourage viewers to reflect on their relationship with nature.

His aerial images cover fields of ice, water and earth, to experience the natural wonders of our planet, and to bear witness to the scars and scale of environmental degradation. In his wildlife images, Beltrá captures the immediacy of trauma caused by oil spills, deforestation, desertification and climate change, and tells the stories of the feral victims of those tragedies. Over the past two decades, his work has taken him to all seven continents, including several expeditions to the Brazilian Amazon, the Arctic, the Southern Oceans and the Patagonian ice fields.

'Water Scarcity' by Mustafah Abdulaziz

4.76 A long-term photographic project documenting the global water crisis, including the effects of climate change on water availability and quality. The project raises awareness about the interconnectedness of climate change and water issues, emphasising the human and ecological consequences.

Performance and interactive art

'Climate Symphony' by Leah Barclay

4.77 An interactive sound installation that translates climate data into music. The piece uses real-time environmental data to create an evolving soundscape. The auditory experience helps audiences understand climate data in an emotional and intuitive way, bridging science and art.

'Sun & Sea (Marina)' by Rugilė Barzdžiukaitė, Vaiva Grainytė and Lina Lapelytė

4.78 An operatic performance set on an artificial beach, where singers perform songs about climate change and environmental degradation while sunbathing. The piece uses the juxtaposition of a leisurely beach scene with urgent environmental themes to provoke reflection on human behaviour and climate inaction.

Digital and media art

'Plastic Reflectic' by Thijs Biersteker

4.79 An interactive installation that visualises the impact of plastic pollution on the environment. Users interact with a screen to see the accumulation of plastic waste. The interactive nature engages viewers and educates them about the severity of plastic pollution and its links to climate change.

'Delta' by Refik Anadol

4.80 A digital artwork that uses AI to process climate data and create dynamic visualisations. The work reflects changes in climate patterns and environmental data. The piece bridges technology and art, making complex climate data accessible and visually compelling to a broad audience.

These examples illustrate the diverse ways in which artists are addressing climate change through various mediums, helping to raise awareness and inspire action.

Literature/Novels

4.81 Climate change has become a significant theme in contemporary literature, where authors explore its impacts, causes, and moral implications through various genres and styles. This emerging body of work is often referred to as 'climate fiction' or 'cli-fi'. Here are some notable examples of how climate change is portrayed in literature.

'The Water Knife' by Paolo Bacigalupi

4.82 Set in a near-future US ravaged by climate change, the novel follows a 'water knife' (a person who cuts off water supplies) navigating a desperate landscape where water is a scarce and valuable resource. The book explores themes of scarcity, survival, and the sociopolitical consequences of environmental degradation.

'Parable of the Sower' by Octavia Butler

4.83 Set in a dystopian future where climate change has led to societal collapse, the story follows a young woman with hyper-empathy who leads a group of survivors in search of a safe haven. The novel explores themes of survival, community and resilience in the face of environmental and social upheaval.

'Flight Behaviour' by Barbara Kingsolver

4.84 A young mother in rural Tennessee discovers a valley filled with millions of monarch butterflies, which have deviated from their usual migration pattern due to climate change. The novel examines the clash between scientific understanding and local scepticism, as well as the broader implications of climate change on nature and human communities.

'Weather' by Jenny Offill

4.85 The story centres on a librarian who becomes increasingly involved in climate change activism as she grapples with personal and global anxieties. It delves into the psychological impact of climate change awareness and the struggle to balance personal life with the urgency of activism.

'The Overstory' by Richard Powers

4.86 This is a Pulitzer Prize-winning novel which intertwines the lives of several characters who are brought together by their deep connection to trees and the natural world, culminating in environmental activism. It addresses deforestation, environmental activism and the intricate relationships between humans and nature.

Poetry

'Ecopoetry: A Critical Introduction' edited by J. Scott Bryson

4.87 This anthology includes poems that explore ecological themes, with many addressing climate change and environmental degradation. The collection reflects on the beauty and fragility of nature, the impact of human activity, and the urgent need for environmental stewardship.

'Field Notes from a Catastrophe: Man, Nature, and Climate Change' by Elizabeth Kolbert

4.88 Though primarily a non-fiction book, it includes poignant passages that read like poetry, reflecting on the devastating effects of climate change. The work addresses the scientific and human dimensions of climate change, offering both lyrical and factual perspectives.

Non-fiction

'This Changes Everything: Capitalism vs. The Climate' by Naomi Klein

4.89 A critical examination of the relationship between capitalism and climate change, arguing that substantial systemic changes are necessary to address the crisis. The book addresses the economic and political barriers to climate action and advocates for transformative solutions.

'The Uninhabitable Earth: Life After Warming' by David Wallace-Wells

4.90 A detailed and alarming account of the potential future impacts of climate change based on current scientific projections. It covers a wide range of topics, including natural disasters, economic collapse, and societal changes due to climate change.

Young adult and children's literature

'Floodland' by Marcus Sedgwick

4.91 In a future world flooded by rising sea levels, a young girl searches for her lost parents and a place of safety. It addresses climate change, survival, and the search for hope in a transformed world.

'The Last Wild' by Piers Torday

4.92 Set in a world where animals are almost extinct due to a mysterious virus, a young boy discovers he can communicate with the remaining animals and sets out to save them. The novel explores themes of environmentalism, adventure and the importance of biodiversity.

CHALLENGES AND SOLUTIONS: MISINFORMATION AND DISINFORMATION

4.93 Climate misinformation is the spread inaccurate information about climate change that can arise from human error. Climate disinformation is driven by a deliberate intent to spread knowingly false information. Regardless of intent, 'scientifically misleading information' can have 'negative implications for climate policy', the IPCC has said.

In a global risk report[12] misinformation and disinformation were cited as the new leaders in the top 10 rankings in 2024 as the biggest short-term risks to human society and long-term risks to extreme weather events. This is worsened by the likelihood that the information is shared.

Climate misinformation can arise from a genuine misunderstanding, drawing conclusions from incomplete information or misinterpreting data. Individuals may inadvertently share misconceptions about climate science, which, while not intended to be malicious, still contribute to the spread of inaccurate information. Climate disinformation is a more insidious form of misinformation as its distributors are knowingly sharing falsehoods and may intend to protect their own interests to the detriment of others. One example is that they may use deceptive tactics to undermine the scientific consensus on climate change or cast doubt on the severity of its impact.

In practice, it can be difficult to determine whether there is deliberate intent to mislead, especially given the increase in false climate information which finds its way onto social media platforms, as identified by multiple studies (for example by the BBC and Stop Funding Heat). Additionally, a post originally created and shared with deceitful motives can unwittingly be circulated further, without harmful intention. Therefore, disinformation can be viewed as a subset of misinformation, whereby all disinformation can be classified as misinformation but not vice versa.

Climate denial

4.94 Climate denial is the dismissal of human-caused climate change and its effects on the environment. This is often the case despite a lot of evidence and recent climate disasters that prove its existence.

Climate delayism

4.95 There is also a shift towards using people's nuanced understanding of disinformation to thwart climate action. People supporting Climate delayism or 'new denial' do not reject that climate change is happening, but instead will diminish and discredit evidence to push the case for delaying climate action.

The Meractor Research institute on Global Commons and Climate Change has identified 12 categories in discourses on climate delay and grouped these under four overarching strategies.

Redirect responsibility

4.96 This uses the discourse of individualism to suggest that addressing climate change is the sole responsibility of individuals rather than governments, industry, companies or society. An example could be that individuals should

12 *Global Risks Report 2024* (19th edn, Marsh McLennan and Zurich, 2024).

renovate homes for energy efficiency or buy a more fuel-efficient car. Not to suggest that individual actions are futile, but this stance might also use 'whataboutism', which counters the importance of individual action by questioning what others are doing. This can involve pointing to larger emitters of carbon and deflecting action on them.

Push non-transformative solutions

4.97 This involves the offering of 'trivial' solutions that are ineffective in reducing greenhouse gas emissions, rather than addressing the root-causes: for instance, relying solely on technologies such as carbon capture, without attempting to drive down consumption of fossil fuels.

Emphasise the downsides

4.98 This is often used to misrepresent the potential consequences of climate policies, solely highlighting the short-term costs. Policy statements can become discourses of delay when they emphasise the downsides of climate action and imply that these carry an even greater burden for society than the consequences of inaction.

Surrender

4.99 This is a narrative that says it is not possible to mitigate climate change effectively given societal structures and human nature, or that it is now too late to act, and thus we should just adapt or accept our fate. Policy statements can become discourses of delay if they raise doubt that mitigation is (still) possible, pointing to seemingly insurmountable political, social or biophysical challenges. *Doomism* further argues that any actions we take are too little, too late.

Chapter 5

Approaches to Climate Change: UK

5.01 In the UK, legislation and regulations related to climate change are structured around several key frameworks and pieces of legislation designed to address:

- greenhouse gas (GHG) emissions;
- promote sustainability; and
- facilitate adaptation to climate impacts.

CLIMATE CHANGE ACT 2008 (CCA)

5.02 The Climate Change Act[1] gained royal assent on the 26 of November 2008. The Act sets up the framework for the UK to achieve its long-term goals of reducing GHG emissions and to ensure steps are taken towards adapting to the impacts of climate change.

Carbon budgets

5.03 Part 1 of the Act gives the Secretary of State a duty to reduce the net UK carbon account for the year 2050 to at least 80 per cent below the level of net UK emissions of targeted GHGs in 1990. The term 'targeted greenhouse gas' is defined in s 24, the term 'net UK carbon account' is defined in s 27 and the term 'net UK emissions' is defined in s 29.

The Act also requires the Secretary of State to set 'carbon budgets' representing UK emissions for five-year periods beginning with the period 2008–12 and taking account of any 'carbon units' which are credited or debited to the net UK carbon account under a system of 'carbon accounting'. Part 1 of the Act also includes a duty on the Secretary of State to report UK emissions levels to Parliament, and to report on the measures the UK Government will take to meet the carbon budgets in Part 1.

Part 1 makes further provision relating to the target and to budgets, including provision on how to calculate whether the target for 2050 has been met and

1 Climate Change Act 2008, https://www.legislation.gov.uk/ukpga/2008/27/contents

how carbon budgets are to be set. It requires that the carbon budget for 2018–22 is set in a way that is consistent with the Government's target to reduce emissions of carbon dioxide (CO_2) by at least 26 per cent by 2020, against 1990 levels. It requires the Secretary of State to have regard to the need for UK domestic action on climate change when considering how to meet the 2050 target and each carbon budget. It also makes provision for the amendment of certain aspects of Part 1 of the Act in certain circumstances and imposes a duty to make regulations about how carbon units are to be used to ensure that the net UK carbon account is within budget.

2050 target

5.04 The UK has committed to reaching net zero by 2050, which means that total GHG emissions would be equal to the emissions removed from the atmosphere, with the aim of limiting global warming and the resultant climate change.

The 2021 Net Zero Strategy set out policies and commitments designed to enable the UK to reach net zero by 2025. The 2023 Net Zero Plan set out an update to the existing strategies, focusing on the scale up and deployment of technologies for decarbonising homes, power, industry and transport. This update also fulfilled the 2022 high court judgment[2] for the government to set out in detail how it aims to reach net zero.

Climate Change Committee (CCC)

5.05 The CCC was established under the CCA and is in place to provide the UK with emission targets and report on progress made in reducing GHG emissions and preparing for and adapting to the impacts of climate change to Parliament.

The key reports that the CCC makes are:

- those giving advice on carbon budgets and long-term emissions targets;
- progress reports on meeting carbon budgets and targets;
- assessment reports of UK climate change risks; and
- progress reports on adapting and preparing for climate change.

In addition the Minister can request advice on specific topics and issues.

Climate Change Risk Assessment (CCRA)

5.06 The CCA requires the UK Government and devolved administrations to undertake a Climate Change Risk Assessment every five years. The latest one was undertaken in 2022. This report to Parliament outlines the key climate change risks and opportunities that the UK faces. It is based on an independent

2 *R (on the application of (1) Friends of the Earth Ltd (2) ClientEarth and (3) Good Law Project and Joanna Wheatley) v Secretary of State for Business, Energy and Industrial Strategy* [2022] EWHC 1841 (Admin).

assessment of UK climate risk based on the statutory advice provided by the Climate Change Committee (CCC).

The 2022 (third) CCRA[3] considered 61 UK-wide climate risks and opportunities across multiple sectors of the economy and prioritised the following eight risk areas for action in the following two years:

- risks to the viability and diversity of terrestrial and freshwater habitats and species from multiple hazards;
- risks to soil health from increased flooding and drought;
- risks to natural carbon stores and sequestration from multiple hazards;
- risks to crops, livestock and commercial trees from multiple climate hazards;
- risks to supply of food, goods and vital services due to climate-related collapse of supply chains and distribution networks;
- risks to people and the economy from climate-related failure of the power system;
- risks to human health, well-being and productivity from increased exposure to heat in homes and other buildings; and
- multiple risks to the UK from climate change impacts overseas.

The second CCRA was in 2017.[4]

The first CCRA was in 2012.[5]

THE CLIMATE CHANGE AGREEMENTS (AMENDMENT OF AGREEMENTS) (EU EXIT) REGULATIONS 2018

5.07 These regulations[6] amend existing climate legislation post-Brexit, maintain the carbon budgeting framework and strengthen targets under the Climate Change Act 2008 post-Brexit. They also adjust references to EU legislation to ensure continued application of the UK's climate framework.

THE UK'S NET ZERO STRATEGY

5.08 Published in October 2021,[7] the Strategy sets out policies and proposals for decarbonising all sectors of the UK by 2050.

3 *UK Climate Change Risk Assessment 2022* (HM Government, 17 January 2022) https://assets.publishing.service.gov.uk/media/61e54d8f8fa8f505985ef3c7/climate-change-risk-assessment-2022.pdf
4 *UK Climate Change Risk Assessment 2017* (HM Government, January 2017) https://assets.publishing.service.gov.uk/media/5a7f6e5ae5274a2e8ab4c23d/uk-climate-change-risk-assess-2017.pdf
5 *UK Climate Change Risk Assessment: Government Report* (HM Government, January 2012) https://assets.publishing.service.gov.uk/media/5a78a060e5274a277e68e336/pb13698-climate-risk-assessment.pdf
6 Climate Change (Agreement of Amendments) (EU Exit) Regulations 2018 (SI 2018/1205) https://www.legislation.gov.uk/uksi/2018/1205/contents
7 *Net Zero Strategy: Build Back Greener* (HMSO, 2021) https://assets.publishing.service.gov.uk/media/6194dfa4d3bf7f0555071b1b/net-zero-strategy-beis.pdf

The Strategy has four key principles:

- 'We will work with the grain of consumer choice: no one will be required to rip out their existing boiler or scrap their current car';
- 'We will ensure the biggest polluters pay the most for the transition through fair carbon pricing';
- 'We will ensure that the most vulnerable are protected through Government support in the form of energy bill discounts, energy efficiency upgrades, and more'; and
- 'We will work with businesses to continue delivering deep cost reductions in low carbon tech through support for the latest state of the art kit to bring down costs for consumers and deliver benefits for businesses.'

CARBON BUDGETS

5.09 The Climate Change Act 2008 established a series of carbon budgets defining the maximum GHG emissions the UK can produce over five-year periods.

First Carbon Budget – covering the period of 2008–12
Second Carbon Budget – covering the period of 2013–17
Third Carbon Budget – covering the period of 2018–22
Fourth Carbon Budget – covering the period of 2023–27
Fifth Carbon Budget – covering the period of 2028–32
Sixth Carbon Budget – covering the period of 2033–37

The Carbon Plan – reducing greenhouse gas emissions (2011)

5.10 In 2011 the government[8] set out scenarios as to how it would meet the first four carbon budgets from 2008–27.

The plan looked at a number of sectors:

- low-carbon buildings
- energy efficiency
- low-carbon heating
- low-carbon transport
- low-carbon industry
- low-carbon electricity
- agriculture, land use, forestry and waste

Clean energy transition

5.11 In 2022 82 per cent of emissions in the UK came from the burning of fossil fuels for energy use. This is due to generating electricity, heat for industry and buildings and transporting people and goods. Less than 20 per cent of all

8 *The Carbon Plan – reducing greenhouse gas emissions* (HM Government, 2011)

emissions were non-energy related and came from land use, F-Gases, waste and agriculture.

The Climate Change Act 2008 mandated the phasing out of coal-fired power stations in the UK. As a result, emissions from electricity supply dropped by nearly three-quarters between 1990 and 2022. Emissions from offshore oil and gas activities in the North Sea have also fallen since 2004 as reserves are gradually depleted.

The next phase of decarbonising the energy supply needs to focus on substituting natural gas with low-carbon sources of power generation.

ENVIRONMENT ACT 2021

5.12 This Act[9] introduces a framework for environmental governance in England post-Brexit, with a strong emphasis on climate change.

The Environment Act 2021 is in two themes, the first being the legal framework for environmental governance and the second making provision for specific improvement of the environment, which includes measures on waste and resource efficiency, air quality and environmental recall,[10] water, nature, and biodiversity and conservation covenants.

The remainder of the Act makes provision for a range for environmental improvements.

Environmental governance (Part 1)

5.13 Part 1 includes provisions to:

- allow the government to set long-term targets (of at least 15 years' duration) in relation to the natural environment and people's enjoyment of the natural environment via statutory instrument;
- require the government to meet long-term targets, and to prepare remedial plans where long-term targets are not met;
- require the government to set, by October 2022, at least one long-term target in each of the priority areas of air quality, water, biodiversity, and resource efficiency and waste reduction;
- require the government to set and meet an air quality target for fine particulate matter in ambient air (PM2.5);
- require the government to set and meet a target relating to the abundance of species;
- require the government to periodically review all environmental targets to assess whether meeting them would significantly improve the natural environment in England;

9 Environment Act 2021, https://www.legislation.gov.uk/ukpga/2021/30/contents
10 Environmental recall – recall of a product which does not meet environmental standards.

- establish the process by which a long-term target is set and amended, as well as an enhanced process where a long-term target is lowered or revoked;
- require the government to have, and maintain, an Environmental Improvement Plan, a plan to significantly improve the natural environment, which sets out the steps the government intends to take to improve the natural environment, and which sets out interim targets towards meeting the long-term targets;
- require the government to produce an annual report on the Environmental Improvement Plan, to consider progress towards improving the natural environment and meeting the targets;
- require the government to review the plan periodically, to consider progress and whether further or different steps are needed to improve the natural environment and meet the targets, and, if appropriate, revise the plan;
- require the government to collect and publish data used to measure progress in improving the natural environment and meeting the targets;
- require the publication of a policy statement on environmental principles setting out how environmental principles specified under the Act are to be interpreted and applied by Ministers of the Crown during the policymaking process;
- create a new, statutory and independent environmental body, the Office for Environmental Protection (OEP), to hold the government to account on environmental law and its Environmental Improvement Plan now that the UK has left the EU;
- define the scrutiny, complaints and enforcement functions of the OEP and their scope;
- establish an enforcement process of environmental review for the OEP;
- define the nature of the OEP, including considerations of membership, remuneration, staffing, powers, reporting, funding, accounts and other issues;
- require the government to publish a report on the impact of all new environmental primary legislation; and
- require the government to undertake a report on environmental legislation across the world every two years.

Environmental governance Northern Ireland (Part 2)

5.14 This part includes provisions to extend the application of the OEP to Northern Ireland and makes separate provision for Environmental Improvement Plans and environmental principles in Northern Ireland.

Waste and resource efficiency (Part 3)

5.15 Part 3 includes provisions to:

- require producers to pay the full net cost of managing their products at end of life to incentivise more sustainable use of resources;
- allow deposit return schemes to be established, whereby a deposit is included in the price of an in-scope item (such as a drink in a bottle or can) which is redeemed when the item is returned to a designated point;

- enable producer responsibility obligations to be applied at all levels of the waste hierarchy to, for example, facilitate the prevention of food waste and increase the redistribution of food surplus;
- enable charges to be applied to specified single-use items;
- require local authorities in England to collect the same range of materials for recycling from households;
- ensure households have a weekly separate food waste collection;
- ensure businesses and public bodies in England present recyclable materials for separate collection and arrange for its separate collection;
- enable the government to set resource-efficient product standards and information and labelling requirements, in order to drive a shift in the market towards durable, repairable and recyclable products;
- improve the proportionality and fairness of litter enforcement, by issuing statutory guidance on the use of enforcement powers and extending an existing power to set out conditions to be met by all those carrying out enforcement activity;
- improve the management of waste, by enabling the Secretary of State and the Devolved Administrations to make regulations in relation to tracking waste digitally;
- improve the regulators' effectiveness in tackling waste crime, reducing the cost of that criminal activity on the wider economy, environment and society;
- allow the Environment Agency to be more flexible and responsive in managing exempt waste sites and ensure proportionate controls are in place to avoid environmental harm or illegal activity as waste market practices change;
- fill a gap in existing powers to ensure that waste can be collected and disposed of when normal processes fail;
- enable the Secretary of State to make regulations to amend the permitted range of penalties for existing Fixed Penalty Notices; and
- enable the Secretary of State to regulate the import, export or transit of waste for export, and hazardous waste.

Air quality and environmental recall (Part 4)

5.16 Part 4 includes provisions to:

- amend Part 4 of the Environment Act 1995 (which creates the Local Air Quality Management Framework) to strengthen the requirements in respect of the National Air Quality Strategy, including a requirement for it to be regularly reviewed;
- amend the Local Air Quality Management Framework to clarify duties and enable greater cooperation between different levels of local government, and other relevant public bodies, in the preparation of Local Air Quality Action Plans;
- amend Part 3 of the Clean Air Act 1993 to enable quicker, simpler and more proportionate enforcement of Smoke Control Areas, a key means by which local authorities can control pollution from domestic solid fuel burning; and
- provide for mandatory recall notices for vehicles and equipment that do not comply with relevant environmental standards and for fines to be issued when a minimum recall rate is not met.

Water (Part 5)

5.17 This part includes provisions to:

- change the procedural requirements for Water Resources Management Plans and Drought Plans, and enable increased collaboration between different water undertakers to better manage water resources;
- require the preparation of Drainage and Sewerage Management Plans by sewerage undertakers, to better plan for the management of wastewater;
- place new duties on government, the Environment Agency and sewerage undertakers to require actions for reducing the frequency and harm of discharges from storm overflows on the environment, set requirements for monitoring the quality of water potentially affected by those discharges, and for reporting on those discharges, annually and in real time;
- modernise the process for modification of water and sewerage undertaker licence conditions by the Water Services Regulation Authority (Ofwat) to bring it in line with other utilities, and to strengthen Ofwat's ability to improve water and sewerage undertakers' operations;
- change the circumstances in which a licence to abstract water from the environment can be revoked or varied without paying compensation, to prevent damage to the environment;
- enable future updates to the lists of priority substances in water quality legislation, and enable the reallocation of regulatory responsibilities in the Solway Tweed river basin district; and
- enable updates to be made to the valuation calculations relevant to the apportionment of internal drainage board (IDB) charges in secondary legislation, allowing for the creation of new or expansion of existing IDBs where there is a local desire to do so.

Nature and biodiversity (Part 6)

5.18 Part 6 includes provisions to:

- amend Natural Environment and Rural Communities Act 2006, s 40 to strengthen and improve the duty on public bodies to conserve and enhance biodiversity, in accordance with the proper exercise of their functions;
- mandate net gain in biodiversity through the planning system, requiring a 10 per cent increase in biodiversity after development, compared to the level of biodiversity prior to the development taking place, as measured by a metric set out by the Department for Environment Food and Rural Affairs (Defra);
- require the preparation and publication of Local Nature Recovery Strategies, a tool to direct action for nature, and place an emphasis on supporting local leadership of nature improvement;
- provide for Species Conservation and Protected Site Strategies to improve the conservation and protection of the most vulnerable species and habitats;
- provide powers to amend Conservation of Habitats and Species Regulations 2017 (SI 2017/1012), reg 9 and Part 6 to refocus the Regulations to support delivery of domestic biodiversity priorities;

- provide greater enforcement powers to the Forestry Commission to reduce illegal tree felling, and require local authorities to consult local residents prior to the felling of street trees; and
- address illegal deforestation in supply chains by placing requirements on larger businesses operating in the UK to establish, implement and report on a due diligence system to ensure forest risk commodities produced on land that was illegally occupied or used do not enter their supply chain, and by prohibiting the use of forest risk commodities that have not been produced in accordance with local laws relating to land use and land ownership.

Conservation covenants (Part 7)

5.19 Part 7 includes provisions to provide for Conservation Covenants: voluntary, legally binding private agreements between landowners and responsible bodies, designated by the Secretary of State, which conserve the natural or heritage features of the land, enabling long-term conservation.

CLEAN GROWTH STRATEGY

5.20 Published in 2017, this strategy supports the UK's transition to a low carbon economy. It outlines approaches to promote clean growth and emissions reductions, addressing sectors such as energy efficiency, low-carbon technologies, and decarbonisation of transportation.

THE ENERGY ACT 2013

5.21 This Act[11] includes provisions to support low-carbon energy generation and improve energy security. It establishes a legislative framework for the following.

Decarbonisation

5.22 The Act allows the Secretary of State to set a 2030 decarbonisation target for the electricity sector in mandatory legislation.

Electricity Market Reform (EMR)

5.23 The Act includes provisions[12] for:

11 Energy Act 2013, https://www.legislation.gov.uk/ukpga/2013/32/contents

12 'Appendix 5: Electricity Market Reform', Gov.uk, https://www.gov.uk/government/publications/2010-to-2015-government-policy-uk-energy-security/2010-to-2015-government-policy-uk-energy-security#appendix-5-electricity-market-reform-emr

- Contracts for Difference (CfD): long-term contracts to provide stable and predictable incentives for companies to invest in low-carbon generation;
- a Capacity Market: to ensure the security of electricity supply, including provisions to allow Electricity Demand Reduction to be delivered;
- conflicts of interest and contingency arrangements: to ensure the institution which will deliver these schemes is fit for purpose;
- investment contracts: long-term contracts enabling early investment in advance of the 2014 CfD regime;
- access to markets: this includes Power Purchase Agreements (PPAs), to ensure the availability of long-term contracts for independent renewable generators, and liquidity measures to enable the government to take action to improve the liquidity of the electricity market, should it prove necessary;
- renewables transition: transitional arrangements for investments under the Renewables Obligation scheme; and
- the Emissions Performance Standard (EPS): to limit CO_2 emissions from new fossil fuel power stations.

Nuclear regulation

5.24 The Act gives the Office of Nuclear Regulation (ONR) a statutory footing.

Government pipeline storage system

5.25 The Act enables the sale of the Government Pipe-line and Storage System (GPSS).

Strategy and Policy Statement

5.26 The Act improves regulatory certainty by ensuring that the government and the Office of Gas and Electricity Markets (Ofgem) are aligned at a strategic level through a Strategy and Policy Statement (SPS), as recommended in the Ofgem Review of July 2011.

Consumer protection

5.27 The Act includes provisions to:

- set a limit on the number of energy tariffs offered to domestic consumers; require the automatic move of customers from poor value closed tariffs to cheaper deals; require the provision of information by suppliers to consumers on the best alternative deals available to them from them;
- allow Ofgem to extend its licence regime to third-party intermediaries, such as switching websites;
- provide a new enforcement power for Ofgem to require energy businesses that breach gas or electricity licence conditions, or other relevant regulatory

requirements, to provide redress to consumers who suffer detriment as a result of the breach; and

- amend the Warm Homes and Energy Conservation Act 2000 to propose a new target for fuel poverty that would be set through secondary legislation.

THE TEN POINT PLAN FOR A GREEN INDUSTRIAL REVOLUTION (2020)

5.28 This plan outlines key policies to accelerate the transition to a green economy.[13] The ten points are:

- Advancing Offshore Wind
- Driving the Growth of Low Carbon Hydrogen
- Delivering New and Advanced Nuclear Power
- Accelerating the Shift to Zero Emission Vehicles
- Green Public Transport, Cycling and Walking
- Jet Zero and Green Ships
- Greener Buildings
- Investing in Carbon Capture, Usage and Storage
- Protecting Our Natural Environment
- Green Finance and Innovation

THE 25 YEAR ENVIRONMENT PLAN

5.29 This plan[14] aims to improve the natural environment and is compatible with climate change goals. The *25 Year Environment Plan* sets out government actions to help the natural world regain and retain good health. It aims to deliver cleaner air and water in cities and rural landscapes, protect threatened species and provide richer wildlife habitats.

The actions to be be taken include:

- Using and managing land sustainably
- Recovering nature and enhancing the beauty of landscapes
- Connecting people with the environment to improve health and well-being
- Increasing resource efficiency and reducing pollution and waste
- Securing clean, healthy, productive and biologically diverse seas and oceans
- Protecting and improving our global environment

13 *The Ten Point Plan for a Green Industrial Revolution* (HM Government, 2020) https://assets.publishing.service.gov.uk/media/5fb5513de90e0720978b1a6f/10_POINT_PLAN_BOOKLET.pdf

14 *A Green Future: Our 25 Year Plan to Improve the Environment* (HM Government, 2018) https://assets.publishing.service.gov.uk/media/5ab3a67840f0b65bb584297e/25-year-environment-plan.pdf

CLIMATE CHANGE LEVY

5.30 The Climate Change Levy (CCL) is provided for in the Finance Act 2000.[15] This is a tax on business energy use in the UK. The main rates for CCL are set out in para 42(1) of Sch 6 to the Finance Act 2000.

Legislation was introduced in the Finance Bill 2024–25 to amend the CCL main rates on electricity, gas, and solid fuels in para 42 of Sch 6 to Finance Act 2000.

Climate Change Agreements (CCAs)

5.31 The Finance Act 2010 amended the CCL to offer a reduced rate of 35 per cent to participants in CCAs. These are voluntary agreements between UK industry and the Environment Agency to reduce energy use and CO_2 emissions. As a result of a CCA, operators receive a discount on the CCL – a tax added to electricity and fuel bills. The Environment Agency administers the scheme of behalf of the whole of the UK.

CCAs are available for a wide range of industries where there are major energy-intensive processes such as chemicals and paper, supermarkets and agricultural businesses such as intensive poultry and pig farming.

Umbrella agreements

5.32 The Department of Energy and Climate Change and industry sectors negotiated energy efficiency targets for each sector, these are the sector commitments. The targets were then included in umbrella agreements held between sector associations and the Environment Agency. Umbrella agreements also list the processes that are eligible for a CCA. In 2020 the Department for Business, Energy and Industrial Strategy (BEIS) (encompassing the Department of Energy and Climate Change and now the Department for Energy Security and Net Zero) negotiated new targets for 2021 and 2022.

Underlying agreements

5.33 An underlying agreement is one held by an operator for a site, or group of sites, within a particular sector. It contains energy or carbon efficiency targets appropriate for their type of operation derived from the umbrella agreement.

How CCAs work

5.34 The current CCA scheme started in April 2013 and runs until 31 March 2025, after which it will be replaced by a new six-year scheme starting in early 2025, running until the end of 2030, with the first target period starting in January 2026.

15 Finance Act 2000, https://www.legislation.gov.uk/ukpga/2000/17/contents

An operator with a CCA had to measure and report its energy use and carbon emissions against agreed targets over two-year target periods up to the end of 2022.

If an operator has more than one eligible facility in the same sector it can hold an individual CCA for each facility or choose to group them together under one CCA.

When a facility or group of facilities is included in a CCA it is referred to as a target unit.

If the target unit meets its targets at the end of each reporting period, the facilities continue to be eligible for the discount on the CCL. The reduced rate certificate lists facilities entitled to claim a discount on the CCL and is updated on the last working day of each month.

CCAs: consultation on a new scheme

5.35 Following the consultation which closed in February 2024, a new CCA scheme will be introduced.

The new scheme will begin its first Target Period on 1 January 2026, with set targets extending through to the end of 2030. Participants meeting their energy efficiency goals will benefit from reduced CCL rates until March 2033.

Existing participants will not automatically be rolled into the new scheme. Each facility must reconfirm its eligibility before the new scheme begins, and a proportion of participants will be subject to audits to verify compliance with the eligibility requirements.

Businesses in sectors already participating in the scheme will be able to join between 1 January and 31 August each year, with no waiting period for certification to receive CCL reductions. Also, a special application window from 1 May to 31 August 2025 will allow new entrants to join the scheme in time for its official launch.

Industrial sectors seeking to join the scheme will be assessed based on eligibility criteria. To qualify, sectors must demonstrate that:

- their energy expenses account for at least 10 per cent of production value (Energy Intensity (EI) ≥ 10%) or
- their energy costs represent between 3 per cent and 10 per cent of production value, with an Import Penetration (IP) ratio of at least 50 per cent (3% ≤ EI < 10% and IP ≥ 50%).

SCOTLAND'S CLIMATE CHANGE LAWS AND REGULATIONS

Climate Change (Scotland) Act 2009

5.36 This Act[16] sets interim and annual targets for reducing GHG emissions.

16 Climate Change (Scotland) Act 2009, https://www.legislation.gov.uk/asp/2009/12/contents

Climate Change (Emissions Reduction Targets) (Scotland) Act 2019

5.37 This Act[17] increased the ambition of Scotland's emissions reduction targets to net zero by 2045.

Climate Change (Emissions Reduction Targets) (Scotland) Act 2024

5.38 This further Act[18] introduced a carbon budget-based approach for setting emissions reduction targets.

Carbon budgets

5.39 These cover a five-year period and set out the amount of GHG emissions allowed during that period. Carbon budget targets should not be exceeded.

Climate Change Committee (CCC)

5.40 Ministers must consider the CCC's advice before finalising regulations to set carbon budget levels.

Climate Change Plan

5.41 The deadline for the first Climate Change Plan was changed so it can align with the process for setting the new carbon budgets.

The legislation also requires:

- local authorities to act sustainably, contribute to carbon emissions reduction targets, and contribute to climate change adaptation;
- the creation of a Citizens Assembly and a Scottish Nitrogen Balance Sheet.

The UK Government also introduced the Climate Change Levy (CCL) to incentivise energy efficiency and reduce carbon emissions. The CCL applies to electricity and gas used for business purposes.

17 Climate Change (Emissions Reduction Targets) (Scotland) Act 2019, https://www.legislation.gov.uk/asp/2019/15

18 Climate Change (Emissions Reduction Targets) (Scotland) Act 2024, https://www.legislation.gov.uk/asp/2024/15/section/1/enacted#section-1-3

WALES'S CLIMATE CHANGE LAWS AND REGULATIONS

Environment (Wales) Act 2016

5.42 This Act[19] establishes a framework for managing natural resources in a sustainable way and includes a statutory framework for climate change action. The Act gives Welsh Ministers the power to set emission reduction targets, including a goal of reducing emissions to net zero by 2050.

Climate Change (Interim Emissions Targets) (Wales) (Amendment) Regulations 2021

5.43 These Regulations[20] introduce carbon budgets to help achieve the net-zero goal. They also set interim emissions targets, including:

- a 27 per cent reduction by 2020;
- a 45 per cent reduction by 2030; and
- a 67 per cent reduction by 2040.

Net Zero Wales

5.44 This is the Welsh Government's plan to achieve net-zero emissions. It includes targets for emissions reductions in areas such as:

- electricity and heat generation
- transport
- homes
- industry and business
- agriculture
- land use
- waste management

Shoreline Management Plans (SMPs)

5.45 These plans outline policies for managing coastal risk. They break the coastline into sections and identify sustainable approaches to managing risks.

19 Environment (Wales) Act 2016, https://www.legislation.gov.uk/anaw/2016/3/contents
20 Climate Change (Interim Emissions Targets) (Wales) (Amendment) Regulations 2021 (SI 2021/338), https://www.legislation.gov.uk/wsi/2021/338/note/made

NORTHERN IRELAND'S CLIMATE CHANGE LAWS AND REGULATIONS

Climate Change Act (Northern Ireland) 2022

5.46 This Act[21] sets targets for reducing GHG emissions in Northern Ireland, including a 100 per cent reduction by 2050. The Act also requires all Northern Ireland departments to contribute to the Act's targets, carbon budgets, and climate action plans.

Climate Change (Reporting Bodies) Regulations (Northern Ireland) 2024

5.47 These Regulations[22] establish a reporting regime for climate change in Northern Ireland by requiring certain public bodies to report on climate change. The regulations also require the Department of Agriculture, Environment and Rural Affairs (DAERA) to produce guidance and publish climate change reports. The Regulations came into effect on 3 May 2024.

Other climate change regulation

5.48 Other aspects of Northern Ireland's climate change laws and regulations include:

- a climate change levy (CCL) that encourages businesses to reduce their energy consumption or use renewable energy sources;
- sectoral targets, such as at least 80 per cent of electricity consumption from renewable sources by 2030;
- a target for at least 70 per cent of waste to be recycled by 2030; and
- a target for a minimum spend of 10 per cent of overall transport budgets on active travel.

LOCAL AUTHORITY INITIATIVES

5.49 Many local authorities have introduced their own climate change strategies and action plans, focusing on localised emissions reduction efforts and adaptation.

Examples include:

- the Net Zero Innovation Programme: a partnership between researchers and council climate change officers to help tackle climate change;

21 Climate Change Act (Northern Ireland) 2022, https://www.legislation.gov.uk/nia/2022/31/contents/enacted

22 Climate Change (Reporting Bodies) Regulations (Northern Ireland) 2024 (SI 2024/93), https://www.legislation.gov.uk/nisr/2024/93/body/made

- the Local Action For Our Environment: a podcast series that offers advice to council officers and members on engaging communities on climate change;
- the LGA Climate Change Sector Support Programme: a training programme that helps council officers develop the skills and tools to grow the retrofit sector;
- the Design in Public Sector Programme: a partnership between the LGA and the Design Council that helps councils develop design skills to address climate challenges;
- Cosy Homes in Lancashire: an initiative that focuses on improving domestic energy efficiency in low-income households;
- Bristol City Council: a council that developed and owns wind turbines;
- the Crindau Flood Management Scheme: a scheme in Newport that built defences along the Crindau Pill to protect homes from river flooding;
- Lancashire County Council: a council that converted 152,000 streetlights to energy saving LEDs;
- Portsmouth City Council: a council that launched 'Switched On Portsmouth', a service to help residents save energy and money in their homes; and
- Waltham Forest Council: a council that retrofitted sheltered housing schemes with a solar-powered system.

INTERNATIONAL COMMITMENTS

5.50 The UK is committed to international agreements such as the Paris Agreement and is taking steps to uphold its commitments.

Chapter 6

Climate Change Litigation Cases: UK

INTRODUCTION

6.01 Climate change litigation cases within the UK fall into three areas.

Cases against the government

6.02 Many climate change cases in the UK are challenges to government and public bodies (both local and central). Following the Paris Agreement, the UK Government made a number of policy changes to implement its adherence to the Agreement. These included the emissions reduction target being amended to 100 per cent by 2050 (under an amendment to the Climate Change Act 2008) and the creation of an independent, advisory body to the government: the Climate Change Committee (CCC).

Cases against corporations

6.03 There are a growing number of high-profile litigation cases against corporations for their climate-related actions. Climate change science has allowed the potential attribution of climate change-caused damages to those who emit the greenhouse gases. For sectors such as the oil and gas industry, litigation can occur at many points in the life of a project, from an initial board decision to initiate a project through to the approach to implementation and the implementation process itself. All steps or decisions taken are open to scrutiny, complaint and dispute.

Shareholder activists

6.04 Many cases have been brought by 'activist' shareholders, a trend where company shares are purchased by those who wish to see change in a business and use that shareholding to challenge the company.

Shareholder activism is a way that shareholders can influence a corporation's behaviour by exercising their rights as partial owners. Classes of shares allow for distinct voting privileges, in addition to dividend entitlements.

While minority shareholders don't run the day-to-day operations, there are several ways they can influence a company's board of directors and executive management actions. This can range from dialogue with managers to formal proposals, which are voted on by all shareholders at a company's annual meeting. Shareholder activists can employ a variety of offensive tactics to force changes:

- they might make use of the media to publicise their demands and prompt greater pressure from other shareholders;
- they can also threaten companies with lawsuits if they are not allowed to have their say.

Some of the issues addressed by shareholder activists are for social change and ask for divestment from politically sensitive parts of the world, for example, greater support of workers' rights (moving away from 'sweatshops') and/or more accountability for environmental degradation.

Responsive cases (where challenges to climate change are brought)

6.05 The courts have seen many disputes as a result of climate action. Groups such as Extinction Rebellion, Just Stop Oil and Insulate Britain have been the subject of significant media attention due to their unconventional protesting strategies. Multiple claims have been brought against climate protestors to reduce disruption caused by their protests and this has resulted in a series of 'persons unknown' cases.

CASES AGAINST GOVERNMENT: PUBLIC LAW CASES

R (on the application of Friends of the Earth Ltd) v Secretary of State for International Trade/UK Export Finance (UKEF) and Another[1]

6.06 In this case the Court of Appeal rejected Friends of the Earth's application for a judicial review of the UK Government's decision to provide $1.15 billion in export finance for a liquified natural gas project in Mozambique. This continued a trend for the UK courts in declining to find that emissions-intensive projects are unlawful (see the Supreme Court's rejection of Friends of the Earth's challenge to the Heathrow Airport expansion in 2020[2]).

In this case, the Court found that the Government was only required to reach a 'tenable' view that funding the project was aligned with the UK's obligations under the Paris Agreement, and that it was not irrational for the Government to conclude that the investment decision was compatible with the Paris Agreement. The Court also considered that the Government was not required to obtain a quantification of the indirect emissions (besides purchased energy) occurring in the project's value chain (Scope 3 emissions) before making its investment decision.

1 *R (on the application of Friends of the Earth Ltd) v Secretary of State for International Trade/ UK Export Finance (UKEF) and Another* [2023] EWCA Civ 14.
2 *R (on the application of Friends of the Earth Ltd and Others) v Heathrow Airport Ltd* [2020] UKSC 52.

Friends of the Earth appealed:

- the Government was required to adopt a view that its decision was aligned with the UK's obligations under the Paris Agreement and that there was no rational basis on which the respondents could conclude that the investment decision was compatible with the Paris Agreement (the Paris Agreement challenge); and
- the respondents failed in their duty of enquiry to obtain a quantification of the project's Scope 3 emissions (the Scope 3 challenge).

At the time the investment decision was made the Government considered that the project was aligned with the UK's obligations under the Paris Agreement because it would help Mozambique transition away from more damaging fossil fuels in line with its Nationally Determined Contribution and Paris Agreement commitments. The gas from the project would replace more polluting fuels and there would be some net reduction in emissions.

Although the Court was not prepared to give a definitive interpretation of the provisions of the Paris Agreement or their legal effect, it did find that the Government's view that its decision was in alignment with the UK's obligations under the Paris Agreement was tenable, and that was sufficient.

The Court did not accept Friends of the Earth's argument that the investment decision was irrational because the Government later acknowledged that the financing of the project did not align with the UK's obligations under the Paris Agreement.

The uncertainty and complexity of the project meant that the Government could not predict a precise outcome of the project's emissions. The Government had to make a decision considering all relevant and material factors, including the UK's obligations under the Paris Agreement.

R (on the application of Sarah Finch on behalf of the Weald Action Group) v Surrey CC[3]

6.07 This case involved whether the UK regulations require Environmental Impact Assessments (EIAs) for fossil fuel production to assess the Scope 3/end-use greenhouse gas (GHG) emissions arising from these developments.

Under Directive 2011/92 EU[4] of the European Parliament and of the Council and the Town and Country Planning (Environmental Impact Assessment) Regulations 2017 (SI 2017/571), was it unlawful for the Council not to require the EIA for a project of crude oil extraction for commercial purposes to include an assessment of the impacts of downstream GHG emissions resulting from the eventual use of the refined products of the extracted oil?

3 *R (on the application of Sarah Finch on behalf of the Weald Action Group) v Surrey CC* [2022] EWCA Civ 187, https://www.supremecourt.uk/cases/uksc-2022-0064.html

4 Directive 2011/92/EU of the European Parliament and of the Council of 13 December 2011 on the assessment of the effects of certain public and private projects on the environment (codification) [2011] OJ L26/1 (as amended), https://eur-lex.europa.eu/legal-content/en/ALL/?uri=CELEX:31992L0011

In December 2018, Horse Hill Developments Ltd sought planning permission from Surrey County Council to retain and expand an existing onshore oil well site (comprising two wells) and to drill for four new wells, enabling the production of hydrocarbons from six wells over a period of 25 years. Planning permission was granted. Sarah Finch applied for judicial review of the Council's decision, acting on behalf of the Weald Action Group. Her claim was unsuccessful before the High Court and the Court of Appeal. The appellant then appealed to the Supreme Court.

Finch related to the requirements for EIAs in the Town and Country Planning (Environmental Impact Assessment) Regulations 2017 (SI 2017/571). These Regulations, which originally implemented EU Directive 92/11/EU (as amended) require certain categories of projects to prepare EIAs and submit them in Environmental Statements alongside planning applications. The EIA process is designed to ensure that authorities cover environmental issues in discretionary assessments of the acceptability of relevant projects. An EIA does not impose restrictions on which projects can or cannot be approved.

Supreme Court decision

6.08 The Supreme Court reversed the decisions of the lower courts and allowed the appeal by a 3-2 majority finding that the Council's decision was unlawful as it relied on an insufficient EIA.

As a result of *Finch*, the government withdrew its defence of the proposed coal mine in Cumbria, but the developer, West Cumbria Mining, continued to defend the decision to approve planning permission for the mine. In *Friends of the Earth Ltd v Secretary of State for Levelling Up, Housing and Communities and Others* [2024] EWHC 2349 (Admin) the judge quashed the Secretary of State's decision to grant planning permission for a new coal mine in Cumbria. See **6.17**.

R (on the application of ClientEarth) v Financial Conduct Authority[5]

6.09 ClientEarth's judicial review of the Financial Conduct Authority's decision to approve the prospectus of Ithaca Energy plc was refused permission after a renewed application. The judge also held that the challenge was not an Aarhus Convention claim.

Aarhus convention claim: The Aarhus Convention grants the public rights regarding access to information, public participation and access to justice in governmental decision-making processes on matters concerning the local, national and transboundary environment. It focuses on interactions between the public and public authorities

ClientEarth said it was essential for the protection of investors that, when fossil fuel companies seek to list on the London Stock Exchange, the

5 *R (on the application of ClientEarth) v Financial Conduct Authority* [2023] EWHC 3301 (Admin).

prospectus should include full and transparent disclosure of climate-related risks. ClientEarth said this would allow investors to make informed decisions and encourage finance flows to shift to support net zero. ClientEarth said that otherwise there were risks that investors would be left with unviable stranded assets and investments losing value in the face of net zero.

The judge concluded that Ithaca's prospectus did address risks to Ithaca's business and securities arising out of climate change factors, associated regulatory measures and changes in consumer use. The result was that the FCA's judgement that the Regulation (EU) 2017/1129, art 16[6] requirements were met was not arguably unlawful. The judge also held that there was no obligation in Article 16 to disclose Ithaca's risk assessment.

R (on the application of (1) Friends of the Earth Ltd (2) ClientEarth (3) Good Law Project) v Secretary of State for Energy Security and Net Zero (SSESNZ)[7]

6.10 In May 2024, the High Court held that the government's Carbon Budget Delivery Plan (CBDP), which the Secretary of State for Business, Energy and Industrial Strategy (BEIS) had devised under Climate Change Act 2008 (CCA 2008), s 13, was unlawful. (The CBDP now falls under the purview of the Department for Energy Security and Net Zero (DESNZ).)

The CBDP was a revised version of the Net Zero Strategy, which had been quashed by a judge two years earlier and aimed to remedy its legal flaws (*R (on the application of (1) Friends of the Earth Ltd (2) ClientEarth and (3) Good Law Project and Joanna Wheatley) v Secretary of State for Business, Energy and Industrial Strategy*[8]). In the judgment, the Secretary of State had still not lawfully demonstrated the government could meet the targets of their sixth carbon budget.

Five grounds of challenge were given:

- ground 1 – the Secretary of State failed to consider mandatory material considerations when purporting to comply with CCA 2008, s 13;
- ground 2 – the Secretary of State proceeded on the basis of an assumption that all of the quantified proposals and policies would be delivered in full, and this assumption was not supported by the information as to risk to delivery with which the Secretary of State was provided;
- ground 3 – the Secretary of State's conclusion that the proposals and policies would enable the carbon budgets to be met was irrational;
- ground 4 – the Secretary of State applied the wrong legal test to CCA 2008, s 13(3) (sustainable development);

6 Regulation (EU) 2017/1129 of the European Parliament and of the Council of 14 June 2017 on the prospectus to be published when securities are offered to the public or admitted to trading on a regulated market, and repealing Directive 2003/71/EC [2017] OJ L168, https://eur-lex.europa.eu/legal-content/EN/TXT/?uri=CELEX%3A32017R1129&qid=1743081576265

7 *R (on the application of (1) Friends of the Earth Ltd (2) ClientEarth (3) Good Law Project) v Secretary of State for Energy Security and Net Zero (SSESNZ)* [2024] EWHC 995 (Admin).

8 *R (on the application of (1) Friends of the Earth Ltd (2) ClientEarth and (3) Good Law Project and Joanna Wheatley) v Secretary of State for Business, Energy and Industrial Strategy* [2022] EWHC 1841 (Admin).

- ground 5 – the Secretary of State failed to include in the CBDP information that he was required to include.

The judge disposed of grounds 1 to 3 together because were about the Secretary of State having inadequate evidence concerning the delivery risk to policies, and so he could not rationally conclude the policies would achieve their projected emissions reductions. Ground 4 was a self-contained issue of statutory interpretation concerning s 13(3). Ground 5 concerned the Secretary of State's duty to publish a consultation document under s 14.

The judge found that grounds 1–4 had all been made out.

Ground 4: Sustainable development

6.11 Ground 4 concerned the question of statutory interpretation, whether the Secretary of State misconstrued CCA 2008, s 13(3), which requires them to certify that his policy plan 'taken as a whole, must be such as to contribute to sustainable development'.

The Secretary of State confirmed that, in his view, the 'overall contribution' of the proposals was 'likely' to contribute to sustainable development. The claimants argued this was an error as the standard was certainty, denoted by 'must', not likelihood. The judge agreed, given the phrasing 'connotes a degree of certainty that a particular outcome will eventuate'. He concluded that 'no reasonable view, could it be said that "likely" means "must"'.

Ground 5: Section 14

6.12 Under ground 5, the claimants argued that the Secretary of State's duty under CCA 2008, s 14, to publish a report for public consultation setting out his proposals and policies, needed to include delivery risk analysis for each policy. The court rejected this as the sector level delivery risk analyses were sufficient.

R (on the application of Friends of the Earth Ltd and Others) v Heathrow Airport Ltd[9]

6.13 The Supreme Court unanimously allowed an appeal concerning whether the Secretary of State for Transport's failure to take account of the UK's climate change commitments under the Paris Agreement rendered the designation of the Airports National Policy Statement[10] (ANPS) favouring the development of a third runway at Heathrow Airport unlawful.

9 *R (on the application of Friends of the Earth Ltd and Others) v Heathrow Airport Ltd* [2020] UKSC 52.

10 Airports National Policy Statement, https://www.gov.uk/government/publications/airports-national-policy-statement

On 26 June 2018, the Secretary of State designated the ANPS under Planning Act 2008, s 5(1).[11] The ANPS supports the development of a third runway at Heathrow Airport to deliver additional hub airport capacity in the southeast of England.

The Court dismissed the respondents' argument that the Secretary of State breached this duty on the ground that he failed to have proper regard to the Paris Agreement when designating the ANPS. The evidence shows that the Secretary of State took the Paris Agreement into account and to the extent that its obligations were already covered by the measures in the CCA 2008 ensured that these were incorporated into the ANPS framework.

The Court dismissed the respondents' argument that the Secretary of State separately breached his s 10 duty by failing to have regard to, firstly, the effect of GHG emissions created by the North West Runway (NWR) scheme after 2050 and, secondly, the effect of non-CO_2 emissions.

Bristol Airport Action Network Co-ordinating Committee v Secretary of State for Levelling Up, Housing and Communities[12]

6.14 In this case, the High Court dismissed a challenge brought primarily on climate change grounds by various local environmental groups and residents to the grant of planning permission for the expansion of Bristol Airport.

- Planning authorities are entitled to consider in a generalised way whether emissions from a proposed development would materially affect the UK's ability to meet its carbon budgets and targets.
- Local decision makers may assume that separate pollution control regimes will operate effectively in respect of the emissions from a proposed development.
- Aviation carbon emissions are primarily to be considered at a national, rather than local, level in accordance with government policy.

The first interested party, Bristol Airport Ltd (BAL), applied to North Somerset Council for planning permission to increase the airport's capacity by about two million passengers per year. The application was refused by the Council, but BAL's appeal against that refusal was allowed, following an inquiry by a panel of planning inspectors.

The claimant alleged that, in relation to climate change issues, the panel erred in:

- its interpretation that the Council's development plan policies did not directly address aviation emissions;
- its interpretation of the national policy 'Making Best – Use of Existing Runways' (MBU);
- finding that it was required to 'assume' that the Secretary of State would comply with his duty under the CCA 2008, as per paragraph 188 of the National Planning Policy Framework;

11 Planning Act 2008, https://www.legislation.gov.uk/ukpga/2008/29/contents

12 *Bristol Airport Action Network Co-ordinating Committee v Secretary of State for Levelling Up, Housing and Communities* [2023] EWHC 171 (Admin).

- failing to consider the impact on the local carbon budget for the Council; and
- its conclusion that the impact of non-carbon dioxide (CO_2) emissions could be excluded from the EIA prepared by BAL and should not weigh in the balance against the proposed expansion.

The claimant submitted that the panel failed to give adequate reasons.

The judge dismissed each of the grounds raised by the claimant, including the reasons challenge. The key question underpinning the inquiry (to which there was no substantial dissent) was whether emissions from the proposal would be so significant that they would materially affect the ability of the UK to meet its carbon budgets and the target of net zero by 2050.

R (on the application of Packham) v Secretary of State for Energy Security and Net Zero and Secretary of State for Transport (challenge to the 'new approach to Net Zero')

6.15 Mr Packham wrote to the Prime Minister, the Energy Secretary and the Transport Secretary to challenge the policy U-turn, saying the Prime Minister does not have the legal right to change at will the timeline to help the UK meet net zero because the actioning of policies in the CBDP is governed by statute. If those policies were delivered in full, the country would make all the carbon savings needed to meet previous budgets and 97 per cent of the carbon savings needed to fulfil carbon budget six. Any changes have to be made according to a process in CCA 2008, s 6.

In the absence of a satisfactory response to his pre-action protocol letter, Mr Packham filed his legal claim at the High Court.[13]

In October 2024 Mr Packham agreed a settlement with the government over two legal challenges against a decision to remove or delay some environmental policies.

R (on the application of (1) Greenpeace Ltd (2) Uplift) v (1) Secretary of State for Energy Security and Net Zero (2) Oil and Gas Authority (North Sea oil and gas licensing)[14]

6.16 The UK High Court dismissed two judicial review claims brought by environmental non-governmental organisations (NGOs), Greenpeace and Uplift, on the government decisions relating to new oil and gas exploration and production in the North Sea.

13 *R (on the application of Packham) v Secretary of State for Energy Security and Net Zero and Secretary of State for Transport* (challenge to the 'new approach to Net Zero'), unreported as settled out of court.

14 *R (on the application of (1) Greenpeace Ltd (2) Uplift) v (1) Secretary of State for Energy Security and Net Zero (2) Oil and Gas Authority* [2023] EWHC 2608 (Admin) (North Sea oil and gas licensing).

The challenges were brought due to concerns over the compatibility of a further licensing round with the UK's climate objectives. The High Court dismissed the claims, holding that the issues in dispute were 'plainly a matter of judgment and not law'.

The claims primarily concerned decisions taken by the Secretary of State for Business, Energy and Industrial Strategy (now under the purview of the Secretary of State for Energy Security and Net Zero) and the Oil and Gas Authority (OGA).

Petroleum Act 1998, s 3[15] permits the OGA to grant licences to search and bore for petroleum. A licence holder must also obtain the OGA's consent before starting a project, and that cannot be given without the Secretary of State's agreement, usually following an EIA.

An issue for the court was whether the Secretary of State had acted unlawfully by not considering, as part of Offshore Energy Strategic Environmental Assessment 4 (OESEA4) or the Checkpoint, downstream emissions of GHGs from the end use by consumers of oil and gas as a fuel ('Scope 3' emissions).

On 7 September 2022, the Secretary of State adopted the Plan as assessed in OESEA4, approved the final design of the Checkpoint (omitting test 5) on the following day, and agreed that the Checkpoint should be applied ahead of the next licensing round. The Secretary of State also decided that a further licensing round would be compatible with the UK's climate objectives.

The challenges brought by Greenpeace and Uplift failed on all seven grounds raised.

(1) Friends of the Earth (2) South Lakeland Action on Climate Change v (1) Secretary of State for Levelling Up, Housing and Communities (2) West Cumbria Mining Ltd (3) Cumbria CC (Whitehaven coalmine) [16]

6.17 The High Court held that the decision to grant planning permission without first assessing the effect of downstream combustion emissions was an error of law.

But the High Court judgment also vindicated Friends of the Earth's (FoE's) decision to challenge the grant of planning permission on three further grounds:

- First, the decision was found to be unlawful because the Secretary of State's approach to the issue of substitution was muddled and irrational. West Cumbria Mining Ltd (WCM) claimed that the mine would not cause any net increase in global GHG emissions because every ton of coal mined

15 Petroleum Act 1998, s 3, https://www.legislation.gov.uk/ukpga/1998/17/section/3#:~:text=3%20 Licences%20to%20search%20and,to%20which%20this%20section%20applies.

16 *(1) Friends of the Earth (2) South Lakeland Action on Climate Change v (1) Secretary of State for Levelling Up, Housing and Communities (2) West Cumbria Mining Ltd (3) Cumbria* CC [2024] EWHC 2349 (Admin), https://www.judiciary.uk/judgments/friends-of-the-earth-and-another-v-secretary-of-state-for-levelling-up-housing-and-communities-and-others/

in Cumbria would replace or 'substitute' coal that would otherwise have been extracted elsewhere. FoE disputed that claim and produced evidence to show it was false. The High Court agreed with FoE that the Secretary of State failed to resolve this dispute adequately in his decision letter, giving inconsistent and irrational conclusions on the degree of 'substitution' that might take place.

- Second, the decision was found to be unlawful because the Secretary of State wrongly accepted WCM's claim that the development would represent 0 per cent of UK carbon budgets. That claim was based on WCM's legal commitment to purchase carbon credits on the international voluntary carbon market to 'offset' the mine's operational emissions. However, the High Court agreed with FoE that WCM's legal commitment did not have the claimed effect. Carbon credits purchased on the international voluntary carbon market do not count towards the UK carbon budgets so the legal commitment did not ensure (as the Secretary of State wrongly believed) that the mine would be 'net zero' for the purposes of UK carbon budgets.
- Third, the decision was found to be unlawful because the Secretary of State's conclusion regarding the international impacts of granting consent was legally flawed on two bases. First, the Secretary of State's conclusion that the Whitehaven mine would set a positive precedent to which other mineral extraction projects could aspire was premised on the legally flawed conclusion that it would be a net zero mine. Second, even if that conclusion were not flawed, the Secretary of State failed to grapple with FoE's alternative contention that it was fundamentally undesirable to encourage the use offsets (a finite resource) to justify the expansion of fossil fuel extraction internationally.

The judgment is an important plank in UK jurisprudence on decision-making in the context of fossil fuel extraction. It may also stand as persuasive authority in other jurisdictions, in particular in relation to issues of substitution and offsetting.

R (on the application of Coal Action Network) v (1) Welsh Ministers (2) Coal Authority (3) Energybuild Mining Ltd[17]

6.18 Whether the Coal Authority, when granting an application to deconditionalise a coal licence, had misunderstood its powers, and whether the Welsh Ministers had any powers, under devolution legislation, in respect of that application.

On 19 May 2023, the judge handed down judgment in *R (on the application of Coal Action Network) v (1) Welsh Ministers (2) Coal Authority (3) Energybuild Mining Ltd* dismissing the Coal Action Network's challenge to the authorisation of coal-mining operations at Aberpergwm, an underground drift mine, in the Vale of Neath.

17 *R (on the application of Coal Action Network) v (1) Welsh Ministers (2) Coal Authority (3) Energybuild Mining Ltd* [2024] EWCA Civ 168, https://www.judiciary.uk/wp-content/uploads/2024/02/Coal-Action-Network-v-Welsh-Ministers.pdf

The claimant unsuccessfully challenged the decision of the Welsh Ministers, dated 10 January 2022, that they did not have the power under Coal Industry Act 1994, s 26A to approve or refuse the authorisation of coal-mining operations granted in a licence that was issued in 1996 and subsequently varied by the Coal Authority, most recently in 2013.

The claim gave rise to two points of statutory interpretation under the 1994 Act as to whether:

- the Welsh Ministers erred in law in deciding that s 26A was inapplicable to applications relating to a licence granted in 1996 and varied in 2013; and
- whether the Coal Authority unlawfully fettered its discretion and/or failed to consider material considerations in approving the operator's application.

The judge dismissed the challenge to the Welsh Ministers' decision. In particular it held that the claimant's interpretation of s 26A 'gives the provision a degree of retrospective force'. The judge also agreed with the Welsh Ministers' submission that, if a licence is granted subject to conditions precedent, 'ordinarily, the recipient of the licence is entitled to expect that if they satisfy those conditions, the authorisation contained in the licence will take effect'.

On the second ground, the judge held that, as the Coal Authority had issued an authorisation subject to the satisfaction of conditions, it was confined to determining whether, in its reasonable opinion, the conditions precedent had been fulfilled. Ultimately, it would be inconsistent with the provisions of the 1994 Act for the Coal Authority 'to treat an application for a determination that conditions imposed in a licence have been satisfied as a fresh opportunity to determine whether, or on what conditions, coal-mining operations should be authorised'.

Trump International Golf Club Scotland Ltd and The Trump Organization LLC v Scottish Ministers[18]

6.19 Trump International Golf Club Scotland Ltd (TIGC) developed a golf resort at Menie Estate and Menie Links, Balmedie, Aberdeenshire. In 2011, Aberdeen Offshore Wind Farm Ltd applied for consent under Electricity Act 1989 (the 1989 Act), s 36 to construct and operate the European Offshore Wind Deployment Centre in Aberdeen Bay. The application concerned the construction of up to 11 wind turbines, which might be of different sizes, with a maximum power generation of 100 MW. The proposed windfarm would be located about 3.5 km from the golf resort and would be seen by people at the resort. TIGC opposed the application. In March 2013, the Scottish Ministers granted consent (the consent) for the development and operation of the windfarm subject to conditions.

TIGC challenged the consent on various grounds in the Scottish courts without success.

TIGC appealed to the Supreme Court on two remaining grounds, arguing that the consent should be quashed:

18 *Trump International Golf Club Scotland Ltd and The Trump Organization LLC v Scottish Ministers* [2015] UKSC 74.

- because the Scottish Ministers had no power under the 1989 Act to grant consent to the windfarm application as only the holder of a licence to generate, transmit, or supply electricity granted under s 6, or a person exempted under s 5 from holding such a licence may apply under s 36 (the Section 36 Challenge); and
- because condition 14 of the consent, which requires the submission and approval of a design statement, is void for uncertainty (the Condition 14 Challenge).

The Supreme Court unanimously dismissed the appeal by TIGC.

CASES AGAINST CORPORATIONS: ACTIVIST COMPANY LAW CLAIMS

ClientEarth v Shell plc and Others[19]

6.20 In *ClientEarth v Shell Plc* [2023] EWHC 1137 (Ch) and *Client Earth v Shell Plc* [2023] EWHC 1897 (Ch), the High Court dismissed ClientEarth's attempt to launch a derivative action against the directors of Shell plc in respect of their alleged failures to properly address the risks of climate change. These decisions indicate that claims of this nature, at least insofar as they are brought by minority shareholders who are not typical investors (eg NGOs and other non-profits such as the claimant in these cases), will face significant challenges.

Notably, in these cases, the court held that:

1. Courts will place significant weight on the fact that directors (especially those of large multinationals) have to balance a myriad of competing considerations when seeking to promote the success of the company for the benefit of the members as a whole. Courts are reluctant to interfere with the proper balancing of these factors, making it harder for claimants to establish that the directors have breached their statutory duties.
2. Claimants bear the burden of showing that the primary purpose of the derivative claim is not for an ulterior motive. It may be challenging for claimants such as NGOs or activist organisations to prove that they are bringing the claim in good faith. This issue is likely to be even more acute where the claimant only holds a *de minimis* shareholding in the company.

Following the second High Court judgment, the court ordered ClientEarth to pay the costs of the proceedings on the standard basis, disapplying the derogation generally applicable to the prima facie stage of derivative actions.

19 *ClientEarth v Shell plc and Others* [2023] EWHC 2182 (Ch).

(1) McGaughey (2) Davies v Universities Superannuation Scheme Ltd and Others[20]

6.21 This is a UK company law, climate litigation, and pension law case, that sought permission for a derivative claim to enforce duties of the directors of the UK university pension fund, USS Ltd. This case was the first to sue directors of a major UK corporation to divest fossil fuels and the first case of beneficiaries of a pension corporation bringing a derivative claim for breaches of directors' statutory duties.

The High Court[21] accepted that the claimants had standing to bring a derivative claim, but refused permission based on *Foss v Harbottle*.[22] The claimants secured permission to appeal to the Court of Appeal with a hearing in June 2023, but were unsuccessful, as the judge held that the appropriate procedure was a 'beneficiary derivative claim' where directors' duties may be held on trust. The fossil fuel risk claim was not addressed in substance but 'well suited' for being brought as an action for breach of trust.

The judge in the High Court held that, while beneficiaries of a pension fund corporation could bring derivative claims, the Court of Appeal decision in *Harris v Microfusion*[23] and the rule in *Foss v Harbottle* meant that the claimants had to show they suffered loss reflected by a loss to the company, and that the directors 'benefited themselves from the breach of duty'. It followed that the claimants' claims for breach of duty to act for proper purposes could not be brought, including the claims alleging misconduct in the valuation and discrimination, and claims alleging a significant risk of financial detriment in the failure to divest fossil fuels or have a plan. The judge added that the claimants had failed to state sufficiently what the losses from fossil fuels were.

Court of Appeal

6.22 The claimants applied for permission to appeal to the Court of Appeal and received permission for a hearing in 2023. The claimants alleged that the High Court applied the wrong legal tests, that all duties under the Companies Act 2006 must be capable of enforcement, and that key parts of their evidence on the imprudent valuation assumptions, and the risk of significant financial detriment from fossil fuels were not considered.

The Court of Appeal held that the claimants ought to have pursued a 'beneficiary derivative claim' rather than a common law company derivative claim. The judge held it was 'not unarguable' that certain directors' duties that the claimants alleged were breached were capable of being held on trust

20 *(1) McGaughey (2) Davies v Universities Superannuation Scheme Ltd and Others* [2023] EWCA Civ 873, https://www.bailii.org/ew/cases/EWCA/Civ/2023/873.html

21 *(1) McGaughey and (2) Davies v Universities Superannuation Scheme Ltd and Directors Others* [2022] EWHC 1233 (Ch).

22 *Foss v Harbottle* (1843) 67 ER 189, https://lawprof.co/company/derivative-action-cases/foss-v-harbottle-1843-67-e-r-189/

23 *Harris v Microfusion and Others* [2016] EWCA Civ 1212, https://www.bailii.org/cgi-bin/format.cgi?doc=/ew/cases/EWCA/Civ/2016/1212.html&query=(Harris)+AND+(v)+AND+(Microfusion)

by the trust fund (USS) for the benefit of the beneficiaries and were therefore capable of enforcement by the claimants. However, this was separate from the company (USS Ltd) that was the corporate trustee where the directors sat, and the rules of procedure differed, in particular with more requirements to gather the views of other beneficiaries. The Court of Appeal did not analyse the substantive claims, including the risks associated with fossil fuel investment, but held that this was particularly apt for a beneficiary claim.

The case was the first in the UK to bring actions against directors personally for their failure to divest fossil fuels in light of climate risk. Solicitors at Ince stated that, despite the High Court's rejection, the case showed 'there is an increasing momentum by activists, shareholders and others to hold them accountable for climate change'.

On appeal to the Court of Appeal the case was described as having 'immense significance' for the future of fossil fuels.

'RESPONSIVE' CASES

National Highways Ltd v Person Unknown and Others[24]

6.23 The Court of Appeal allowed the appeal in this case, a judgment which will assist claimants seeking to conclude claims involving precautionary injunctions, particularly in relation to protestors.

National Highways had obtained a series of interim precautionary injunctions restraining apprehended trespass or nuisance linked to protest activity in response to a series of protests carried out by 'Insulate Britain' activists. The protests received wide media coverage, and involved protestors sitting on, and gluing themselves to, various roads on the strategic road network, with the M25 and southeast being particularly targeted.

National Highways made an application for summary judgment. The application sought final injunctions in materially the same form as the interim injunctions already granted.

After a two-day hearing in May 2022, the High Court judge found that while National Highways had made out its case for a precautionary injunction, the application for summary judgment could not succeed in relation to the majority of the named and unnamed defendants because it had failed to show that, on the balance of probabilities, those defendants had already committed the relevant torts which were threatened.

The Court of Appeal, however, has confirmed that there is no need for a claimant seeking a final precautionary injunction to demonstrate that defendants have actually committed those torts, confirming that the essence of a precautionary prohibitory injunction (whether interim or final) is that the tort is threatened and the claimant's course of action is not complete.

24 *National Highways Ltd v Person Unknown and Others* [2023] EWCA Civ 182.

The Court of Appeal also confirmed that, where a defendant has not served a defence, any evidence, or otherwise engaged with the proceedings, that is of 'considerable relevance' to the test of whether the defendant had a real prospect of successfully defending the claim. As a result, the Court of Appeal allowed the appeal and granted the final injunction.

Transport for London v Persons Unknown and Others[25]

6.24 Transport for London (TfL) brought a claim under the Highways Act 1980, to protect the rights of the public to the 'use and enjoyment' of the highways. Transport for London was successful, and the judge found the defendants' acts had constituted trespass and both private and public nuisance. The environmental activist group Insulate Britain (IB) carried out London protests designed to cause serious disruption. These protest tactics included activists deliberately blocking highways by sitting down in the road, and many gluing themselves to the road's surface and/or locking themselves to each other to make their removal more time-consuming. IB repeatedly stated that these protests will continue until its demands are met.

TfL sought a final injunction against 129 of 138 named defendants and certain defined persons unknown. The injunction sought an order preventing protesters from the blocking of specified roads and areas in a significant part of the TfL strategic road network. The locations in question include bridges or 'junctions of great importance' and surrounding access roads, as well as certain longer protected stretches of road such as the A4 and the North Circular. The case came before Morris J on 29–30 March and on 3 May he gave judgment.

TfL made its injunction claim pursuant to its duty under Highways Act 1980, s 130 (protection of public rights) 'to assert and protect the rights of the public to the use and enjoyment of any highway for which [it is] the highway authority' and on the basis that the conduct of the defendants in participating in the IB protests constituted:

- trespass;
- private nuisance; and/or
- public nuisance.

For the persons unknown in the light of the guidelines specified in *Canada Goose UK Retail Ltd v Persons Unknown*,[26] the court was also 'satisfied that it is just and convenient to grant the final injunction against the persons unknown'.

The judge considered (among other things) that the aims of preventing obstruction of the public on the relevant highways and preventing violence and danger which occur when this is jeopardised are sufficiently important to justify interference with the defendants' rights. There was also no less restrictive or alternative means to achieve the prevention of obstructive and disruptive protests other than a final injunction. The court gave judgment for

25 *Transport for London v Persons Unknown and Others* [2023] EWHC 1038 (KB), https://content.tfl.gov.uk/1-sealed-judgment-order-in-tfl-insulate-britain-case-aa.pdf
26 *Canada Goose UK Retail Ltd v Persons Unknown and Another* [2020] EWCA Civ 303.

the claimant for a final injunction in the terms of the draft order before the court. To protect the public and the claimant's rights, the final injunction will last for five years, with the court reviewing yearly 'for supervisory purposes'.

Shell UK Ltd and Others v Persons Unknown[27]

6.25 In this case, Shell's UK entity brought this case against 'Persons Unknown' to restrict protesting at their petrol stations. They were successful and subsequently an Order was produced, restricting anyone 'in connection with protest campaigns' from 'disrupting the sale or supply of fuel' at Shell petrol stations in England and Wales.

The claimants, Shell UK Ltd and two others, sought interim injunctions against Persons Unknown to restrain unlawful protests by environmental activists at petrol stations known as the Haven and the Tower. The claimants objected to the third claimant, Shell UK Oil Products Ltd, being heard at the hearing due to late documentation. Despite submissions inviting the court to uphold the judge's reasoning, no transcript of his judgment was obtained by the claimants.

A number of issues were considered:

- validity of interim injunctions against Persons Unknown for unlawful protests;
- rights of defendants under ECHR, Articles 10 and 11 in light of the injunctions;
- application of the tort of conspiracy to injure by unlawful means;
- consideration of balancing rights of assembly and expression against business interests
- compliance with Human Rights Act 1998, s 12(3) regarding communication restraints;
- propriety of alternative service methods for the injunctions; and
- granting a third-party disclosure order against the Commissioner.

The court granted interim injunctions against Persons Unknown to restrain unlawful protests at Shell Petrol Stations, finding them necessary and proportionate to protect the claimants' rights. The court also considered the application of the tort of conspiracy to injure and compliance with communication restraints under Article 10. Additionally, alternative service methods were approved, and a third-party disclosure order against the Commissioner was considered.

27 *Shell UK Ltd and Others v Persons Unknown* [2023] EWHC 1229 (KB), https://www.landmarkchambers.co.uk/wp-content/uploads/2023/05/QA-2022-001241-001259-and-001420-Shell-UK-v-Persons-Unknown_Final-judgment-of-Hill-J26.pdf

Chapter 7

Approaches to Climate Change: EU

INTRODUCTION

7.01 The European Union (EU) has adopted a comprehensive approach to climate change law, a combination of regulatory frameworks, policy initiatives, and legislative acts designed to mitigate climate change impacts, promote sustainability, and transition towards a low-carbon economy.

EUROPEAN CLIMATE LAW

7.02 Enacted in 2021,[1] this law sets legally binding targets for the EU to become climate-neutral by 2050. It establishes a framework for achieving intermediate targets and ensures that national policies contribute to the overall goals. This writes into law the goal set out in the European Green Deal. It also sets the intermediate target of reducing net greenhouse gas (GHG) emissions by at least 55 per cent by 2030, compared to 1990 levels.

Objectives

7.03 The European Climate Law:

- sets the long-term direction for meeting the 2050 climate neutrality objective through all policies, in a socially fair and cost-efficient manner;
- sets a more ambitious EU 2030 target, to set Europe on a responsible path to becoming climate-neutral by 2050;
- creates a system for monitoring progress and taking further action if needed;
- provides predictability for investors and other economic actors; and
- ensures that the transition to climate neutrality is irreversible.

Key elements

7.04 The European Climate Law sets a legally binding target of net-zero GHG emissions by 2050. The EU institutions and the Member States are bound to take the necessary measures at EU and national level to meet the target, considering the importance of promoting fairness and solidarity among

1 Regulation (EU) 2021/1119 of the European Parliament and of the Council of 30 June 2021 establishing the framework for achieving climate neutrality and amending Regulations (EC) No 401/2009 and (EU) 2018/1999 ('European Climate Law') [2024 OJ L243/1, https://eur-lex.europa.eu/legal-content/EN/TXT/?uri=CELEX:32021R1119

Member States. The Climate Law includes measures to keep track of progress and adjust the EU's actions, based on existing systems such as the governance process for Member States' national energy and climate plans (NECPs), regular reports by the European Environment Agency, and the latest scientific evidence on climate change and its impacts.

Progress will be reviewed every five years, in line with the global stocktake exercise under the Paris Agreement.

The European Climate Law also addresses the necessary steps to get to the 2050 target:

- Based on an impact assessment, the EU has set a new target for 2030 of reducing net GHG emissions by at least 55 per cent compared to levels in 1990. The new EU 2030 target is included in the law.
- In July 2021, the Commission adopted a series of proposals to revise all relevant policy instruments to deliver the additional emissions reductions for 2030.
- The law also includes a process for setting a 2040 climate target.

The European Climate Law includes:

- a legal objective for the EU to reach climate neutrality by 2050;
- a 2030 climate target of at least 55 per cent reduction of net emissions of GHGs as compared to 1990, with clarity on the contribution of emission reductions and removals;
- recognition of the need to enhance the EU's carbon sink through a more ambitious land use, land use change and forestry (LULUCF) regulation, for which the Commission made a proposal in July 2021 and which entered into force in May 2023;
- a process for setting a 2040 climate target, considering an indicative GHG budget for 2030–50 to be published by the Commission;
- a commitment to negative emissions after 2050;
- the establishment of a European Scientific Advisory Board on Climate Change, that will provide independent scientific advice;
- stronger provisions on adaptation to climate change;
- strong coherence across EU policies with the climate neutrality objective; and
- a commitment to engage with sectors to prepare sector-specific roadmaps charting the path to climate neutrality in different areas of the economy.

The European Climate Law was published in the *Official Journal* on 9 July 2021 and entered into force on 29 July 2021.

Implementation

7.05 Each year the Commission publishes the EU Climate Action Progress report, which shows the progress towards the EU's emission reduction targets. The report covers actual (historic) emissions and projected future emissions for the EU as a whole and for every EU Member State. It includes information on different climate policy areas, EU legislative progress, climate finance and adaptation.

The latest information published is:

- *EU Climate Action Progress Report 2024. Leading the way: from plans to implementation for a green and competitive Europe*[2]
- *EU Climate Action Progress Report 2024*[3]
- Technical information accompanying the *Climate Action Progress Report 2024*[4]

Commission recommendations: progress on climate neutrality and adaptation

7.06 These are recommendations under the European Climate Law for Member States that did not submit a draft updated NECP in time for the Commission recommendations in December 2023.

EUROPEAN GREEN DEAL

7.07 The European Green Deal,[5] introduced in December 2019, outlines the EU's ambition to reduce GHG emissions by at least 55 per cent by 2030 compared to 1990 levels. This deal serves as a roadmap for various sectors, including energy, transportation, agriculture, and biodiversity.

In order to achieve this there are a number of initiatives.

REPowerEU

7.08 In response to the hardships and the disruption of the global energy market caused by Russia's invasion of Ukraine, the European Commission is implementing its REPowerEU Plan[6] to phase out Russian fossil fuel imports.

Launched in May 2022, REPowerEU is helping the EU to

- save energy;

2 *EU Climate Action Progress Report 2024. Leading the way: from plans to implementation for a green and competitive Europe*, https://climate.ec.europa.eu/document/download/7bd19c68-b179-4f3f-af75-4e309ec0646f_en?filename=CAPR-report2024-web.pdf

3 Report from the Commission to the European Parliament and the Council EU Climate Action Progress Report 2024 COM/2024/498 final, https://eur-lex.europa.eu/legal-content/EN/TXT/?uri=CELEX:52024DC0498

4 Commission Staff Working Document Technical information Accompanying the document Report from the Commission to the European Parliament and the Council EU Climate Action Progress Report 2024 SWD/2024/249 final, https://eur-lex.europa.eu/legal-content/EN/TXT/?uri=CELEX:52024SC0249

5 Communication from the Commission to the European Parliament, the European Council, the Council, the European Economic and Social Committee and the Committee of the Regions The European Green Deal COM/2019/640 final, https://eur-lex.europa.eu/legal-content/EN/TXT/?uri=CELEX%3A52019DC0640&qid=1743696391792

6 Communication from the Commission to the European Parliament, the European Council, the Council, the European Economic and Social Committee and the Committee of the Regions REPowerEU Plan COM/2022/230 final, https://eur-lex.europa.eu/legal-content/EN/TXT/?uri=CELEX%3A52022DC0230&qid=1743696440491

- diversify energy supplies; and
- produce clean energy.

The Green Deal Industrial Plan

7.09 The Green Deal Industrial Plan[7] enhances the competitiveness of Europe's net-zero industry and is accelerating the transition to climate neutrality. It does this by creating a more supportive environment for scaling up the EU's manufacturing capacity for the net-zero technologies and products required to meet Europe's ambitious climate targets.

There are four pillars of the plan:

- a predictable and simplified regulatory environment;
- faster access to funding;
- enhancing skills; and
- open trade for resilient supplies.

There are a number of initiatives within this.

Net-Zero Industry Act[8]

7.10 This aims to scale up the manufacturing of clean technologies in the EU which means increasing the EU's manufacturing capacity of technologies that support the clean energy transition and release extremely low, zero or negative GHG emissions when they operate.

Critical Raw Materials Act[9]

7.11 To meet its climate and digital objectives, sourcing, processing and recycling critical raw materials in Europe and securing supply chains are the challenges ahead:

- lithium, cobalt and nickel are used to produce batteries;
- gallium is used in solar panels;

7 Communication from the Commission to the European Parliament, the European Council, the Council, the European Economic and Social Committee and the Committee of the Regions A Green Deal Industrial Plan for the Net-Zero Age COM/2023/62 final, https://eur-lex.europa.eu/legal-content/EN/TXT/?uri=CELEX%3A52023DC0062

8 Proposal for a Regulation of the European Parliament and of the Council on establishing a framework of measures for strengthening Europe's net-zero technology products manufacturing ecosystem (Net Zero Industry Act) COM/2023/161 final; European Commission, 'Net-Zero Industry Act', https://eur-lex.europa.eu/legal-content/EN/TXT/?uri=CELEX%3A52023PC0161&qid=1743154282992

9 Regulation (EU) 2024/1252 of the European Parliament and of the Council of 11 April 2024 establishing a framework for ensuring a secure and sustainable supply of critical raw materials and amending Regulations (EU) No 168/2013, (EU) 2018/858, (EU) 2018/1724 and (EU) 2019/1020 [2019] OJ L2024/1252; European Commission, 'European Critical Raw Materials Act', https://eur-lex.europa.eu/legal-content/EN/TXT/?uri=CELEX%3A32024R1252&qid=1743154356057

- raw boron is used in wind technologies; and
- titanium and tungsten are used in the space and defence sectors.

The EU aims to ensure secure and sustainable supply of critical raw materials for Europe's industry and significantly lower the EU's dependency on imports from single-country suppliers.

Reform of the electricity market design[10]

7.12 Through common energy market rules and cross-border infrastructure, energy can be produced in one EU country and delivered to consumers in another. Boosting competition, improving the long-term markets and allowing consumers to choose energy suppliers keeps prices in check.

EU Action to address the energy crisis

7.13 To protect EU businesses and households from episodes of excessively high gas prices in the EU, the Commission has proposed a Market Correction Mechanism,[11] a temporary and targeted instrument to automatically intervene on the gas markets in case of extreme gas price hikes. The new mechanism aims to reduce the volatility on European gas markets while safeguarding the security of gas supply.

EMISSION TRADING SYSTEM (ETS)

7.14 The EU ETS[12] is a cornerstone of the EU's climate policy, allowing companies to buy and sell emission allowances for GHGs. This cap-and-trade system incentivises businesses to reduce emissions, as they can profit from selling surplus allowances.

The system:

- requires polluters to pay for their GHG emissions;

10 Directive (EU) 2024/1711 of the European Parliament and of the Council of 13 June 2024 amending Directives (EU) 2018/2001 and (EU) 2019/944 as regards improving the Union's electricity market design [2024] OJ L2024/1711, https://eur-lex.europa.eu/legal-content/EN/TXT/?uri=CELEX%3A32024L1711&qid=1743154468296; Regulation (EU) 2024/1747 of the European Parliament and of the Council of 13 June 2024 amending Regulations (EU) 2019/942 and (EU) 2019/943 as regards improving the Union's electricity market design [2024] OJ L2024/1747, https://eur-lex.europa.eu/legal-content/EN/TXT/?uri=CELEX%3A32024R1747&qid=1743154524716; European Commission, 'Electricity market design' https://energy.ec.europa.eu/topics/markets-and-consumers/electricity-market-design_en

11 Proposal for a Council Regulation Establishing a market correction mechanism to protect citizens and the economy against excessively high prices COM/2022/668 final, https://eur-lex.europa.eu/legal-content/EN/TXT/?uri=CELEX%3A52022PC0668&qid=1669911853248

12 European Commission, 'Development of the EU ETS (2005-2020)', https://climate.ec.europa.eu/eu-action/eu-emissions-trading-system-eu-ets/development-eu-ets-2005-2020_en

- launched in 2005, as the world's first carbon market and is amongst the largest ones globally;
- helps bring overall EU emissions down while generating revenues to finance the green transition;
- covers emissions from the electricity and heat generation, industrial manufacturing and aviation sectors – which account for roughly 40 per cent of total GHG emissions in the EU;
- started covering emissions from maritime transport in 2024; and
- operates in all EU countries plus Iceland, Liechtenstein and Norway, and is linked to the Swiss ETS (since 2020).

The EU ETS is based on a 'cap and trade' principle. The cap is the limit set on the total amount of GHG that can be emitted by installations and operators covered under the scope of the system. This cap is reduced annually in line with the EU's climate target, ensuring that overall EU emissions decrease over time. The EU ETS cap is expressed in emission allowances with one allowance giving the right to emit one ton of CO_2e (ie carbon dioxide equivalent). Allowances are sold in auctions and they can be traded. As the cap decreases, so does the supply of allowances to the EU carbon market.

Under the system, companies must monitor and report their emissions on an annual basis and surrender enough allowances to fully account for their annual emissions. If these requirements are not met then fines can be imposed. Whilst the allowances are mainly sold in auctions, companies receive some allowances for free.

Companies may also trade allowances amongst themselves. If an installation or operator reduces emissions, the company can either sell the spare allowances and/or keep them to use in the future. All these operations are recorded in the Union Registry.

Aviation – long haul flights excluded from monitoring scheme

7.15 Under the EU ETS, all airlines operating in Europe, European and non-European alike, are required to monitor, report and verify their emissions, and to surrender allowances against those emissions. They receive tradeable allowances covering a certain level of emissions from their flights each year.

Under the EU ETS 'cap and trade' system, aviation contributed to reducing the carbon footprint of other sectors by around 160 million tons during the third trading period (2013–20), according to the 2022 *European Aviation Environmental Report*. The compliance rate in the aviation sector is high, as over 99.5 per cent of emissions are usually covered by surrender of allowances.

However the EU Commission had pressure from legacy airlines to exclude long-haul flights from the scope of an aviation emission monitoring scheme, which means that 67 per cent of aviation's contrail[13] climate impact is ignored.[14]

13 Contrail – or condensation train, is a line-shaped cloud that forms when an aircraft's exhaust mixes with cold air.

14 Teoh et al, 'Global aviation contrail climate effects from 2019 to 2021', EGU sphere, https://egusphere.copernicus.org/preprints/2023/egusphere-2023-1859/

FIT FOR 55 PACKAGE

7.16 Launched in July 2021, this legislative package contains proposals to align EU legislation with its 2030 climate target. It includes revisions to existing policies, such as the ETS, the Renewable Energy Directive and the Energy Efficiency Directive.

It includes:

- EU Emissions Trading System (ETS) reform;
- a new EU Emissions Trading System for building and road transport fuels;
- the Social Climate Fund;
- the Effort Sharing Regulation;[15]
- a Regulation on land use, land use change, forestry and agriculture (LULUCF);[16]
- CO_2 emissions standards for cars and vans;[17]
- the Carbon Border Adjustment Mechanism (CBAM);
- the Renewable Energy Directive;[18]
- the Energy Efficiency Directive;[19]
- the Alternative Fuels Infrastructure Regulation (AFIR);[20]
- the ReFuel EU Aviation Regulation;[21]

15 Regulation (EU) 2023/857 amending Regulation (EU) 2018/842 on binding annual greenhouse gas emission reductions by Member States from 2021 to 2030 contributing to climate action to meet commitments under the Paris Agreement, and Regulation (EU) 2018/1999 [2023] OJ L2023/111, https://www.europeansources.info/record/proposal-for-a-regulation-amending-regulation-eu-2018-842-on-binding-annual-greenhouse-gas-emission-reductions-by-member-states-from-2021-to-2030-contributing-to-climate-action-to-meet-commitments-u/

16 Consolidated text: Regulation (EU) 2018/841 of the European Parliament and of the Council of 30 May 2018 on the inclusion of greenhouse gas emissions and removals from land use, land use change and forestry in the 2030 climate and energy framework, and amending Regulation (EU) No 525/2013 and Decision No 529/2013/EU [2018] OJ L2018/156, https://eur-lex.europa.eu/legal-content/EN/TXT/?uri=CELEX:02018R0841-20230511

17 Consolidated text: Regulation (EU) 2019/631 of the European Parliament and of the Council of 17 April 2019 setting CO2 emission performance standards for new passenger cars and for new light commercial vehicles, and repealing Regulations (EC) No 443/2009 and (EU) No 510/2011 (recast) [2019] OJ L2019/111, https://eur-lex.europa.eu/legal-content/EN/TXT/?uri=CELEX%3A02019R0631-20231203

18 Directive (EU) 2023/2413 of the European Parliament and of the Council of 18 October 2023 amending Directive (EU) 2018/2001, Regulation (EU) 2018/1999 and Directive 98/70/EC as regards the promotion of energy from renewable sources, and repealing Council Directive (EU) 2015/652 [2023] OJ L2023/2413, https://eur-lex.europa.eu/legal-content/EN/TXT/?uri=CELEX%3A32023L2413&qid=1699364355105

19 Directive (EU) 2023/1791 of the European Parliament and of the Council of 13 September 2023 on energy efficiency and amending Regulation (EU) 2023/955 (recast) [2023] OJ L2023/231, https://eur-lex.europa.eu/legal-content/EN/TXT/?uri=OJ%3AJOL_2023_231_R_0001&qid=1695186598766

20 Regulation (EU) 2023/1804 of the European Parliament and of the Council of 13 September 2023 on the deployment of alternative fuels infrastructure, and repealing Directive 2014/94/EU [2023] OJ L2023/234, https://eur-lex.europa.eu/legal-content/EN/TXT/?uri=CELEX%3A32023R1804

21 Regulation (EU) 2023/2405 of the European Parliament and of the Council of 18 October 2023 on ensuring a level playing field for sustainable air transport (ReFuelEU Aviation) [2023] OJ L2023/2405,https://eur-lex.europa.eu/legal-content/EN/TXT/?uri=CELEX%3A32023R2405

- the FuelEU Maritime Regulation;[22]
- the Energy Performance of Buildings Directive;[23]
- updated EU rules to decarbonise gas markets and promote hydrogen; and
- EU Methane Regulation for the energy sector.

ADAPTATION STRATEGY[24]

7.17 The EU has also developed a strategy focusing on climate adaptation, recognising the need to enhance resilience to the impacts of climate change. This includes guidance for Member States on developing national adaptation strategies. This strategy sets out how the EU can adapt to the unavoidable impacts of climate change and become climate resilient by 2050.

The strategy has four principle objectives:

- Smarter adaptation – adaptation actions must be informed by data and risk assessment tools that are available to all, from families building homes, to businesses in coastal regions and farmers planning their crops. The strategy proposes actions that push the frontiers of knowledge on adaptation so that better data on climate-related risks and losses can be gathered and enhance Climate-ADAPT[25] as the European platform for adaptation knowledge.
- Swifter adaptation – the strategy focuses on developing and rolling out adaptation solutions to help reduce climate-related risk, increase climate protection and safeguard the availability of fresh water.
- More systematic adaptation – climate change will have impacts at all levels of society and across all sectors of the economy, so adaptation actions must also be systemic. It will support the further development and implementation of adaptation strategies and plans at all levels of governance with three cross-cutting priorities:
  — integrating adaptation into a micro-fiscal policy;
  — nature-based solutions for adaptation; and
  — local adaptation action.
- Stepping up international action for climate resilience – the EU will increase support for international climate resilience and preparedness through the provision of resources, by prioritising action and increasing effectiveness, through the scaling up of international finance and through stronger global engagement and exchanges on adaptation.

22 Regulation (EU) 2023/1805 of the European Parliament and of the Council of 13 September 2023 on the use of renewable and low-carbon fuels in maritime transport, and amending Directive 2009/16/EC [2023] OJ L2023/234, https://eur-lex.europa.eu/legal-content/EN/TXT/?uri=CELEX%3A32023R1805

23 Directive (EU) 2024/1275 of the European Parliament and of the Council of 24 April 2024 on the energy performance of buildings (recast) [2024] OJ L2024/1275, https://eur-lex.europa.eu/legal-content/EN/TXT/?uri=OJ:L_202401275&pk_keyword=Energy&pk_content=Directive

24 Communication from the Commission to the European Parliament, the Council, the European Economic and Social Committee and the Committee of the Regions Forging a climate-resilient Europe – the new EU Strategy on Adaptation to Climate Change COM/2021/82 final, https://eur-lex.europa.eu/legal-content/EN/TXT/?uri=COM:2021:82:FIN

25 Climate-ADAPT, https://climate-adapt.eea.europa.eu/en

SECTORAL REGULATIONS

7.18 The EU has implemented specific regulations targeting key sectors such as energy (including renewable energy directives), transport, agriculture and waste management to reduce emissions and promote sustainable practices.

EU Emission Trading System (ETS)

7.19 See 7.14.

Effort Sharing Regulation (ESR)

7.20 The Effort Sharing Regulation[26] establishes a national target for each EU Member State for the reduction of GHG emissions by 2030 in the following sectors:

- domestic transport (excluding aviation);
- buildings, agriculture; and
- small industry and waste.

The emissions covered by the Effort Sharing Regulation account for almost 60 per cent of total domestic EU emissions. It was initially adopted in 2018 and was amended in 2023. With new national targets Member States will collectively contribute to an emission reduction at EU level, in the Effort Sharing sectors, of 40 per cent compared to 2005 levels. The revision was adopted as part of a package of proposals aimed at reducing the EU's emissions by 55 per cent by 2030 (compared to 1990 levels) and delivering the European Green Deal.

Renewable Energy Directive (RED II)

7.21 The Renewable Energy Directive[27] is the legal framework for the development of clean energy across all sectors of the EU economy, supporting cooperation between EU countries towards this goal. Since its introduction, the share of renewable energy sources in EU energy consumption has increased from 12.5 per cent in 2010 to 23 per cent in 2022. Sweden had the highest share of renewables in its consumption (66 per cent), ahead of Finland (47.9 per cent) and Latvia (43.3 per cent).[28]

26 Regulation (EU) 2018/842 of the European Parliament and of the Council of 30 May 2018 on binding annual greenhouse gas emission reductions by Member States from 2021 to 2030 contributing to climate action to meet commitments under the Paris Agreement and amending Regulation (EU) No 525/2013 [2018] OJ L156/26, https://eur-lex.europa.eu/legal-content/EN/TXT/?uri=CELEX%3A32018R0842&qid=1743155524684

27 Directive (EU) 2023/2413 of the European Parliament and of the Council of 18 October 2023 amending Directive (EU) 2018/2001, Regulation (EU) 2018/1999 and Directive 98/70/EC as regards the promotion of energy from renewable sources, and repealing Council Directive (EU) 2015/652 [2023] OJ L2024/2413, https://eur-lex.europa.eu/eli/dir/2023/2413/oj

28 Eurostat, 'Shedding light on energy in the EU – 2023 edition', https://ec.europa.eu/eurostat/web/interactive-publications/energy-2023#renewable-energy

Energy Efficiency Directive (EED)

7.22 The Energy Efficiency Directive is a key driver in Europe's energy transition. The revised Energy Efficiency Directive[29] raises the EU's ambition on energy efficiency and establishes 'energy efficiency first' as a fundamental principle of EU energy policy, giving it legal standing for the first time. This means that energy efficiency must be considered by EU countries in all relevant policy and major investment decisions taken in the energy and non-energy sectors. The 2023 revision follows a proposal for a recast directive on energy efficiency put forward by the Commission in July 2021, as part of the EU Green Deal package. The 2021 proposal was further enhanced as part of the REPowerEU plan (see **7.08**) presented by the Commission in May 2022, aiming to decrease the EU's dependency on fossil fuel imports from Russia.

Regulation on the Governance of the Energy Union and Climate Action

7.23 For the EU to reach its 2030 climate and energy targets, the Regulation on the Governance of the Energy Union and Climate Action[30] sets common rules for planning, reporting and monitoring. The Regulation also ensures that EU planning and reporting are synchronised with the ambition cycles under the Paris Agreement.

Integrated national energy and climate plans

7.24 Under the Regulation on the Governance of the Energy Union and Climate Action,[31] EU Member States develop integrated NECPs based on a common template.

29 Directive (EU) 2023/1791 of the European Parliament and of the Council of 13 September 2023 on energy efficiency and amending Regulation (EU) 2023/955 [2023] OJ L231/1, https://eur-lex.europa.eu/legal-content/EN/TXT/?uri=OJ%3AJOL_2023_231_R_0001&qid=1695186598766

30 Regulation (EU) 2018/1999 of the European Parliament and of the Council of 11 December 2018 on the Governance of the Energy Union and Climate Action, amending Regulations (EC) No 663/2009 and (EC) No 715/2009 of the European Parliament and of the Council, Directives 94/22/EC, 98/70/EC, 2009/31/EC, 2009/73/EC, 2010/31/EU, 2012/27/EU and 2013/30/EU of the European Parliament and of the Council, Council Directives 2009/119/EC and (EU) 2015/652 and repealing Regulation (EU) No 525/2013 of the European Parliament and of the Council [2018 OJ L328/1, https://eur-lex.europa.eu/legal-content/EN/TXT/?toc=OJ:L:2018:328:TOC&uri=uriserv:OJ.L_.2018.328.01.0001.01.ENG

31 Regulation (EU) 2018/1999 of the European Parliament and of the Council of 11 December 2018 on the Governance of the Energy Union and Climate Action, amending Regulations (EC) No 663/2009 and (EC) No 715/2009 of the European Parliament and of the Council, Directives 94/22/EC, 98/70/EC, 2009/31/EC, 2009/73/EC, 2010/31/EU, 2012/27/EU and 2013/30/EU of the European Parliament and of the Council, Council Directives 2009/119/EC and (EU) 2015/652 and repealing Regulation (EU) No 525/2013 of the European Parliament and of the Council [2018 OJ L328/1, https://eur-lex.europa.eu/legal-content/EN/TXT/?toc=OJ:L:2018:328:TOC&uri=uriserv:OJ.L_.2018.328.01.0001.01.ENG

The plans cover the five dimensions of the Energy Union:

- decarbonisation (greenhouse gas reduction and renewables);
- energy security;
- energy efficiency;
- internal energy market; and
- research, innovation and competitiveness.

Member States submitted their 2021–30 final plans in 2019. The Commission has assessed these both at EU and Member State level. Member States had to update their NECPs by the end of June 2023 in a draft form. The Commission assessed the Member States' draft updated NECPs and issued recommendations to ensure their ambitions were in line with EU targets for 2030. Member States submitted their final updated plans, taking account of the Commission's assessment and recommendations, by 30 June 2024. Member States can adapt national policies and measures at any time, provided such changes are included in the biennial integrated national energy and climate progress reports to the Commission.

Regulation on Land Use, Land Use Change, and Forestry (LULUCF)

7.25 The land use sector covers the management of cropland, grassland, wetlands, forests and settlements, as well as changes in land use, including afforestation (ie planting trees), deforestation or draining of peatlands. With agricultural and forest lands covering more than three-quarters of the EU's territory, the land use sector offers significant carbon sequestration and emission reduction opportunities.

To address these challenges and leverage opportunities for climate action, the EU has implemented legislative frameworks. One of these is the revised Regulation on Land Use, Land Use Change, and Forestry (LULUCF),[32] which aims to enhance governance, promote transparency, and strengthen the link between climate mitigation and environmental protection measures.

The key provisions are:

- ambitious net carbon removal targets;
- synergies for climate and biodiversity;
- simplified reporting rules; and
- advanced monitoring techniques.

Transport and aviation regulations

7.26 Aviation – airlines are subject to the EU ETS, see **7.15**.

32 Regulation (EU) 2018/841 of the European Parliament and of the Council of 30 May 2018 on the inclusion of greenhouse gas emissions and removals from land use, land use change and forestry in the 2030 climate and energy framework, and amending Regulation (EU) No 525/2013 and Decision No 529/2013/EU [2018] OJ L156/1, https://eur-lex.europa.eu/legal-content/EN/TXT/?uri=CELEX:02018R0841-20230511

Cars and vans

CO_2 emissions

7.27 To help reduce emissions, the EU has a Regulation that sets CO_2 emission performance standards for new passenger cars and vans (Regulation (EU) 2019/631).[33]

With stricter CO_2 emission targets in place since 2020, the average CO_2 emissions from all new passenger cars registered in Europe fell by 27 per cent between 2019 and 2022, while the average emissions from new vans dropped by 10 per cent. The main driver of this decrease in emissions is the surge in zero-emission vehicles, which respectively amounted to 13.4 per cent and 6 per cent of the 2022 EU (and Norway and Iceland) new car and van fleet.

On 19 April 2023, the European Parliament and the Council amended the Regulation to strengthen the CO_2 emission performance standards for new passenger cars and vans, and bring them in line with the EU's ambition to reach climate neutrality by 2050. This amendment strengthened the emission targets applying from 2030 and set a 100 per cent emission reduction target for both cars and vans from 2035 onwards.

Fuel Quality Directive

7.28 EU Member States annually report information on the volumes, energy content and life cycle GHG emissions of fuels used in road transport and non-road mobile machinery, as well as the quality of automotive petrol and diesel, in line with their obligations under the Fuel Quality Directive 98/70/EC,[34] Articles 7a and 8.

Circular Economy Action Plan

7.29 The European Commission adopted the Circular Economy Action Plan (CEAP)[35] in March 2020. It is one of the main building blocks of the European Green Deal, Europe's agenda for sustainable growth. The EU's transition to a circular economy will reduce pressure on natural resources and will create sustainable growth and jobs. It is also important to achieve the EU's 2050

33 Regulation (EU) 2019/631 of the European Parliament and of the Council of 17 April 2019 setting CO2 emission performance standards for new passenger cars and for new light commercial vehicles, and repealing Regulations (EC) No 443/2009 and (EU) No 510/2011 [2019] OJ L111/13, https://eur-lex.europa.eu/legal-content/EN/TXT/?uri=CELEX%3A02019R0631-20231203

34 Directive 2009/30/EC of the European Parliament and of the Council of 23 April 2009 amending Directive 98/70/EC as regards the specification of petrol, diesel and gas-oil and introducing a mechanism to monitor and reduce greenhouse gas emissions and amending Council Directive 1999/32/EC as regards the specification of fuel used by inland waterway vessels and repealing Directive 93/12/EEC [2009] OJ L140/88, https://eur-lex.europa.eu/eli/dir/2009/30/oj/eng

35 Communication from the Commission to the European Parliament, the Council, the European Economic and Social Committee and the Committee of the Regions A new Circular Economy Action Plan For a cleaner and more competitive Europe, COM/2020/98 final, https://eur-lex.europa.eu/legal-content/EN/TXT/?qid=1583933814386&uri=COM:2020:98:FIN

climate neutrality target and to halt biodiversity loss. The action plan has initiatives along the entire life cycle of products and targets how products are designed, promotes circular economy processes, encourages sustainable consumption, and aims to ensure that waste is prevented and the resources used are kept in the EU economy for as long as possible.

The objectives are to introduce measures to:

- make sustainable products the norm in the EU;
- empower consumers and public buyers;
- focus on the sectors that use most resources and where the potential for circularity is high such as: electronics and ICT, batteries and vehicles, packaging, plastics, textiles, construction and buildings, food, water and nutrients;
- ensure less waste;
- make circularity work for people, regions and cities; and
- lead global efforts on circular economy.

Biodiversity Strategy for 2030

7.30 The EU's Biodiversity Strategy for 2030 is a comprehensive and long-term plan to protect nature and reverse the degradation of ecosystems. The Strategy aims to put Europe's biodiversity on a path to recovery by 2030 and contains specific actions and commitments.

The biodiversity strategy aims to put Europe's biodiversity on the path to recovery by 2030 for the benefit of people, climate and the planet. In the post-Covid-19 context, the strategy aims to build our societies' resilience to future threats such as:

- the impacts of climate change;
- forest fires;
- food insecurity; and
- disease outbreaks – including by protecting wildlife and fighting illegal wildlife trade.

INTERNATIONAL COOPERATION

7.31 The EU actively engages in international climate negotiations, such as the Paris Agreement. It has committed to supporting developing countries in their climate change efforts through financial and technical assistance.

Climate change is a global challenge that requires a response from all countries in order to achieve the objectives of the Paris Agreement to limit global temperature rise to 1.5°C.

CO_2 emissions within the EU decreased by approximately 7.6 per cent in 2023, to 2.5 billion metric tons ($GtCO_2$). This is the lowest they have been for 58 years. However the emissions of many countries are still rising.[36] As a result the

36 Statista, 'Carbon dioxide emissions in the European Union 1965-2023', https://www.statista.com/statistics/450017/co2-emissions-europe-eurasia/#:~:text=Carbon%20dioxide%20(CO2)%20emissions%20from,in%20more%20than%2058%20years

EU is actively engaging with third countries to promote the green transition and decoupling growth from emissions.

Climate action is a part of the EU's foreign policy agenda. Through diplomacy and cooperation initiatives, the EU aims to advance global climate action and support partner countries in their efforts to tackle climate change. This includes the promotion of policy measures that support the transition towards climate neutrality or low-carbon economies (mitigation), as well as helping countries build climate resilience (adaptation). The European Green Deal serves as an internal compass to deepen the EU's engagement in relation to climate action worldwide and to share best practices with like-minded countries.

To increase climate cooperation with other countries, the EU has a range of instruments and tools.

High-level dialogues

7.32 High-level dialogues on climate-related issues with selected partner countries are used to prepare multilateral climate negotiations and to move towards more ambitious domestic climate action. High-level dialogues are a beneficial instrument for fostering new or deepening existing technical cooperation at bilateral level.

Green Alliances and Green Partnerships

7.33 Green Alliances and Green Partnerships are bilateral frameworks to enhance dialogue and cooperation with key EU partner countries on:

- climate action;
- a clean and fair energy transition;
- environment protection; and
- other areas of relevance to the green transition.

There are Green Alliances with Canada, Japan and Norway and Green Partnerships with Morocco and the Republic of Korea

Just Energy Transition Partnerships (JETPs)

7.34 These are bilateral frameworks to help mobilise financial resources to support a country towards new and more ambitious climate targets and lower GHG emissions. JETPs also assist the communities who need the most support with the transition as they depend on the production of fossil fuels. JETPs are bilateral frameworks between the International Partners Group, also known as the G7 (Canada, Denmark, the EU, France, Germany, Norway, the UK, the US) and another country.

There are JETPs with Indonesia, Senegal, South Africa and Vietnam.

EU Climate Dialogues

7.35 These are used to spread European know-how to support peer-to-peer learning. The projects build upon and complement the climate policy dialogues and cooperation with major economies and foster exchanges and collaboration among national and sub-national administrations, business communities, academia and civil society stakeholders, supporting progress toward the Paris Agreement goals.

RESEARCH AND INNOVATION

7.36 The EU promotes investments in research and innovation to develop new technologies that facilitate the transition to a low-carbon economy, as outlined in programmes like Horizon Europe.

To limit warming to 1.5°C, immediate emission reductions are urgently needed across all productive sectors. Science has also provided the number of available responses for both mitigation and adaptation. The EU is committed to providing the best available scientific evidence, such as that in the Intergovernmental Panel on Climate Change (IPCC) assessments.[37] The European Green Deal is providing a momentum for ambitious climate action. The European Climate Law means that reaching climate neutrality in the EU by 2050 and reducing net GHG emissions by 2030 by at least 55 per cent compared to 1990 is now legally binding. The EU Strategy on Adaptation to Climate Change[38] sets out how the EU can adapt to the unavoidable impacts of climate change and become climate resilient by 2050.

Science plays a key role in ensuring that policies are effective, the European Climate Law also provides for the establishment of a European Scientific Advisory Board on Climate Change[39] to inform the design and implementation of EU climate action. The results of EU-funded research are an important source of information for the Board.

To ensure scientific evidence is available to guide design and implementation of climate strategies in Europe and globally, the EU continues to be a key funder of world-class climate science. The high quality and relevance of EU-funded research is also reflected by the contributions of EU projects to the work of the IPCC.[40] Current research and innovation activities supported through Horizon Europe Cluster 5 – Destination 1 – 'Climate sciences and responses' – focus on the following.

Earth system science

7.37 The Earth system includes a complex network of physical, chemical, and biological processes that interact with each other in various ways, not yet fully understood.

37 *IPCC Sixth Assessment Report*, https://www.ipcc.ch/assessment-report/ar6/

38 Communication from the Commission to the European Parliament, the European Council, the Council, the European Economic and Social Committee and the Committee of the Regions Forging a climate-resilient Europe – the new EU Strategy on Adaptation to Climate Change COM/2021/82 final, https://eur-lex.europa.eu/legal-content/EN/TXT/?uri=CELEX%3A52021DC0082&qid=1743696599680

39 European Scientific Advisory Board on Climate Change, https://climate-advisory-board.europa.eu

40 European Commission, 'Intergovernmental Panel on Climate Change', https://research-and-innovation.ec.europa.eu/research-area/environment/climate-change-science/intergovernmental-panel-climate-change-ipcc_en

For example, the Earth's atmosphere, oceans, land surfaces and ice sheets are all interconnected, and changes in one system can have ripple effects throughout the entire planet.

Earth system science is about understanding these complex interactions, which requires sustained research effort across different disciplines and overcoming challenges associated with technological capacity to gather and process the necessary data.

By studying the Earth system, researchers can develop more accurate climate models that can help us predict how the planet will respond to different levels of GHG emissions and other human activities.

For instance, by comparing scenarios, models show that Earth's temperature would not have changed if it were not for human activities. Such information is essential for policymakers who are working to develop effective strategies for mitigating climate change and adapting to its impacts.

Climate change mitigation, pathways to climate neutrality

7.38 With the European Green Deal and the European Climate Law, the EU is committed to becoming climate neutral by 2050. This is necessary to avoid the dangerous consequences of climate change by limiting global warming to well below 2°C, ideally to 1.5°C, as agreed in the Paris Agreement. Scientific evidence is clear that immediate and drastic emissions reductions across all sectors are needed to keep these goals within reach and this decade will be decisive.

Science will continue to play a central role in defining evidence-based, economically effective and socially just pathways aligned with the global temperature targets and evidence from the research community is needed to drive ambition, mobilise action, guide policy responses, and clarify the roles of different areas from governments, through businesses, to local communities.

Climate change impacts and adaptation

7.39 Adaptation to climate change is about adjusting to a warmer world, to protect people, nature, our prosperity and way of life. The Earth has already warmed by over 1.1°C since the late 19th century with far-reaching impacts on every region of the world, causing more frequent and intense extreme events such as heatwaves or droughts, changing rainfall patterns, melting ice, and altering both natural and human habitats.

Adaptation feasibility and effectiveness depends on the level of warming and communities' readiness. Making immediate and deep cuts in the emissions of GHGs is the best adaptation strategy, but, in parallel, there must be preparation for the unavoidable climate impacts which are already occurring and are likely to continue. Adaptation will be necessary in agriculture, biodiversity, coastal areas, energy, finance, forestry, health, infrastructure, marine and fisheries, transport, urban, water management and many others.

Social science, citizen science and behavioural science for climate action

7.40 Integrating social and behavioural sciences into climate change research is crucial for a better understanding of human interactions with the environment, promoting behavioural change, informing policy decisions, and engaging the public.

Policy and social sciences are looking at climate solutions by exploring non-technical aspects of technologies and helping to navigate the complex landscape of human values, interests and trade-offs, and power dynamics.

This makes a strong case for better integrating Social Sciences and Humanities (SSH) disciplines into climate-related research as well as a more interdisciplinary approach where social and climate scientists work to understand climate in the pursuit of the most effective solutions.

International cooperation

7.41 International cooperation in climate science research is essential due to the inherently global nature of climate change. In addition, climate research often relies on expensive infrastructure and observation systems that call for effective burden sharing mechanisms across jurisdictions. Collaborative efforts help facilitate filling the knowledge and data gaps by pooling resources and expertise from many countries and regions. This enables a more comprehensive, robust and context-specific understanding of climate dynamics and their impacts.

Scientific cooperation is especially necessary to improve consensus between the Global North and the Global South within the UN Framework Convention on Climate Change process. The work of the IPCC is a prime example of how instrumental scientific cooperation is for shaping effective mitigation and adaptation responses. The IPCC reports not only represent an essential source of information about climate change, but they also mainstream science into policy processes and help to forge consensus among governments, creating the necessary momentum for the implementation of the Paris Agreement.

Cross-cutting issues related to climate science

7.42 Climate change and climate action increasingly intersect with multiple dimensions of human and natural world. Not only are mitigation and adaptation two sides of the same coin, but their interactions are inherently complex. Progress on mitigation will largely determine the demand for, and the effectiveness of, adaptation, with limits being reached at higher levels of warming. At the same time, mitigation pathways themselves must be resilient to the changing climate, particularly the occurrence of extremes.

The IPCC stresses the urgency of advancing climate-resilient development that combines deep emissions reductions and climate adaptation together, making a strong case for better coordination and integration of climate policies and actions. The IPCC also emphasises that more integration is needed between mitigation, adaptation and sustainable development, while accounting for the fairness dimension. Also, strong links exist between climate change and biodiversity loss, with climate-related impacts on ecosystems and biodiversity likely to limit our future ability to adapt and mitigate.

EU-funded research aims at providing a more complete overview of how adaptation and mitigation interact with each other and with other policy objectives, forming a basis for a more strategic and comprehensive approach to policy design and implementation.

The cross-cutting category also includes other projects of horizontal nature, including coordination and support actions.

Chapter 8

Climate Change Litigation Cases: EU

THE EUROPEAN COURT OF HUMAN RIGHTS

8.01 On 9 April 2024, the European Court of Human Rights handed down its judgments in three cases:

- *Verein KlimaSeniorinnen Schweiz and Others v Switzerland (KlimaSeniorinnen)*
- *Carême v France (Carême)*
- *Duarte Agostinho and Others v Portugal and Others (Duarte Agostinho).*

In each case there were alleged breaches of the European Convention on Human Rights (EHCR) by the respondent States on the basis of their inaction on climate change. These cases represent the Court's first substantive assessment of the interplay between the ECHR and climate change.

Carême and *Duarte Agostinho* were held to be inadmissible; the Court found in favour of the applicants (in part) in *KlimaSeniorinnen*, holding that a European

Convention on Human Rights (ECHR) Convention state's inaction on climate change (here, Switzerland's) could amount to a breach of the ECHR.

KlimaSeniorinnen

8.02 In the case of *Verein KlimaSeniorinnen Schweiz and Others v Switzerland*[1] the European Court of Human Rights (ECtHR or the Court) ruled that Switzerland had breached the ECHR by not taking sufficient action against climate change. In particular, it found a breach of the right to respect for private and family life contained in Article 8 of the Convention, based on Switzerland's failure to mitigate the impact of climate change on the lives, health, well-being and quality of life of its citizens. It also ruled that Switzerland had breached the right to a fair trial in terms of Article 6, in that the domestic courts failed to examine the merits of the applicants' complaints, including the scientific evidence.

The application was brought by four individuals and an association of 2,500 women, KlimaSeniorinnen, all of whom were concerned about the impacts climate change was having on their health, well-being, and quality of life. In particular the applicants, whose average age was 73, cited evidence regarding the disproportionately adverse effects climate change has on older women.

In November 2016, the applicants submitted a request to the Swiss Federal Department of the Environment, Transport, Energy and Communications (DETEC) to try and compel the Swiss authorities to take all necessary measures required by the Swiss Constitution and the Convention to prevent the increase of global temperatures. DETEC rejected their request based on a lack of standing, indicating that the applicants were pursuing general public interests which did not provide them with victim status under the Convention.

Both appeals to the Federal Administrative Court and the Federal Supreme Court were dismissed. This was on the basis that the applicants hadn't shown that their rights had been sufficiently and directly affected by climate change in a way that was different to the rest of the population.

Their next application was to the ECtHR, claiming that the Swiss authorities had breached Article 8 of the Convention by failing to ensure respect for their private and family life, including their home. They said that their rights under Article 6 had been breached because the Swiss courts had not responded to their requests for effective mitigating measures to be implemented against climate change.

On the 9 April 2024, the ECtHR handed down its judgment in three cases, including *KlimaSeniorinnen*: *Duarte Agostinho* and *Carême* were dismissed. However in the case of *KlimaSeniorinnen* the courts made a number of important rulings.

KlimaSeniorinnen argued that Article 8 was engaged by Switzerland's failure to take the necessary steps to reduce emissions and combat the immediate risk posed to its vulnerable elderly female citizens by the climate crisis. The Swiss Government's response was that climate change is a global problem

1 *Verein KlimaSeniorinnen Schweiz and Others v Switzerland* (App no 53600/20), https://hudoc.echr.coe.int/eng#{%22itemid%22:[%22002-14304%22]}

and therefore, the applicants could not attribute causation specifically to Switzerland. The government also stated that, given the technical and complex nature of climate change, states should be afforded a wide margin of appreciation. The living-instrument doctrine[2] did not allow for the Convention to be interpreted in a way that undermined the principle of subsidiarity.[3]

The Court acknowledged that this kind of claim is a new departure from the Court's environmental case law which has dealt with situations involving specific sources of environmental harm as opposed to the wider problem of climate change, for which there is no single or specific source of harm. However 'failure by the Court to maintain a dynamic and evolutive approach would risk rendering it a bar to reform or improvement'. The Court's environmental jurisprudence means that the Court recognised the 'intergenerational burden' of the climate crisis and the rights of future generations.

However, applying the principle of subsidiarity, the Court reiterated that states have freedom to decide the specific steps they will take to comply with their positive obligations.

The Court held that Switzerland had failed to comply with its positive obligations under Article 8 to put in place relevant legislative and administrative frameworks to quantify, through a carbon budget or otherwise, national greenhouse gas (GHG) emissions limitations.

Following the case the Swiss authorities will now be supervised by the Committee of Ministers to adopt measures aimed at ensuring compliance with its Convention obligations. The Swiss State was ordered to pay KlimaSeniorinnen €80,000 towards costs.

Carême

8.03 The case in *Carême v France*[4] concerned a complaint by a former inhabitant and mayor of the municipality of Grande-Synthe, who said that France has taken insufficient steps to prevent global warming and that this failure is a violation of the right to life and the right to respect for private and family life. The Court declared inadmissible the application, on the ground that the applicant did not have victim status within the meaning of Article 34 of the Convention.

Duarte Agostinho

8.04 The case *Duarte Agostinho and Others v Portugal and Others*[5] concerned the current and future severe effects of climate change, which the

2 A judicial interpretation method used by the ECtHR to interpret the ECHR means that the European Convention on Human Rights (ECHR) should be interpreted in light of present-day conditions and evolving standards, rather than a static interpretation form its inception.

3 Subsidiarity – a principle that aims to ensure that decisions are made at the level of government closest to the people.

4 *Carême v France* (App no 7189/21) CE:ECHR:2024:0409DEC000718921 (2024) 79 EHRR SE1 (relinquishment), https://hudoc.echr.coe.int/eng#{%22itemid%22:[%22002-13678%22]}

5 *Duarte Agostinho and Others v Portugal and Others* (App no 39371/20) (2024) 78 EHRR SE9, https://hudoc.echr.coe.int/eng#{%22itemid%22:[%22002-13724%22]}

applicants attributed to the respondent states, and which, they claim, impact their lives, well-being, mental health and the peaceful enjoyment of their homes. As it concerned the extraterritorial jurisdiction of respondent states other than Portugal, the Court found that there were no grounds in the Convention for the extension of their extraterritorial jurisdiction in the manner requested by the applicants. Having regard to the fact that the applicants had not pursued any legal avenue in Portugal concerning their complaints, the applicants' complaint against Portugal was also inadmissible for non-exhaustion of domestic remedies. The Court declared inadmissible the applications lodged against Portugal and the other states on the issue of climate change.

ALIGNMENT WITH THE PARIS AGREEMENT

Milieudefensie and Others v Royal Dutch Shell plc[6]

8.05 In April 2019, six environmental associations and non-governmental organisations (NGOs):

- Milieudefensie (Greenpeace Netherlands Foundation),
- Environmental Defense Association (Amsterdam),
- National Association for the Conservation of the Wadden Sea (Harlingen),
- Foundation for the Promotion of the fossil free movement (Amsterdam),
- Both ENDS Foundation, and
- Association of Young Environmentally Active,

together with 17,319 individual co-claimants brought a case before the Hague District Court alleging that Shell's contributions to climate change violated its duty of care under Dutch law and human rights law.

The question before the court was whether Shell should be required to make further changes to the Shell Group's existing corporate policy to reduce the carbon dioxide (CO_2) emissions for the entire group's energy portfolio to achieve lower emission levels by the end of 2030, relative to 2019 levels.

In May 2021, the court handed down its judgment, stating that, as a matter of Dutch law, Shell was subject to a duty of care in respect of the harmful effects of climate change and was required it to reduce its carbon emissions. This decision was made on a range of legal and factual bases, including:

- the provisions of the Dutch Civil Code;
- scientific evidence regarding climate change; and
- human rights instruments including the ECHR and soft law instruments such as:
  - — the UN Guiding Principles on Business and Human Rights (UNGPs) and
  - — the Organisation for Economic Co-operation and Development (OECD) Guidelines for Multinational Enterprises.

6 *Milieudefensie and Others v Royal Dutch Shell plc* (C/09/571932/HA ZA 19-379) NL:RBDHA:2021:5339, https://climatecasechart.com/wp-content/uploads/non-us-case-documents/2019/20190405_8918_summons.pdf

The Hague District Court reached the significant conclusion that Shell, as a corporate entity had an obligation to protect the claimants' human rights as part of complying with the implied standard of care contained in Section 6:162 of the Dutch Civil Code,[7] and that this involved an obligation to limit the human rights impacts associated with climate change.

Shell appealed against the 2021 ruling and raised ten grounds for appeal and also sought recovery for its costs from both sets of proceedings.

Shell argued that corporate emissions reductions were not a matter for the courts but a matter belonging to legislators. It argued that lawmakers had not imposed any obligations on companies to reduce their CO_2 emissions by a certain percentage, and that the court's decision should therefore be reversed on appeal.

The Court of Appeal upheld Shell's appeal[8] in respect of the specific percentage reduction which had been imposed by the court in 2021, overturning the Court's order.

The Court of Appeal made a number of other significant findings:

- the role of the state: the court acknowledged the important role of the state in setting policy but concluded that businesses have parallel obligations;
- the appropriate forum: the court rejected Shell's argument that the courts were not the appropriate forum for questions about the energy transition. The court found that assessing whether Shell has the alleged legal obligation and deciding on the claims based on that obligation is a task of the court; and
- choice of law: the court applied Dutch law on the basis that one of the events giving rise to the damage was the corporate decision-making of Shell. Importantly, the court found that the reduction obligation falls on Royal Dutch Shell, as the parent company establishing the Shell group's climate change policies and strategies.

Unwritten duty of care

8.06 Shell's reduction obligation was established under the general tort provision of Dutch Civil Code (DCC), Article 6:162, which contains a duty of care for natural persons and legal entities. Breaching this duty of care results in a liability for damages suffered as a result of the breach. Milieudefensie claimed a declaratory judgment that such a duty of care for Shell existed and, that under this duty of care, Shell was legally obliged to contribute to the prevention of dangerous climate change by reducing its carbon emissions through its corporate group policy. Milieudefensie's claim was solely about Shell's future carbon emissions. No monetary damages were claimed.

7 Section 6:162 of the Dutch Civil Code Definition of a 'tortious act' – 1. A person who commits a tortious act (unlawful act) against another person that can be attributed to him, must repair the damage that this other person has suffered as a result thereof.

8 *Milieudefensie and Others v Royal Dutch Shell plc* (C/09/571932/HA ZA 19-379) NL:GHDHA:2024:2100, https://climatecasechart.com/wp-content/uploads/non-us-case-documents/2024/20241112_8918_judgment.pdf

Marlene Lemme and Others v State of Bavaria

8.07 Ten people brought a complaint against the State of Bavaria, Germany,[9] claiming that the state's failure to set adequate climate protection goals and emission reduction paths was in violation of domestic environmental law and constitutional law. They alleged that this failure to mitigate would have an effect on the plaintiffs' human rights and health, as well as damaging animals and nature.

Following the decision in *Neubauer and Others v Germany* (see **8.09**) and the Federal Climate Protection Act (Bundes-Klimaschutzgesetz (KSG)), it was contended that the State of Bayern could be in breach of its duty to protect the fundamental rights of the claimants under the Basic Law of the Federal Republic of Germany (Germany's Constitution) and, by failing to stipulate, a GHG reduction pathway that was adequate and complied with the targets set out in the KSG.

The plaintiffs' claimed that their constitutional rights were being violated on two counts:

- due to the inadequacy of the existing climate protection laws; and
- because of the failure of some state legislatures to create a uniform reduction path for GHG emissions.

They also raised that some of the federal states in Germany (State of Brandenburg, State of Hesse) had not specified any reduction paths at all, or that the chosen pathways were insufficient.

To ensure that the plaintiffs' losses of freedom are reasonable and that the burden of GHG emissions is not placed solely upon future generations, the legislature is obliged to implement the necessary reductions in CO_2 emissions and changes in lifestyle, as required by the Constitution and the provisions in the KSG. As the constitutional petition was not admitted for adjudication, the arguments of the respondents were not presented.

The court emphasised how states have a limited amount of influence in the area of climate protection, which is managed by the federal government. Therefore it is difficult to determine state-specific reduction requirements, especially taking into consideration that emission reduction coordination is currently being approached horizontally through individual emission sectors. On this basis the court rejected the claims, finding that it was not possible to determine the extent to which the state legislature had the necessary powers to reduce or prevent any future violations of the rights contained in Articles 2, 14 and 20a of the Constitution.

9 *Marlene Lemme and Others v Bavaria* (German Bundesverfassungsgericht, constitutional complaint of 30 June 2021), https://climatecasechart.com/wp-content/uploads/non-us-case-documents/2021/20210630_14619_petition.pdf

GOVERNMENTS

Urgenda Foundation v State of the Netherlands[10]

8.08 Urgenda set out the facts of climate change in their summons and explained why emissions needed to be radically reduced to avert catastrophic harm. It provided the grounds upon which it claimed the Dutch state was legally obliged to take action to reduce Dutch GHG emissions.

In its defence, the state acknowledged all of the facts of climate change, including the potentially devastating consequences if no action was taken. The state implicitly acknowledged that it was not doing its share to avoid dangerous climate change but rejected the idea that it could be legally obliged to act. It argued that there is no legal obligation on the basis of which it is legally bound to reduce GHG emissions.

On 14 April 2015, oral arguments were presented at the Hague District Court. The Hague District Court issued its judgment on the 24 June 2015, ordering the Dutch State to lower its emission by at least 25 per cent before 2020 compared to 1990 levels.

The appeal at the Hague Court of Appeal took place on 28 May 2018.[11] The judgment was delivered on 9 October 2018: the Hague Court of Appeal upheld the 2015 court decision.

On 8 January 2019, the state filed its grounds of appeal to the Supreme Court. Despite its initial announcement to file the appeal because of its disagreement with the Court of Appeal's approach to the question of 'separation of powers', the state challenged a wide range of findings that were made by the Court of Appeal. This included the finding that the state had a human rights-based obligation to reduce emissions and the necessity to reduce Dutch emissions by at least 25 per cent by 2020 compared to 1990 levels in order to prevent global warming from exceeding 2°C.

On 12 April 2019, Urgenda filed its written defence to the Supreme Court. The case was heard at the Supreme Court on 24 May 2019. On 21 June 2019 Urgenda filed its rejoinder in which it responded to the pleadings and the written submissions of the state.

The final judgment of the Supreme Court, on the 20 December 2019, stated that the Dutch Government must reduce emissions immediately in line with its human rights obligation.

Neubauer and Others v Germany

8.09 Luisa Neubauer, along with nine youth climate activists, brought a case[12] against the German Federal Government for its failure to enact adequate

10 *Urgenda Foundation v State of the Netherlands* (19/00135) NL:HR:2019:2007, https://uitspraken.rechtspraak.nl/details?id=ECLI:NL:HR:2019:2007

11 *State of the Netherlands v Urgenda Foundation* NL:GHDHA:2018:2610, https://uitspraken.rechtspraak.nl/details?id=ECLI:NL:GHDHA:2018:2610

12 *Neubauer and Others v Germany* (BvR 2656/18), https://climatecasechart.com/non-us-case/neubauer-et-al-v-germany/

climate legislation. The plaintiffs argued that the existing climate legislation, the 2019 German Federal Climate Change Act (Bundes-Klimaschutzgesetz (KSG)) – not only didn't meet Germany's responsibilities under the Paris Agreement, but also didn't uphold the claimants' fundamental rights under the German Constitution (German Basic Law).

The plaintiffs argued that some provisions of the KSG were unconstitutional and incompatible with fundamental rights because they lacked a detailed plan for reducing GHG emissions, therefore moving the burden of combating climate change onto future generations. They sought declaratory relief that the law's inadequate emissions reduction targets were unconstitutional and that the German Government must set new targets for reducing GHG emissions.

The plaintiffs alleged that the current legislation violated the of the duty of protection arising from fundamental rights, including:

- the right to freedom;
- the right to a future consistent with human dignity; and
- the right to an ecological minimum standard of living.

The Paris Agreement, to which Germany is a party, binds states to enact and enforce specific provisions for reducing GHG emissions. Under the Paris Agreement, states commit to limiting the increase in the global average temperature to well below 2°C above pre-industrial levels and to pursue efforts to limit the temperature increase to 1.5°C above pre-industrial levels. The Agreement leaves the specifics of how each state party will achieve the above-stated requirements to the states.

The German Federal Constitutional Court was unanimous in deciding that the KSG was partially unconstitutional, as it failed to protect future generations from future infringements of their rights. The court ordered the legislature to amend the KSG by the end of 2022. Specifically, it ordered the German Government to correct and tighten up the KSG provisions to strengthen future mitigation pathways with specific provisions for limiting global warming to 2°C but preferably 1.5°C.

The German Government complied with the court's judgment, enhancing the climate protection policy and raising its GHG emissions reduction targets. Amendments to the KSG now include a 64 per cent reduction of GHG emissions by 2030; an 88 per cent reduction by 2040; and achieving climate neutrality by 2045.

PUBLIC PARTICIPATION IN DECISION-MAKING

Kaiser and Others v Volkswagen AG

8.10 In a judgment of 14 February 2023,[13] the Braunschweig Regional Court dismissed the action brought by climate activists and supported by

13 *Kaiser and Others v Volkwagen AG* (Braunschweig Regional Court, 14 February 2023), https://climatecasechart.com/wp-content/uploads/non-us-case-documents/2021/20211111_16019_petition.pdf

Greenpeace that sought an order to prohibit the distribution of Volkswagen (VW) vehicles with combustion engines from 2030 and to make VW reduce its CO_2 emissions by 65 per cent by 2023 compared to 2018 levels.

The court dismissed the action and referred to another decision from the German Constitutional Court dated 18 January 2022, which held that the German legislature complied sufficiently with its climate-related constitutional obligations by enacting the German Climate Protection Act (Bundes-Klimaschutzgesetz (KSG))[14] on 31 August 2021.

EU TRADING SCHEME

Schaefer Kalk GmbH & Co KG v Germany

8.11 This case[15] challenged the treatment of CO_2 that becomes chemically bound as emitted for the purposes of the European Union Emissions Trading Scheme (EU ETS).

A German company operating a facility covered by the EU ETS argued that CO_2 that is transferred to a non-covered facility and becomes chemically bound and is therefore not released into the atmosphere should not be considered 'emitted'.

The European Court of Justice agreed, invalidating an EU regulation as it systematically included CO_2 that becomes chemically bound in the trading scheme regardless of whether that CO_2 is actually emitted into the atmosphere.

Schaefer Kalk GmbH & Co KG (Schaefer Kalk) operated an installation for the calcination of lime in Hahnstätten, Germany, which was subject to the EU ETS. During the lime calcination process CO_2 was emitted, which Schaefer Kalk transferred to an installation that was not covered by the EU ETS for the production of precipitated calcium carbonate (PCC). As Schaefer Kalk needed to get their monitoring plan approved, they applied for authorisation to subtract the CO_2 transferred for PCC production from the amount of GHG emissions in the company's emissions report. They argued that the transferred CO_2 is chemically bound in the PCC and cannot be emitted into the atmosphere and therefore cannot be regarded as 'emissions' as defined in Article 3(b) of Directive 2003/87/EC.[16]

The legal issues surrounding carbon capture and utilisation (CCU) within the EU are moving rapidly to align with the goal of achieving carbon neutrality by 2050. Under the EU ETS, recent amendments and court rulings have expanded the scope of accepted CCU applications, particularly looking at the importance of permanent chemical binding of CO_2 in products. However, there is still the

14 German Climate Protection Act, https://www.gesetze-im-internet.de/englisch_ksg/englisch_ksg.html

15 *Schaefer Kalk GmbH & Co v Germany* (C-460/15) EU:C:2017:29, https://eur-lex.europa.eu/legal-content/EN/TXT/?uri=CELEX%3A62015CJ0460

16 Directive 2003/87/EC of the European Parliament and of the Council of 13 October 2003 establishing a scheme for greenhouse gas emission allowance trading within the Community and amending Council Directive 96/61/EC [2003] OJ L275/32, https://eur-lex.europa.eu/eli/dir/2003/87/oj/eng

definition issue of what 'permanently chemically bound' means and the criteria for assessing the duration of carbon storage in products.

GREEN WASHING (CLIMATE WASHING CASES)

Vegetarian Society of Denmark v Danish Crown 2021

8.12 In the case of *Vegetarian Society and Others of Denmark v Danish Crown*,[17] Danish NGOs, including the Danish Vegetarian Association and the Climate Movement in Denmark sued Danish Crown, a leading pork producer in the EU. They brought the claim in May 2021 when the NGOs claimed the company deceived consumers through one of its marketing campaigns. The campaign said that pork is 'more climate-friendly than you would think' and that its pork production was 'climate controlled'.

In March 2024, the Western High Court ruled that the first phrase was not considered misleading, but it found the second phrase violated Danish Marketing Practices Act, s 5 for misrepresenting the environmental impact of the company's products.

FossielVrij NL v KLM

8.13 Here, FossielVrij NL sued Dutch airline, KLM, for alleged greenwashing in its advertising campaigns.[18] The case was supported by other organisations, including ClientEarth, and could provide an international precedent.

On 24 May 2022, campaigners for FossielVrij NL issued a summons to Dutch aviation company KLM at a shareholder meeting of AirFrance-KLM. The letter stated that KLM would be sued in violation of European consumer law if it did not stop the misleading advertisement claims under its 'Fly Responsibly' campaign to the effect that CO_2 compensation measures and alternative fuels could make flying sustainable. The Fly Responsibly ads presented the airline as 'creating a more sustainable future' and on track to reduce its emissions to net zero by 2050.

The Amsterdam District Court at first instance ruled that the airline KLM had violated Dutch consumer law by making misleading environmental claims in its advertisements and marketing.

FossielVrij NL argued that some 19 statements made by KLM in their advertisements and marketing campaign misled consumers about the environmental benefits of their products and violated the Dutch Unfair Commercial Practices Act (which implemented the EU Unfair Commercial Practices Directive).

17 *Vegetarian Society and Others of Denmark v Danish Crown* (Western High Court Viborg, March 2024) BS-472/2022-VLR; 1009/23, https://climatecasechart.com/wp-content/uploads/non-us-case-documents/2021/20210529_15251_summons.pdf

18 *FossielVrij NL v KLM* (C/13/71948/HA ZA 22-524) NL:RBAMS:2024:1512, https://climatecasechart.com/wp-content/uploads/non-us-case-documents/2024/20240320_17244_judgment.pdf

The statements were made as part of KLM's 'Fly Responsibly' campaign and 'CO2ZERO' service whereby customers were encouraged to make a financial contribution to reforestation projects selected by KLM as a way reduce the impact of their flights on the environment. KLM, in their defence, claimed that it was free to publish information about its sustainability efforts and claimed that, whilst it realised that its main business activities were not currently sustainable, it was working on a number of projects to make its operations more sustainable.

However, while the court was satisfied making a declaratory judgment that 15 of the statements were misleading and unlawful, it was not willing to award the pleaded 'penalty' of €100,000 each time KLM violated the Act, although it did order KLM to pay FossielVrij NL's costs.

TURNING OFF THE TAPS

In Re Tax Benefits for Aviation[19]

8.14 The applicant, a consumer utilising both rail and air services, applied for relief, citing a diagnosis of multiple sclerosis and health issues exacerbated by the climate crisis. She argued that existing Austrian tax laws favoured aviation over rail travel and this contributed to environmental problems and violated her constitutional rights, including:

- the right to equality before the law;
- the right to life; and
- the right to private and family life.

On 27 June 2023, the Constitutional Court of Austria dismissed the application as inadmissible. The court cited the amendment to the Value-Added Tax Act as of 1 January 2023, which extended value-added tax (VAT) exemptions from aviation and maritime shipping to cross-border rail transport. The court determined that the contested provision was no longer in force, leading to a lack of standing for the applicants. Additionally, the court held that the obligation to pay VAT was directed at businesses, excluding consumers from challenging relevant provisions.

POLLUTER PAYS

Luciano Lliuya v RWE[20]

8.15 Saúl Luciano Lliuya is an Andean farmer and mountain guide from Peru and he, with more than 50,000 inhabitants of the Andean city of Huaraz,

19 *Re Tax Benefits for Aviation* [2022] G 106-107/2022-10, V 140/2022-10 (Constitutional Court of Austria), https://climaterightsdatabase.com/2024/01/09/in-re-tax-benefits-for-aviation/

20 *Luciano Lliuya v RWE* (Case No. 2 O 285/15), https://climatecasechart.com/wp-content/uploads/non-us-case-documents/2021/20210927_Case-No.-2-O-28515-Essen-Regional-Court_order.pdf

are threatened by a flood wave due to the consequences of global warming. A glacial lake above the city has grown due to glacial melt. An ice avalanche could cause the lake to overflow and trigger a destructive tidal wave.

In November 2015, he filed a lawsuit against the energy company RWE in a German civil court.

Evidence presented in the case includes:

- a scientific study linking flood risk in the Peruvian Andes to global warming; and
- a study in the scientific journal Remote Sensing that found there was 'no evidence of significant glacial instability'.

In May 2022, judges and experts from the German city of Hamm visited the Palcacocha Lake area in Peru to assess the risk of flooding. RWE maintains the position that a single company cannot be held responsible for the consequences of climate change.

The case is still ongoing.

Asmania and Others v Holcim

8.16 Four inhabitants of the Indonesian island of Pari have sued Swiss-based major buildings materials company, Holcim (from 2015 to 2021: Lafarge Holcim).[21] In July 2022, they filed a request for conciliation before the Justice of the Peace of the Canton of Zug, Switzerland. This is a step required by the Swiss Civil Procedure Code. The plaintiffs are supported by three NGOs:

- HEKS/EPER (Switzerland);
- the European Center for Constitutional and European Rights (ECCHR); and
- WALHI (Indonesia).

The plaintiffs request proportional compensation for climate change-related damages on Pari, a reduction in CO_2 emissions by 43 per cent by 2030 and by 69 per cent by 2040, relative to 2019 levels, and a financial contribution towards adaptation measures on Pari.

The claim combines two approaches, reduction of GHGs and compensation. In February 2023, following a Conciliation Hearing before the Justice of the Peace in October 2022 where no settlement was reached, the NGOs supporting the plaintiffs announced that the plaintiffs had formally lodged a lawsuit against Holcim with the Cantonal Court of Zug (Kantonsgericht Zug). The Conciliation Hearing failed.

Hugues Falys, FIAN, Greenpeace, Ligue des Droits Humains v TotalEnergies (The Farmer Case)[22]

8.17 Hugues Falys, a farmer from the Hainaut province in Belgium is taking legal action before the Tournai Commercial Court, on the border with France, against TotalEnergies for its responsibility for climate change.

21 *Asmania and Others v Holcim* (Cantonal Court of Zug (Kantonsgericht Zug)).

22 *Hugues Falys, FIAN, Greenpeace, Ligue des Droits Humains v TotalEnergies* (Commercial Court of Tournai), https://climatecasechart.com/wp-content/uploads/non-us-case-documents/2024/20240301_54998_petition.pdf

Falys' legal action is the first climate case ever brought in Belgium against a multinational company. Three Belgian NGOs, FIAN, Greenpeace, and the Ligue des Droits Humains (LDH) have joined forces to intervene in the case, with support from the Belgian Climate Coalition. The case seeks recognition for the damages suffered by Hugues Falys, but also TotalEnergies's compliance with the targets of the Paris Agreement. The case asks the court to request TotalEnergies to implement a credible transition plan, which includes a halt to new investments in fossil fuel projects, a 47 per cent reduction in gas and oil production by 2030, and a more stringent 75 per cent reduction by 2040.

The first hearing took place on 16 April 2024 in the Commercial Court of Tournai. During the hearing, the five parties agreed on a schedule for the exchange of pleadings, which will take place on the 19 and 26 November 2025.

Chapter 9

Approaches to Climate Change: US

9.01 The United States (US) approaches climate change through a combination of federal, state, and local policies, initiatives, and international commitments.

President Biden made an executive order Protecting Public Health and the Environment and Restoring Science to Tackle the Climate Crisis.[1] The

1 Executive Order 13990, 'Protecting Public Health and the Environment and Restoring Science to Tackle the Climate Crisis', https://www.federalregister.gov/documents/2021/01/25/2021-01765/protecting-public-health-and-the-environment-and-restoring-science-to-tackle-the-climate-crisis

Environment Protection Agency (EPA) is considering rule-making proposals to address some of the largest sources of both climate- and health-harming pollution, such as the transportation, oil and natural gas, and power sectors. We await what changes President Trump may make.

ROLE OF THE SUPREME COURT

9.02 Article III of the Constitution establishes the federal judiciary. Article III, Section I states that 'The judicial Power of the United States, shall be vested in one supreme Court, and in such inferior Courts as the Congress may from time to time ordain and establish'. Although the Constitution establishes the Supreme Court, it permits Congress to decide how to organise it. Congress first exercised this power in the Judiciary Act of 1789. This Act created a Supreme Court with six justices. It also established the lower federal court system.

The Justices

9.03 Various Acts of Congress have altered the number of seats on the Supreme Court: today, there is one Chief Justice and eight Associate Justices of the US Supreme Court. Like all federal judges, justices are appointed by the President and are confirmed by the Senate. They, typically, hold office for life.

The Court's jurisdiction

9.04 Article III, Section II of the Constitution establishes the jurisdiction (legal ability to hear a case) of the Supreme Court. The Court has original jurisdiction (a case is tried before the Court) over certain cases, eg suits between two or more states and/or cases involving ambassadors and other public ministers.

The Court has appellate jurisdiction (the Court can hear the case on appeal) on almost any other case that involves a point of constitutional and/or federal law. Some examples include cases to which the US is a party, cases involving treaties, and cases involving ships on the high seas and navigable waterways (admiralty cases).

Cases

9.05 When exercising its appellate jurisdiction, the Court, with a few exceptions, does not have to hear a case. The Certiorari Act of 1925 gives the Court the discretion to decide whether or not to do so. In a petition for a writ of certiorari, a party asks the Court to review its case.

Judicial review

9.06 The best-known power of the Supreme Court, judicial review, or the ability of the Court to declare a legislative or executive act in violation of the Constitution, is not found within the text of the Constitution itself.

Role

9.07 The Supreme Court is the highest court in the land, it is the court of last resort for those looking for justice.

- Due to its power of judicial review, it has an essential role in ensuring that each branch of government recognises the limits of its own power.
- It also protects civil rights and liberties by striking down laws that violate the Constitution.
- It sets appropriate limits on democratic government by ensuring that popular majorities cannot pass laws that harm and/or take undue advantage of unpopular minorities.
- The decisions of the Supreme Court have an important impact on society at large, not just on lawyers and judges.

FEDERAL STATE CLAIMS

9.08 The US Court of Federal Claims has jurisdiction over claims seeking money judgments against the US.

The federal courts have jurisdiction over:

- cases that raise a 'federal question' involving the US Government, the US Constitution, or other federal laws; and
- cases involving 'diversity of citizenship', which are disputes between two parties not from the same state or country, and where the claim meets a set dollar threshold for damages,
- more specifically, federal courts hear criminal, civil, and bankruptcy cases. And once a case is decided, it can often be appealed.

See (**9.10**) *Mayor & City Council of Baltimore v BP plc.*

See (**9.10**) *Board of County Commissioners of Boulder County v Suncor Energy (USA) Inc.*

CONSTITUTIONAL CLAIMS

9.09 Constitutional claims in the US involve the rights and protections guaranteed by the Constitution. Constitutional claims can only be brought against a 'state actor'. The State Action Doctrine provides guidelines for who can be a defendant.

Federal courts are courts of limited jurisdiction, meaning they can only hear cases authorised by the Constitution or federal statutes. The relevant federal district court is the starting point for cases arising under the Constitution.

To bring a claim in federal court, the plaintiff must demonstrate that:

- they suffered a distinct injury;
- the injury is traceable to the defendant's conduct; and
- the requested relief is likely to redress the injury.

The Supreme Court has the final say over when a right is protected by the Constitution. The Court can strike down state laws that violate the Constitution.

State courts can provide greater liberty under state constitutions by declining to follow decisions of the Supreme Court that undermine recovery of damages. State constitutions can fill in the gaps left by the federal constitution.

Constitutional remedies include:

- the jurisdiction of a court to hear a claim (in the US, a court's jurisdiction is a remedy because it establishes the power of a court to hear a case and grant relief, meaning it's the legal foundation for a party to seek and obtain a court order to address a wrong or dispute, whether through monetary damages or other forms of relief);
- the existence of a cause of action; and
- the availability of judicial relief.

See (**10.04**) *Held v State of Montana*.

STATE LAW CLAIMS

9.10 State law is the law of each separate US state. Each state has its own state constitution, state government and state courts. Each state has a legislative branch that promulgates state regulations following statutory authorisation and a judicial branch which applies, interprets and, occasionally, overturns both state and statutes and regulations and local ordinances.

A state law claim is a legal remedy that can be sought in state court. State courts handle most types of laws, including civil, criminal, family, probate and small claims cases.

Points to note concerning US state law claims include:

- State law diversity – to bring a state law claim in federal court, all plaintiffs must be from different states than all defendants, and the amount in controversy must be more than $75,000.
- State law and federal courts – federal courts generally don't interpret state law extensively. Instead, they follow state law as announced by the highest state court.
- State law and the Supreme Court – the Supreme Court rarely tries to interpret state law. However, the Supreme Court can review state court judgments if they aren't based on adequate and independent state grounds.
- State law and the US Constitution – the US Constitution creates a federal system of government, where power is shared between the federal and state governments.
- State law and civil law – some states have inherited civil law features from when they were part of Mexico. For example, many states in the southwest have a community property system for married couples.

These are examples where defendants have sought intervention from the Supreme Court:

- *Minnesota v American Petroleum Institute*[2]

2 *Minnesota v American Petroleum Institute*, 63 F.4th 703 (8th Cir. 2023).

- *Rhode Island v Shell Oil Products Co*[3]
- *City of Hoboken v Chevron Corp'n*[4]
- *Mayor & City Council of Baltimore v BP plc*[5]
- *City & County of Honolulu v Sunoco LP*[6]
- *County of San Mateo v Chevron Corp'n*[7]
- *City of Oakland v BP plc*[8]
- *Board of County Commissioners of Boulder County v Suncor Energy (USA) Inc.*[9] But cf. *City of New York v Chevron Corp'n.*[10]

COMMON LAW CLAIMS

9.11 A simple definition of common law is law based on court decisions rather than codes or statutes.

Common law claims are legal claims that are based on historical tradition and court decisions, rather than written laws. In the US, common law claims can be made in a variety of situations, including:

- Personal injury – an injured party can sue a negligent party for damages caused by their carelessness. For example, if an intoxicated driver causes an accident, the driver can be sued for damages in addition to facing criminal charges.
- Fraud – the Supreme Court has ruled that agencies must bring fraud claims in federal court, rather than in administrative proceedings, because defendants are entitled to a jury trial.
- Federal common law – the US Congress gives courts the power to create federal common law in areas like antitrust, bankruptcy, and civil rights. Courts can create federal common law when Congress has not addressed a situation, or when applying state laws would create uncertainty.

PUBLIC TRUST CLAIMS

9.12 The public trust doctrine (PTD) is a legal principle that establishes the government's responsibility to hold certain resources in trust for the benefit of the public. The PTD limits the government's ability to transfer resources to private parties and the private use of those resources. The PTD has been used in a variety of cases, including those related to:

3 *Rhode Island v Shell Oil Products Co*, 35 F.4th 44 (1st Cir. 2022).
4 *City of Hoboken v Chevron Corp'n*, 45 F.4th 699 (3d Cir. 2022).
5 *Mayor & City Council of Baltimore v BP plc*, 31 F.4th 178 (4th Cir. 2022).
6 *City & County of Honolulu v Sunoco LP*, 39 F.4th 1101 (9th Cir. 2022).
7 *County of San Mateo v Chevron Corp'n*, 32 F.4th 733 (9th Cir. 2022).
8 *City of Oakland v BP plc*, 969 F.3d 895 (9th Cir. 2020).
9 *Board of County Commissioners of Boulder County v Suncor Energy (USA) Inc*, 25 F.4th 1238 (10th Cir. 2022).
10 *City of New York v Chevron Corp'n*, 993 F.3d 81 (2d Cir. 2021).

- Public access – the PTD has been used to provide public access to land that was previously filled in, such as land under tidally influenced waters.
- Public interest – the PTD has been used to assert public interest in oil resources and to prevent the private ownership of fish stocks and crustacean beds.
- Drinking and recreation – in most US states, the PTD is used to maintain lakes and navigable streams for drinking and recreation.

Some examples of public trust claims include:

- *Sierra Club v California Department of Water Resources*[11]: a 2024 filing;
- *Neighbours for a True Oasis v Village of Port Washington North*[12]: a 2024 filing challenging a plan to sell a forested area for development;
- *In re Hawai'i Electric Light Co*[13]: a 2023 filing that rejected a power purchase agreement for a biomass facility; and
- *Protect the Public's Trust v US Department of State*[14]: a Freedom of Information Act lawsuit seeking documents related to the Special Presidential Envoy for Climate.

SECURITIES AND FINANCIAL REGULATION

9.13 Securities and financial regulation claims in the US can include:

- Misleading statements – individuals who intentionally make misleading statements in an official Securities and Exchange Commission (SEC) document can be held liable. People who rely on these false statements can sue for damages.
- Violating securities laws or regulations – the SEC can bring civil actions against those it alleges broke securities laws or regulations.
- Shareholder class action lawsuits – these lawsuits can allege claims under various sections of the Exchange Act and the Securities Act.
- Mergers and acquisitions litigation.
- Racketeer Influenced and Corrupt Organizations Act (RICO) violations.

Other aspects of securities and financial regulation include:

- Enforcement proceedings – firms that are found to be non-compliant with rules can face enforcement proceedings.
- Resolution – the process of restructuring or winding down a financial institution in a way that minimises harm to the economy.

11 *Sierra Club v California Department of Water Resources* (24WM000008), https://climatecasechart.com/case/sierra-club-v-california-department-of-water-resources-3/

12 *Neighbours for a True Oasis v Village of Port Washington North* (609509/2024), https://climatecasechart.com/case/neighbors-for-a-true-oasis-v-village-of-port-washington-north/

13 *In re Hawai'i Electric Light Co* (SCOT-22-0000418), https://climatecasechart.com/case/in-re-hawaii-electric-light-co-3/

14 *Protect the Public's Trust v US Department of State* (1:22-cv-02231), https://climatecasechart.com/case/protect-the-publics-trust-v-us-agency-for-international-development/#:~:text=Protect%20the%20Public's%20Trust%2C%20which,conduct%20to%20all%20public%20servants%2C"

- An early warning system – states can alert the public, policymakers, and other regulators to problems.
- The Commodities Futures Trading Commission (CFTC) – the CFTC was founded in 1974 to regulate the futures contracts market.

Environmental, social and governance (ESG) disclosure mandates

9.14 In March 2022, the US SEC released its proposed rules on mandating certain climate-related disclosures for listed companies. The SEC finalised 'The Enhancement and Standardization of Climate Related Disclosures for Investors'[15] Rule on 6 March 2024. The SEC is adopting amendments to its rules under the Securities Act of 1933 and Securities Exchange Act of 1934 that will require registrants to provide certain climate-related information in their registration statements and annual reports. The final rules will require information about a registrant's climate-related risks that have materially impacted or are reasonably likely to have a material impact on, its business strategy, results of operations, or financial condition. In addition, under the final rules, certain disclosures related to severe weather events and other natural conditions will be required in a registrant's audited financial statements.

LEGISLATION AND REGULATORY FRAMEWORK

Clean Air Act

9.15 The Clean Air Act is the law that defines the EPA's responsibilities for protecting and improving the nation's air quality and the stratospheric ozone layer. The last major change in the law, the Clean Air Act Amendments, was enacted by Congress in 1990. Legislation passed since then has made several minor changes.

The Clean Air Act, like other laws enacted by Congress, was incorporated into the US Code as Title 42, Chapter 85.[16] The House of Representatives maintains a current version of the US Code, which includes Clean Air Act changes enacted since 1990.

The Clean Air Act covers:

- Title I – Air Pollution Prevention and Control
  - — Part A – Air Quality and Emission Limitations
  - — Part B – Ozone Protection (replaced by Title VI)
  - — Part C – Prevention of Significant Deterioration of Air Quality
  - — Part D – Plan Requirements for Nonattainment Areas
- Title II – Emission Standards for Moving Sources

15 'The Enhancement and Standardization of Climate Related Disclosures for Investors', Federal Register, https://www.federalregister.gov/documents/2024/03/28/2024-05137/the-enhancement-and-standardization-of-climate-related-disclosures-for-investors

16 42 U.S.C. 85, https://uscode.house.gov/browse/prelim@title42/chapter85&edition=prelim

- — Part A – Motor Vehicle Emission and Fuel Standards
- — Part B – Aircraft Emission Standards
- — Part C – Clean Fuel Vehicles
- Title III – General
- Title IV – Noise Pollution
- Title IV-A – Acid Deposition Control
- Title V – Permits
- Title VI – Stratospheric Ozone Protection

Clean Water Act

9.16 The Clean Water Act (CWA) establishes the basic structure for regulating discharges of pollutants into the waters of the US and regulating quality standards for surface waters. The basis of the CWA was enacted in 1948 and was called the Federal Water Pollution Control Act, but the Act was significantly reorganised and expanded in 1972. The 'Clean Water Act' became the Act's common name with the amendments in 1972.

Under the CWA, the EPA has implemented pollution control programmes such as setting wastewater standards for industry. The EPA has also developed national water quality criteria recommendations for pollutants in surface waters.

The CWA made it unlawful to discharge any pollutant from a point source into navigable waters, unless a permit was obtained.

The EPA's National Pollutant Discharge Elimination System (NPDES) permit programme controls discharges.

Point sources are discrete conveyances such as pipes or man-made ditches.

To note:

- individual homes that are connected to a municipal system, use a septic system, or do not have a surface discharge do not need an NPDES permit;
- industrial, municipal, and other facilities must obtain permits if their discharges go directly to surface waters.

Endangered Species Act and other wildlife protection statutes

9.17 The Endangered Species Act (ESA)[17] provides a programme for the conservation of threatened and endangered plants and animals and the habitats in which they are found. The lead federal agencies for implementing the ESA are:

- the US Fish and Wildlife Service (FWS) – the FWS maintains a worldwide list of endangered species, including birds, insects, fish, reptiles, mammals, crustaceans, flowers, grasses and trees; and
- the US National Oceanic and Atmospheric Administration (NOAA) Fisheries Service.

17 The Endangered Species Act (ESA), https://www.fws.gov/sites/default/files/documents/endangered-species-act-accessible_7.pdf

The law requires federal agencies, in consultation with the US FWS and/or the NOAA Fisheries Service, to ensure that actions they authorise, fund, or carry out are not likely to jeopardise the continued existence of any listed species or result in the destruction or adverse modification of designated critical habitat of such species. The law also prohibits any action that causes a 'taking' of any listed species of endangered fish or wildlife. Likewise, import, export, interstate and foreign commerce of listed species are all generally prohibited.

The Office of Pesticide Programs (OPP) implements key portions of the ESA. The OPP regulates the use of all pesticides in the US and establishes maximum levels for pesticide residues in food, thereby safeguarding the nation's food supply.

FREEDOM OF INFORMATION ACT AND OTHER STATUTES AND REGULATIONS

9.18 The Freedom of Information Act (FOIA) is a law that gives the public access to federal agency records, including information related to climate change:

- US EPA – the EPA uses the FOIA to promote transparency and accountability in its work on climate change. The EPA recently updated its FOIA regulations to make it easier for the public to access information about the agency's actions and activities
- US Department of State – an FOIA lawsuit was filed against the Department of State to compel the release of documents related to the Special Presidential Envoy for Climate. The plaintiff argued that the documents would provide the public with greater insight into the federal government's climate priorities
- Council on Environmental Quality (CEQ) FOIA Reading Room – the CEQ FOIA Reading Room provides information on environmental issues, including reports, publications, and environmental laws and regulations.

The FOIA allows agencies to withhold certain information from the public if it would harm government or private interests. However, administrative and judicial remedies are available to those who are denied access to records. See:

- *Friends of the Earth v Council on Environmental Quality*;[18]
- *Massachusetts v Environmental Protection Agency*;[19] and
- *Sackett v Environmental Protection Agency*.[20]

18 *Friends of the Earth v Council on Environmental Quality* (1:22-cv-01128), https://climatecasechart.com/wp-content/uploads/case-documents/2023/20231130_docket-122-cv-001128_stipulation.pdf

19 *Massachusetts v Environmental Protection Agency*, 549 U.S. 497 (2007), https://supreme.justia.com/cases/federal/us/549/497/

20 *Sackett v EPA*, 598 U.S. 651 (2023), https://supreme.justia.com/cases/federal/us/598/21-454/

NEPA (National Environmental Policy Act)

9.19 The National Environmental Policy Act (NEPA) was one of the first laws ever written that establishes the broad national framework for protecting our environment. The NEPA's basic policy is to assure that all branches of government consider the environment prior to undertaking any major federal action that significantly affects the environment.

NEPA requirements are invoked when airports, buildings, military complexes, highways, parkland purchases, and other federal activities are proposed. Environmental Assessments (EAs) and Environmental Impact Statements (EISs), which are assessments of the likelihood of impacts from alternative courses of action, are required from all federal agencies and are the most visible NEPA requirements.

Energy Policy Act and Clean Power Plan

9.20 Designed to encourage energy efficiency and renewable energy, though the Clean Power Plan faced legal challenges and has been replaced by other initiatives in recent administrations.

Energy Policy Act

9.21 The Energy Policy Act addresses energy production in the US and concerns:

- energy efficiency;
- renewable energy;
- oil and gas;
- coal;
- tribal energy;
- nuclear matters and security;
- vehicles and motor fuels, including ethanol;
- hydrogen;
- electricity;
- energy tax incentives;
- hydropower and geothermal energy; and
- climate change technology.

For example, the Act provides loan guarantees for entities that develop or use innovative technologies that avoid the by-production of greenhouse gases (GHGs). Another provision of the Act increases the amount of biofuel that must be mixed with gasoline sold in the US.

Clean Power Plan

9.22 On 3 August 2015, President Obama and the EPA announced the Clean Power Plan, an important step in reducing carbon pollution from power plants.

The aim of the Clean Power Plan is to:

- reduce carbon pollution from power plants, while maintaining energy reliability and affordability. The EPA issued final Carbon Pollution Standards for new, modified, and reconstructed power plants, and proposed a Federal Plan and model rule to assist states in implementing the Clean Power Plan. These are the first ever national standards that address carbon pollution from power plants;
- cut significant amounts of power plant carbon pollution and the pollutants that cause the soot and smog that harm health, while advancing clean energy innovation, development and deployment, and laying the foundation for the long-term strategy needed to tackle the threat of climate change. This gives states and utilities the flexibility and time needed to achieve these pollution cuts; and
- acknowledge that fossil fuels continue to be a critical component of the US's energy future. The Clean Power Plan simply makes sure that fossil fuel-fired power plants will operate more cleanly and efficiently, while expanding the capacity for zero- and low-emitting power sources.

In 2009, the EPA determined that GHG pollution threatens US health and welfare by leading to long-lasting changes in climate that can have a range of negative effects on human health and the environment. Carbon dioxide (CO_2) is the most prevalent GHG pollutant, accounting for nearly three-quarters of global GHG emissions and 82 per cent of US GHG emissions.

The Clean Air Act – under s 111(d) – creates a partnership between the EPA, states, tribes and US territories, with the EPA setting a goal and states and tribes choosing how they will meet it.

The final Clean Power Plan follows that approach. The EPA has established interim and final CO_2 emission performance rates for two subcategories of fossil fuel-fired electric generating units (EGUs):

- fossil fuel-fired electric steam generating units (generally, coal- and oil-fired power plants); and
- natural gas-fired combined cycle generating units.

To maximise the range of choices available to states in implementing the standards and to utilities in meeting them, the EPA has established interim and final statewide goals in three forms:

- a rate-based state goal measured in pounds per megawatt hour (lb/MWh);
- a mass-based state goal measured in total short tons of CO_2; and
- a mass-based state goal with a new source complement measured in total short tons of CO_2.

States then develop and implement plans that ensure that the power plants in their state – either individually, together or in combination with other measures – achieve the interim CO_2 emissions performance rates over the period from 2022 to 2029 and the final CO_2 emission performance rates, rate-based goals or mass-based goals by 2030.

Under Clean Air Act, s 111(d), the EPA determines the best system of emissions reduction (BSER) that has been demonstrated for a particular pollutant and a particular group of sources by examining technologies and measures already being used.

Consistent with previous BSER determinations in s 111(d) rule-makings, the EPA considers the types of strategies, technologies and measures that states and utilities are already using to reduce CO_2 from fossil fuel-fired power plants.

In the final Clean Power Plan, the EPA determined that BSER consists of three building blocks:

- Building Block 1 – reducing the carbon intensity of electricity generation by improving the heat rate of existing coal-fired power plants;
- Building Block 2 – substituting increased electricity generation from lower-emitting existing natural gas plants for reduced generation from higher-emitting coal-fired power plants; and
- Building Block 3 – substituting increased electricity generation from new zero-emitting renewable energy sources (like wind and solar) for reduced generation from existing coal-fired power plants.

In determining the BSER, the EPA considered the ranges of reductions that can be achieved at coal, oil and gas plants at a reasonable cost by application of each building block, considering how quickly and to what extent the measures encompassed by the building blocks could be used to reduce emissions.

EXECUTIVE ORDERS AND POLICY INITIATIVES

9.23 Various administrations have used executive orders to implement climate initiatives. For instance, the Biden Administration prioritised climate action through an executive order aimed at achieving net-zero emissions by 2050 and promoting clean energy.

In 2021 the Instrument of Acceptance was deposited with the UN Secretary-General, indicating the US's desire to rejoin the Paris Agreement.

Following this there were a number of Executive Orders:

- EO 14008 Executive Order on Tackling the Climate Crisis at Home and Abroad
- EO 13990 Executive Order on Protecting Public Health and the Environment and Restoring Science to Tackle the Climate Crisis
- EO 14013 Rebuilding and Enhancing Programs to Resettle Refugees and Planning for the Impact of Climate Change on Migration
- EO 14007 Executive Order on Establishing President's Council of Advisors on Science and Technology
- Memorandum on Restoring Trust in Government Through Scientific Integrity and Evidence-Based Policymaking.

In November 2020, President-Elect Biden appointed John Kerry as his special presidential envoy for climate which reinforced his commitment to tackling the global crisis. In December 2020 President-Elect Biden appointed Gina McCarthy as head of the new White House Office of Domestic Climate Policy (officially created in Executive Order 14008).

On his first day in office President Donald Trump issued several executive orders that reversed the Biden Administration policies on climate change, this included withdrawing from the Paris Agreement, terminating the New

Green Deal, promoting fossil fuels while blocking clean energy initiatives and withdrawing support for electric vehicles.

INTERNATIONAL ENGAGEMENT

Paris Agreement

9.24 The US rejoined the Paris Agreement under the Biden Administration in 2021,[21] committing to reduce GHG emissions by 50–52 per cent below 2005 levels by 2030.

After his inauguration in 2025, President Donald Trump signed an executive order directing the US to withdraw from the Paris Climate Agreement. This echoed his directive in 2017, when he announced that the US would abandon the global Paris Accord. President Trump also signed a letter to the United Nations indicating his intention to withdraw from the 2015 agreement.

He also rescinded the US International Climate Finance Plan, which was established following an Executive Order from former President Biden to channel support from multilateral and bilateral institutions to assist developing countries in climate mitigation and adaptation.

Investment in clean energy

9.25 There has been significant investment in renewable energy technologies, including solar, wind and energy storage through initiatives like the Infrastructure Investment and Jobs Act and the Inflation Reduction Act.

According to the International Energy Agency (IEA) report on World Energy Investment 2024[22] the US has taken steps to scale up investments in clean energy. These investments overtook the spending that went to fossil fuels in 2020, when oil and gas investments fell sharply and increased to $280 billion in 2023 from $200 billion in 2020. The country also invests a significant amount in oil and gas: for every $1.4 spent on clean energy in 2023, US investors directed $1 to fossil fuels.

There are new legislative vehicles supporting clean energy investment in the US – see below.

Bipartisan Infrastructure Investment and Jobs Act of 2021

9.26 The law authorises $1.2 trillion for transportation and infrastructure spending with $550 billion of that figure going toward 'new' investments and

21 US Department of State, 'The United States Officially rejoins the Paris Agreement' press statement (19 February 2021), https://2021-2025.state.gov/the-united-states-officially-rejoins-the-paris-agreement/

22 IEA, *World Energy Investment 2024*, https://www.iea.org/reports/world-energy-investment-2024/united-states

programmes. This bipartisan law strengthens the Pipelines and Hazardous Materials Safety Administration's (PHMSA's) safety authority and includes many provisions that will help PHMSA fulfil its mission of protecting people and the environment by advancing the safe transportation of energy and other hazardous materials.

US Inflation Reduction Act (IRA) of 2022

9.27 The President's Inflation Reduction Act (IRA) of 2022 makes the single largest investment in climate and energy in US history, enabling the US to tackle the climate crisis, advancing environmental justice, securing the US's position as a world leader in domestic clean energy manufacturing, and putting the US on a pathway to achieving net zero by 2050.

CLIMATE ADAPTATION AND RESILIENCE

9.28 There has been development of national and state adaptation strategies to enhance the resilience of communities, ecosystems and infrastructure to climate impacts, as outlined in the National Climate Assessment

The EPA's 2024–27 Climate Adaptation Plan[23] focuses on priority actions the agency will take over the next four years to allow it to deliver on its mission to protect human health and the environment, even as the climate changes. The plan integrates consideration of climate risks into multiple actions as appropriate and where consistent with the EPA's statutory authority, such as in the development of rules, policy and guidance; permitting and environmental reviews; monitoring, enforcement and compliance activities; and grant making.

Highlights from the plan include priority actions the EPA is taking to:

1. foster a climate-ready workforce;
2. build facility resilience;
3. develop climate-resilient supply chains; and
4. integrate climate resilience into external funding opportunities.

STATE AND LOCAL ACTIONS

9.29 Many states and municipalities have implemented their own climate policies and renewable energy goals. States like California and New York are recognised for ambitious climate initiatives aimed at reducing emissions and promoting clean energy.

23 US EPA, *2024-2027 Climate Adaptation Plan*, https://www.epa.gov/system/files/documents/2024-06/epas-2024-2027-climate-adaptation-plan-508-compliant.pdf

In 2023, under the first phase of the $5 billion programme, the EPA made a total of $250 million in grants available to 45 states, the District of Columbia, Puerto Rico, 80 Metropolitan Statistical Areas (MSAs), four territories, and over 200 tribes and tribal consortia to develop ambitious climate action plans that address GHG emissions across their communities and economies.

The EPA publishes a list of Priority Climate Action Plans for States, MSAs, tribes, and territories, it includes links to the Priority Climate Action Plans (PCAPs) developed for each state, MSA, tribe and territory.

ENVIRONMENTAL JUSTICE

9.30 'Environmental justice' means the just treatment and meaningful involvement of all people, regardless of income, race, colour, national origin, tribal affiliation or disability in agency decision-making and other federal activities that affect human health and the environment so that people:

- are fully protected from disproportionate and adverse human health and environmental effects (including risks) and hazards, including those related to climate change, the cumulative impacts of environmental and other burdens, and the legacy of racism or other structural or systemic barriers; and
- have equitable access to a healthy, sustainable, and resilient environment in which to live, play, work, learn, grow, worship and engage in cultural and subsistence practices.

Integrating environmental justice at the EPA

9.31 Since the Office of Environmental Justice (OEJ) was created, and with the creation of the Office of Environmental Justice and External Civil Rights (OEJECR), there have been significant efforts across the EPA to integrate environmental justice into day-to-day operations. Every regional and headquarter office has an environmental justice coordinator who serves as a focal point within that organisation.

Chapter 10

Climate Change Litigation Cases: US

INTRODUCTION

10.01 Much debate has taken place about which courts should be hearing cases brought against alleged polluters and greenhouse gas (GHG) emitters. In 1984 the case of *Chevron USA Inc v Natural Resources Defense Council (NRDC)*[1] brought about a doctrine known as the 'Chevron deference'. This consists of a two-part test that gives deference to government agencies:

- whether Congress has spoken directly to the precise issue in question; and
- whether the agency's answer is based on a permissible construction or statute.

The case was a challenge over the government's interpretation of the word 'source' in the Clean Air Act of 1963. The Act didn't precisely define what constituted a 'source' of air pollution. The Environment Protection Agency (EPA) initially defined 'source' to cover any significant change or addition to a plant or factory. In 1981, the EPA changed its definition to mean only an entire plant or factory, allowing companies to build new projects without

1 *Chevron USA Inc v NRDC*, 467 U.S. 837 (1984), https://supreme.justia.com/cases/federal/us/467/837/

going through the EPA's review process if they simultaneously modified other parts of their plant to reduce emissions, avoiding any net change. The NRDC, an environmentalist advocacy group, challenged the legality of the EPA's new definition. NRDC won the case in a federal court, but the Supreme Court overturned that decision and ruled in favour of Chevron on the grounds that the courts should broadly defer to the EPA and other independent regulatory agencies. *Chevron* has been cited in many cases but, 40 years later, in June 2024, the Supreme Court overruled *Chevron* in the case of *Loper Bright Enterprises v Raimondo*[2] on the ground that it conflicted with administrative procedure.

In the case of *Loper Bright Enterprises v Raimondo*, Loper Bright Enterprises, a New Jersey-based family-owned herring fishing company worked in the waters of New England and estimated that the cost of federal monitoring was $700 per day. In February 2020 Loper Bright filed a lawsuit in the United States (US) District Court for the District of Columbia alleging that the Magnuson-Stevens Fishery Conservation and Management Act (MSA) did not authorise the US National Oceanic and Atmospheric Administration (NOAA) Fisheries Service[3] to mandate industry-funded monitoring of herring fisheries. The District Court applied *Chevron* and granted summary judgment in favour of the NOAA Fisheries Service.

Despite *Chevron* providing for deference in the case of an ambiguously worded statute, the District Court found that the MSA unambiguously provides for industry-funded monitoring of herring fisheries, and therefore concluded its analysis at the first step of *Chevron*. The court acknowledged Loper Bright's arguments regarding ambiguity in the statutory language but noted that, even if these contentions successfully argued the existence of ambiguity in the text, the NOAA Fisheries Service's interpretation of the MSA would have been a reasonable reading of the statute.

A three-judge panel of the US Court of Appeals for the District of Columbia Circuit heard oral arguments in the case in February 2022. The court affirmed the judgment of the district court. However, the circuit court did not rest its analysis at the first step of *Chevron*, saying that the language of the MSA was not completely unambiguous about whether or not it provided for industry-funded monitoring of herring fisheries. Instead, it concluded its analysis at the second step of *Chevron*, stating that the NOAA Fisheries Service reasonably interpreted the MSA when it came to what the court deemed the 'silence on the issue of cost of at-sea monitoring'.

Loper Bright petitioned the Supreme Court in November 2022. In its petition for a writ of certiorari, Loper Bright presented two questions to the Court:

- it asked the Court to rule on whether granting the NOAA Fisheries Service the power to require domestic vessels to pay the salaries of monitors it carries was based on a proper application of *Chevron*; and
- it asked the Court to rule on whether *Chevron* should be overruled outright, or at least limited in its scope.

2 *Loper Bright Enterprises v Raimondo* (22-451), 603 U.S. 369 (2024), https://www.supremecourt.gov/opinions/23pdf/603us1r54_o7jp.pdf

3 *Loper Bright Enterprises v Raimondo* (21-5166) (D.C. Cir 2022), https://law.justia.com/cases/federal/appellate-courts/cadc/21-5166/21-5166-2022-08-12.html

Loper Bright was heard alongside *Relentless, Inc* in January 2024. On 28 June 2024, the Supreme Court issued its decision striking down *Chevron* deference.

With this ruling in June 2024, the Supreme Court handed that power back to individual judges who lack the same breadth or depth of expertise. The decision overruled a 40-year precedent that has shaped how US Government functioned.

This ruling applies across the board to much of the work of the federal government. Courts now take the lead on interpreting law for technical issues pertaining to pollution. This was made clear in the case of *Sackett v EPA* (see **10.12**) when the Supreme Court issued its judgment. The decision changed which bodies of water are protected by the Clean Water Act, with the Court ignoring robust agency science and declaring that wetlands shouldn't qualify for the same protections as other waterways, like rivers, lakes, or streams.

FEDERAL STATE CLAIMS

BP plc and Others v Mayor & City Council of Baltimore

10.02 In this case[4] starting in July 2017, state and local governments started to file lawsuits against oil and gas companies alleging that their exploration, production and marketing of fossil fuels was contributing to the plaintiff's climate-related injuries. For many years the decision was about whether the case should be heard in the federal courts or not.

In 2018, the Mayor and City Council of Baltimore (City) filed suit against 26 oil and gas companies in the Circuit Court for Baltimore City. They alleged that the defendants' conduct in promoting and selling fossil fuels, despite their awareness of the associated hazards, that their campaign against regulations was on deception and misinformation and their failure to develop less dangerous alternatives had contributed to the City's climate change-related injuries. The City's complaint asserted eight causes of action, seven based on state tort law and one based on the Maryland Consumer Protection Act.

The court issued its decision on 17 May 2021. In a 7-1 ruling, the court vacated the Fourth Circuit's decision and remanded the case for further review. The majority agreed with BP and others that the Fourth Circuit erred in considering all factors for review in denying the change of jurisdiction requested by the City, therefore vacating their decision and not ruling on the merits of Baltimore's complaints related to the petitioners.

In May 2021, the Court granted review of three other similar cases in which a city or state had successfully changed jurisdiction in an environmental lawsuit, vacating the circuit court rulings that allowed these changes to proceed on the basis of the *BP* opinion, and remanding these cases for further review.

4 *BP plc and Others v Mayor & City Council of Baltimore*, 593 U.S. _ (2021), https://www.supremecourt.gov/opinions/20pdf/19-1189_p86b.pdf

Suncor Energy (USA) Inc v Board of County Commissioners of Boulder County

10.03 In this case the issues were:

- whether federal common law necessarily and exclusively governs claims seeking redress for injuries allegedly caused by the effect of interstate GHG emissions on the global climate; and
- whether a federal district court has jurisdiction under 28 U.S.C. § 1331[5] over claims necessarily and exclusively governed by federal common law but labelled as arising under state law.

The defendants sought dismissal, asserting that the plaintiff's claims should be dismissed because they were governed by federal common law, pre-empted by federal common law, impaired the federal foreign affairs power, violated the separation of powers doctrine, violated the Commerce Clause and the Due Process Clause, amongst other claims.

On 21 June 2024, the Court granted in part and denied in part the Motion to Dismiss, finding that defendants' arguments as to pre-emption lacked merit and the claims were not pre-empted by federal common law or the Clean Air Act. The Court emphasised that the Clean Air Act does not contain an express pre-emption clause, and, in the Court's view, Congress did not intend to 'occupy' the entire field of GHG emissions (leaving space for state regulation). The Court also rejected the defendants' other arguments, which argued that the complaint violated the Commerce Clause, the Due Process Clause, and other related clauses.

The defendants petitioned the Colorado Supreme Court for permission to appeal the question of whether federal law precludes state law claims for injuries allegedly caused by global climate change. The Court granted review and ordered briefing. A ruling from the Colorado Supreme Court remains pending.

CONSTITUTIONAL CLAIMS

Held v State of Montana

10.04 This case[6] was brought by 16 youth plaintiffs and was the first in the US to be brought on the basis of a constitutional right to a healthy environment. The youths specifically argued that Montana had pursued an energy policy that 'permits' and 'encourages' the promotion and extraction of fossil fuels, without having regard for the negative impacts that rising GHG emissions have on climate change. Additionally, they argued that a provision within the Montana Environmental Policy Act (MEPA) that prevents state agencies from considering GHG emissions or the potential impacts on the climate when conducting environmental reviews interferes with their constitutional rights.

5 *Suncor Energy (USA) Inc v Board of County Commissioners of Boulder County* (21-1550), https://www.supremecourt.gov/DocketPDF/21/21-1550/259222/20230316134530410_21-1550%20Suncor.pdf

6 *Held v State of Montana* (DA 23-0575), https://climatecasechart.com/case/11091/

When the first Montana state constitution was ratified in 1889, Montana was a 'sparsely populated frontier state'. By the 1960s, a growing population was matched by growing calls for greater protection of the environment and for civil rights. This led to the establishment of a constitutional convention with 100 'ordinary' Montanans elected to be involved in the process. Motivated by the environmental movement and the fact that Montana's natural resources would be exploited if not protected by law, the delegates actively sought to include the right to a clean and healthy environment within the new constitution. The plaintiffs challenged the provision within MEPA that forbids the state and state agencies from considering the impacts of climate change or GHG emissions in their environmental reviews.

After considering the scientific evidence that GHG emissions are a significant contributor to human-made climate change, and the extent to which state agencies have been aware of the risks posed by GHG emissions, the judge concluded that the plaintiffs are being harmed by climate change, and these harms can be directly attributed to Montana's energy policies and the state's failure to consider GHG emissions in its environmental reviews. The judgment has the effect of invalidating any state statutes that prohibit consideration of GHG emissions and their impacts.

Counsel for the state of Montana deemed the case a 'publicity stunt' and promptly filed a notice of appeal. In January 2024, the Montana Supreme Court declined a motion to stay judgment, finding that the district court had not abused its discretion.

STATE LAW CLAIMS

10.05 In April the US Supreme Court declined to consider five cases in which fossil fuel companies had argued that climate change-related civil action should be heard in federal and not state courts.

There were five cases originally filed in the state courts where the defendants asked that the cases be heard in federal court as this would pre-empt the state law claims and end the lawsuits.

The five cases were:

- *Suncor Energy (USA) Inc and Others v Board of County Commissioners of Boulder City and Others* (see **10.03**);
- *County of San Mateo v Chevron Corp'n* (see **10.06**);
- *State of Rhode Island v Shell Oil Products Co and Others* ;[7]
- *BP plc and Others v Mayor and City Council of Baltimore* (see **10.02**); and
- *Sunoco LP and Others v City and County of Honolulu and Others*.[8]

7 *State of Rhode Island v Shell Oil Products Co and Others*, 35 F.4th 44 (1st Cir. 2022), https://law.justia.com/cases/federal/appellate-courts/ca1/19-1818/19-1818-2022-05-23.html

8 *Sunoco LP and Others v City and County of Honolulu and Others*; *Shell plc, FKA Royal Dutch Shell plc and Others v City and County of Honolulu and Others* Nos 23-947 and 23-952, https://www.supremecourt.gov/DocketPDF/23/23-947/334791/20241210173557425_23-947_and_23-952_Sunoco_FINAL.pdf

County of San Mateo v Chevron Corp'n

10.06 This case[9] was an action by California counties and cities seeking damages and other relief from fossil fuel companies for the rise in sea level. The action was against 32 fossil fuel companies to hold them accountable for climate deception and make them pay for damages they knowingly caused including increased flooding, sea level rise and coastal erosion.

Among the allegations were:

- that defendants went to great lengths to understand, and either knew or should have known, the dangers associated with their fossil fuel products;
- that, in contrast to their denial and downplaying of the risks of climate change in public, the defendants' internal actions demonstrated their awareness of, and intent to profit from, uses of fossil fuel products they knew were hazardous; and
- that the defendants' deceit only recently came to light, and that their misconduct was ongoing.

As result San Mateo County had suffered, is still suffering and will continue to suffer injuries from the defendants' tortious conduct from:

- sea level rise-related conditions and injuries;
- extreme precipitation and landslide-related conditions and injuries;
- extreme wildfires;
- drought-related conditions and injuries; and
- public health conditions and injuries.

In April 2023, the US Supreme Court denied fossil fuel industry defendants' petitions for writ of certiorari seeking review of decisions affirming remand orders that sent climate change cases brought by state and local governments back to state courts. The fossil fuel companies had asked the Court to consider whether there was federal jurisdiction over state-law claims seeking redress for injuries allegedly caused by the effects of interstate or transboundary GHG emissions on the global climate because federal common law necessarily governs such claims.

City of Oakland v BP plc

10.07 In this case[10] public nuisance actions were brought by the City of Oakland and the City of San Francisco against fossil fuel companies.

On 8 January 2021, fossil fuel companies filed a petition for writ of certiorari seeking review of the Ninth Circuit's May 2020[11] reversal of the district

9 *County of San Mateo v Chevron Corp'n*, 32 F.4th 733 (9th Cir. 2022), https://www.govinfo.gov/app/details/USCOURTS-ca9-18-15499

10 *City of Oakland v BP plc*, 969 F.3d 895 (9th Cir. 2020), https://climatecasechart.com/wp-content/uploads/case-documents/2023/20231127_docket-22-16810-22-16812_memorandum.pdf

11 Ninth Circuit May 2020: (3.17-cv-06011-WHA), https://climatecasechart.com/wp-content/uploads/case-documents/2020/20201110_docket-317-cv-06011_statement.pdf

court's 2018 denial[12] of Oakland's and San Francisco's motions to remand their climate change nuisance cases to California state court.

The petition requested that the court considered the questions of:

- whether putative state-law tort claims alleging harm from global climate change are removable because they arise under federal law; and
- whether a plaintiff is barred from challenging removal on appeal after curing any jurisdictional defect and litigating the case to final judgment.

In their brief opposing certiorari, the cities framed the questions presented as:

- whether a California state law public nuisance claim alleging wrongful and deceptive promotion of hazardous consumer goods 'arises under' a congressionally displaced body of federal common law regarding interstate air pollution for the purposes of removal jurisdiction; and
- whether the respondents waived their right to appeal an erroneously denied remand motion by filing an amended complaint to conform to that erroneous ruling while expressly preserving their appellate rights, and then opposing petitioners' motion to dismiss that amended complaint.

The cities' renewed motion for remand is pending in the district court, with the cities arguing against the companies' remaining grounds for removal: federal-officer removal, Outer Continental Shelf Lands Act, enclave jurisdiction, and bankruptcy removal. The cities have also filed a motion to amend their complaints to withdraw federal common law public nuisance claims that they added after the district court denied remand.

PUBLIC TRUST CLAIMS

Sierra Club v California Department of Water Resources: A 2024 filing

10.08 This case[13] involved a challenge to California Department of Water Resources' (DWR's) approval of the Delta Conveyance Project (DCP), which would divert water from the Sacramento River for export to southern areas of the state. Though the DCP was only recently approved by the DWR after completing the California Environmental Quality Act (CEQA) process, the DCP faced new obstacles to its implementation.

In August 2020, the DWR adopted three bond resolutions which would have authorised revenue bond financing as the mechanism to fund the DCP.

The DWR contended that the planning and construction of the Delta Program was within the authority granted to the Department by Water Code, § 11260 (last amended in 1959) to modify the Facility Response Plan (FRP), which, at

12 District Court 2018: (3.17-cv-06011-WHA), https://climatecasechart.com/wp-content/uploads/case-documents/2018/20180824_docket-317-cv-06011_notice-of-appeal.pdf

13 *Sierra Club v California Department of Water Resources* (24WM000008), https://climatecasechart.com/wp-content/uploads/case-documents/2024/20240119_docket-24WM000008_petition-for-writ-of-mandate.pdf

one time, included a Delta Cross Channel to move water from the Sacramento River to pumping facilities in the south delta. The Department argued that the Delta Program facilities would serve the same function as the facilities described in § 11260, as the facilities would be transporting water from the Feather River and Sacramento River to the south delta for export. The court held that the DWR's definition of the Delta Program ignores the scope of the FRP's objectives and could theoretically provide for the DWR to approve facilities that would serve purposes other than those set forth in the reports.

The court found that § 11260 does not delegate to the DWR the authority to adopt the bond resolutions and, as such, the DWR's actions exceeded the scope of its authority. Because the DWR lacks the authority to adopt the Delta Program as a 'modification' of the FRP unit, the court found that 'it necessarily follows that DWR lacks the authority to issue revenue bonds to finance the Delta Program'. In accordance with this holding, the court denied and dismissed the Department's Validation Action.

Other public trust cases

10.09

- *Neighbours for a True Oasis v Village of Port Washington North*:[14] a 2024 filing challenging a plan to sell a forested area for development (see **9.12**).
- *In re Hawai'i Electric Light Co*:[15] a 2023 filing that rejected a power purchase agreement for a biomass facility (see **9.12**).
- *Protect the Public's Trust v US Department of State*:[16] a Freedom of Information Act (FOIA) lawsuit seeking documents related to the Special Presidential Envoy for Climate (see **9.12**).

FREEDOM OF INFORMATION

Friends of the Earth v Council on Environmental Quality

10.10 In this case[17] a Freedom of Information Act (FOIA) lawsuit sought information related to the preparation of a US Department of the Interior report on federal oil and gas leasing, including the programmes' impacts on climate change.

14 *Neighbours for a True Oasis v Village of Port Washington North* (609509/2024) (a 2024 filing challenging a plan to sell a forested area for development), https://climatecasechart.com/wp-content/uploads/case-documents/2024/20240531_docket-6095092024_petition-1.pdf

15 *In re Hawai'i Electric Light Co* (SCOT-22-0000418) (a 2023 filing that rejected a power purchase agreement for a biomass facility), https://climatecasechart.com/wp-content/uploads/case-documents/2019/20190510_docket-SCOT-17-0000630_opinion.pdf

16 *Protect the Public's Trust v US Department of State* (1:22-cv-02231) (an FOIA lawsuit seeking documents related to the Special Presidential Envoy for Climate), https://climatecasechart.com/wp-content/uploads/case-documents/2022/20220323_docket-122-cv-00799_complaint.pdf

17 *Friends of the Earth v Council on Environmental Quality* (1:22-cv-01128), https://climatecasechart.com/wp-content/uploads/case-documents/2023/20231130_docket-122-cv-001128_stipulation.pdf

Friends of the Earth (FOE) filed an FOIA lawsuit against the Council on Environmental Quality (CEQ) to compel disclosure of information that FOE alleged might reveal 'potential political interference' in the preparation of a report by the US Department of Interior on federal oil and gas permitting and leasing practices, 'including potential climate and other impacts associated with oil and gas activities on public lands or in offshore waters'.

After the production of records, FOE agreed to a dismissal of the FOIA suit concerning the Biden Administration review of the federal oil and gas leasing programme. In January 2021 President Biden directed the US Department of the Interior to conduct a review of the federal oil and gas permitting and leasing programme and paused new oil and gas leasing pending completion of the review. The Secretary of the Interior was directed to consider whether to adjust royalties associated with extracted coal, oil, and gas resources or to take other action to account for corresponding climate costs.

In November 2023, the parties stated that the CEQ had issued a final response to FOE's FOIA request in January 2023 and that the parties had reached an agreement in principle after engaging in settlement discussions regarding the merits and attorneys' fees and costs since FOE completed its review of the records produced.

CLEAN AIR ACT

Massachusetts v Environmental Protection Agency

10.11 Massachusetts and several other states petitioned[18] the Environmental Protection Agency (EPA), asking the EPA to regulate emissions of carbon dioxide and other gases that contribute to global warming from new motor vehicles. Massachusetts argued that the EPA was required to regulate these GHGs by the Clean Air Act (CAA) – which states that Congress must regulate 'any air pollutant' that can 'reasonably be anticipated to endanger public health or welfare'.

The EPA denied the petition, claiming that the CAA does not authorise the Agency to regulate GHG emissions. Even if it did, the EPA argued, the Agency had discretion to defer a decision until more research could be done on 'the causes, extent and significance of climate change and the potential options for addressing it'. Massachusetts appealed the denial of the petition to the Court of Appeals for the DC Circuit, and a divided panel ruled in favour of the EPA.

In 2003, the EPA made two determinations:

- it lacked authority under the CAA to regulate carbon dioxide and other GHGs for climate change purposes; and
- even if it did have such authority, it would decline to set GHG emissions standards for vehicles.

18 *Massachusetts v Environmental Protection Agency*, 549 U.S. 497 (2007), https://supreme.justia.com/cases/federal/us/549/497/

The US Court of Appeals for the District of Columbia Circuit decided, in September 2005, to uphold the decision for the EPA. However, appellate judges were at odds in their reasoning for reaching the majority conclusion.

CLEAN WATER ACT

Sackett v Environmental Protection Agency

10.12 In this case[19] Michela and Chantell Sackett ran an excavation company that wanted to develop a property several hundred feet from Priest Lake, a popular vacation site in the Idaho Panhandle. Sackett began backfilling an Idaho lot with gravel to build a home. The EPA, in response to a neighbour's complaint, halted the work, informed Sackett that the property contained federally protected wetlands and that the backfilling violated the Clean Water Act (CWA), which prohibits discharging pollutants into 'the waters of the United States'.[20] The EPA ordered Sackett to remove the gravel and stop any further construction without a permit. The EPA threatened penalties of over $40,000 per day.

The EPA classified the Sackett wetlands as 'waters of the United States' because they were near a ditch that fed into a creek, which fed into Priest Lake, a navigable, intrastate lake.

The Sacketts sued in 2008 and the case made its way through the federal courts system for the next 14 years. The lawyers argued that the wetland the Sacketts had filled was not a protected 'water of the United States' merely because there was a dry land between it and other bodies of water and so wasn't subject to EPA regulation.

The Ninth Circuit affirmed summary judgment in favour of the EPA. However, the Supreme Court reversed this decision. Clean Water Act jurisdiction over an adjacent wetland requires that the adjacent body of water constitutes waters of the US (a relatively permanent body of water connected to traditional interstate navigable waters) and a continuous surface connection between the wetland and that water, making it difficult to determine where the 'water' ends and the 'wetland' begins.

19 *Sackett v EPA*, 598 U.S. 651 (2023) https://supreme.justia.com/cases/federal/us/598/21-454/
20 33 U.S.C. 1362(7).

Chapter 11

Climate Change Litigation Cases: Australia and New Zealand

AUSTRALIA

Net Zero Plan

11.01 This plan is to guide Australia's transition to net-zero greenhouse gas (GHG) emissions by 2050. It covers all major parts of the economy and establishes policies to reduce emissions. It articulates Australia's transition to net zero. The Plan ensures consistency with international and domestic commitments. It sets out government priorities, establishes policies and measures to drive down emissions and supports ongoing and new investment in low emissions and renewable activities.

Alongside the Net Zero Plan, the Australian Government has set an ambitious and achievable 2035 emissions reduction target. This means Australia is accelerating climate action, consistent with global peers.

The Net Zero Plan builds on the government's current emissions reduction policies – examples are below.

Safeguard Mechanism

11.02 This policy sets limits on GHG emissions from Australia's largest industrial facilities. The limits are designed to gradually decrease to help Australia achieve its emissions reduction targets.

The Safeguard Mechanism[1] commenced in 2016 and was reformed in 2023 to ensure that facilities covered by the mechanism contribute to meeting these targets. The reforms also help strengthen Australia's competitiveness as the world moves to net zero. The Safeguard Mechanism factsheet sets out the scheme's design settings, including the reforms.

82 per cent renewable electricity target

11.03 The Australian Government's Powering Australia plan aims to create jobs, reduce pressure on energy bills, and lower emissions by boosting renewable energy. The Australian Government's emissions reduction targets are 43 per cent by 2030 and net zero by 2050.

Capacity Investment Scheme

11.04 The Capacity Investment Scheme (CIS) is an Australian Government revenue underwriting scheme to accelerate investment in:

- renewable energy generation, such as wind and solar; and
- clean dispatchable capacity, such as battery storage.

1 Department of Climate Change, Energy, the Environment and Water, 'Safeguard mechanism', https://www.dcceew.gov.au/sites/default/files/documents/safeguard-mechanism-reforms-factsheet.pdf

The scheme provides a long-term revenue safety net that decreases financial risk for investors. This ensures more renewable energy projects get built.

New Vehicle Efficiency Standard

11.05 The Standard applies to new cars sold in the Australian market.

> 'The Standard will incentivise car companies to supply new cars that use less fuel per kilometre. Each vehicle manufacturer has a set average CO_2 target for the vehicles they produce, which they must meet or beat. Over time, the CO_2 target is lowered and in order to continue to meet or beat the target, companies must provide more choices of fuel-efficient, low or zero emissions vehicles.
>
> The target will be applied nationally on average. Suppliers can still sell any vehicle type they choose but they'll need to sell more fuel-efficient models to offset any less efficient models they sell. If suppliers meet or beat their target, they'll receive credits. If they sell more polluting cars than their target, they will have two years to either trade credits with a different supplier, or generate credits themselves, before a penalty becomes payable. For example, if a supplier is above the target in 2025, it will be able work in 2026 and 2027 to generate credits to offset this.'[2]

Mandatory climate reporting

11.06 This law requires large and medium-sized companies to disclose climate-related risks and opportunities, and GHG emissions. The largest companies must begin reporting in 2025.

From 1 January 2025, many large Australian businesses and financial institutions will be preparing annual sustainability reports containing mandatory climate-related financial disclosures, following the passage of a major bill through Parliament.

The Treasury Laws Amendment (Financial Market Infrastructure and Other Measures) Bill 2024 passed through Parliament on the 9 September 2024 and received Royal Assent on the 17 September 2024.

The mandatory climate reporting requirements will be phased in over the next three years across three groups of reporting entities, with the first reporting cohort required to prepare annual sustainability reports for the financial year commencing on or after 1 January 2025. The second and third reporting cohorts are required to prepare annual sustainability reports for the financial years commencing on or after 1 July 2026 and 1 July 2027 respectively.

2 Australian Government, Department of Infrastructure, Transport, Regional Development, Communications and the Arts, 'What is the New Vehicle Efficiency Standard (the Standard)?', https://www.infrastructure.gov.au/infrastructure-transport-vehicles/vehicles/new-vehicle-efficiency-standard/australias-new-vehicle-efficiency-standard-frequently-asked-questions#:~:text=through%20the%20Standard%3F-,What%20is%20the%20New%20Vehicle%20Efficiency%20Standard%20(the%20Standard)%3F,they%20must%20meet%20or%20beat

The Australian Securities and Investment Commission (ASIC) is urging all reporting entities, including those in the second and third reporting cohorts, to begin preparing for the new climate disclosure regime.

The ASIC's dedicated sustainability reporting page includes information regarding:

- the sustainability reporting obligations;
- its role in administering the regime;
- its approach to enforcement in the regime's early days; and
- its approach to relief and its forward work plan.

Reporting Entities	Group 1	Group 2	Group 3
Large entities and their controlled entities meeting at least two of three criteria	Consolidated revenue: $500 million or more End of financial year (EOFY) consolidated gross assets: $1 billion or more EOFY employees: 500 or more	Consolidated revenue: $200 million or more EOFY consolidated gross assets: $500 million or more EOFY employees: 250 or more	Consolidated revenue: $50 million or more EOFY consolidated gross assets: $25 million or more EOFY employees: 100 or more
National Greenhouse and Energy Reporting (NGER) Reporters	Above NGER publication threshold in s 13(1)(a) of the NGER Act 2007	All other NGER reporters	N/A
Registered schemes, Registrable Superannuation Entities and retail Corporate Collective Investment Vehicles	N/A	$5 billion assets under management or more	N/A

Climate Change Act 2022

11.07 This Act[3] outlines Australia's GHG emissions reduction targets and requires the minister to prepare an annual climate change statement.

The Act has three key functions:

- to set out Australia's GHG emissions reduction targets in domestic law (Part 2);

3 Climate Change Act 2022, https://www.legislation.gov.au/C2022A00037/latest/text

- to require annual ministerial statements to Parliament regarding climate change and progress towards achievement of emissions reduction targets (Part 3); and
- to provide advisory functions regarding these targets and statements to the Climate Change Authority (CCA) (Part 4).

Blue Carbon Conservation, Restoration and Accounting Program

11.08 This programme supports coastal blue carbon ecosystems[4] through conservation and restoration projects.

> 'Coastal blue carbon ecosystems provide essential breeding grounds for commercial fish, habitat for threatened marine species such as turtles and dugongs, feeding and staging grounds for migratory birds, and filter water flowing into ocean and reef systems. They play a vital role in food security and sustaining coastal livelihoods, including by supporting fishing and tourism.
>
> Coastal blue carbon ecosystems also provide a natural barrier that can reduce the impact of storm surges reducing coastal inundation, infrastructure damage and protecting coastal communities. Scientific assessments show that blue carbon ecosystems can store two to four times more carbon per hectare and sequester it 30-50 times faster than terrestrial forests, and thereby can make a significant contribution to global action on climate change. Blue carbon ecosystems are recognised as an important nature-based solution to climate change.
>
> Australia is considered a global "blue carbon hotspot". Australia harbours about 12 per cent of the World's blue carbon ecosystems, which hold about 5-11 per cent of global blue carbon stock. The seagrass meadows surrounding the coral reefs in the Great Barrier Reef alone host an estimated 11 per cent of the world's seagrass blue carbon.
>
> The Australian Government recognises the importance of blue carbon ecosystems for climate change mitigation and adaptation, protection of biodiversity and threatened species, disaster risk reduction and livelihoods of coastal communities.
>
> With a view to conserve and restore blue carbon ecosystems, the Australian Government is supporting research, on-ground restoration projects, capacity building and global partnerships through various initiatives.'

National Electric Vehicle Strategy

11.09 This strategy aims to increase the uptake of electric vehicles to reduce emissions.

> 'The Strategy sets out 3 key objectives:
>
> - increase the supply of affordable and accessible EVs
> - establish the resources, systems and infrastructure to enable rapid EV uptake
> - encourage increased EV demand.

4 Australian Government, Department of Climate Change, Energy, the Environment and Water, 'Coastal Blue Carbon Ecosystems', https://www.dcceew.gov.au/environment/marine/coastal-blue-carbon-ecosystems#:~:text=Australia%20leads%20the%20International%20Partnership,manage%20global%20blue%20carbon%20ecosystems

Implementing initiatives under the objectives will help us deliver the following outcomes:

- expand EV availability and choice
- reduce road transport emissions
- make it easy to charge EVs across Australia
- increase local manufacturing and recycling
- make EVs more affordable
- reduce the cost to Australians of running their vehicles.'[5]

Safeguard Mechanism

11.10 See **11.02**.

Powering Australia

11.11

'The Australian Government's Powering Australia plan is focused on creating jobs, reducing pressure on energy bills and reducing emissions by boosting renewable energy.

Powering Australia is a comprehensive plan with commitments on:

- National climate leadership
- Energy
- Industry, agriculture and carbon farming
- Transport'[6]

Emissions reduction incentives

11.12 There are a number of programmes and initiatives encouraging businesses, industries and consumers to reduce their emissions:

- the Australian Carbon Credit Unit (ACCU) scheme[7] aims to provide incentives for a range of organisations and individuals to adopt new practices and technologies to reduce their emissions and store carbon;
- Climate Active[8] encourages Australian businesses to become carbon neutral by awarding the Climate Active Carbon Neutral Standard certification;

5 Australian Government, Department of Climate Change, Energy, the Environment and Water, 'National Electric Vehicle Strategy', https://www.dcceew.gov.au/energy/transport/national-electric-vehicle-strategy#:~:text=Implementing%20initiatives%20under%20the%20objectives,reduce%20road%20transport%20emissions

6 Australian Government, Department of Climate Change, Energy, the Environment and Water, 'Australia's energy strategies and frameworks Powering Australia', https://www.dcceew.gov.au/energy/strategies-and-frameworks#:~:text=Powering%20Australia%20is%20a%20comprehensive,Industry%2C%20agriculture%20and%20carbon%20farming

7 Australian Government, Department of Climate Change, Energy, the Environment and Water, 'Australian Carbon Credit Unit (ACCU) scheme', https://www.dcceew.gov.au/climate-change/emissions-reduction/accu-scheme

8 Climate Active, https://www.climateactive.org.au

- the Renewable Energy Target (RET) scheme[9] reduces emissions by encouraging more electricity generation from renewable sources.

Annual Climate Change Statement

11.13 The Annual Climate Change Statement to Parliament provides a summary of the Australian Government's progress responding to climate change. It highlights achievements through the year and identifies areas for further action.

The statement includes:

- progress made towards achieving Australia's GHG emissions reduction targets;
- international developments relevant to addressing climate change;
- climate change policy developments;
- the effectiveness of policies to meet targets and reduce emissions, particularly the alignment of safeguard emissions with the safeguard outcomes;
- the impact of policies on rural and regional Australia;
- risks to Australia from climate change impacts, including to national security; and
- adaptation action.

Adapting to climate change

11.14

> 'While Australia works to limit future climate change through our Powering Australia plan and emissions reduction and reporting, we are also increasing the country's capacity to adapt to the climate crisis.
>
> - Roles and Responsibilities for Climate Change Adaptation in Australia 2012[10] outlines the responsibilities of each level of Australian government to plan and implement adaptation activities.
> - National Climate Resilience and Adaptation Strategy 2021 – 2025[11] outlines how the Australian Government will fulfil its 2012 COAG Roles and Responsibilities.'[12]

9 Australian Government, Department of Climate Change, Energy, the Environment and Water, 'Renewable Energy Target (RET) scheme', https://www.dcceew.gov.au/energy/renewable/target-scheme

10 Australian Government, Department of Climate Change, Energy, the Environment and Water, *Roles and Responsibilities for Climate Change Adaptation in Australia* (2012), https://www.dcceew.gov.au/sites/default/files/documents/coag-roles-respsonsibilities-climate-change-adaptation_0.pdf

11 Australian Government, Department of Climate Change, Energy, the Environment and Water, 'National Climate Resilience and Adaptation Strategy 2021 – 2025', https://www.dcceew.gov.au/climate-change/policy/adaptation/strategy

12 Australian Government, Department of Climate Change, Energy, the Environment and Water, 'Australia's climate change strategies', https://www.dcceew.gov.au/climate-change/strategies

Climate change agencies

11.15 There are a number of agencies, organisations and partnerships working on climate change initiatives in Australia:

- the Australian Energy Infrastructure Commissioner[13] manages complaints about wind farms, large-scale solar farms, energy storage facilities and new major transmission projects;
- the Australian Renewable Energy Agency (ARENA)[14] finances low-emissions technology and renewable energy projects;
- the Commonwealth Scientific Industrial Research Organisation (CSIRO)[15] uses climate simulations to project future climate;
- the Clean Energy Finance Corporation (CEFC)[16] finances clean energy projects;
- the Clean Energy Regulator[17] administers the National Greenhouse Energy Reporting (NGER), Emission Reduction Fund (ERF), and Renewable Energy Target (RET) schemes;
- the Climate Change Authority[18] advises the government on Australia's climate change policies and future emissions reduction targets;
- the Bureau of Meteorology[19] monitors, analyses and communicates observed and future changes in Australia's climate; and
- the Australian Climate Service[20] works across Australian government agencies to develop climate information to support better planning and preparedness for climate and natural hazards.

Climate change cases

Investor or activist led

11.16 These (including funded) claims are designed not to extract compensation, but to obtain declaratory and injunctive relief in an effort to change corporate, government and boardroom behaviour.

O'Donnell v Commonwealth of Australia

In this case[21] Equity Generation Lawyers filed a lawsuit in the Federal Court on behalf of Kathleen (Katta) O'Donnell against the Australian Government. The lawsuit alleged that Australia's economy and reputation in international financial markets would be significantly affected by the adequacy of the

13 Australian Energy Infrastructure Commissioner, https://www.aeic.gov.au
14 Australian Renewable Energy Agency (ARENA), https://arena.gov.au
15 Commonwealth Scientific Industrial Research Organisation (CSIRO), https://www.csiro.au
16 Clean Energy Finance Corporation (CEFC), https://www.cefc.com.au
17 Clean Energy Regulator, https://cer.gov.au
18 Climate Change Authority, https://www.climatechangeauthority.gov.au
19 Bureau of Meteorology, http://www.bom.gov.au
20 Australian Climate Service, https://www.acs.gov.au
21 *O'Donnell v Commonwealth of Australia* (Federal Court of Australia, Proceeding No. VID482/2020) [2021] FCA 1223, https://climatecasechart.com/wp-content/uploads/non-us-case-documents/2021/20211008_Case-number-VID4822020-Judgment-citation-2021-FCA-1223_judgment-1.pdf

Australian Government's response to climate change, and, as a result, investors who trade in Australian government bonds faced material risks from climate change that should be disclosed. The lawsuit also alleged that the government has misled or deceived investors and continued to mislead or deceive investors in failing to disclose such risks.

Ms O'Donnell, in the class action, represented all retail bondholders who, during the period 7 July 2020 and 20 December 2022, acquired, and continued to hold, one or more units of Australian:

- exchange-traded Treasury Indexed Bonds (eTIB) maturing in 2050 with ASX code GSIC50; and
- exchange-traded Treasury Bonds (eTB) maturing in 2047 with ASX code GSBE47.

Sovereign bonds are issued by nation states to fund government expenditure and the Commonwealth raises debt through a wholesale market for Australian Government Bonds, in which financial institutions participate. Retail investors, like Ms O'Donnell, participate indirectly in the wholesale market for Australian Government Bonds by obtaining 'depository interests' of wholesale bonds. Those depositary interests are traded on the Australian Securities Exchange (ASX). The prices for retail and wholesale bonds are linked.

On 11 March 2021 the Commonwealth filed an application to strike out Ms O'Donnell's claim.

The court permitted the claim in misleading or deceptive conduct to proceed and refused the Commonwealth's application to disband the class action. Ms O'Donnell's claims for a duty of disclosure and against Commonwealth officials were struck out.

The decision sets out details of the applicant's claim, including the allegations that:

- physical and transitional risks from climate change are material risks for bondholders;
- transitional risks will be exacerbated the longer Australia takes to commit to a net-zero emissions target and the longer it takes to implement effective measures to reach net zero; and
- not disclosing climate change risks to bond investors is misleading or deceptive under Australian Securities and Investments Commission Act 2001, s 12DA.

On 7 August 2023, the parties informed the court that, subject to the court's approval, they had agreed to settle the proceeding in terms set out in a Heads of Agreement.

McVeigh v Retail Employees Superannuation Pty Ltd

11.17 In this case[22] the parties reached a settlement where the Australian pension fund agreed to incorporate climate change financial risks in its

22 *McVeigh v Retail Employees Superannuation Pty Ltd* [2019] FCA 14, https://climatecasechart.com/wp-content/uploads/non-us-case-documents/2019/20190117_NSD13332018_judgment.pdf

investments and implement a net-zero by 2050 carbon footprint goal. The case was about Mr McVeigh's action relating to climate change risk assessment and discourse obligations against one of Australia's largest superannuation funds, the Retail Employees Superannuation Trust (Rest).

Mr McVeigh (a member, beneficiary and financial contributor to the Rest fund), claimed that Rest had breached its obligations under the Superannuation Guarantee (Administration) Act 1992 and the Corporations Act 2001 with regard to its management and disclosure of climate change-related business risks.

Mr McVeigh had made requests for information from Rest in August 2017 regarding Rest's knowledge and opinion of its climate change business risks (including both the physical impacts and transitional impacts of climate change), and the actions taken by Rest to respond to such risks. While some information was provided by Rest to McVeigh, it was alleged that this was insufficient to allow him to understand or make an informed judgement about the management and financial condition of Rest, or its investment performance.

The matter did not proceed to trial, but Rest made a number of important acknowledgements in its public statement on 2 November 2020.[23] Other Australian superannuation funds (and other managed funds globally) are likely to follow this or risk facing a similar action by their members or other key stakeholders.

Regulatory prosecution

11.18 These are claims relating to the accuracy of reporting of environmental credentials and/or plans to achieve emissions targets

Minister for Environment v Sharma

11.19 In September 2020, eight young people filed a class action in Australia's Federal Court to block a coal project. The lawsuit sought an injunction to stop the Australian Government from approving an extension of the Whitehaven Vickery coal mine. The plaintiffs claimed to represent all people under 18 and argued that Federal Minister Sussan Ley has a common law duty of care for young people. They further said that digging up and burning coal would exacerbate climate change and harm young people in the future. The plaintiffs sought an injunction to prevent the Minister from approving the project under the Environment Protection and Biodiversity Conservation Act 1999 (EPBC).

The appeal[24] concerns the orders made by the primary judge declaring that the Commonwealth Minister for the Environment had a duty of care at common law when exercising her power under EPBC Act 1999, ss 130 and 133 to consider and approve an extension of a coal mine in New South Wales.

23 Rest, 'Rest reaches settlement with Mark McVeigh' (2 November 2020), https://rest.com.au/why-rest/about-rest/news/rest-reaches-settlement-with-mark-mcveigh

24 *Minister for the Environment v Sharma* [2022] FCAFC 65, https://climatecasechart.com/wp-content/uploads/non-us-case-documents/2022/20220422_VID-389-of-2021-2021-FCA-560-2021-FCA-774-2022-FCAFC-35-2022-FCAFC-65_judgment.pdf

The Chief Justice was of the view that the duty should not be imposed for a number of reasons:

- the content and scope of the duty would call forth at the point of assessment of breach the need to re-evaluate, change or maintain high public policy, the assessment of which is unsuited to decision by the judicial branch in private litigation;
- the imposition would be inconsistent with the decision-making in question under the EPBC Act 1999 according to its terms, as understood in its context as part of Commonwealth and State responsibilities for the protection of the environment; and
- taken in conjunction with these two matters, the lack of control over the harm (as distinct from over the tiny contribution to the overall risk of damage from climate change), a lack of special vulnerability in the legal sense, the indeterminacy of liability and the lack of proportionality between the tiny increase in risk and lack of control and liability for all damage by heatwaves, bushfires and rising sea levels to all Australians under the age of 18, ongoing into the future, mean that the duty in tort should not be imposed.

The plaintiffs announced that they would not appeal the decision and asked the court to make orders that the proceeding not continue as a representative proceeding.

Challenges to government authorisations

11.20 These cases relate to energy and resources projects, alleging unacceptable climate change, Aboriginal cultural heritage, and human rights impacts.

Cooper v National Offshore Petroleum Safety and Environmental Management Authority (NOPSEMA)

11.21 In this case[25] Mardudhunera Traditional Custodian, Raelene Cooper, represented by the Environmental Defenders' Office, filed a case in the Federal Court of Australia seeking judicial review of the NOPSEMA's decision to approve Woodside's application to carry out seismic blasting for the Scarborough Gas Project. Woodside said that they were ready to begin seismic blasting, this was despite objections from Traditional Custodians that they had not been consulted.

Despite finding that Woodside's consultation with First Nations stakeholders was inadequate, the NOPSEMA gave approval for the testing on 31 July.

> 'Conditions were attached to the approval that further consultation needed to be carried out before commencement of the blasting. Ms Cooper argues that NOPSEMA cannot grant the approval until she has been properly consulted; and alternatively that Woodside cannot begin seismic testing until Woodside has

25 *Cooper v National Offshore Petroleum Safety and Environmental Management Authority (No 2)* [2023] FCA 1158, https://www.judgments.fedcourt.gov.au/judgments/Judgments/fca/single/2023/2023fca1158

> consulted with her, as required under the conditions of Woodside's approval from NOPSEMA.'

On 14 September, an interim injunction was granted until 28 September and the hearing of the matter was brought forward to later in September.

Munkara v Santos NA Barossa Pty Ltd

11.22 In this case[26] a member of the Jikilaruwu clan, filed proceedings and applied for an urgent injunction to prevent Santos commencing pipeline work on the Barossa gas project. The Tiwi Traditional Owner argued that Santos had not properly assessed submerged cultural heritage along the route of its Barossa export pipeline. On 15 January 2024, the judge dismissed the case.

In this case the Federal Court set the standard of proof required to support an assertion as to whether a particular project was likely to cause a significant risk to Aboriginal cultural heritage. A number of significant findings were made about the evidence that would be required to establish the existence of intangible Aboriginal cultural heritage such as Dreaming stories and songlines, and the extent to which that intangible heritage was likely to be harmed by a proposed development.

In determining whether the pipeline posed a 'significant' risk to 'cultural heritage', it was necessary to look at the degree of chance of impact to the cultural heritage and the nature or the gravity of that impact. Therefore, the test for a significant risk is one about sufficiency requiring the injunction applicant to demonstrate a risk of significant adverse impact upon the cultural heritage. The burden of proof falls on the party seeking to assert the risk, the Tiwi Islanders had to establish that, on the balance of probabilities, the pipeline posed a risk to cultural heritage, that being an impact that was both significant and new, which could be one involving mathematical chance of less than 50 per cent.

The judge said:

> '55. Regulation 11A requires an operator to consult with a range of Commonwealth, State or Northern Territory Departments and agencies to which the activities to be carried out under the environment plan, or revision of the environment plan, may be relevant. Also to be consulted are persons or organisations whose functions, interests or activities may be affected by the activities. In addition, the operator is required to consult the Department of the responsible State Minister or responsible Northern Territory Minister, as applicable, and any other person or organisation that the operator considers relevant. The operator is required to give each such person ("relevant person") sufficient information to allow the person to make an informed assessment of the possible consequences of the activity on the functions, interests or activities of the person. (Note that NOPSEMA will have to make an assessment of the sufficiency of the information in each case.)'

It was not sufficient to prove that the cultural features 'may exist' or that the Tiwi Islanders 'might have' a spiritual connection to sea country, or beliefs in song lines and Dreamings. The Federal Court held that the existence of such

26 *Munkara v Santos NA Barossa Pty Ltd (No 5)* [2024] FCA 717, https://www.judgments.fedcourt.gov.au/judgments/Judgments/fca/single/2024/2024fca0717

burial grounds was found to have no more than a negligible chance of existing, and therefore they were incapable of forming a cultural heritage risk. There was also insufficient evidence to prove that the Tiwi Islanders, as a people, held a communal belief that extended to two spirits in the vicinity of the pipeline route. Therefore, as there was no proof that the cultural features existed, there was no cultural heritage risk posed by the pipeline.

Greenwashing

Australasian Centre for Corporate Responsibility v Santos Ltd

11.23 In this case[27] the Australasian Centre for Corporate Responsibility (ACCR) made greenwashing claims against Santos Ltd.

In August 2021, the ACCR[28] commenced proceedings in the Federal Court alleging Santos Ltd had breached the Corporations Act 2001 and the Australian Competition and Consumer Act[29] by engaging in misleading or deceptive conduct relating to representations contained in its 2020 Annual Report.

In August 2022, the ACCR amended its case to include alleged greenwashing in Santos Ltd's *2020 Investor Day Briefing*[30] and *Australia State of the Environment Climate Report*,[31] following additional information produced by Santos Ltd in the litigation discovery process.

The representations concerned three major areas:

- representations that Santos Ltd had a clear and credible pathway to:
  - reduce its Scope 1 and 2 GHG emissions by 26–30 per cent by 2030 (from its 2019–20 baseline);
  - achieve 'net-zero' Scope 1 and 2 GHG emissions by 2040;
- representations that Santos Ltd is a producer of 'clean energy', and that natural gas is a 'clean fuel'; and
- representations that hydrogen produced from natural gas with carbon capture and storage (blue hydrogen) is 'clean' and 'zero emission'.

The ACCR asked the Federal Court to:

1. make declarations that Santos Ltd had engaged in misleading or deceptive conduct, or conduct that was likely to mislead or deceive;
2. grant an injunction prohibiting Santos Ltd from engaging in the same misleading or deceptive conduct in the future; and
3. grant an injunction requiring Santos Ltd to issue a corrective statement regarding the environmental impacts of its operations.

27 *Australasian Centre for Corporate Responsibility v Santos Ltd* (Federal Court of Australia, Proceeding No. NSD858/2021).

28 ACCR, 'Greenwashing Proceedings in Federal Court' (24 October 2024), https://www.accr.org.au/news/greenwashing-proceedings-in-federal-court/

29 Australian Competition and Consumer Act, https://consumer.gov.au/legislation/current-legislation

30 Santos Ltd, *Investor day briefing 2020*, https://www.santos.com/wp-content/uploads/2020/12/2020-Investor-Day-FINAL.pdf

31 Australian Government, Department of Climate Change, Energy, the Environment and Water, *Australia State of the Environment Climate Report*, https://soe.dcceew.gov.au/sites/default/files/2022-07/soe2021-climate.pdf

Australian Securities and Investments Commission v LGSS Pty Ltd

11.24 In this case[32] the Federal Court found that LGSS Pty Ltd, as trustee of the superannuation fund Active Super, contravened the law in connection with various misleading representations concerning its environmental, social and governance (ESG) credentials.

Active Super had claimed in its marketing that it eliminated investments that posed too great a risk to the environment and the community, including gambling, coal mining and oil tar sands. Following the invasion of Ukraine, Active Super also made representations that Russian investments were 'out'.

The Federal Court found that, from 1 February 2021 to 30 June 2023, Active Super invested in various securities that it had claimed were eliminated or restricted by ESG investment screens. These securities were held by Active Super both directly and indirectly (via managed funds or Exchange Traded Funds (ETFs)).

The judge rejected Active Super's claims that an ordinary or reasonable consumer would draw a distinction between holding shares in a company and indirect exposures through a pooled fund.

The judge found that the use of the terms such as such as 'not invest', 'No Way' and 'eliminate' were unequivocal and not the subject of any potential qualifications under LGSS's 'Sustainable and Responsible Investment Policy'.

At the time of publishing these representations, Active Super held direct and indirect investments in companies such as:

- SkyCity Entertainment Group Ltd and Pointsbet Holdings Ltd (gambling);
- Gazprom PJSC and Sberbank of Russia (Russian entities);
- ConocoPhillips and Shell Plc (oil tar sands); and
- Whitehaven Coal Ltd (see **6.17**) and Coronado Global Resources (coal mining).

The matter has been listed for a further hearing to consider the appropriate form of declaratory relief and the court will consider the pecuniary penalty to impose for the conduct at a later date.

Torres Strait Islanders Petition

11.25 In this case[33] the Indigenous peoples of the Torres Strait Islands brought a petition against Australia for violations of the International Covenant on Civil and Political Rights (ICCPR).[34] This provides people worldwide with an important avenue for redress of violations of human rights related to climate

32 *Australian Securities and Investments Commission v LGSS Pty Ltd* [2024] FCA 587, https://download.asic.gov.au/media/ticl0q1b/24-121mr-asic-v-lgss-pty-ltd-2024-fca-587.pdf

33 *Daniel Billy and Others v Australia (Torres Strait Islanders Petition)* (CCPR/C/135/D/3624/2019), https://climatecasechart.com/wp-content/uploads/non-us-case-documents/2019/20190513_CCPRC135D36242019_complaint.pdf

34 International Covenant on Civil and Political Rights (ICCPR), General Assembly Resolution 2200A (XXI), https://www.ohchr.org/en/instruments-mechanisms/instruments/international-covenant-civil-and-political-rights

change. They argued that Australia's insufficient climate action violated their human rights under ICCPR Articles:

- 6 (right to life);
- 17 (right to private, family and home life);
- 24(1) (right of the child to protective measures); and
- 27 (right to culture).

The eight Torres Strait Islanders were Indigenous inhabitants of Boigu, Poruma, Warraber and Masig, four small low-lying islands in Australia. The Torres Strait Islands are a group of over 100 islands off the northern tip of Queensland, between Australia and Papua New Guinea. They are home to a diverse Indigenous population comprised of over 7,000 people in 19 communities across 16 of the islands. Each community is distinct, with their own traditions, laws, and customs.

This was the first legal action grounded in human rights brought by climate-vulnerable inhabitants of low-lying islands against a nation state and alleged that Australia's insufficient climate action had violated their fundamental human rights under the ICCPR.

The Islanders argued that these violations stemmed from insufficient climate mitigation targets, as well as a general failure to cease to promotion of fossil fuel extraction and use. The Islanders also argued that the state had failed to adopt adaptation measures, despite numerous requests for assistance and funding by or on behalf of the Islanders.

The United Nations Human Rights Committee asked Australia to compensate the Indigenous Islanders for the harm suffered, engage in meaningful consultations with their communities to assess their needs, and take all necessary measures to continue to secure the communities' safe existence on their respective islands.

NEW ZEALAND

Climate Change Response Act 2002

11.26 This Act puts in place a legal framework to enable New Zealand to meet its international obligations under the United Nations Framework Convention on Climate Change, the Kyoto Protocol and the Paris Agreement.

The Act includes powers for the Minister of Finance to manage New Zealand's holdings of units that represent New Zealand's target allocation for GHG emissions under the Protocol. It enables the Minister to trade those units on the international market. It establishes a registry to record holdings and transfers of units. The Act also establishes a national inventory agency to record and report information relating to GHG emissions in accordance with international requirements.

In 2019, the Act was amended by the Climate Change Response (Zero Carbon) Amendment Act 2019. These amendments provide a framework by which

New Zealand can develop and implement clear and stable climate change policies that:

- contribute to the global effort under the Paris Agreement to limit the global average temperature increase to 1.5°C above pre-industrial levels; and
- allow New Zealand to prepare for, and adapt to, the effects of climate change.

This Act is administered by the Ministry for the Environment.

There are also regulations which are made under the Act:

- Climate Change (Agriculture Sector) Regulations 2010[35]
- Climate Change (Eligible Industrial Activities) Regulations 2010[36]
- Climate Change (Emissions Rulings: Fees and Charges) Regulations 2010[37]
- Climate Change (Forestry Sector) Regulations 2008[38]
- Climate Change (Liquid Fossil Fuels) Regulations 2008[39]
- Climate Change (Other Removal Activities) Regulations 2009[40]
- Climate Change (Stationary Energy and Industrial Processes) Regulations 2009[41]
- Climate Change (Synthetic Greenhouse Gas Levies) Regulations 2013[42]
- Climate Change (Unique Emissions Factors) Regulations 2009[43]
- Climate Change (Unit Register) Regulations 2008[44]
- Climate Change (Waste) Regulations 2010[45]

35 Climate Change (Agriculture Sector) Regulations 2010 SR 2010/335), https://www.legislation.govt.nz/regulation/public/2010/0335/latest/DLM3253001.html?search=ts_regulation%40deemedreg_climate+change_resel_25_a&p=1
36 Climate Change (Eligible Industrial Activities) Regulations 2010 (SR 2010/189), https://www.legislation.govt.nz/regulation/public/2010/0189/latest/DLM3075101.html?search=ts_regulation%40deemedreg_climate+changeresel_25_a&p=1
37 Climate Change (Emissions Rulings: Fees and Charges) Regulations 2010 (SR 2010/213), https://www.legislation.govt.nz/regulation/public/2010/0213/latest/DLM3087506.html?search=ts_regulation%40deemedreg_climate+change_resel_25_a&p=1
38 Climate Change (Forestry Sector) Regulations 2008 (SR 2008/355), https://www.legislation.govt.nz/regulation/public/2008/0355/latest/DLM1633759.html?search=ts_regulation%40deemedreg_climate+change_resel_25_a&p=1
39 Climate Change (Liquid Fossil Fuels) Regulations 2008 (SR 2008/356), https://www.legislation.govt.nz/regulation/public/2008/0356/latest/DLM1635601.html?search=ts_regulation%40deemedreg_climate+change_resel_25_a&p=1
40 Climate Change (Other Removal Activities) Regulations 2009 (SR 2009/284), https://www.legislation.govt.nz/regulation/public/2009/0284/latest/DLM2381201.html?search=ts_regulation%40deemedreg_climate+change_resel_25_a&p=1
41 Climate Change (Stationary Energy and Industrial Processes) Regulations 2009 (SR 2009/285), https://www.legislation.govt.nz/regulation/public/2009/0285/latest/DLM2394207.html?search=ts_regulation%40deemedreg_climate+change_resel_25_a&p=1
42 Climate Change (Synthetic Greenhouse Gas Levies) Regulations 2013 (SR 2013/46), https://www.legislation.govt.nz/regulation/public/2013/0046/latest/DLM5093451.html?search=ts_regulation%40deemedreg_climate+change_resel_25_a&p=1
43 Climate Change (Unique Emissions Factors) Regulations 2009 (SR 2009/286), https://www.legislation.govt.nz/regulation/public/2009/0286/latest/DLM2378401.html?search=ts_regulation%40deemedreg_climate+change_resel_25_a&p=1
44 Climate Change (Unit Register) Regulations 2008 (SR 2008/357), https://www.legislation.govt.nz/regulation/public/2008/0357/latest/DLM1634227.html?search=ts_regulation%40deemedreg_climate+change_resel_25_a&p=1
45 Climate Change (Waste) Regulations 2010 (SR 2010/338), https://www.legislation.govt.nz/regulation/public/2010/0338/latest/DLM3249508.html?search=ts_regulation%40deemedreg_climate+change_resel_25_a&p=1

Climate Change Response (Zero Carbon) Amendment Act 2019

11.27 The amendments brought in by the Act do four key things:

- set a new domestic GHG emissions reduction target for New Zealand to:
  - — reduce net emissions of all greenhouse gases (except biogenic methane) to zero by 2050;
  - — reduce emissions of biogenic methane to 24–47 per cent below 2017 levels by 2050, including to 10 per cent below 2017 levels by 2030;
- establish a system of emissions budgets to act as stepping stones towards the long-term target;
- require the government to develop and implement policies for climate change adaptation and mitigation; and
- establish a new, independent Climate Change Commission to provide expert advice and monitoring to help keep successive governments on track to meeting long-term goals.

Climate Change (Auctions, Limits, and Price Controls for Units) Regulations 2020

11.28 The Regulations[46] help New Zealand meet its:

- 2050 emissions target; and
- emissions targets under the Paris Agreement.

The Regulations also provide for auctions to sell New Zealand units by setting out the schedule and rules for auctions.

Climate change cases

Lawyers for Climate Action NZ Inc v Climate Change Commission

11.29 In this case[47] the Climate Change Response Act 2002 (as amended in 2019) which sets a goal of net-zero emissions by 2050 and creates a Climate Change Commission to provide periodic advice to the government in meeting that goal, was challenged when, on the 1 July 2021, a group of hundreds of New Zealand lawyers sued the country's Climate Change Commission and the Minister for Climate Change, James Shaw, arguing that several pieces of advice provided by the Climate Change Commission had violated New Zealand administrative law.

The proceedings concerned the Commission's recommended emissions budgets and its advice to the Minister on New Zealand's Nationally Determined

46 Climate Change (Auctions, Limits, and Price Controls for Units) Regulations 2020 (LI 2020/264) https://www.legislation.govt.nz/regulation/public/2020/0264/latest/LMS375230.html

47 *Lawyers for Climate Action NZ Inc. v Climate Change Commission* [2022] NZHC 3064, https://climatecasechart.com/wp-content/uploads/non-us-case-documents/2022/20221123_2022-NZHC-3064_judgment.pdf

Contributions (NDCs) under the Paris Agreement and the United Nations Framework Convention on Climate Change.

In the claim they alleged that the Commission made legal and logical errors, which resulted in advice that was irrational, unreasonable and inconsistent with the purpose of the Climate Change Response Act 2002. They specifically argued that it:

- used incorrect measures to calculate reductions;
- incorrectly prioritised considerations;
- adopted an incorrect carbon accounting method; and
- incorrectly allowed for offshore mitigation.

Following agreement between the parties, the court ordered that the Amendment Regulations be reconsidered to ensure that, as per the principal Act, they were:

- in accordance with New Zealand's 2050 target; and
- strictly in accordance with New Zealand's emissions budgets and NDC, or alternatively, in accordance with them, with discrepancies justified by matters set out in the principal Act.

The Minister had to reconsider the Amendment Regulations by the 30 September 2023.

Smith v Fonterra Cooperative Group Ltd and Others

11.30 In this case[48] Michael Smith brought tort claims against New Zealand's seven largest GHG emitters, collectively responsible for one-third of all New Zealand's GHGs. He argued their activities amounted to torts of public nuisance, negligence and a novel climate duty. Smith further argued that these emissions affected him personally. As a Māori leader with an interest in customary land, Smith argued that the defendants' actions would harm him through impacts related to rising sea levels, loss of sites of cultural and spiritual significance, damage to fisheries and adverse health impacts. Smith asked the court to issue declarations against the defendants, and to require them to reduce emissions. Notably, Smith did not seek damages. His case was against: Fonterra Cooperative Group Ltd, Genesis Energy Ltd, Dairy Holdings Ltd, New Zealand Steel Ltd, Z Energy Ltd, Channel Infrastructure NZ Ltd and BT Mining.

The claimant brought claims in:

- public nuisance;
- negligence; and
- a new climate change duty.

The claimant brought the claim both as an individual who is impacted by climate change and in his capacity as a community elder who was representing vulnerable Māori living in coastal areas of New Zealand. The defendants were seven significant GHG emitters across a range of sectors although, as

48 *Smith v Fonterra Cooperative Group Ltd and Others* [2024] NZSC 5, https://www.courtsofnz.govt.nz/assets/cases/2024/2024-NZSC-5.pdf

the claimant acknowledged, there was no principled basis for singling out the seven defendants in particular.

The New Zealand High Court declined to strike the claim out on the basis that the defendants may have breached an 'inchoate' climate change duty of care. The New Zealand Court of Appeal struck out the claim on the basis that it was inconsistent with fundamental principles of New Zealand (and English) common law

However, the Supreme Court allowed Mr Smith's claims in these three areas to proceed to trial.

The Supreme Court was only considering whether the claims should be struck out and emphasised that 'a refusal to strike out a cause of action is not a commentary on whether or not the claim ultimately will succeed'.

Students for Climate Solutions Inc v Minister of Energy and Resources

11.31 In this case[49] in 2021, Students for Climate Solutions brought a case against the Minister of Energy and Resources. They argued that the defendant Minister, in granting petroleum exploration permits under the Crown Minerals Act (CMA) 1991, had failed to adequately consider the effects of the exploration on climate change. Specifically, the plaintiff claimed that:

- climate change was a mandatory relevant consideration for the purposes of New Zealand administrative law; and
- that the failure to consider climate change rendered the decision unreasonable and that the Minister had failed to have proper regard for the Treaty of Waitangi, New Zealand's founding document.

They were unsuccessful in the Court of Appeal challenging the decision of the Minster of Energy and Resources to grant two permits under the petroleum exploration permits in Taranaki under CMA 1991, s 25(1). They argued that the decision to grant the permits was unlawful because the Minister had failed to consider the climate change implications of the decision, as required either as a mandatory relevant consideration or to have proper regard to the principles of the Treaty of Waitangilte Tiriti o Waitangi.

The Court unanimously rejected the challenge on the 7 May 2024, the majority observing that climate change was not an explicit consideration listed under the factors the Minister was required to consider under CMA 1991, s 29A and it further rejected the Students for Climate Solutions' argument that climate change considerations were impliedly required by the Act's purpose, relying instead on the CMA 1991's legislative history to determine that the Act was intended to:

- support mineral exploration and mining for New Zealand's economic benefit; and

49 *Students for Climate Solutions Inc v Minister of Energy and Resources* [2024] NZCA 152, https://climatecasechart.com/non-us-case/students-for-climate-solutions-inc-v-minister-of-energy-and-resources/

- allow for petroleum exploration in the Taranaki region in the interests of facilitating a 'just transition'.

While the Court acknowledged the seriousness of climate change, it found that climate change implications were not a mandatory relevant consideration under the CMA 1991. The Court considered that the purpose of the CMA 1991 was focused on mining for the economic 'benefit of New Zealand'. In reaching this conclusion, the Court noted that it 'cannot strain legislation to the point that it no longer gives effect to Parliament's intention'.

Chapter 12

Climate Change Litigation Cases: China, India, Brazil and the African Nations

CHINA

Carbon Neutrality Goal

12.01 In June 2015, Premier Li Keqiang of the People's Republic of China, on a visit to France, announced that China's carbon dioxide (CO_2) emissions would peak around 2030. In September 2022 President Xi Jinping proposed a goal to become carbon neutral by 2060. China therefore aims to achieve carbon neutrality by 2060 and peak carbon emissions before 2030. The country is investing heavily in renewable energy, particularly solar and wind, becoming a global leader in the production of clean energy technologies.

China's Achievements, New Goals and Measures for Nationally Determined Contributions is published in English on the United Nations website.[1]

1 *China's Achievements, New Goals and New Measures for Nationally Determined Contributions*, https://unfccc.int/sites/default/files/NDC/2022-06/China's%20Achievements%2C%20New%20Goals%20and%20New%20Measures%20for%20Nationally%20Determined%20Contributions.pdf

In March 2021 the early government work report[2] highlighted the importance for China of achieving carbon neutrality, indicating that China has made this an important objective next to others:

> 'In a bid to make the urgently needed improvements to the legal systems for people's wellbeing, education and culture, social governance, environmental protection, and green and low-carbon development, we will formulate an anti-food waste law, a law for the promotion of the cultural industry, a family education law, a preschool education law, a personal information protection law, a social assistance law, a legal aid law, a law for the protection of wetlands, and a law on activities and environmental protection in Antarctica. We will revise the Sports Law, the Education Law, the Vocational Education Law, the Law on the Protection of the Rights and Interests of Women, the Public Security Administrative Penalty Law, the Law on Administrative Review, and the Law on the Prevention and Control of Environmental Noise Pollution. We will speed up legislative work on the protection of the Yellow River. We will waste no time in researching laws and regulations relating to new technologies and applications such as those in the areas of the digital economy, internet finance, artificial intelligence, big data, and cloud computing, so as to ensure that the law both promotes and protects the healthy development of new business forms and models.'

Five-Year Plans

12.02 The 14th Five-Year Plan[3] emphasises reducing carbon intensity (emissions per unit of GDP) and increasing the proportion of non-fossil fuels in the energy mix.

> **'Article XXVIII Continue to improve environmental quality**
>
> We will deepen the fight for pollution prevention and control, establish a sound environmental governance system, promote accurate, scientific, legal, and systematic pollution control, promote pollution reduction and carbon reduction in a coordinated manner, continuously improve the quality of the air and water environment, and effectively control the risks of soil pollution.'

Lawsuits concerning climate change

Beijing Grassland Alliance Environmental Protection Center v Xingyi Shangcheng Power Generation Co Ltd

12.03 In this case,[4] Beijing Grassland Alliance Environmental Protection Center, supported by three other non-governmental organisations (NGOs), sued Xingyi Shangcheng Power Generation Co Ltd.

2 *Report on the Work of the Standing Committee of the National People's Congress* (2021), https://npcobserver.com/wp-content/uploads/2020/11/NPCSC-2021-Work-Report_Eng.pdf

3 *Outline of the People's Republic of China of China's 14th Five-Year Plan for Economic and Social Development and Long-Range Objectives for 2035* (2021), https://cset.georgetown.edu/wp-content/uploads/t0284_14th_Five_Year_Plan_EN.pdf

4 *Beijing Grassland Alliance Environmental Protection Center v Xingyi Shangcheng Power Generation Co Ltd* (unreported), https://climatecasechart.com/non-us-case/beijing-grassland-alliance-environmental-protection-center-v-xingyi-shangcheng-power-generation-company-limited/

There were eight demands, focusing on three key issues:

- **Environmental damages:** The defendant was accused of engaging in long-term practices that included:
  - — emitting waste gas, dust, and key pollutants above standard levels;
  - — tampering with or forging pollution monitoring data; and
  - — failing to maintain automatic monitoring equipment.
- **Carbon emissions:** It was alleged that the defendant exceeded the permissible limits for CO_2 emissions and the court was asked to evaluate the atmospheric damage caused by these excessive emissions and that the defendant was to be held accountable for the ecological damage and to provide compensation.
- **Carbon quotas:** The plaintiff argued that the defendant failed to pay for 821,596 tons of carbon emission quotas during the first compliance period of the carbon trading system, despite exceeding the allowable CO_2 emissions. The court was asked to order the defendant to pay for 818,148 tons of carbon credits and implement energy-saving measures. It was pointed out that the defendant had only purchased 3,448 tons in January 2022.

The decision of the court: 7 June 2024:

- **Environmental tort:** The court found that the defendant's emissions of sulphur dioxide and dust, which exceeded the legal limits, constituted an environmental tort.
- **Carbon emissions and quotas:** The court ruled that the defendant had not exceeded emissions standards for waste gas or nitrogen oxides (except during equipment malfunctions), and that the plaintiff had failed to prove that the defendant's non-payment for additional carbon quotas had caused environmental damage.

The court concluded that the defendant's repeated failure to fulfil its carbon trading obligations, despite multiple reminders, was unlawful and contrary to the goals of mitigating climate change and protecting the legal rights of current and future generations.

The court ruled that it has jurisdiction over failure to comply with carbon trading obligations.

Although Chinese law does not currently classify CO_2 as a pollutant, its emissions are still subject to stringent controls, and entities responsible for excess emissions must fulfil their obligations accordingly. This case shows that NGOs in China have started to drive changes in the country's carbon market development.

Friends of Nature Institute v Ningxia State Grid

12.04 The case[5] was about whether Ningxia State Grid had violated China's Renewable Energy Law[6] by failing to purchase all electricity from renewable energy sources so as to protect the environment.

5 *Friends of Nature Institute v Ningxia State Grid* (unreported), https://climatecasechart.com/non-us-case/the-friends-of-nature-institute-v-ningxia-state-grid/

6 Renewable Energy Law No 33 of 2006, https://policy.asiapacificenergy.org/node/43#:~:text=CHINA%3A%20Renewable%20Energy%20Law%20No,33%20of%202006&text=Overall%20Summary%3A,of%20the%20economy%20and%20society

On 24 January 2018, the Friends of Nature Institute (FON)[7] sued the state-owned enterprise, Ningxia State Grid for its abandonment of wind and solar power in violation of Articles 2 and 14 of the Renewable Energy Law. Article 2 provides a definition of 'renewables', and Article 14 requires that the grid companies 'purchase all electricity generated from renewable energy sources' and 'provide connection service'.

In this case, Ningxia State Grid failed to purchase all electricity generated by wind and solar energy.

On 4 April 2023, the court ruled that Ningxia State Grid had not violated Article 14 of the Renewable Energy Law and dismissed the majority of the FON's claims. The court confirmed that the State Grid has the general obligation to protect the environment in accordance with the law, regulation, and business standards. However, the court found that the defendant had met its specific obligation in purchasing wind and solar power. According to the Measures for the Guaranteed Full Purchase of Renewable Electric Power issued by the National Development and Reform Commission on 24 March 2016, grid companies are required to 'purchase all electricity' under Article 14 only if the electricity consumption is safe.

The court also stressed that the State Grid still has social responsibility for facilitating the use of the renewables and shall effectively implement its low-carbon transition plans under the scrutiny of responsible governmental agencies. Also, the court confirmed FON's active participation in environmental litigation. In light of the public interest character of the plaintiff's lawsuit and the defendant's social responsibility, the court ordered Ningxia State Grid to cover 350,000 RMB (US $49,000) of the plaintiff's litigation costs.

The FON has appealed.

Friends of Nature Institute v Gansu State Grid

12.05 This case[8] was regarding whether a company's failure to connect renewable energy to the grid is unlawful as it generates additional greenhouse gas (GHG) emissions.

On 6 June 2017, FON sued the state-owned enterprise, Gansu State Grid for its high abandonment rate of wind power in violation of Renewable Energy Law, Articles 2 and 14. Article 2 provides a definition of 'renewables', and Article 14 requires that the grid companies 'purchase all electricity generated from renewable energy sources' and 'provide connection service'. In this case, Gansu State Grid purchased the electricity generated by wind power and solar energy, but did not connect it to the grid. The defendant provided a strict interpretation of Article 14 indicating that a grid company does not have a duty to put all the renewable electricity it purchases on the grid. Though under Article 29 of the same law, a grid company is responsible for failure to purchase all electricity produced from renewable sources only if such failure

7 Friends of Nature (China) is the People's Republic of China's oldest NGO. In 1994 the organisation was officially registered under the name Green Culture Institute.

8 *Friends of Nature Institute v Gansu State Grid* (unreported), https://climatecasechart.com/non-us-case/the-friends-of-nature-institute-v-gansu-state-grid/

were to cause economic damage to the producer, FON argued for an extensive explanation of Article 29 in that the defendant's high curtailment of wind and photovoltaic power, resulting in GHG emissions, should have been prevented, and that the Gansu State Grid should be held responsible for the environmental damage caused by its use of coal-fired power.

On 14 August 2018, the Lanzhou Intermediate People's Court rejected the NGO's claims on procedural grounds. The court reasoned that the Gansu State Grid, because it is solely responsible for the acquisition and distribution of electricity, does not engage in activities that directly cause pollution or degradation. As a result, the applicant failed to meet the conditions for instituting an action. Unsatisfied by this decision, FON appealed to the High Court of Gansu Province.

On 28 December 2018, the High Court of Gansu Province overruled the decision of the lower court on the ground of Civil Procedure Law, Article 119,[9] as there was a specific defendant and claim, and ordered the Gansu Mining Area Intermediate Court to hear the case.

On 5 June 2019, the Gansu Mining Area Intermediate People's Court accepted the case and published the court's notice to inform the parties.

On 10 April 2023, a mediation agreement was signed between Gansu State Grid and FON under the supervision of the Gansu Mining Area Intermediate People's Court. According to the agreement, Gansu State Grid agreed to (a) invest 1.98 billion CNY at first and then at least 913 million CNY to put the renewable electricity on the grid before 2025; (b) submit a report annually during the implementation of the above-mentioned project to the Gansu Mining District People's Court, the copy of which shall also be transferred by the court to FON; and (c) disclose information related to the consumption of clean energy, subject to public supervision.

Beijing Fengfujiuxin Marketing and Technology Co Ltd v Zhongyan Zhichuang Blockchain Co Ltd

12.06 The plaintiffs asserted claims of breach of contract and sought to recover damages from the defendant.[10]

In May 2019, Beijing Fengfujiuxin Marketing and Technology Co Ltd (the plaintiff) and Zhongyan Zhichuang Blockchain Co Ltd (the defendant) signed three contracts that stated that the plaintiff would purchase 1,542 micro data storage servers for bitcoin mining and transfer 93 per cent of the profits from the mining to the plaintiff as either fiat currency or bitcoin.

The plaintiff paid RMB 100 million to purchase the facilities and maintain their operation. The defendant paid 18.3463 BTC but stopped sharing the profits

9 Civil Procedure Law, http://www.npc.gov.cn/zgrdw//englishnpc/Law/2007-12/12/content_1383880.htm

10 *Beijing Fengfujiuxin Marketing and Technology Co Ltd v Zhongyan Zhichuang Blockchain Co Ltd* (unreported), https://climatecasechart.com/non-us-case/beijing-fengfujiuxin-marketing-and-technology-co-ltd-v-zhongyan-zhichuang-blockchain-co-ltd/

from the mining operation afterward. Therefore, the plaintiff sued and sought damages of 278.1655 BTC or US $95.5 million (roughly RMB 67 million).

On 14 December 2021, the District Court of Chaoyang in Beijing rejected the plaintiff's claims, as the contractual arrangement was voided. According to Contract Law, Article 52(4),[11] a contract is void if it harms public interests.

The court found that, according to these policy documents, cryptocurrency-related activities consume an immense amount of energy and can create instability in the financial market, therefore going against public interests. As a result, the contractual arrangements between the parties are invalid because they jeopardised public interests. Unsatisfied by this decision, the plaintiff appealed to the Intermediate People's Court.

On 7 July 2022, the Beijing Third Intermediate People's Court dismissed the plaintiff's appeal. It upheld both the decision and the reasoning of the court of first instance.

INDIA

National Action Plan on Climate Change (NAPCC)

12.07 This plan outlines a framework for climate action, focusing on sustainable development and renewable energy. India has committed to increasing its non-fossil energy capacity to 500 GW by 2030.

The National Action Plan was launched on 30 June 2008[12] and outlines eight National Missions on Climate change:

- National Solar Mission
- National Mission for Enhanced Energy Efficiency
- National Mission for Sustainable Habitat
- National Water Mission
- National Mission for Sustaining the Himalayan Eco-system
- National Mission for a Green India
- National Mission for Sustainable Agriculture
- National Mission for Strategic Knowledge for Climate Change

International Solar Alliance

12.08 India has taken leadership in promoting solar energy through initiatives like the International Solar Alliance (ISA), aiming to enhance solar energy deployment globally.

11 Contract Law, https://english.cnipa.gov.cn/transfer/lawpolicy/relatedawsregulations/915598.htm

12 Ministry of Environment, Forest and Climate Change, *National Action Plan on Climate Change (NAPCC)* (2021), https://static.pib.gov.in/WriteReadData/specificdocs/documents/2021/dec/doc202112101.pdf

The ISA[13] is an alliance of countries which mostly lie between the Tropic of Cancer and the Tropic of Capricorn. The ISA was conceived as a joint effort by India and France to mobilise efforts against climate change through the deployment of solar energy solutions. Its aim is to develop and deploy cost-effective and transformational energy solutions powered by the sun. At present 199 countries are signatories to the ISA Framework Agreement of which 99 countries submitted information for ratification to become full members.

Lawsuits concerning climate change

12.09 In an article, 'Litigating Climate Claims in India',[14] the authors looked at suits which were brought where people have challenged the impacts of government decisions or government inability to regulate specific activities, or sought to force government bodies to comply with the law.

In one case nine-year-old Ridhima Pandey[15] brought a case against the Indian Government before the National Green Tribunal.[16] She argued that her rights were being violated and the state should do more to mitigate its emissions. Her petition was dismissed in 2019 as climate change was already covered in the impact assessment process.

In another case brought by lawyer and activist Nuggehalli Jayasimha against the government,[17] the National Green Tribunal examined the climate impact of dairy farming and subsequently directed the central pollution control board to develop a methane inventory for dairies throughout India and set sustainability guidelines for the industry.

There have also been cases where the government defended a policy decision to increase the license fee[18] for timber as deforestation is responsible for significant GHG emissions.

MK Ranjitsinh and Others v Union of India and Others

12.10 This case[19] was brought to look at balancing the need to safeguard biodiversity in the preservation of the Great Indian Bustard and mitigating the impacts of climate change through interpretation of Indian Constitutional Provisions and other legal frameworks in India as well as international commitments.

13 International Solar Alliance, https://isolaralliance.org

14 Peel and Lin, 'Litigating Climate Claims in India' (2020) 114 AJIL Unbound 45–50, https://www.cambridge.org/core/journals/american-journal-of-international-law/article/litigating-climate-claims-in-india/4BF1BFCD33474A8E7370425F3014BE26?ref=the-wave.net

15 *Ridhima Pandey v Union of India* (Original Application No. 187/2017; Civil Appeal No. 388/2021), https://climatecasechart.com/non-us-case/pandey-v-india/

16 National Green Tribunal (India) https://www.greentribunal.gov.in

17 *Nuggehalli Jayasimbha v Government of NCT of Delhi* (unreported, 20 May 2020), https://indiankanoon.org/doc/159137499/?ref=the-wave.net

18 *M/S Singh Timber Traders and Others vs State of UP and Others*, Allahabad High Court (unreported, 8 July 2020), https://indiankanoon.org/doc/159982119/

19 *MK Ranjitsinh and Others v Union of India and Others* (unreported, 21 March 2024), https://climatecasechart.com/non-us-case/mk-ranjitsinh-ors-v-union-of-india-ors/

A petition was filed asking the Supreme Court of India to invoke its jurisdiction to issue an order to protect two endangered birds, the Great Indian Bustard (GIB) and the Lesser Florican. The number of Great Indian Bustards is at around 200 individuals and the loss is mainly due to the degradation of its habitat as well as hunting for sport and food. It is also at risk from the construction of infrastructure, such as roads, wind turbines, solar energy projects and electricity pylons.

The original case was brought by MK Ranjitsinh a well-known conservationist who was concerned with the plight of the Great Indian Bustard and its smaller cousin, the Lesser Florican. He succeeded in a judgment of the Supreme Court dated 19 April 2021 in which the Supreme Court blocked the installation of overhead transmission lines over a wide area and mandated that the lines should be dug underground instead. Viewing this order as impractical the Indian Government appealed. The Ministry of Environment, Forests, and Climate Change, the Ministry of Power, and the Ministry of New and Renewable Energy (MNRE) requested that the judgment dated 19 April 2021, should be modified as its implementation would cause adverse implications for the power sector and India's international commitment for energy transition as well as its fulfilment of its promise under the Paris Agreement signed by India in 2015 under the United Nations Framework Convention on Climate Change (UNFCCC). In this case there were two major issues:

- whether to modify the directions issued under the earlier judgment dated 19 April 2019; and
- balancing the preservation of the Great Indian Bustard with India's commitment to control climate change through just transition (moving fossil fuels to renewable energy).

The court reviewed the factors causing threats to Great Indian Bustards, the actions taken by the Government of India, specifically the programme Habitat Improvement and Conservation Breeding of the Great Indian Bustard[20] launched in 2016 and other measures. The court also discussed the impacts of climate change and India's commitments and efforts to control it. An observation was that the promotion of renewable energy sources is crucial for also promoting social equity by ensuring access to clean and affordable energy for all segments of society therefore fostering inclusive growth and development across the country. The court emphasised the duty on the part of the state under Article 48[21] and the fundamental duty of citizens under Article 51A of the Constitution of India[22] as constitutional commitments to ensure protection of the natural world and compassion for living creatures. The court related these Articles to Indian Constitution, Articles 21 and 14 and

20 Wildlife Institute of India, 'Habitat improvement and conservation breeding of the great Indian bustard: an integrated approach', https://wii.gov.in/campa_gib

21 Indian Constitution, Article 48 Invocation of Responsibility for a Breach of an Obligation to the International Community as a Whole. Article 48 provides:

'1. Any State other than an injured State is entitled to invoke the responsibility of another State in accordance with paragraph 2 if:

(a) the obligation breached is owed to a group of States including that State, and is established for the protection of a collective interest of the group; or

(b) the obligation breached is owed to the international community as a whole.'

https://legal.un.org/legislativeseries/pdfs/chapters/book25/english/book25_part3_ch1_art48.pdf

22 Indian Constitution, Article 51A, https://indiankanoon.org/doc/867010/

declared that the right to a clean environment and the right against the adverse effects of climate change have their bases in Article 21 which recognises the right to life and personal liberty and Article 14 which indicates equality before law and equal protection of law. These Articles justified the actions of the state. The court dealt with intersection between climate change and human rights as well as a novel issue raising the issue of the intricate interface between the conservation of an endangered species, such as the Great Indian Bustard, and the imperative of protecting against climate change. Power lines now need to be underground in areas where the Great Indian Bustard lives.

Sukhdev Vihar Welfare Residents Association v State of NCT of Delhi

12.11 This case[23] concerned the GHG emissions of an operating waste-to-energy plant in a densely populated area.

In 2013, the applicants, a residents welfare association, challenged the construction and operation of the waste-to-energy plant run by the Municipal Corporation of Delhi (MCD). The plant was to be built in a densely populated residential area and would affect the lives of the residents. The incineration of unsegregated municipal solid waste emits large quantities of GHGs, including CO_2 and nitrogen oxide which contribute to global climate change. MCD argued that the plant was a state-of-the-art facility and offered a clean, efficient and effective alternative to the dumping of municipal solid waste in landfill sites. It was in the public interest that the plant operated.

On 2 February 2017, the National Green Tribunal (NGT) allowed the operation of the plant. The need was to ensure processing of municipal waste with least residue by developed and tested technologies. Examining public health and interest in conjunction with environmental protection, the balance tilted in favour of permitting the plant to continue its operation for the processing of municipal solid waste from waste to energy. Applying the precautionary principle through monitoring and adhering to standards would ensure that there were no adverse impacts on public health and environment.

According to the tribunal, the project adopted anti-pollution measures, improved technology, introduced new mechanisms for segregation and brought emissions not only within the prescribed limits but within even stricter standards imposed by the regulatory authorities. Based on the scientific evidence and inspection reports, the waste-to-energy plant was permitted to operate.

Society for Protection of Environment & Biodiversity v Union of India

12.12 This case[24] concerned quashing those parts of environmental impact assessment (EIA) regulation that exempted construction sector from environmental clearance.

23 *Sukhdev Vihar Welfare Residents Association v. State of NCT of Delhi,*No 22 (THC) of 2013 (MA No 19 of 2014), https://www.wwfindia.org/?26210/Sukhdev-Vihar-Residents-Welfare-Association-and-ors-Vs-The-State-of-NCT-of-Delhi-and-ors

24 *Society for Protection of Environment & Biodiversity v Union of India* (No 490/2016 (Principle Bench)), https://www.wwfindia.org/?25902/Society-For-Protection-Of-Environment-and-Biodiversity-SPENBIO-Vs-Union-of-India--Ors

In 2016, the applicant, an environmental society, filed a case before the NGT raising objections to the 2016 draft notification that exempted building and construction projects from the environmental clearance requirement. According to the applicant, unregulated building and construction activities would cause irreversible damage to the environment, thereby having serious repercussions for climate change. The exemption was also in derogation of India's international commitments to the Rio Declaration 1992 and Paris Agreement 2015, especially when read in the light of the precautionary principle. The respondent, the Ministry of Environment and Forests, contended that the draft notification was a policy decision taken by the Government of India to provide affordable housing to the weaker sections of society under the 'Housing for All by 2022' scheme. The NGT, exercising its jurisdiction, upheld the applicant's contention. The 2016 draft notification considerably diluted the regime of environmental clearance in building and construction activities, thereby, leading to severe environmental impacts. The principle of non-regression, an accepted norm in international environmental law, mandates that environmental law should not be modified to the detriment of environmental protection.

An EIA evaluates carbon emissions associated with the construction project, its adverse impact on the environment, and best practice strategies to reduce these emissions. This helps in achieving the ambitious targets and is directly linked to climate change and the Sustainable Development Goals.

Indian Council for Enviro-Legal Action (ICELA) v Ministry of Environment, Forest and Climate Change

12.13 In 2014, ICELA, an environmental NGO, filed an application against the Ministry of Environment, Forest and Climate Change, and companies producing HCFC-2 to stop emitting HFC-23.[25] The emission of this by-product has 14,800 times more global warming potential (being a GHG) than CO_2 thereby leading to ozone depletion. The petitioner relied on constitutional mandates, namely Indian Constitution, Articles 48A (duty of the state to protect the environment) and 51A(g) (fundamental duty of the citizen to protect and improve the environment), and Environment Protection Act 1986, s 3 that give powers to Central Government to take such measures as deemed necessary or expedient for the purpose of protecting and improving quality of the environment and preventing, controlling and abating environmental pollution.

The NGT acknowledged that, undisputedly, HFC-23 has an effect on global warming, it being one of the GHGs, and that, at present, there was a gap in scientific understanding of HFC-23's toxic impact on the air and its categorisation as a pollutant. The tribunal further observed 'international conventions and treaties have to provide a path for domestic legislation and in any case it has failed and it has to be regulated without further delay'. Accordingly, the NGT directed the regulatory authorities and expert bodies to

25 *Indian Council for Enviro-Legal Action (ICELA) v Ministry of Environment, Forest and Climate Change* (App no 170/2014), https://www.casemine.com/judgement/in/5c06107cb338d16e11efe67f

conduct a comprehensive database study on HFC-23, it being a pollutant, and assess the extent of its impact on global warming, it being one of the GHGs. On 27 September 2021, India ratified the Kigali Amendment of the Montreal Protocol, to reduce and phase out the use of hydrofluorocarbons (HFCs) by 80 per cent by 2050.

In re Court on its own motion v State of Himachal Pradesh and Others

12.14 Here, the NGT, on its own motion, issued restrictions to curb black carbon emissions, among other things.[26]

In February 2014, India's NGT issued a ruling on its own motion imposing a number of restrictions on activity around the Rohtang Pass,[27] an environmentally sensitive area in the Himalayan state of Himachal Pradesh.

The NGT has jurisdiction pursuant to a 2010 statute 'over all civil cases where a substantial question relating to environment … is involved and such question arises out of [one or more of seven environmental protection statutes enacted between 1974 and 2002'.[28]

Although the NGT described how GHG emissions cause global warming, and affirmed the applicability of the 'polluter pays' principle to the respondents in this case, the tribunal did not assign Himachal Pradesh responsibility for mitigating global warming per se. It did, however, order the government of Himachal Pradesh to undertake sweeping measures to reduce pollution, including random pollution checks, restricting transport in certain areas to compressed natural gas and electric buses, and implementing a reforestation programme. These measures were to be overseen by a Monitoring Committee that should make quarterly reports to the court.

Ridhima Pandey v Union of India

12.15 Ridhima Pandey, a nine-year-old from the Uttarakhand region, is the named plaintiff in a climate change case filed in March 2017 with the NGT.[29] The plaintiff's petition argues that the Public Trust Doctrine,[30] India's commitments under the Paris Agreement, and India's existing environmental laws and climate-related policies oblige greater action to mitigate climate change. It also argues that the term 'environment', as used in the Environment (Protection) Act 1986, necessarily encompasses the climate.

26 *In re Court on its own motion v State of Himachal Pradesh and Others* (CWPIL No. 23/2019), https://climatecasechart.com/non-us-case/sher-singh-v-state-of-himachal-pradesh/

27 Himalayan Wonders, 'Rohtang Pass', https://www.himalayanwonders.com/content/attractions/rohtang-pass.html?selocation=UK

28 *In re Court on its own motion v State of Himachal Pradesh and Others* (CWPIL No. 23/2019), https://climatecasechart.com/non-us-case/sher-singh-v-state-of-himachal-pradesh/

29 *Ridhima Pandey v Union of India*, No 187/2017 https://greentribunal.gov.in/caseDetails/DELHI/0701109011512017?page=order

30 Manupatra Academy, 'Public Trust Doctrine', http://www.manupatracademy.com/legalpost/public-trust-doctrine#

The case was brought under National Green Tribunal Act 2010, s 2(m), which authorises claims that raise 'a substantial question relating to the environment'. In addition to those legal provisions, the petition cites the principles of sustainable development, precaution, and intergenerational equity, as well as judicial decisions based on similar legal principles in the Netherlands (*Urgenda Foundation v Kingdom of the Netherlands*[31]), Pakistan (*Leghari v Pakistan*[32]), and the US (*Juliana v US*[33]). Pandey argued that she, along with all children and future generations, had the right to a healthy environment under the principle of intergenerational equity.

On 15 January 2019, the NGT dismissed the case, reasoning that climate change is already covered in the process of impact assessments under the Environment Protection Act of 1986, and therefore, 'There is no reason to presume that Paris Agreement and other international protocols are not reflected in the policies of the Government of India or are not taken into consideration in granting environment clearances'.

BRAZIL

12.16 Brazil is already seeing the effects of climate change. In a report from the Centro Euro-Mediterraneo sui Cambiamenti Climatici (CMCC)[34] it is shown that, without urgent action to reduce emissions, heatwaves in Brazil will last longer and there will be an increase in heat-related excess deaths. There will also be sea level rise, coastal erosion and fiercer weather.

Amazon protection

12.17 Brazil's climate strategy involves protecting the Amazon rainforest, which is a critical carbon sink. Although deforestation rates have fluctuated, there are ongoing efforts to combat illegal logging and promote sustainable land use.

Renewable energy growth

12.18 Brazil has made significant investments in renewable sources, especially hydropower, along with a growing emphasis on wind and solar energy.

31 *Urgenda Foundation v The Netherlands* (19/00135) NL:HR:2019:2007, see Urgenda, 'Landmark decision by Dutch Supreme Court', https://www.urgenda.nl/en/themas/climate-case/#:~:text=Landmark%20decision%20by%20Dutch%20Supreme%20Court&text=The%20Urgenda%20Climate%20Case%20against%20the%20Dutch%20Government%20was%20the,to%20prevent%20dangerous%20climate%20change.

32 *Leghari v Pakistan* ((2015) WP No. 25501/201), https://climatecasechart.com/non-us-case/ashgar-leghari-v-federation-of-pakistan/

33 *Juliana v US* (unreported), https://climatecasechart.com/case/juliana-v-united-states/

34 CMCC, *G20 Climate Risk Atlas Brazil*, https://files.cmcc.it/g20climaterisks/Brazil.pdf

Lawsuits concerning climate change

Instituto Arayara v ANP and Others (on auction of oil exploration blocks in the Amazon Basin)

12.19 On 6 December 2023, the NGO Instituto Arayara de Educação e Cultura para a Sustentabilidade filed a public civil action (environmental class action) against the National Agency for Petroleum, Natural Gas and Biofuels (ANP), Brazil's Federal Environmental Agency (Instituto Basileiro do Meio Ambiante e Recursos (IBAMA)), and the Federal Government. This lawsuit[35] is one of a set of six environmental class actions filed regarding the 4th Bid Cycle for oil exploration blocks.

One day after the COP 28 climate summit closed in Dubai, where Brazil's president reinforced the need to slash GHG emissions, ANP put up 602 oil and gas exploration blocks for auction, including 21 in the Amazon River Basin. The blocks violate state environmental guidelines and overlap with protected areas and Indigenous and Quilombola territories, according to an analysis by the Arayara International Institute.

The plaintiff argued that the climate emergency requires an energy transition towards clean energies and a reduction in GHG emissions, which is incompatible with the expansion of oil exploration. It requested that the offer, in the 4th Permanent Offer Cycle, of the blocks in the Amazon Basin in Sector AM-T-82 should be suspended until technical analysis that demonstrates the socioenvironmental viability is carried out, in particular with reasoned opinions from bodies such IBAMA. On a definitive basis, they request that the contested blocks be excluded from the Bid Cycle.

The ANP clarified that it promotes social participation before bidding for oil and natural gas exploration rights. It emphasised that simply holding an auction process does not impose a risk on the environment.

On 1 March 2024, the Federal Government filed its defence. In addition to addressing the licensing issues already dealt with by other federal bodies, it claimed that the offer of the contested blocks is technically supported by the rules issued by the competent bodies. In March 2024, Atem Participações SA filed a defence in which it stressed that the bidding process does not pose a risk to the environment and that all the impacts of the projects to be explored will be assessed during the environmental licensing phase.

35 *Instituto Arayara v ANP and Others* (unreported), https://climatecasechart.com/non-us-case/instituto-arayara-vs-anp-and-others-on-auction-of-oil-exploration-blocks-in-the-amazon-bazin/

Public Defender's Office of the State of Pará v Associação dos Ribeirinhos e Moradores and Others (Project 2620 carbon credits and 'forest carbon grabbing')

12.20 A case concerning whether there were established illegal carbon credit projects in extractivist land areas in the Pará state.[36]

On 19 July 2023, the Public Defender's Office of the State of Pará (DPE-PA) filed a public civil action (ACP) with a request for injunctive relief against:

- the Associação dos Ribeirinhos e Moradores,
- the Sindicato dos Produtores Rurais de Portel,
- the Amigos dos Ribeirinhos Assessoria Ambiental Eireli,
- Brazil Agfor LLC, and
- the Municipality of Portel,

concerning a project that generates illegal carbon credits sold on the voluntary market.

This ACP is part of a set of four lawsuits filed by the DPE-PA on the same grounds, but questioning different carbon credit projects. The companies and association are being sued for being responsible, being developers of the project or being alleged owners of the rural properties where it is located.

On the merits, the plaintiff requests:

- confirmation of the requests for an injunction;
- recognition of the right to the traditional territory;
- the annulment of Project 2620;
- the annulment of legal transactions derived from it;
- an order to prohibit the defendants from entering the territories;
- a declaration that the Public Utility Decree issued by the Municipality of Portel is null and void; and
- an order to pay collective moral damages in the amount of R$ 5,000,000.00 to be paid into the Eastern Amazon Fund in favour of the communities of the extractivist territories of Portel.

Flexpetro Distribuidora de Derivados de Petróleo Ltda v ANP and Federal Union (Acquisition of CBios)

12.21 This case[37] concerns whether the National Biofuels Policy complies with the commitments assumed under the Paris Agreement.

This lawsuit was filed as an Ordinary Action, with a request for injunctive relief, by Flexpetro Distribuidora de Derivados de Petróleo Ltda in the face

36 *Public Defender's Office of the State of Pará v Associação dos Ribeirinhos e Moradores and Others* (Public Civil Action (ACP) 0806505-59.2023.8.14.0015), https://climatecasechart.com/non-us-case/public-defenders-office-of-the-state-of-para-vs-associacao-dos-ribeirinhos-e-moradores-and-others-project-2620-carbon-credits-and-forest-carbon-grabbing/

37 *Flexpetro Distribuidora de Derivados de Petróleo Ltda v ANP and Federal Union* (ProcedCom 5057055-20.2020.4.04.7000), https://climatecasechart.com/non-us-case/flexpetro-distribuidora-de-derivados-de-petroleo-ltda-v-anp-and-federal-union-acquisition-of-cbios/

of the ANP and the Federal Union aiming to move away from the goal of acquiring Decarbonisation Credits (CBios) for the plaintiff company.

CBios were established by the National Biofuels Policy (Federal Law 13.576/2017), known as RenovaBio.[38] The Policy seeks to contribute to the commitments assumed by Brazil under the Paris Agreement (enacted by Federal Decree 9,073/2017), to promote the expansion of biofuels in the energy matrix and the reduction of GHGs in the production, commercialisation and use of biofuels.

The Policy established annual national decarbonisation targets for the fuel sector, which are, each year, individualised for fuel distributors and fulfilled by companies through the acquisition of CBios available on the Stock Exchange. The annual reduction targets are set by the National Energy Policy Council (CNPE). The individual goals are indicated by the ANP. CBios are issued by biofuel producers or exporters authorised by the ANP, and the issuance of these assets by all of them is not mandatory.

The plaintiff company alleges that, when establishing the decarbonisation targets in June and July 2019 (referring to the year 2019 and the decade 2020–29), the ANP acted in conflict with the RenovaBio Law,[39] since it published the targets without any information about the availability of CBios in the market and without the regulation of the certification process.

The injunction was granted, suspending the compulsory goals regarding the acquisition of CBios, as well as restraining the defendants from imposing fines and/or sanctions due to non-compliance with the goals, until further decision.

The decision was subsequently revoked due to the judgment of Interlocutory Appeal 5059210-44.2020.4.04.0000 filed by the ANP.

On the merits, ANP states:

- the propositional competence of the CNPE to set annual decarbonisation targets;
- that the creation of CBios is in line with environmental rules, constituting CBios an economic instrument aimed at protecting the environment and providing quality of life for present and future generations, especially in view of the reduction of pollutant emissions;
- the absence of delay in the disclosure of annual targets;
- the validity, timeliness and legitimacy of the rules that regulate the CBios;
- that there was sufficient time for the acquisition of CBios and their full availability in the market;
- that any granting of the initial requests negatively interferes with the fulfilment of international carbon emission reduction agreements; and
- that the claim contained in the initial filing constitutes interference by the Judiciary in the performance of the Executive Power.

A decision was made to dismiss the request based on the following reasoning: CNPE Resolution 15/2019 allowed the 2019 target, effective from 24 December, to be proven in 2020, along with the target for the following year, proportionate

38 Governo Federal, 'RenovaBio (English)', https://www.gov.br/mme/pt-br/assuntos/secretarias/petroleo-gas-natural-e-biocombustiveis/renovabio-1/renovabio-ingles

39 ANP, 'RenovaBio Law', https://www.gov.br/anp/pt-br/assuntos/renovabio/renovabio-legislation-english

to the number of days it was in effect. The fact that the CBios trading platform began operating in mid-2020 did not impact the acquisition of credits by companies in the sector, as reported by the ANP, with most companies fully meeting the set target.

AFRICAN NATIONS

12.22 Several African countries are investing in renewable energy, such as wind and solar power, to address energy poverty while also pursuing climate goals. Initiatives like the African Renewable Energy Initiative aim to significantly increase renewable energy capacity.

According to a report from the World Metrological Organisation (WMO), Africa is responsible for only a small part of global GHG emissions but is suffering disproportionally from climate change. The *State of the Climate in Africa 2022 Report*[40] indicates:

- temperature increase is accelerating;
- extreme weather worsens food insecurity, displacement and conflict;
- agricultural productivity is falling;
- adaptation financing is insufficient;
- losses and damages are rising; and
- early warnings must reach everyone.

Countries enacting climate change laws

12.23 Climate change laws have been enacted in six African countries:

- Kenya
- Benin Republic
- Nigeria
- Uganda
- Mauritius
- South Africa

Many of these are relatively new (between 2016 and 2023).

Kenya

12.24 Kenya's subnational governments, called counties, are semi-autonomous which has led to the Climate Change Act 2016 (CCA) paying particular attention to climate federalism.[41] The CCA aims to 'integrate climate

40 WMO, *State of the Climate in Africa 2022 Report* (2023), https://wmo.int/publication-series/state-of-climate-africa-2022

41 Fenna et al., *Climate Governance and Federalism* (Cambridge University Press, 2023), https://www.cambridge.org/core/books/climate-governance-and-federalism/climate-governance-and-federalism/DDD2BE3A9C507EEFE1CE7E99D30E9290

change into the exercise of power and functions of all levels of governance'. This requires that the 'county government may enact legislation that further defines implementation of its obligations under this Act'. In response most counties in Kenya have passed their own climate laws.

The process works through three institutional levels.

- The County Climate Change Planning Committee (CCCPC) oversees all adaptation-related projects in a given county.
- A Ward Climate Change Planning Committee (WCCPC) drafts proposals on adaptation needs on the ground.
- The Steering Committee (SC), which is sometimes chaired by the Governor, is in charge of oversight, and has the final say on fund allocation for an adaptation project, after it has been approved by County Assembly members.

Lawsuits concerning climate change

Legal Advice Centre T/A Kituo cha Sheria and Another v Attorney General and Others (Iten ELC Petition No. 007 of 2022)

12.25 A climate change petition by the Illchamus and Tugen communities in Kenya essentially suing the government for the impacts of climate change flooding in Lake Baringo.[42]

Members of Ilchamus and Tugen communities living on the shores of Lake Baringo in Kenya together with Kituo cha Sheria (a Kenyan Human Rights NGO) filed a climate change petition before the Environment and Land Court (ELC) in Iten.

The petitioners alleged the violation of several rights under the Constitution of the Republic of Kenya 2010.[43] They sought to enforce the climate change duties of public officials under the Climate Change Act[44] and other related constitutional rights under the Constitution of the Republic of Kenya 2010.

The petitioners claimed that they were victims of climate change-related flooding which had caused displacement and loss of life and property.

The petitioners said that the flooding had been caused by hydro-meteorological variables due to climate change.

The petitioners sought 12 substantive orders; among them:

42 *Legal Advice Centre T/A Kituo cha Sheria and Another v Attorney General and Others* (Iten ELC Petition No. 007 of 2022) [2024] KEELC 1521 (KLR), https://climatecasechart.com/non-us-case/iten-elc-petition-no-007-of-2022-legal-advice-centre-t-a-kituo-cha-sheria-anor-v-attorney-general-and-7-others/

43 Constitution of the Republic of Kenya 2010, http://www.parliament.go.ke/sites/default/files/2023-03/The_Constitution_of_Kenya_2010.pdf

44 Climate Change Act No. 11 of 2016, Laws of Kenya, [2019] eKLR Net 196 of 2016, http://kenyalaw.org:8181/exist/rest/db/kenyalex/Kenya/Legislation/English/Acts%20and%20Regulations/C/Climate%20Change%20Act%20-%20No.%2011%20of%202016/docs/ClimateChangeAct11of2016.pdf

- a declaration that relevant government officials failed, refused and/ or neglected to take precautionary measures to anticipate, prevent or minimise the causes of climate change and mitigate its adverse impacts;
- a declaration that relevant government officials failed, refused and/or neglected to avert, minimise and address effects of climate change suffered by the petitioners;
- an order to compel relevant government officials to rehabilitate, relocate, and restore damaged infrastructure; and
- an order for compensation for climate change damage; and an order for resettlement of flood victims.

Save Lamu and Others v National Environmental Management Authority and Amu Power Co Ltd

12.26 This case[45] concerned whether the National Environmental Management Authority (NEMA) violated public participation requirements in issuing a license to construct a coal-fired power plant and whether a coal company's EIA adequately considered climate change and other factors.

Kenya's National Environmental Tribunal set aside the issuance of a license by the NEMA to Amu Power Co for the construction of the Lamu Coal-fired Power Plant (Lamu Plant). The Lamu Plant would be the first coal-fired power plant in Kenya. The tribunal found that the NEMA violated the Environmental Impact Assessment and Audit Regulations (EIA Regulations) by granting an Environmental Impact Assessment License without proper and meaningful public participation in the process. The tribunal also found that Amu Power Co's Environmental and Social Impact Assessment was incomplete and scientifically insufficient in violation of the EIA Regulations.

Benin Republic

12.27 According to the Intergovernmental Panel on Climate Change's (IPCC's) 'mid emission' projection, the mean sea level on West Africa's Gulf of Guinea is expected to rise between 0.15 m and 0.31 m by 2050.[46] The Benin Government recognises that, without adaptive measures, the rising sea levels would destroy one-third of the current coastline settlements over the coming decade. In 2018 the Benin Parliament passed legislation for the prevention and control of climate consequences.[47] Benin also adopted a National Action Plan (NAP) for climate change adaptation the objective of which is to increase the resilience and adaptive capacity of local communities impacted by climate change by 2030.

45 *Save Lamu and Others v National Environmental Management Authority and Amu Power Co Ltd*, Tribunal Appeal No Net 196 of 2016 [2019] KEELC 4739 (KLR), http://kenyalaw.org/caselaw/cases/view/176697/

46 IPCC, *Special report on Ocean and Cryosphere in a Changing Climate*, https://www.ipcc.ch/srocc/

47 Law No. 2018-18 regulating climate change actions (Climate Change Act), https://climate-laws.org/document/law-no-2018-18-regulating-climate-change-actions_6373#

Nigeria

12.28 President Muhammadu Buhari of Nigeria signed the country's Climate Change Bill into law on the 18 November 2021. The Nigerian Climate Change Act established the National Council for Climate Change which can develop policies and make decisions on all matters concerning climate change in Nigeria.

Lawsuits concerning climate change

Oronto Douglas v Shell Petroleum Development Co Ltd and Others

12.29 This case[48] turned on whether there was evidence that the right of the appellant was affected, or direct injury done to him.

The appellant was an environmental activist who filed a claim against the respondents and the Federal Environmental Protection Agency. The claim was for a declaration and an injunction to stop the respondents from continuing with a liquefied natural gas project until an EIA was conducted. The respondents filed a preliminary objection and argued that the appellant lacked the necessary standing and that the procedure of the claim was defective. The trial judge ruled in favour of the respondents, stating that the appellant had no legal standing and that the procedure was confused.

The appeal was allowed as the Court of Appeal concluded that the trial judge misdirected himself and set aside his decision, remitting the matter back to the Federal High Court for a retrial before another judge.

Centre for Oil Pollution Watch (COPW) v Nigerian National Petroleum Corp'n (NNPC) (2018) Supreme Court of Nigeria

12.30 This case[49] concerned whether an oil spill affected the human rights of communities.

On 13 May 2005, the COPW started legal action against the NNPC. The case was brought in the Federal High Court, Lagos Division, over an oil spillage in the ACHA Community of Abia State of Nigeria. The oil spillage was allegedly caused by the defendant's negligence resulting from its pipeline corroding due to lack of maintenance, rupturing and spewing hydrocarbon mineral oil into the surrounding streams and river of lneh/Aku. This resulted in contamination of two community streams that were the major sources of water supply to the community.

The plaintiff alleged that, although the defendant contained the spillage on the surface, it failed to clean up or reinstate the Ineh/Aku streams/river.

48 *Oronto Douglas v Shell Petroleum Development Co Ltd and Others* (1999) 2 NWLR (Pt.591) 466, https://climatecasechart.com/non-us-case/oronto-douglas-v-shell-petroleum-development-company-ltd-ors/

49 *Centre for Oil Pollution Watch (COPW) v Nigerian National Petroleum Corp'n (NNPC)* (2018) Supreme Court of Nigeria (unreported), https://climatecasechart.com/non-us-case/centre-for-oil-pollution-watch-copw-vs-nnpc-2018-supreme-court-of-nigeria/

Furthermore, the plaintiff said that they were negligent in both the causation and containment of the oil spillage and that the spillage had harmful effects on living resources, marine life, human health and other usage of the streams.

The Supreme Court of Nigeria (SCN) held that the appellant NGO had the standing to sue the respondent, thereby liberalising or broadening the rule of standing.

The SCN further clarified that:

> 'Accordingly, every person, including NGOs, who bonafide seek the due performance of statutory functions or enforcement of statutory provisions or public laws, especially laws designed to protect human lives, public health and the environment, should be regarded as proper persons clothed with standing in law to request adjudication on such issues of public nuisance.'

The SCN also acknowledged that recognising public interest litigation will help address some other barriers to access to justice, noting particularly, for the first time, that:

> 'there is no gain saying in the fact that there is increasing concern about climate change, depletion of the ozone layer, waste management, flooding and global warming etc ... Both nationally and internationally, countries and organisations are adopting stronger measures to protect and safeguard the environment for the benefits of the present and future ... it is on account of this, inter alia, that I am of the firm view that this court, being a court of policy should expand the locus standi of the Plaintiff/Appellant to sue.'

Finally, the SCN decision in the above case aligns with the constitutional human rights approach to environmental and climate protection taken earlier by the Lower Court/Federal High Court in *Gbemre v Shell and Others* (see **12.31**). It demonstrated a significant positive paradigm shift in the attitude of the SCN to environmental and climate change-related claims. It provided additional human rights and constitutional tools for potential climate litigation in Nigeria.

Gbemre v Shell Petroleum Development Co of Nigeria Ltd and Others

12.31 This case[50] concerned a challenge to the practice of gas flaring in the Niger Delta by oil and gas companies.

The applicant, Gbemre, a representative of the Niger Delta where a community instituted an action against the Nigerian Government for its failure to stop the oil and gas company, Shell, in gas flaring for decades and Shell for engaging in massive and unceasingly intense gas flaring in the community, in the course of its exploration and production activities (joint respondents).

The Federal Hight Court held that these constitutionally guaranteed rights inevitably include the rights to a clean, poison- and pollution-free environment. The federal judge ruled that the actions of the respondents in allowing and continuing to flare gas in the applicant's community were a violation of the community's fundamental rights to a clean and healthy environment. The

50 *Gbemre v Shell Petroleum Development Co of Nigeria and Others* (Suit No FHC/B/CS/53/05) (2005) 6 AHRLR 152 (Nigeria), https://climatecasechart.com/non-us-case/gbemre-v-shell-petroleum-development-company-of-nigeria-ltd-et-al/

judge further ruled that Shell's failure to carry out an EIA was a clear violation of the EIA Act[51] and a violation of said rights. The judge ordered them to take immediate steps to stop gas flaring. The judge further ordered the Attorney General of Nigeria to ensure speedy amendment of the Associated Gas Re-injection Act[52] to be in line with Nigeria's human rights obligations under both the Constitution and the African Charter. The judge made no award of damages, costs, or compensation.

(1) Alame and Others, (2) Chief Minapakama and Others, (3) Okpabi and Others, (4) Ejire Awala and Others and (5) Okochi Nwoko Ododo and Others v (1) Shell plc (formerly known as Royal Dutch Shell plc) and (2) Shell Petroleum Development Co of Nigeria Ltd

12.32 In this case[53] the Court of Appeal delivered judgment in two linked appeals concerning claims brought by tens of thousands of residents of two communities in the Niger Delta against the parent company of the Shell Group, Shell Plc, and its Nigerian subsidiary, the Shell Petroleum Development Co of Nigeria Ltd. The claimant residents of the Ogale and Bille Communities in the Niger Delta, alleged that there had been a large number of oil spills from infrastructure operated by the defendants, and that these caused extensive environmental damage. The Court of Appeal judgment overturned the High Court's ruling that found that, because the claimants had been unable to link particular areas of damage to over a 100 individual oil spills, the claims should be treated as a 'global claim' – which is a type of legal action used in contractual disputes in the construction industry.

Under a global claim the Bille and Ogale communities would have had to prove that Shell was responsible for 100 per cent of the pollution that had impacted their environment. If there were any other sources of pollution for which Shell was not responsible, the claim would fail.

This substantial group litigation therefore could not be progressed by way of the selection and trial of lead claims. The High Court reached this conclusion despite the claimants having repeatedly and expressly disavowed any reliance on a 'global claim'.

The Court of Appeal unanimously allowed the claimants' appeal against the 'global claims' order. The Court of Appeal held that:

> 'No judge or court is entitled to require a party to establish their case by a particular method. A party should be permitted to formulate their claims as they wish, not forced into a straitjacket (or corner or cul-de-sac of the judge's or their opponent's choosing.'

51 Environmental Impact Assessment Act, https://www.placng.org/lawsofnigeria/laws/E12.pdf

52 Associated Gas Re-injection Act, https://placng.org/lawsofnigeria/view2.php?sn=40

53 *(1) Alame and Others, (2) Chief Minapakama and Others, (3) Okpabi and Others, (4) Ejire Awala and Others and (5) Okochi Nwoko Ododo and Others v (1) Shell plc (formerly known as Royal Dutch Shell plc), and (2) Shell Petroleum Development Company of Nigeria Ltd* [2024] EWCA Civ 1500, https://www.judiciary.uk/wp-content/uploads/2024/12/Alame-v-Shell.pdf

Uganda

12.33 The Uganda National Climate Change Act 2021,[54] has seven parts and four schedules and its scope is detailed in Part 1. The Act was adopted to give force in law to the UNFCCC, the Kyoto Protocol and the Paris Agreement to:

- provide climate change response measures;
- provide for participation in climate change mechanisms;
- provide for the measuring of emissions, reporting and verification of information;
- provide for the institutional arrangements for coordinating and implementing climate change response measures; and
- provide for the financing for climate change response measures.

Lawsuits concerning climate change

Tsama William and Others v Uganda's Attorney General and Others

12.34 This case[55] concerns whether Uganda has failed to fulfil its positive obligations under climate change and disaster management law to manage the risk of landslides in the Bududa District.

On 14 October 2020, the applicants (victims of recurring landslides in Bududa District, Uganda) filed a suit against:

- the Attorney General (representing the Government);
- the National Environment Management Authority; and
- the Bududa Local Government Council,

alleging that the respondents have failed to put in place an effective machinery against landslides in Bududa District, and that the respondents' acts and/or omissions have led to the violation of applicants' fundamental rights.

The applicants argue that the infringement of the their fundamental rights could have been avoided if the respondents had discharged their respective obligations under the law. They further point out that Bududa District is likely to suffer from more landslides in the future due to factors such as changing rainfall patterns and increasing extreme weather events caused by climate change and environmental degradation. If the affected people are not urgently relocated and resettled, further loss of life, loss of property and infringement of human rights is likely to occur.

Mbabazi and Others v Attorney General and National Environmental Management Authority

12.35 This case[56] concerns the Ugandan Government's obligations to mitigate climate change pursuant to the public trust doctrine

54 The National Climate Change Act 2021, https://www.preventionweb.net/media/93572/download?startDownload=20241023

55 *Tsama William and Others v Uganda's Attorney General and Others* (024 of 2020), https://climatecasechart.com/non-us-case/tsama-william-and-others-v-ugandas-attorney-general-and-others/

56 *Mbabazi and Others v Attorney General and National Environmental Management Authority* (Civil Suit No. 283 of 2012), https://climatecasechart.com/non-us-case/mbabazi-et-al-v-attorney-general-et-al/

In 2012, the plaintiffs sought declaratory and injunctive relief on behalf of four Ugandan minors. They argued that Article 237 of the Ugandan Constitution makes the Government of Uganda a public trustee of the nation's natural resources, including its atmosphere and that Articles 39 and 237 require the government to preserve those resources from degradation for both present and future generations.

After a preliminary hearing, the High Court ordered the parties to undertake a 90-day mediation process but has taken no further action as of October 2017.

Mauritius

12.36 Mauritius' framework climate law is set out in the Climate Change Act 2020.[57] Parts II, III and IV of the Act create climate-focused institutions and bodies and set their goals. Part II creates the Inter-Ministerial Council on Climate Change which is charged with setting national objectives, goals and targets with a view to making Mauritius a climate change-resilient and low-emission country. Part III creates the Department of Climate Change within the Ministry responsible for climate matters.

The Department's role encompasses broad policymaking duties, including the following:

- promoting adaptation and mitigation measures in all sectors;
- establishing mitigation procedures and reporting mechanisms;
- establishing and maintaining a climate change database;
- promoting the implementation of UNFCCC, Article 6 on education, training and public awareness on climate change and related matters;
- monitoring the implementation of mitigation and adaptation policies; and
- annually publishing the National Inventory Report on GHG emission by sources and removal by sinks.

Part IV creates the Climate Change Committee and charges it with a range of coordination and recommendation missions.

Part V mandates the Department, in collaboration with other executive bodies, to formulate a National Climate Change Adaptation Strategy and Action Plan, a National Climate Change Mitigation Strategy and Action Plan, and a National Inventory Report

Part VI defines the legal applicability of the Act to the island of Rodrigues, for which dedicated institutional bodies will be created, and strategies and policies will be developed.

Part VII contains implementation, enforcement, liability, consequences of liability and confidentiality clauses. It also amends the Beach Authority Act,[58] the Environment Protection Act,[59] the Local Government Act,[60] the Pas

57 Climate Change Act 2020 (no 11/2020), https://www.fao.org/faolex/results/details/fr/c/LEX-FAOC204415/

58 Beach Authority Act, https://faolex.fao.org/docs/pdf/mat210091.pdf

59 Environment Protection Act 2002, https://environment.govmu.org/Documents/Legislations/A. Acts/EPA 2002.pdf

60 Local Government Act 1989, https://la.govmu.org/downloads/LGA%201989.pdf

Géométriques Act,[61] the Planning and Development Act,[62] the State Lands Act[63] and the Tourism Authority Act[64] with climate-related clauses.

South Africa

12.37 South Africa's dependence on coal as a primary fuel source for electricity generation makes the country one of the top 15 GHG emitters. The South African cabinet has approved the country's first Climate Change Bill and created a presidential Climate Commission. It has also been developing key policy documents, such as a Low Emissions Strategy and the National Climate Change Adaptation Strategy, and implementing carbon tax, a Just Transition Framework and an Implementation Plan.

On 23 July 2024, President Ramaphosa signed the Climate Change Act[65] into law. The Act, however, is not yet operational and will only come into effect when the President issues a proclamation. The Bill was first tabled in 2018 which was 13 years after the *National Climate Change Response White Paper*.

The Act takes precedence over other climate-related laws, requiring all government policies and measures to align with its goals. It mandates all levels of government to map, plan for, and address climate adaptation needs, recognising the urgent nature of climate change.

Lawsuits concerning climate change

EarthLife Africa Johannesburg v Minister of Environmental Affairs and Others

12.38 This case[66] concerned a challenge to environmental review of coal-fired power plant development for failure to adequately consider climate change-related impacts.

In this case South Africa's High Court was asked to determine whether, under the National Environmental Management Act,[67] 'relevant' considerations for environmental review of plans for a new 1,200 MW coal-fired Thabametsi Power Project[68] included the project's impacts on global climate change. The project would operate until about 2060.

61 Pas Géométriques Act, https://www.fao.org/faolex/results/details/en/c/LEX-FAOC041846/

62 Planning and Development Act 2004, https://faolex.fao.org/docs/pdf/mat166412.pdf

63 State Lands Act, https://faolex.fao.org/docs/pdf/mat52827.pdf

64 Tourism Authority Act 2006, https://www.tourismauthority.mu/wp-content/uploads/2023/03/THE-TOURISM-AUTHORITY-ACT-2006.pdf

65 Climate Change Act (no 22 of 2024), https://www.gov.za/sites/default/files/gcis_document/202407/50966climatechangeact222024.pdf

66 *EarthLife Africa Johannesburg v Minister of Environmental Affairs and Others*, https://climatecasechart.com/non-us-case/4463/

67 National Environmental Management Act (no 107 of 1998), https://www.gov.za/documents/national-environmental-management-act#main-content

68 Power Technology, 'Thabametsi Coal Power Plant, Limpopo Province', https://www.power-technology.com/projects/thabametsi-coal-power-plant-limpopo-province/

The court noted that the statute does not expressly consider climate change but said that such considerations are relevant and that the absence of any environmental review of the project made its approval unlawful. This issue came before the court as a result of EarthLife Africa[69] Johannesburg's appeals.

The first appeal was submitted to the Minister of Environmental Affairs challenging the adequacy of the project's environmental review; EarthLife argued that the review was invalid because it largely ignored climate change.

The second appeal, in the High Court in Pretoria, challenged the Minister's determination that the review was legally valid even though it would have to be supplemented by a climate change analysis because issues related to climate mitigation and adaptation had not been 'comprehensively assessed and/or considered'.

The court cited several reasons, including South Africa's commitments under the Paris Agreement, that climate change was a relevant consideration for the environmental review of the Thabametsi Project. As the review, which was approved by the Minister, effectively ignored climate change, the court held it to be legally invalid.

On 19 November 2020, the High Court issued an order setting aside all governmental authorisations for the coal-fired power plant. The court also ordered the defendants to pay court costs.

Trustees for the Time Being of GroundWork v Minister of Environmental Affairs, ACWA Power Khanyisa Thermal Power Station RF (Pty) Ltd and Others

12.39 This case[70] revolved around environmental law and the duty of the state to protect the environment.

The environmental organisation, GroundWork, filed a motion requesting that South Africa's High Court review and set aside the Department of Environmental Affair's authorisation to develop a 600 MW coal-fired power plant, the 'Khanyisa Project', without first considering the climate change impacts of the plant. It also challenged the Minister of Environmental Affairs' rejection of GroundWork's application to appeal the authorisation.

GroundWork argued that this dismissal directly contradicted the court's decision in *EarthLife Africa Johannesburg v Minister of Environmental Affairs and Others* handed down on 8 March 2017. That case considered a similar authorisation for a 1,200 MW coal-fired plant called the Thabametsi Project.

As the litigation unfolded, it emerged that the Khanyisa Project had breached the conditions of its environmental authorisation and that its authorisation had expired. The Department of Forestry, Fisheries and Environment (DFFE) agreed that the authorisation was no longer valid. The Khanyisa Project's

69 EarthLife Africa, https://earthlife.org.za

70 *Trustees for the Time Being of GroundWork v Minister of Environmental Affairs, ACWA Power Khanyisa Thermal Power Station RF (Pty) Ltd and Others* (61561/17) (27 May 2021, unreported), https://climatecasechart.com/non-us-case/groundwork-v-minister-environmental-affairs-others/

developer, ACWA, did not file answering papers and the matter proceeded on an unopposed basis.

On 27 May 2021, the High Court declared that the environmental approval for the planned 600 MW Khanyisa coal-fired power station had expired. It ordered ACWA to pay the costs of the litigation.

Chapter 13

How Effective has Climate Change Law Been?

INTRODUCTION

13.01 Climate change law is a set of laws and policies which govern how to address climate change. These can include acts, decrees and policies that are passed by the legislative and executive branches of government. In recent years, since the late 1990s, the number of climate change laws has rapidly increased due to a number of factors:

- pressure from governments, society and international organisations – since the 2009 Copenhagen summit many countries have made national pledges. According to a study published in Nature Climate Change, 19 out of the 34 countries surveyed failed to meet their 2020 climate change commitments set in Copenhagen;[1]
- growing awareness of climate change – climate change became a prominent issue as people became frustrated by a lack of action; and
- increased litigation – more people are now acting against governments and organisations for their role in climate change.

1 'Actions before agreement' (2025) 15(1) Nat. Clim. Chang., https://www.nature.com/articles/s41558-024-02223-8

This means more laws have been passed, existing laws are being strengthened and there are more court rulings on climate change. Currently there are two further global opinions expected in 2025 to join the one from the International Tribunal for the Law of the Sea (ITLOS) (see **14.02**). New areas of litigation are also emerging, such as greenwashing and transition risk. Transition risk cases are those associated with the speed and extent to which an organisation manages and adapts to the internal and external pace of change to reduce greenhouse gas (GHG) emissions and transition to renewable energy.

Climate change laws have focused on:

- energy;
- transport;
- economy-wide issues;
- land use, land use change, and forestry (LULUCF);
- social development;
- gender and equality;
- human rights; and
- food security.

It is important, therefore, to consider the effectiveness of climate change law as individuals and organisations have applied it to climate change litigation through court cases and legal or regulatory complaints to hold institutions and governments accountable for climate damaging ways of working.

FRAMEWORKS AND AGREEMENTS

International climate agreements

13.02 The Paris Agreement (2015) (see **3.05**) established a framework for countries to set and strengthen their climate commitments (Nationally Determined Contributions (NDCs)) every five years and, as the world moves closer to 2030, countries are expected to update their commitments to enhance ambition in reducing emissions. The countries that signed the Paris Agreement also enacted legislation to translate these commitments into law. Unlike other climate summits and conferences, it resulted in real and legally binding commitments in the many countries that signed the Agreement. This has led to an increasing pressure to secure binding commitments to achieve net-zero emissions and focus on loss and damage due to climate impacts, as highlighted at COP 26 and COP 27.

Framework for evaluation

13.03 The Paris Agreement includes a transparency framework requiring countries to report on their emissions and progress towards their commitments regularly. This provides an accountability mechanism which puts pressure on countries to meet their targets.

Enhanced Transparency Framework

13.04 Parties that adopted the Paris Agreement in 2015 have established the Enhanced Transparency Framework (ETF) and work is has been carried out to establish the necessary arrangements to implement the ETF and establish how the equipment, activities and systems under the current measurement, reporting and verification system under the Convention and the Kyoto Protocol (see **3.04**) will transition to the ETF.

The ETF guides countries on reporting on their GHG emissions and progress toward NDCs, climate change impacts and adaptation, support provided and mobilised, and support needed and received. The ETF also includes processes that allow technical experts to review the reported information and a multilateral peer review where countries can ask questions of one another.

For the Rulebook negotiations, countries had to agree on when the Paris Agreement's ETF would replace the existing transparency arrangements and on the specific provisions, guidelines and processes for reporting and review.

Key Rulebook decisions from COP 24

13.05 Countries adopted the guidelines necessary to operationalise the ETF and agreed to report under the ETF through documents known as biennial transparency reports (BTRs) and agreed that the first BTRs would be due by 31 December 2024. Countries completed their existing transparency reports by 31 December 2022 (for developed countries) and 31 December 2024 (for developing countries).

Many of the specific reporting provisions have been enhanced compared to the previously existing transparency arrangements, particularly for developing countries. The table below illustrates some of the key differences between the new ETF and previous arrangements under the United Nations Framework Convention on Climate Change (UNFCCC).

The ETF under the Paris Agreement builds on the measurement reporting and verification (MRV) system which, for developed countries, consists of GHG inventories and the International Assessment and Review (IAR) and, for developing countries, the International Consultation and Analysis (ICA).

Parties to the Paris Agreement were required to submit their first BTR (BTR1) and national inventory report, if submitted as a stand-alone report, in accordance with the Methane Guiding Principles (MPG), by 31 December 2024 at the latest.[2] By 20 January 2025, 109 countries had submitted their BTRs; 59 of which were from developing countries.[3]

The submission of this information makes the countries' progress towards the Paris Agreement target visible to anyone with an interest. The publication of data also acts as a reminder of what needs to be done to meet the agreed

2 Details of countries which have submitted their BTR1: United Nations Climate Change, 'First Biennial Transparency Reports', https://unfccc.int/first-biennial-transparency-reports

3 UNEP Copenhagen Climate Change Centre, 'CBIT-GSP supports 46 countries in first Biennial Transparency Report submissions', https://unepccc.org/cbit-gsp-supports-46-countries-in-first-biennial-transparency-report-submissions/

targets. When the ETF is fully implemented parties will be able to submit the mandatory information and data in the agreed formats which, in turn, will allow for the comprehensive analysis, review, comparison, and assessment of progress. This involves establishing new reporting and review systems and additional tools for data and information management. A training programme for expert reviewers is also being developed as well as reporting tools. A large number of reviewers is required for this process to function well.

Global cooperation

13.06 International agreements need to be strengthened with cooperative efforts among nations to address climate change collaboratively as climate change is a global issue that requires coordinated efforts. International partnerships can facilitate the sharing of technology, best practices and financial resources, especially for developing nations, and international cooperation is essential to mitigate climate change. This involves countries working together to reduce GHG emissions, sharing their knowledge and adapting to the impacts of climate change.

Building on local and regional initiatives in Europe, the European Union (EU) also extends its leadership to contribute to global action with:

- the Global Covenant of Mayors[4] – a global alliance involving cities, local governments and partners from all sectors of society. Being part of the alliance means contributing to building an inclusive, just, low-emission and climate-resilient future and helping to meet and exceed the Paris Agreement objectives of limiting global warming to 1.5°C. All cities under the EU Covenant are automatically part of the Global Covenant too;
- the International Urban and Regional Cooperation programme[5] (IURC) – this programme promotes decentralised international urban and regional cooperation in sustainable urban development in key partner countries and regions;
- the Urban Transitions Mission[6] (UTM) – a global 'sister' of the EU Mission Climate-Neutral and Smart Cities, this mobilises decision makers across all levels of government to prioritise climate-neutral and net-zero pathways enabled by clean energy and systemic innovation across all sectors and in urban governance. The UTM is one of the seven missions of Mission Innovation; and
- PLATFORMA[7] – a hub of expertise on European local and regional governments' international action, which aims at boosting European local and regional governments' contributions to EU development cooperation policies and international frameworks.

4 The Global Covenant of Mayors, https://www.globalcovenantofmayors.org
5 The International Urban and Regional Cooperation Programme, https://www.iurc.eu
6 The Urban Transitions Mission, https://mission-innovation.net/missions/urban-transitions-mission/
7 PLATFORMA, https://platforma-dev.eu

LEGISLATION AND REGULATORY MECHANISMS

National and regional legislation

13.07 Many countries have proposed more rigorous emissions reductions and committed to energy transition policies. This legislation holds governments legally to account but also organisations affected by these changes. The following are some examples.

- Germany has '*Energiewende*' a long-term energy and climate strategy to move Germany towards a climate-neutral energy system by 2045. Germany aims to have a negative emissions balance, meaning that it will use natural sinks, such as trees or soil, to remove more GHGs than it emits. In the first federal Climate Change Act (from 2019) (Bundes-Klimaschutzgesetz), the net-zero commitment was originally set for 2050. In 2021, however, it was amended and moved up five years after Germany's Constitutional Court declared the German Climate Change Act partly unconstitutional because it shifted the burden of GHG emissions to future generations. The Act lays down specific economy-wide annual reduction targets as well as medium- and long-term targets in all sectors of the economy – energy, buildings, transport, industry, and agriculture. Emission trends are closely monitored and measured against postulated climate goals, which leads to regular revisions of policies and targets. Every two years, the Council of Experts for Climate Matters presents a report, which examines GHG emissions trends, assesses governmental action, and proposes additional measures to close the ambition or implementation gap.
- Australia has also committed to stronger climate goals with:
  - the Net Zero Plan – this will lay out and extend Australia's action on climate change;[8]
  - the Safeguard Mechanism – this sets legislated limits – known as baselines – on the GHG emissions of certain facilities. These emissions limits will decline, predictably and gradually and will help achieve Australia's emission reduction targets of 43 per cent below 2005 levels by 2030 and net zero by 2050. The Safeguard Mechanism commenced in 2016 and was reformed in 2023 to ensure that facilities covered by the mechanism contribute to meeting these targets. The reforms also helped strengthen their competitiveness as the world moves to net zero. The Safeguard Mechanism factsheet sets out the scheme's design settings, including the reforms;
  - an 82 per cent renewable electricity target providing a AU $300 energy bill rebate to every household and additional energy bill relief for small businesses. This expands on the energy bill relief rolled out in 2023–24 (AU $3.5 billion over three years);
  - an agreement to establish a new National Energy Transformation Partnership which will help to transform Australia's energy system to achieve net zero by 2050. This includes expanding the Capacity Investment Scheme (CIS) to target a total of 32 GW of new capacity by 2030;

8 Australian Government, Department of Climate Change, Energy, the Environment and Water, 'Net Zero', https://www.dcceew.gov.au/climate-change/emissions-reduction/net-zero

- — unlocking investment in the electricity grid with Rewiring the Nation (AU $20 billion funding in low-cost finance over four years);
- — the Capacity Investment Scheme (CIS) which is an Australian Government revenue underwriting scheme to accelerate investment in:
  - renewable energy generation (generation), such as wind and solar; and
  - clean dispatchable capacity (dispatchable), such as battery storage;
- — a New Vehicle Efficiency Standard which will help:
  - provide more choice of new cars that are fuel-efficient and low- or zero-emission; and
  - reduce transport emissions, improving the air quality.

  The Standard will apply to new cars sold in the Australian market. The introduction of the Standard keeps Australia on track to achieve net-zero emissions by 2050.

- Chile passed a climate change law containing a net-zero target with a list of key principles including scientific validity, cost-effectiveness, an ecosystem approach, equity and climate justice, and non-regression. This framework helps set the tone for the rest of the Chilean Government's response to climate change and other states are encouraged to take note of it.
- France is tackling greenwashing with a decree relating to claims of carbon neutrality in advertising. An increase in net-zero pledges and commitments from many different parties are positive developments, but France is passing a landmark law to ensure clarity and accountability across the terms 'climate neutral' and 'net zero'.
- Although China doesn't have a recognised framework of climate change law, its five-year plans have integrated climate change within its industrial planning and policy. Its most recent plan lays out the Chinese Development Pathway, which contains a significant amount of climate-relevant information. Although this is not an exclusively climate change-focused document, it is important to recognise that not every country takes the same approach. Some are managing their transition in different but equally effective ways.
- The UK has:
  - — The Climate Change Act 2008 which sets the UK's target of reducing GHG emissions by at least 100 per cent compared to 1990 levels by 2050; and
  - — The Levelling-up and Regeneration Act 2023 which introduced a strengthened duty on relevant authorities to further the purposes of protected landscapes.
- The EU has adopted the European Climate Law in 2021 which sets a target of reducing emissions by 55 per cent by 2030 and achieving climate neutrality by 2050.

More countries are likely to enact legally binding climate laws aiming for transparency and accountability to fulfil international commitments. Where countries fail to meet these legal targets/duties they may face judicial action.

EU support for towns, cities and regions

13.08 The EU has several initiatives to support towns, cities and regions in their efforts to lower their emissions and adapt to climate change.

- The EU Covenant of Mayors[9] for Climate and Energy brings together thousands of municipalities that want to secure a better future for their citizens. By joining the initiative, they voluntarily commit to reduce emissions, build climate resilience and address energy poverty in their territory.
- The EU Mission Climate-Neutral and Smart Cities[10] involves 100 EU cities, together with their citizens and local businesses, as well as regional and national authorities and investors, to deliver climate-neutrality by 2030. These cities act as experimentation and innovation hubs to enable all European cities to follow suit by 2050.
- The EU Mission on Adaptation to Climate Change[11] empowers European regional and local authorities to build climate resilience. It aims to guide at least 150 communities through understanding climate risks, developing action plans, and implementing innovative solutions by 2030.
- The EU Green City Accord[12] is a movement of European mayors committed to making cities cleaner and healthier. By signing the Accord, cities commit to addressing five areas of environmental management: air, water, nature and biodiversity, the circular economy and waste, and noise.
- The LIFE EU City Facility[13] supports local authorities and their groupings with tailor-made financial support and related services to develop investment concepts related to the implementation of their climate and energy action plans.
- The Smart Cities Marketplace[14] helps cities explore solutions, shape sustainable urban projects, and successfully close a deal for financing them.
- The European Urban Initiative[15] provides EU cities with funding, technical assistance and learning opportunities to promote sustainable urban development.

US cases

13.09

- *City of Oakland v BP plc* (see **10.07**). In this case[16] public nuisance actions were brought by the City of Oakland and the City of San Francisco against fossil fuel companies.

9 Covenant of Mayors – Europe, https://eu-mayors.ec.europa.eu/en/home
10 EU Mission: Climate-Neutral and Smart Cities, https://research-and-innovation.ec.europa.eu/funding/funding-opportunities/funding-programmes-and-open-calls/horizon-europe/eu-missions-horizon-europe/climate-neutral-and-smart-cities_en
11 EU Mission on Adaptation to Climate Change, https://climate-adapt.eea.europa.eu/en/mission
12 EU Green City Accord, https://environment.ec.europa.eu/topics/urban-environment/green-city-accord_en
13 LIFE EU City Facility, https://www.eucityfacility.eu
14 The Smart Cities Marketplace, https://smart-cities-marketplace.ec.europa.eu
15 The European Urban Initiative, https://social-economy-gateway.ec.europa.eu/eu-funding-programmes/european-urban-initiative_en
16 *City of Oakland v BP plc*, 969 F.3d 895 (9th Cir. 2020), https://climatecasechart.com/wp-content/uploads/case-documents/2023/20231127_docket-22-16810-22-16812_memorandum.pdf

- *County of San Mateo v Chevron Corp'n* (see **10.06**). This case[17] was an action by California counties and cities seeking damages and other relief from fossil fuel companies for the rise in sea level. The action was against 32 fossil fuel companies to hold them accountable for climate deception and make them pay for damages they knowingly caused including increased flooding, sea level rise and coastal erosion.

Clean Air Act

13.10

- *Massachusetts v Environmental Protection Agency* (see **10.11**). Massachusetts and several other states petitioned[18] the Environmental Protection Agency (EPA), asking the EPA to regulate emissions of CO_2 and other gases that contribute to global warming from new motor vehicles. Massachusetts argued that the EPA was required to regulate these GHGs by the Clean Air Act (CAA) – which states that Congress must regulate 'any air pollutant' that can 'reasonably be anticipated to endanger public health or welfare'.

Clean Water Act

13.11

- *Sackett v Environmental Protection Agency* (see **10.12**). In this case[19] Michela and Chantell Sackett ran an excavation company that wanted to develop a property several hundred feet from Priest Lake, a popular vacation site in the Idaho Panhandle. Sackett began backfilling an Idaho lot with gravel to build a home. The EPA, in response to a neighbour's complaint, halted the work, informed Sackett that the property contained federally protected wetlands and that the backfilling violated the Clean Water Act (CWA), which prohibits discharging pollutants into 'the waters of the United States'.[20] The EPA ordered Sackett to remove the gravel and stop any further construction without a permit. The EPA threatened penalties of over $40,000 per day.

Integration of climate resilience into laws

13.12 Many countries have now started integrating their climate adaptation strategies.

17 *County of San Mateo v Chevron Corp'n*, 32 F.4th 733 (9th Cir. 2022), https://www.govinfo.gov/app/details/USCOURTS-ca9-18-15499

18 *Massachusetts v Environmental Protection Agency*, 549 U.S. 497 (2007), https://supreme.justia.com/cases/federal/us/549/497/

19 *Sackett v EPA*, 598 U.S. 651 (2023), https://supreme.justia.com/cases/federal/us/598/21-454/

20 33 U.S.C. 1362(7).

Canada is integrating climate adaptation strategies into their climate plans while addressing both mitigation and adaptation through their climate frameworks. It has a strong foundation in actioning adaptation with the Indigenous peoples, the private sector, academia, non-governmental organisations (NGOs), youth, citizens and residents who are leading innovative solutions for their communities and regions.

Canada's National Adaptation Strategy outlines a shared path to a more climate-resilient Canada and establishes a shared vision of what Canadians wants their future to look like, setting out a common direction for action across five interconnected systems that are at the heart of lives and communities:

- Disaster Resilience;
- Health and Well-being;
- Nature and Biodiversity;
- Infrastructure; and
- Economy and Workers.

As climate impacts intensify, there will likely be a growing emphasis on laws and regulations that ensure resilience against climate effects, influencing infrastructure, land use planning, and disaster preparedness.

Spain – Climate Change and Energy Transition Law

13.13 Law 7/2021 on Climate Change and Energy Transition promotes the use of clean energy and regulates the obligations of power companies. This includes setting targets for reducing emissions, developing a decarbonisation strategy, and encouraging the use of renewable gases.

UK – Low-Carbon Transition Plan

13.14 This plan sets[21] legally binding targets to reduce emissions through investment in energy efficiency and clean energy technologies.

EU – Energy Efficiency Directive

13.15 The EU's Energy Efficiency Directive[22] requires EU countries to consider energy efficiency in all relevant policy and investment decisions.

21 HM Government, *The UK Low Carbon Transition Plan National strategy for climate and energy*, https://assets.publishing.service.gov.uk/media/5a74b4b1e5274a3cb2866852/9780108508394.pdf

22 Directive (EU) 2023/1791 of the European Parliament and of the Council of 13 September 2023 on energy efficiency and amending Regulation (EU) 2023/955 (the Energy Efficiency Directive) [2023] OJ L231/1. See European Commission, 'Energy Efficiency Directive', https://energy.ec.europa.eu/topics/energy-efficiency/energy-efficiency-targets-directive-and-rules/energy-efficiency-directive_en

UK – energy efficiency laws

13.16 Minimum Energy Efficiency Standards[23] (MEES), in England and Wales, require properties to meet a minimum energy efficiency standard before they can be rented. Landlords cannot grant new leases or renew existing leases for properties with an Energy Performance Certificate (EPC) rating of F or G.

Consequences of non-compliance

13.17 Landlords who violate MEES standards may face penalties. Failing to comply with energy efficiency regulations can contribute to GHG emissions and have legal consequences.

Regulations on carbon markets pricing

13.18 Article 6 of the Paris Agreement allows for voluntary cooperation through market mechanisms, enabling countries to trade emissions reductions. Such mechanisms can incentivise reductions in a cost-effective manner, driving investment into low-carbon technologies and encouraging countries to exceed their targets.

The Center for Climate and Energy Solutions (C2ES) summarised the market mechanisms that can be used for climate policy:[24]

- Technology Mandate – Command and Control
- Performance Standard (rate based, non-tradable)
- Performance Standard (rate based, tradable)
- Performance Standard (mass based, tradable)
- Renewable Clean Energy Portfolio Standard (potentially tradeable)
- Energy Efficiency Resource Standard (potentially tradeable)
- Energy Efficiency Resource Standard (potentially tradeable)

EU Trading Scheme case

13.19

- *Schaefer Kalk GmbH & Co KG v Germany* (see **8.11**). This case[25] challenged the treatment of CO_2 that becomes chemically bound as emitted for the purposes of the European Union Emissions Trading Scheme (EU ETS).

23 HM Government, Department for Energy Security and Net Zero and Department for Business, Energy & Industrial Strategy, *Domestic private rented property: minimum energy efficiency standard – landlord guidance*, https://www.gov.uk/guidance/domestic-private-rented-property-minimum-energy-efficiency-standard-landlord-guidance

24 C2ES, *Market Mechanisms: Options for Climate Policy*, https://www.c2es.org/wp-content/uploads/2020/04/market-mechanisms-options-climate-policy.pdf

25 *Schaefer Kalk GmbH & Co KG v Germany* (C-460/15) EU:C:2017:29, https://eur-lex.europa.eu/legal-content/EN/TXT/?uri=CELEX%3A62015CJ0460

Carbon pricing and market mechanisms

13.20 Implementation of carbon pricing mechanisms, such as carbon taxes or cap-and-trade systems are used to incentivise emissions reductions. By assigning a cost to carbon emissions, businesses and consumers are encouraged to reduce their carbon footprints, invest in cleaner technologies, and adopt sustainable practices.

Technological regulation and innovation

13.21 Regulations around carbon capture technologies and renewable energy subsidies are becoming more common as countries transition to sustainable energy systems.

Future climate laws may increasingly govern emerging technologies, ensuring they contribute positively to climate goals while managing potential risks.

Technological innovation such as:

- renewable energy – solar, wind, and hydropower are examples of renewable energy sources that can reduce GHG emissions;
- energy storage – technologies like lithium-ion batteries and pumped hydro storage can capture and store energy from renewable sources;
- carbon capture and storage (CCS) – this is a technology that can capture and store carbon dioxide (CO_2) emissions;
- sustainable transportation – electric vehicles and other sustainable transportation options can reduce GHG emissions;
- green agriculture – smart farming practices and drought-resistant crops can help reduce GHG emissions and help adapt to climate change;
- early warning systems – these can help people adapt to the adverse effects of climate change; and
- sea walls – these can help people adapt to the adverse effects of climate change.

Technological regulation needs to:

- ensure technology policies are part of a comprehensive approach that includes non-technology policies;
- ensure governments provide supportive policies that encourage the use of climate technologies; and
- allow businesses to invest in and innovate climate technologies.

Communities can adopt and advocate for climate technologies.

ACCOUNTABILITY AND TRANSPARENCY

Encouraging accountability and transparency

13.22 The Paris Agreement includes a transparency framework requiring countries to report on their emissions and progress towards their commitments regularly. This provides an accountability mechanism which puts pressure on countries to meet their targets. Signing the Paris Agreement also meant that many countries created legislation which then gave their carbon reduction targets a legal basis. (See **13.04**.)

Public participation in decision making – case

13.23

- *Kaiser and Others v Volkswagen AG* (see **8.10**). In a judgment of 14 February 2023,[26] the Braunschweig Regional Court dismissed the action brought by climate activists and supported by Greenpeace that sought an order to prohibit the distribution of Volkswagen (VW) vehicles with combustion engines from 2030 and to make VW reduce its CO_2 emissions by 65 per cent by 2023 compared to 2018 levels.

Polluter pays – cases

13.24

- *Asmania and Others v Holcim* (see **8.16**).[27] Four inhabitants of the Indonesian island of Pari have sued Swiss-based major buildings materials company, Holcim (from 2015 to 2021: Lafarge Holcim). In July 2022, they filed a request for conciliation before the Justice of the Peace of the Canton of Zug, Switzerland. This is a step required by the Swiss Civil Procedure Code. The plaintiffs are supported by three NGOs.
- *Hugues Falys, FIAN, Greenpeace, Ligue des Droits Humains v TotalEnergies (The Farmer Case)* (see **8.17**).[28] Hugues Falys, a farmer from the Hainaut province in Belgium is taking legal action before the Tournai Commercial Court, on the border with France, against TotalEnergies for its responsibility for climate change.
- *Luciano Lliuya v RWE* (see **8.15**).[29] Saúl Luciano Lliuya is an Andean farmer and mountain guide from Peru and he, with more than 50,000 inhabitants of the Andean city of Huaraz, are threatened by a flood wave due to the consequences of global warming. A glacial lake above the city has grown due to glacial melt. An ice avalanche could cause the lake to overflow and trigger a destructive tidal wave.

26 *Kaiser and Others v Volkswagen AG* (Braunschweig Regional Court, 14 February 2023).

27 *Asmania and Others v Holcim* (Cantonal Court of Zug (Kantonsgericht Zug)).

28 *Hugues Falys, FIAN, Greenpeace, Ligue des Droits Humains v TotalEnergies (The Farmer Case)* (Commercial Court of Tournai).

29 *Luciano Lliuya v RWE* (Case No 2 O 285/15), https://climatecasechart.com/wp-content/uploads/non-us-case-documents/2021/20210927_Case-No.-2-O-28515-Essen-Regional-Court_order.pdf

Freedom of information – case

13.25

- *Friends of the Earth v Council on Environmental Quality* (see **10.10**).[30] A Freedom of Information Act (FOIA) lawsuit sought information related to the preparation of a US Department of the Interior report on federal oil and gas leasing, including the programmes' impacts on climate change.

Corporate responsibility and climate disclosure

13.26 The EU's Corporate Sustainability Reporting Directive[31] (CSRD) requires larger companies to disclose their environmental impact, including climate risks.

It seems likely that there will be a trend towards mandatory climate-related financial disclosures globally, pushing corporations to align their activities with climate goals and ensuring accountability.

LITIGATION AND JUDICIAL OUTCOMES

Cases related to alignment with the Paris Agreement

13.27

- *Marlene Lemme and Others v State of Bavaria* (see **8.07**).[32] Ten people brought a complaint against the State of Bavaria, Germany, claiming that the state's failure to set adequate climate protection goals and emission reduction paths was in violation of domestic environmental law and constitutional law. They alleged that this failure to mitigate would have an effect on the plaintiffs' human rights and health, as well as damaging animals and nature.
- *Milieudefensie and Others v Royal Dutch Shell plc* (see **8.05**).[33] In April 2019, six environmental associations and NGOs:
  - — Milieudefensie (Greenpeace Netherlands Foundation),
  - — Environmental Defense Association (Amsterdam),

30 *Friends of the Earth v Council on Environmental Quality* (1:22-cv-01128), https://climatecasechart.com/wp-content/uploads/case-documents/2023/20231130_docket-122-cv-001128_stipulation.pdf

31 Directive (EU) 2022/2464 of the European Parliament and of the Council of 14 December 2022 amending Regulation (EU) No 537/2014, Directive 2004/109/EC, Directive 2006/43/EC and Directive 2013/34/EU, as regards corporate sustainability reporting (Corporate Sustainability Reporting Directive) [2022] OJ L322/15, https://eur-lex.europa.eu/legal-content/EN/TXT/?uri=CELEX:32022L2464

32 *Marlene Lemme and Others v Bavaria* (German Bundesverfassungsgericht, constitutional complaint of 30 June 2021).

33 *Milieudefensie and Others v Royal Dutch Shell plc* (C/09/571932/HA ZA 19-379) NL:RBDHA:2021:5339.

- — National Association for the Conservation of the Wadden Sea (Harlingen),
- — Foundation for the Promotion of the fossil free movement (Amsterdam),
- — Both ENDS Foundation, and
- — Association of Young Environmentally Active,

together with 17,319 individual co-claimants brought a case before the Court challenging that Shell's contributions to climate change violated its duty of care under Dutch law and human rights law.

Human rights-based litigation

13.28 These cases rely on human rights enshrined in international law and national constitutions. For example, a case might claim that states have violated the right to life or privacy by not doing enough to address climate change. Rights-based climate litigation is helping to bridge the gap between international pledges and governmental action at the national level, constituting an important 'bottom-up' form of pressure on governments to do their 'fair share' in tackling climate change.

Human rights-based cases against governments are taking a range of formats, including challenging inaction on climate change (as in the *Urgenda* case against the Netherlands: see **8.08**).[34]

Global South countries that have led the way in socioeconomic rights jurisprudence are likely to be areas for human rights-based climate cases in future. It seems that cases against corporations may also increase, helped by the trend in human rights due diligence laws.

An increasing number of rights-based cases are being brought by young people on behalf of future generations, which result in high-profile cases before the European Court of Human Rights (*Duarte Agostinho and Others v Portugal and Others*: see **8.04**).[35]

European Convention on Human Rights – governments have a duty to tackle climate change

13.29 The case concerned a complaint by Verein Klima Seniorinnen Schweiz (Climate Senior Women Association Switzerland: see **8.02**)[36] that Swiss authorities were not taking sufficient action to mitigate the effects of climate change, despite their duties under the European Convention on Human Rights. The ECtHR's verdict is binding and has the power to influence the law in 46 countries in Europe.

34 *Urgenda Foundation v State of the Netherlands* (19/00135) NL:HR:2019:2007.

35 *Duarte Agostinho and Others v Portugal and 32 Others* (App no 39371/20) (2024) 78 EHRR SE9, https://hudoc.echr.coe.int/eng#{%22itemid%22:[%22002-13724%22]}

36 *Verein KlimaSeniorinnen Schweiz and Others v Switzerland* (App no 53600/20) (2024) 79 EHRR 1, https://hudoc.echr.coe.int/eng#{%22itemid%22:[%22002-14304%22]}

The European Court of Human Rights – cases

13.30

- *Carême v France* (*Carême*) (see **8.03**). The case in *Carême v France*[37] concerned a complaint by a former inhabitant and mayor of the municipality of Grande-Synthe, who said that France had taken insufficient steps to prevent global warming and that this failure was a violation of the right to life and the right to respect for private and family life. The Court declared the application inadmissable on the ground that the applicant did not have victim status within the meaning of Article 34 of the Convention.
- *Duarte Agostinho and Others v Portugal and Others* (see **8.04** and **13.28**) The case concerned the current and future severe effects of climate change, which the applicants attributed to the respondent states, and which, they claimed, impacted their lives, well-being, mental health and the peaceful enjoyment of their homes. As it concerned the extraterritorial jurisdiction of respondent states other than Portugal, the Court found that there were no grounds in the Convention for the extension of their extraterritorial jurisdiction in the manner requested by the applicants. Having regard to the fact that the applicants had not pursued any legal avenue in Portugal concerning their complaints, the applicants' complaint against Portugal was also inadmissible for non-exhaustion of domestic remedies. The Court declared inadmissible the applications lodged against Portugal and the other states on the issue of climate change.
- *Verein KlimaSeniorinnen Schweiz and Others v Switzerland* (see **8.02** and **13.29**). In this case the European Court of Human Rights (ECtHR) ruled that Switzerland had breached the ECHR by not taking sufficient action against climate change. In particular, it found a breach of the right to respect for private and family life contained in Article 8 of the Convention, based on Switzerland's failure to mitigate the impact of climate change on the lives, health, well-being and quality of life of its citizens. It also ruled that Switzerland had breached the right to a fair trial in terms of Article 6, in that the domestic courts failed to examine the merits of the applicants' complaints, including the scientific evidence.

Public trust claims – cases

13.31

- *Sierra Club v California Department of Water Resources* (a 2024 filing) (see **10.08**). This case[38] involved a challenge to California Department of Water Resources' (DWR's) approval of the Delta Conveyance Project (DCP), which would divert water from the Sacramento River for export to southern areas of the state. Though the DCP was only recently approved by the DWR after completing the California Environmental Quality Act (CEQA) process, the DCP faced new obstacles to its implementation.

37 *Carême v France* (App no 7189/21) CE:ECHR:2024:0409DEC000718921 (2024) 79 EHRR SE1 (relinquishment), https://hudoc.echr.coe.int/eng#{%22itemid%22:[%22002-13678%22]}

38 *Sierra Club v California Department of Water Resources* (24WM000008), https://climatecasechart.com/wp-content/uploads/case-documents/2024/20240119_docket-24WM000008_petition-for-writ-of-mandate.pdf

Federal state claims – cases

13.32

- *BP plc and Others v Mayor & City Council of Baltimore* (see **10.02**). In this case[39] starting in July 2017, state and local governments started to file lawsuits against oil and gas companies alleging that their exploration, production and marketing of fossil fuels was contributing to the plaintiff's climate-related injuries. For many years the decision was about whether the case should be heard in the federal courts or not.
- *Suncor Energy (USA) Inc v Board of County Commissioners of Boulder County* (see **10.03**). The defendants sought dismissal[40] asserting that plaintiffs' claims should be dismissed because they were governed by federal common law, pre-empted by federal common law, impaired the federal foreign affairs power, violated the separation of powers doctrine, and violated the Commerce Clause and the Due Process Clause, amongst other claims.

State – cases

13.33

- *City of Oakland v BP plc* (see **10.07**). In this case[41] public nuisance actions were brought by the City of Oakland and the City of San Francisco against fossil fuel companies.
- *County of San Mateo v Chevron Corp'n (*see **10.06**). This case[42] was an action by California counties and cities seeking damages and other relief from fossil fuel companies for the rise in sea level. The action was against 32 fossil fuel companies to hold them accountable for climate deception and make them pay for damages they knowingly caused including increased flooding, sea level rise and coastal erosion.

Governments – cases

13.34

- *Bristol Airport Action Network Co-ordinating Committee v Secretary of State for Levelling Up, Housing and Communities*[43]

39 *BP plc and Others v Mayor & City Council of Baltimore*, 593 U.S. _ (2021), https://www.supremecourt.gov/opinions/20pdf/19-1189_p86b.pdf

40 *Suncor Energy (USA) Inc v Board of County Commissioners of Boulder County* (21-1550), https://www.supremecourt.gov/DocketPDF/21/21-1550/259222/20230316134530410_21-1550%20Suncor.pdf

41 *City of Oakland v BP plc*, 969 F.3d 895 (9th Cir. 2020), https://climatecasechart.com/wp-content/uploads/case-documents/2023/20231127_docket-22-16810-22-16812_memorandum.pdf

42 *County of San Mateo v Chevron Corp'n*, 32 F.4th 733 (9th Cir. 2022), https://www.govinfo.gov/app/details/USCOURTS-ca9-18-15499

43 *Bristol Airport Action Network Co-ordinating Committee v Secretary of State for Levelling Up, Housing and Communities* [2023] EWHC 171 (Admin).

- *R (on the application of Friends of the Earth) v Secretary of State for International Trade/UK Export Finance (UKEF) and Another*[44]
- *(1) Friends of the Earth (2) South Lakeland Action on Climate Change v (1) Secretary of State for Levelling Up, Housing and Communities (2) West Cumbria Mining Ltd (3) Cumbria CC*[45] (Whitehaven coalmine)
- *R (on the application of (1) Greenpeace Ltd (2) Uplift) v (1) Secretary of State for Energy Security and Net Zero (2) Oil and Gas Authority*[46] (North Sea oil and gas licensing)
- *Neubauer and Others v Germany*[47]
- *R (on the application of Coal Action Network) v (1) Welsh Ministers (2) Coal Authority (3) Energybuild Mining Ltd*[48]
- *R (on the application of (1) Friends of the Earth Ltd (2) ClientEarth (3) Good Law Project) v Secretary of State for Energy Security and Net Zero (SSESNZ)*[49]
- *R (on the application of ClientEarth) v Financial Conduct Authority*[50]
- *R (on the application of Sarah Finch on behalf of the Weald Action Group) v Surrey CC*[51]
- *R (on the application of Packham) v Secretary of State for Energy Security and Net Zero and Secretary of State for Transport*[52] (challenge to the 'new approach to Net Zero')
- *Urgenda Foundation v State of the Netherlands*[53]

Corporations – cases

13.35

- *R (on the application of Friends of the Earth Ltd and Others) v Heathrow Airport Ltd*[54] (see **6.13**). The Supreme Court unanimously allowed an appeal concerning whether the Secretary of State for Transport's failure to take account of the UK's climate change commitments under the Paris Agreement rendered the designation of the Airports National Policy

44 *R (on the application of Friends of the Earth) v Secretary of State for International Trade/ UK Export Finance (UKEF) and Another* [2023] EWCA Civ 14.

45 *(1) Friends of the Earth (2) South Lakeland Action on Climate Change v (1) Secretary of State for Levelling Up, Housing and Communities (2) West Cumbria Mining Ltd (3) Cumbria CC* [2024] EWHC 2349 (Admin).

46 *R (on the application of (1) Greenpeace Ltd (2) Uplift) v (1) Secretary of State for Energy Security and Net Zero (2) Oil and Gas Authority* [2023] EWHC 2608 (Admin).

47 *Neubauer and Others v Germany* (BvR 2656/18), https://climatecasechart.com/wp-content/uploads/non-us-case-documents/2020/20200206_11817_complaint.pdf

48 *R (on the application of Coal Action Network) v (1) Welsh Ministers (2) Coal Authority (3) Energybuild Mining Ltd* [2024] EWCA Civ 168.

49 *R (on the application of (1) Friends of the Earth Ltd (2) ClientEarth (3) Good Law Project) v Secretary of State for Energy Security and Net Zero (SSESNZ)* [2024] EWHC 995 (Admin).

50 *R (on the application of ClientEarth) v Financial Conduct Authority* [2023] EWHC 3301 (Admin).

51 *R (on the application of Sarah Finch on behalf of the Weald Action Group) v Surrey CC* [2022] EWCA Civ 187.

52 *R (on the application of Packham) v Secretary of State for Energy Security and Net Zero and Secretary of State for Transport.*

53 *Urgenda Foundation v State of the Netherlands* (19/00135) NL:HR:2019:2007.

54 *R (on the application of Friends of the Earth Ltd and Others) v Heathrow Airport Ltd* [2020] UKSC 52.

Statement[55] (ANPS), favouring the development of a third runway at Heathrow Airport, unlawful.

- *Trump International Golf Club Scotland Ltd and The Trump Organization LLC v Scottish Ministers*[56] (see **6.19** and **13.35**). Trump International Golf Club Scotland Ltd (TIGC) developed a golf resort at Menie Estate and Menie Links, Balmedie, Aberdeenshire. In 2011, Aberdeen Offshore Wind Farm Ltd applied for consent under Electricity Act 1989 (the 1989 Act), s 36 to construct and operate the European Offshore Wind Deployment Centre in Aberdeen Bay. The application concerned the construction of up to 11 wind turbines, which might be of different sizes, with a maximum power generation of 100 MW. The proposed windfarm would be located about 3.5 km from the golf resort and would be seen by people at the resort. TIGC opposed the application. In March 2013, the Scottish Ministers granted consent for the development and operation of the windfarm subject to conditions.

Five-year plans

13.36

- *Beijing Grassland Alliance Environmental Protection Center v Xingyi Shangcheng Power Generation Co Ltd* (see **12.03**). Beijing Grassland Alliance Environmental Protection Center,[57] supported by three other NGOs, sued Xingyi Shangcheng Power Generation Co Ltd.
- *Beijing Fengfujiuxin Marketing and Technology Co Ltd. v Zhongyan Zhichuang Blockchain Co Ltd* (see **12.06**).[58] The plaintiffs asserted claims of breach of contract and sought to recover damages from the defendant.
- *Friends of Nature Institute v Ningxia State Grid* (see **12.04**). The case[59] was about whether Ningxia State Grid had violated China's Renewable Energy Law by failing to purchase all electricity from renewable energy sources so as to protect the environment.
- *Friends of Nature Institute v Gansu State Grid* (see **12.05**).[60] Whether a company's failure to connect renewable energy to the grid is unlawful as it generates additional GHG emissions.

55 Airports National Policy Statement, https://www.gov.uk/government/publications/airports-national-policy-statement

56 *Trump International Golf Club Scotland Ltd and The Trump Organization LLC v Scottish Ministers* [2015] UKSC 74.

57 *Beijing Grassland Alliance Environmental Protection Center v Xingyi Shangcheng Power Generation Co Ltd* (unreported), https://climatecasechart.com/non-us-case/beijing-grassland-alliance-environmental-protection-center-v-xingyi-shangcheng-power-generation-company-limited/

58 *Beijing Fengfujiuxin Marketing and Technology Co Ltd. v Zhongyan Zhichuang Blockchain Co Ltd* (unreported), https://climatecasechart.com/non-us-case/beijing-fengfujiuxin-marketing-and-technology-co-ltd-v-zhongyan-zhichuang-blockchain-co-ltd/

59 *Friends of Nature Institute v Ningxia State Grid* (unreported), https://climatecasechart.com/non-us-case/the-friends-of-nature-institute-v-ningxia-state-grid/

60 *Friends of Nature Institute v Gansu State Grid* (unreported), https://climatecasechart.com/non-us-case/the-friends-of-nature-institute-v-gansu-state-grid/

Trends in sustainability and environmental, social and governance (ESG)-focused litigation

13.37 Claims against companies related to 'sustainability' have increased over the years and ESG reporting will highlight waste-related practices due to imposed reporting obligations. In these cases lawsuits seek to hold businesses accountable for their waste-related impacts and to change corporate practices. Cases range from those against governments, NGOs, and company shareholders. Circular economy-focused litigation is of two types.

Waste-related lawsuits

13.38 Challenges have been made to sustainability goals selected by companies themselves and sought to impose external ESG principles to corporate practices.

Product attribute lawsuits

13.39 Product attribute lawsuits tend to focus on claims regarding particular products.

For example, in relation to product recyclability: consumers sued The Glad Products Company[61] and Clorox Company alleging that the companies falsely labelled and advertised their trash bags as 'recyclable' and 'designed for municipal use' in part because 'no municipalities allow the bags, which end up in landfills or incinerators'. The consumers sought injunctive and monetary relief. This case is similar to other lawsuits that have been brought in recent years, including the California federal case of *Smith v Keurig Green Mountain, Inc*,[62] alleging that Keurig wrongfully labelled its Keurig pods as 'recyclable'.

Greenwashing

13.40 *Dwyer v Allbirds, Inc*,[63] is an example of ESG-focused litigation targeting corporate statements on environmental impacts. This consumer class action lawsuit was filed against the clothing company Allbirds and alleged that the company made misleading marketing statements, including ones regarding the welfare of the sheep from which Allbirds sourced its wool. Ultimately, the court dismissed this suit.

61 *Peterson v Glad Products Co* (3:23-cv-00491-TSH), https://climatecasechart.com/wp-content/uploads/case-documents/2023/20230717_docket-323-cv-00491_order.pdf

62 *Smith v Keurig Green Mountain Inc* (4:18-cv-06690-HSG), https://www.govinfo.gov/app/details/USCOURTS-cand-4_18-cv-06690/context

63 *Dwyer v Allbirds, Inc*, 598 F. Supp. 3d 137 (S.D.N.Y. 2022), https://climatecasechart.com/wp-content/uploads/case-documents/2022/20220418_docket-721-cv-05238_opinion-and-order.pdf

Greenwashing – cases

13.41

- *FossielVrij NL v KLM*[64] (see **8.13**). Here, FossielVrij NL sued Dutch airline, KLM, for alleged greenwashing in its advertising campaigns. The case was supported by other organisations, including ClientEarth, and could provide an international precedent.
- *Vegetarian Society of Denmark v Danish Crown* 2021 (see **8.12**). In this case,[65] Danish NGOs, including the Danish Vegetarian Association and the Climate Movement in Denmark sued Danish Crown, a leading pork producer in the EU. They brought the claim in May 2021 when the NGOs claimed the company deceived consumers through one of its marketing campaigns. The campaign said that pork is 'more climate-friendly than you would think' and that Danish Crown's pork production was 'climate controlled'.

Carbon Market Watch v FIFA[66]

13.42 In 2022, Carbon Market Watch[67] filed a complaint against FIFA for misleadingly advertising the 2022 World Cup in Qatar as 'carbon neutral'. The complaint was filed in Belgium, France, the Netherlands, the UK and Switzerland.

Corporate liability cases

13.43 These cases seek to hold corporations responsible for climate harm. For example, a case might claim that a fossil fuel company should be held responsible for contributing to climate change.

TECHNOLOGY AND INNOVATION

13.44 See **13.21**.

Facilitating financial support and technology transfer

13.45 The Green Climate Fund[68] (under the UNFCCC) aims to support developing countries in their climate efforts by providing financial resources

64 *FossielVrij NL v KLM* (C/13/719848/HA ZA 22-524), https://climatecasechart.com/wp-content/uploads/non-us-case-documents/2024/20240320_17244_judgment.pdf
65 *Vegetarian Society of Denmark v Danish Crown 2021* (Western High Court Viborg, March 2024) BS-472/2022-VLR; 1009/23.
66 Complaint to the Belgian Advertising Ethics panel regarding the 'carbon neutrality' communication of the 2022 FIFA World Cup, https://climatecasechart.com/wp-content/uploads/non-us-case-documents/2022/20221201_18356_complaint.pdf
67 Dufrasne, *Poor Tackling: Yellow card for 2022 FIFA World Cup's carbon neutrality claim* (31 October 2022), https://carbonmarketwatch.org/publications/poor-tackling-yellow-card-for-2022-fifa-world-cups-carbon-neutrality-claim/
68 Green Climate Fund, https://www.greenclimate.fund

and facilitating technology transfer, and, by supporting vulnerable nations in implementing climate initiatives, it can help bridge the gap between developed and developing countries thereby accelerating progress toward net zero on a global scale.

Financial support

13.46 The Global Environment Facility[69] (GEF) provides funding for technology needs assessments and other capacity-building activities.

Technology transfer

13.47 The Finance and Technology Transfer Centre for Climate Change (FINTECC) provides incentive grants and technical support to companies in European Bank for Redevelopment (EBRD) countries to implement climate technologies.

Other initiatives

13.48 The UNFCCC promotes and cooperates in the development and transfer of technologies that reduce emissions.

Barriers to technology transfer organisation and knowledge

13.49 There are many barriers, including:

- government and law – politics and the willingness for change;
- investment and finance – changes require investment;
- consumer and market – consumers need to want the changes; and
- infrastructure and development – for example the intention to have renewable energy can be difficult if no one want to have the wind or solar farm near where they live.

The UNFCCC and the World Trade Organization (WTO) agreements contain a range of commitments by developed countries to help Least Developed Countries (LDCs) access technology to support their development and address the impacts of climate change. However, many of these commitments remain unmet.

Advancing technology and innovation

13.50 Investment in research and development of new technologies, such as carbon capture and storage (CCS), advanced nuclear energy, and hydrogen fuel is needed.

69 Green Environment Facility (GEF), https://www.thegef.org

These innovative technologies can facilitate the transition to a low-carbon economy by capturing emissions from industrial processes and providing alternative energy sources.

The 1970s saw the popularisation of the 3 Rs campaign: 'Reduce, Reuse, Recycle'. This shift in emphasis from, 'do what you want, but recycle if you can' to individuals having a broader obligation to minimise product waste is one which is familiar now with extensive recycling schemes in many countries. The development of ESG reporting and litigation has focused organisations and consumers on claims related to product sustainability and the 'circular economy'. ESG reporting also imposes waste minimisation on businesses.

Decarbonising transport in Peru and South Africa

13.51 Lima, Peru, is ranked as one of the world's worst cities for traffic congestion and, although 60 per cent of trips take place on public transport, there has been an increase in the use of private vehicles, causing air pollution and severe road congestion. In 2010, Peru's government issued the first country-wide law to improve conditions for bicycles and promote cycling. During the Covid-19 pandemic, Lima added almost 100 kilometres of bike lanes and separated them from the roadway.

In South Africa many residents in large cities face long commutes to the workplace as a legacy of Apartheid. Bus rapid transit (BRT) is seen as part of the solution under South Africa's National Green Transport Strategy for easing traffic congestion.

Improving energy efficiency of buildings in Türkiye and Colombia

13.52 Buildings and appliances consume about 30 per cent of global energy and are responsible for 27 per cent of CO_2 emissions. Türkiye launched an initiative to renovate as many as 500 central government buildings and develop a market for other public building renovations.

Colombia's mandatory Green Building Code was enacted in 2015. The government introduced tax incentives for solutions such as insulation and energy-efficient air conditioning systems and received catalytic financing from the International Finance Corporation, the private sector arm of the World Bank.

Taxing carbon in British Columbia

13.53 Carbon tax aims to reduce GHG emissions by taxing activities that emit CO_2 but can also be an efficient way for government to raise revenues. In 2008, the Canadian province of British Columbia began adding additional taxes to all fossil fuels purchased for transportation, home heating, and electricity, with the carbon tax covering 70 per cent of GHG emissions. The government also communicated that the tax would not raise the overall tax burden of firms and households but would finance reduction in other (less efficient) taxes.

Restoring soil in the Sahel

13.54 In Africa's Sahel region, where agriculture is the main employment and key for food security, healthy soils are essential. However, soil is also the dominant carbon sink, containing three times more CO_2 than the vegetation above ground. Farmers have adopted low-cost, efficient traditional practices, such as agroforestry and conventional rainwater harvesting techniques, to capture rainfall, reduce runoff, restore soils, and improve agriculture productivity.

Circular economy practices

13.55 'Circular economy' is the transition towards a circular economy that emphasises the reuse, recycling and repurposing of materials. Reducing waste and increasing resource efficiency minimises GHG emissions associated with production and disposal and conserves natural resources. Circular economy litigation challenges companies for their waste-related impacts and aims to change their practices. The goal is to encourage companies to adopt more sustainable practices.

City of Baltimore v Philip Morris (2022)

13.56 The City of Baltimore[70] filed suit against Philip Morris International and other major tobacco manufacturers to hold them accountable for cigarette litter, with charges including public nuisance, trespass, and violations of state and municipal laws. The city sought to recover damages including the past, present, and future costs to the city of cleaning up cigarette litter, as well as punitive damages.

On 3 February 2023, the defendants filed a notice of removal, arguing that the case concerned questions of federal law and requesting that it be removed from the Circuit Court of Baltimore City to the District Court for the District of Maryland. On 19 January 2024, the District Court for the District of Maryland rejected the defendants' arguments that the case concerned questions of federal law and granted the plaintiff's request to remand the case back to the Circuit Court of Baltimore City. On 19 March 2024, the defendants filed a motion to dismiss for failure to state a claim. On 10 May the plaintiff filed a memorandum of law in opposition to the defendants' motion to dismiss. On 24 June the defendants filed a reply in support of their motion to dismiss.

Fostering inclusivity and climate justice

13.57 Agreements often emphasise the importance of including marginalised communities in climate action, as seen in discussions around loss and damage.

70 *City of Baltimore v Philip Morris*, (1:23-CV-00303), https://www.publichealthlawcenter.org/litigation-tracker/baltimore-v-philip-morris-2022

A more inclusive approach addresses the inequities of climate change and builds a global consensus for ambitious action, facilitating broader support for climate initiatives.

Fostering inclusivity and climate justice means ensuring that the benefits of climate action are distributed equitably and that the most vulnerable communities are supported. This involves centring human rights and equity in decision making and action on climate change.

This involves:

- prioritising human rights – climate justice puts human rights at the centre of global development;
- equitable distribution – climate justice demands that the benefits and burdens of climate action are distributed equitably;
- including vulnerable groups – climate justice promotes the participation of vulnerable groups in decision making on climate change; and
- addressing historical responsibility – climate justice acknowledges the unequal historical responsibility that countries and communities have for the climate crisis.

Focus on climate justice and equity

13.58 Climate change is an intergenerational issue where adverse impacts are driven by human activity which presents serious implications for current and future generations. The United Nations[71] has set out that intergenerational climate justice is grounded in the idea that the

> 'Fairness between generations is embedded in the concept of sustainable development: satisfying the needs of the present generation should not come at the expense of generations to come. In broad terms, the pursuit of welfare by current generation should not diminish the opportunities for a good and decent life for succeeding generations.'

In short:

- intergenerational climate justice is a multidimensional concept which covers the responsibility for past and current GHG emissions;
- distributive justice is the distribution of natural resources;
- restorative justice is the displacement and imposition of types of climate risks, the restoration of Earth systems and relationships between humans and nature and governance; and
- procedural justice is justice in the structures of decision making.

Neubauer and Others v Germany

13.59 In this case[72] (see **8.09**), the plaintiffs successfully challenged the constitutionality of Germany's emission reduction targets and claimed the

71 United Nations General Assembly, *Sustainable development – Intergenerational Solidarity and the needs of future generations*, https://sustainabledevelopment.un.org/content/documents/2006future.pdf

72 *Neubauer and Others v Germany (*BvR 2656/18), https://climatecasechart.com/wp-content/uploads/non-us-case-documents/2020/20200206_11817_complaint.pdf

German Climate Protection Law (Bundes-Klimaschutzgesetz) violated the rights of future generations by introducing a legal requirement to meet the goals of the Paris Agreement and an insufficiently strict 2050 emissions reductions target with insufficient details on the plans to meet these target.

Promoting cooperative action

13.60 Agreements like the Kigali Amendment to the Montreal Protocol[73] highlight cooperative efforts to phase down hydrofluorocarbons (HFCs), potent GHGs.

BARRIERS TO EFFECTIVENESS

13.61

- Political and economic barriers – political changes can alter a country's stance on climate change (see **Chapter 1**).
- Societal awareness – people's awareness of the reality of climate change can be influenced by misleading media information.

CONCLUSION

13.62 Periodic conferences of the parties (COP) (see **Appendix III**) to the UNFCCC allow for reassessment of scientific findings and their implications for policies. These assessments can lead to strengthened commitments, as evidenced by enhanced NDCs submitted in line with changing climate science and the exigencies of climate impacts.

Whilst international agreements are critical, several challenges persist:

- enforcement – most international agreements lack binding enforcement mechanisms and instead rely on self-determined commitments, which can lead to non-compliance;
- political will – the success of agreements often needs the political will of nations, which can fluctuate based on domestic priorities, economic conditions and leadership changes; and
- equity issues – there are differing capabilities and responsibilities between countries which can create friction, particularly between developed and developing nations with regard to emissions reductions and support.

Whilst international agreements in climate change law significantly bolster efforts to achieve net-zero emissions, their effectiveness depends on strong

73 Kigali Amendment to the Montreal Protocol https://treaties.un.org/Pages/ViewDetails.aspx?src=IND&mtdsg_no=XXVII-2-f&chapter=27&clang=_en

political commitment, transparent implementation, international collaboration and enforcement mechanisms. The only chance of achieving net-zero is with countries working together.

Addressing climate change is a complex challenge that requires a combination of technological, regulatory, behavioural and ecological solutions. Climate law, however, is proving to have some teeth and is holding governments and organisations to account.

Chapter 14

International Treaties and Opinions – The Future?

INTRODUCTION

14.01 The International Tribunal for the Law of the Sea (ITLOS) has been the first international body to issue an Advisory Opinion on state obligations under the United Nations Convention on the Law of the Sea (UNCLOS) to preserve and protect oceans form the adverse effects of climate change caused by man-made greenhouse gas (GHG) emissions.

Two other international courts, the Inter-American Court of Human Rights (IACtHR) and the International Court of Justice (ICJ) are expected to issue Advisory Opinions in 2025. Climate change law has seen a growing increase in cases against governments and organisations within countries and outside. These Opinions are now bringing into question what obligations states owe to each other. This seems to be happening through a series of Advisory Opinions attempting to clarify the scope of state obligations concerning climate change under international law.

Advisory Opinions are statements or interpretations of law provided by a court or tribunal in response to legal questions submitted by authorised states, agencies, international organisations or other bodies such as the UN Security Council and UN General Assembly (UNGA). An Advisory Opinion is not legally binding on states; however, it can be influential as to the definitive interpretation of state obligations under international law.

There have been previous Advisory Opinions which have formed the basis of a UNGA resolution:

- ICJ 2019 Advisory Opinion on the Legality or Use of Nuclear Weapons[1]
- ICJ 2019 Advisory Opinion on the Chagos Archipelago[2]

The Paris Agreement (see **3.05**) and the United Nations Framework Convention on Climate Change (UNFCCC) (see **3.03**) are significant international law instruments addressing climate change, but they do not address the detailed issue of liability or compensation between states. COP 29 focused on the Loss and Damage Fund and closed in November 2024 with a new finance goal to help countries protect their people and economies against climate disasters and share in the benefits of clean energy.

> '• Triple finance to developing countries, from the previous goal of USD 100 billion annually, to USD 300 billion annually by 2035.
>
> • Secure efforts of all actors to work together to scale up finance to developing countries, from public and private sources to the amount of USD 1.3 trillion per year by 2035.
>
> Known formally as the New Collective Quantified Goal on Climate Finance (NCQG), it was agreed after two weeks of intensive negotiations and several years of preparatory work, in a process that requires all nations to unanimously agree on every word of the agreement.'

INTERNATIONAL TRIBUNAL ON THE LAW OF THE SEAS (ITLOS) – ADVISORY OPINION

14.02 ITLOS handed down its Advisory Opinion[3] concerning state obligations to protect the world's oceans and marine biodiversity from climate change in May 2024.

ITLOS formation

14.03 The ITLOS is an independent judicial body established by the 1982 United Nations Convention on the Law of the Sea (UNCLOS). The ITLOS is composed of 21 independent members elected by secret ballot by the State Parties to the Convention. Each State Party can nominate up to two candidates from people who have a reputation for fairness and integrity and

1 ICJ 2019 Advisory Opinion on the Legality or Use of Nuclear Weapons, https://www.icj-cij.org/case/95#:~:text=From%20a%20consideration%20of%20customary,of%20certain%20weapons%20of%20mass

2 ICJ 2019 Advisory Opinion on the Chagos Archipelago, https://www.icj-cij.org/index.php/node/105778#:~:text=United%20Kingdom%20was%20not%20entitled,other%20maritime%20zones%20because%20Mauritius

3 Request for an Advisory Opinion submitted by the Commission of Small Island States on Climate Change and International Law (Request for Advisory Opinion submitted to the Tribunal), Case No 31, https://www.itlos.org/en/main/cases/list-of-cases/request-for-an-advisory-opinion-submitted-by-the-commission-of-small-island-states-on-climate-change-and-international-law-request-for-advisory-opinion-submitted-to-the-tribunal/

are recognised as competent in the field of sea law. It has jurisdiction over any dispute concerning the interpretation or application of the Convention, and over all matters specifically provided for in any other agreement which confers jurisdiction on the Tribunal. Disputes relating to the Convention may concern the delimitation of maritime zones, navigation, conservation and management of the living resources of the sea, protection and preservation of the marine environment and marine scientific research.

ITLOS Advisory Opinion

14.04 The Opinion was requested in December 2022 by the Coalitions of Small Island States on Climate Change and International Law (COSIS).

States who have the least responsibility for climate change, Small Island Developing States (SIDS), may also be the most likely to bear its worst effects in the short- as well as long-term. It is expected that, over the coming decades, SIDS will encounter 'rising sea levels, extreme weather events, coral bleaching, loss of fisheries and marine biodiversity', as well as the risk of total submersion. The Prime Ministers of Antigua and Barbuda and Tuvalu signed the Agreement for the Establishment of the Commission of Small Island States on Climate Change and International Law (COSIS[4]) on the eve of COP 26.

The Agreement was registered with the United Nations in accordance with Article 102[5] of the Charter of the United Nations. The Republic of Palau acceded to the Agreement in November 2021, Niue in September 2022, Vanuatu in December 2022, and Saint Lucia in December 2022. Membership is open to any member of the Alliance of Small Island States (AOSIS).[6]

Request for an Opinion

14.05 At the time of requesting the Advisory Opinion COSIS included:

- Antigua and Barbuda;
- Tuvalu;
- the Republic of Pilau;
- Niue;
- the Republic of Vanuatu and Saint Lucia (subsequently, acceded to by Saint Vincent and the Grenadines);
- Saint Christopher (Saint Kitts) and Nevis; and
- the Commonwealth of the Bahamas.

All COSIS members are UNCLOS signatories.

4 Commission of Small Island States on Climate Change and International Law, https://www.cosis-ccil.org

5 United Nations, 'Mandate to Register and Publish Treaties and International Agreements', https://treaties.un.org/pages/DB.aspx?path=DB/UNTS/page1_en.xml&menu=UNTS#:~:text=Under%20Article%20102%20of%20the,registered%20treaties%20and%20international%20agreements.

6 Alliance of Small Island States – https://www.aosis.org

The Request was to clarify the specific obligations of State Parties under (but not limited to) Part XII of the UNCLOS regarding:

- impacts caused by human-induced GHG emissions; and
- protecting and preserving the marine environment from these impacts.

On the 21 May 2024, ITLOS delivered an Advisory Opinion[7] which found that states have a legal obligation to protect the world's oceans and marine biodiversity from climate change in accordance with the UNCLOS.

This Opinion clarifies a state's specific obligations in relation to (but not limited to) Part XII of the UNCLOS[8] to prevent, reduce and control pollution of the marine environment caused by the effects of climate change, including through ocean warming, sea level rise and ocean acidification.

Specific obligations of State Parties to the UNCLOS, including Part XII

14.06

- To prevent, reduce and control pollution of the marine environment in relation to the deleterious effects that result or are likely to result from climate change, including through ocean warming and sea level rise, and ocean acidification, which are caused by anthropogenic greenhouse gas emissions into the atmosphere.
- To protect and preserve the marine environment in relation to climate change impacts, including ocean warming and sea level rise, and ocean acidification.

UNCLOS

14.07 UNCLOS was opened for signatures on 10 December 1982 in Montego Bay in Jamaica. It came into force on 14 November 1994 and is a binding agreement for 154 states and the EC (as of 24 July 2008). The UNCLOS established a legal framework for all marine and maritime activities.

During the 17th century there was the concept of the freedom of the sea where national rights were limited to a specified belt of water extending from a country's coastline, usually three nautical miles (5.6 km; 3.5 miles). It was developed as the 'cannon shot' rule.

The canon shot rule

14.08 This is generally credited to Bynkershoek who furthered Hugo Grotius' idea that coastal states should have a right to the adjoining waters

7 ITLOS, 'Tribunal delivers unanimous Advisory Opinion in Case No 31' (21 May 2024), https://www.itlos.org/fileadmin/itlos/documents/press_releases_english/PR_350_EN.pdf

8 Part XII UNCLOS, https://www.un.org/depts/los/convention_agreements/texts/unclos/part12.htm

the width of which corresponds to their capacity of exercising effective control over it. Bynkershoek translated this into practical terms by arguing that this corresponded to the range of a coastal state's weapons '*Terrae potestas finitur ubi finitur armorum vis*'.[9] The Italian, Ferdinand Galliami calculated the range of the most advanced cannon at the time as three nautical miles – and this became known as the cannon shot rule.[10] The cannon shot rule prevailed until the mid-19th century when it gave way to the three nautical mile-limit which has itself been extended and modified. Any waters beyond national waters were considered to be international waters, free for all nations, but belonging to none (principle of *mare liberum*[11]).

Extension of the limits

14.09 In the early 20th century there was a desire, on behalf of some nations, to extend this limit and include mineral resources, provide for the protection of fish stocks and provide the means to enforce pollution control. In 1930 the League of Nations called a conference in The Hague, however no agreements resulted from this meeting.

In 1945, under President Harry S. Truman, the US extended its control to all the natural resources on the continental shelf. This was followed by other countries. Between 1946 and 1950, Chile, Peru and Ecuador extended their rights to a distance of 200 nautical miles (370 km; 230 miles) and covered the Humboldt Current fishing grounds. Other nations followed, extending their territorial seas to 12 nautical miles (22 km; 14 miles).

UNCLOS I

14.10 In 1949 the International Law Commission had both the regime of territorial waters and the high seas as topics for codification. The Commission's work culminated with the conference on the UNCLOS I as part of the Geneva Convention 1958.

This conference resulted in four treaties.

Convention on the Territorial Sea and Contiguous Zone

14.11 The Convention on the Territorial Sea and Contiguous Zone was agreed upon at the first United Nations Conference on the Law of the Sea (UNCLOS I) in 1958, entered into force on 10 September 1964 and is an international treaty that defines maritime zones and boundaries. Many countries have since ratified the 1982 UNCLOS, which supersedes the 1958 Convention for those countries.

9 'Power over the land ends wherever the force of arms ends'.
10 The Scandinavians claimed four nautical miles on the basis of their superior cannon.
11 *Mare liberum* – 'the sea that is open to all nations'.

Territorial sea

14.12 This is the area of sea that extends up to 12 nautical miles from the baseline of a coastal state. The coastal state has jurisdiction over this area, but foreign ships can pass through it under the right of 'innocent passage'.

Contiguous zone

14.13 The area of sea that extends 12 nautical miles beyond that of the territorial sea. The coastal state can enforce laws in this zone on specific matters, such as customs, taxation, immigration and pollution.

Exclusive Economic Zone (EEZ)

14.14 The area of sea that extends up to 200 nautical miles from the baseline. The coastal state has exclusive rights over natural resources in this zone.

Convention on the Continental Shelf

14.15 This came into force on 10 June 1964 and was an international treaty that established the rights of states to explore and exploit the natural resources of the continental shelf that surrounds them. The Convention's purpose was to define and codify the rules of international law relating to continental shelves and it included provisions on the conservation of living resources and oceanographic research.

The Convention was superseded by the 1982 UNCLOS, which contained more clearly defined rules for the continental shelf.

The Convention recognised the 'doctrine of the continental shelf', which states that a littoral state has exclusive rights to exploit the natural resources on and under the continental shelf.

Convention on the High Seas

14.16 This came into force on 30 September 1962 and is an international treaty that defines the rules of international law for the high seas, which are the parts of the ocean that are not within a country's territorial waters. The Convention defines the high seas as open to all nations, and no country can claim sovereignty over any part of them. It also establishes the following freedoms for the high seas:

- freedom of navigation;
- freedom of fishing;
- freedom to lay submarine cables and pipelines; and
- freedom to fly over the high seas.

The high seas are home to a large amount of biodiversity, including plankton, predatory fish, whales, and sharks but are also under threat from unregulated exploitation, such as overfishing, pollution and climate change.

In June 2023, the UNGA adopted the High Seas Treaty, which aims to protect the marine biodiversity of the high seas. The Treaty covers areas beyond national jurisdiction, including the high seas and the seabed beyond continental shelves. The Treaty includes provisions for:

- sharing benefits from marine genetic resources;
- area-based management tools, such as marine protected areas;
- environmental impact assessments; and
- capacity building and the transfer of marine technology.

Convention on Fishing and Conservation of Living Resources of the High Seas

14.17 This came into force on 20 March 1966 and a multilateral agreement that aims to:

- ensure the sustainable use and long-term conservation of fishery resources;
- safeguard the marine ecosystems that these resources exist in;
- ensure a food supply for human consumption; and
- solve problems related to the conservation of living resources in the high seas through international cooperation.

The Convention was adopted in Geneva on 29 April 1958, and entered into force on 20 March 1966. It was created in response to the development of modern technology, which put some of these resources at risk of over-exploitation.

UNCLOS II

14.18 In 1960 the United Nations held a second conference on the laws of the sea, but the six-week conference in Geneva did not result in any new agreements. It was convened to consider topics such as the breadth of the territorial sea and fishery limits, which had not been agreed upon in the said Conventions (Resolution 1307 (XIII) of 10 December 1958). Substantive decisions on the breadth of the territorial sea and the fishery limits were deferred to a later stage.

UNCLOS III

14.19 In New York in 1973 the third UN Conference on the Law of the Sea was convened. The conference used a consensus process, rather than majority vote, to try and reduce the possibility of groups of nation-states dominating the negotiations. More than 160 nations participated and the conference lasted until 1982. The resulting Convention came into force on 16 November 1994, one year after the 60th state, Guyana, ratified the treaty.

The Convention set the limit, in various areas, for a carefully measured baseline. Usually the baseline would be the low-water line but with a deeply indented coast and/or fringing islands or a coast which is highly unstable, then straight lines may be used.

Internal waters

14.20 This covers all water and waterways on the landward side of the baseline. Here, the coastal state is free to set laws, regulate use, and use any resource. Foreign vessels have no right of passage within internal waters. A vessel in the high seas assumes jurisdiction under the internal laws of its flag state.

Archipelagic waters

14.21 The Convention set the definition of 'Archipelagic States'[12] in Part IV, which also defines how the state can draw its territorial borders. A baseline is drawn between the outermost points of the outermost islands, subject to these points being sufficiently close to one another. All waters inside this baseline are designated 'Archipelagic Waters'. The state has sovereignty over these waters to the same extent as it has over internal waters, but subject to existing rights, including traditional fishing rights of immediately adjacent states. Foreign vessels have right of innocent passage through archipelagic waters, but archipelagic states may limit innocent passage to designated sea lanes.

Territorial sea

14.22 Up to 12 nautical miles (22 km; 14 miles) from the baseline, the coastal state is free to set laws, regulate the use of, and use any resource. Vessels were given the right of innocent passage through any territorial sea, with strategic straits allowing the passage of military craft as transit passages. 'Innocent passage' is defined by the Convention as passing through waters in an expeditious and continuous manner, which is not 'prejudicial to the peace, good order or the security' of the coastal state.

Fishing, polluting, weapons practice and spying are not 'innocent', and submarines and other underwater vehicles are required to navigate on the surface and to show their flag. Nations can also temporarily suspend innocent passage in specific areas of their territorial sea, if doing so is essential for the protection of their security.

Contiguous zone

14.23 Beyond the 12-nautical-mile (22 km) limit, a further 12 nautical miles (22 km) from the territorial sea baseline limit constitutes the contiguous zone. Here a state can continue to enforce laws in four specific areas:

- customs;
- taxation;
- immigration; and
- pollution.

12 'Archipelagic State' – composed of groups of islands that form a state as a single unit; the islands and the waters within the baselines are internal waters (archipelagic waters).

Exclusive Economic Zones (EEZs)

14.24 These extend 200 nautical miles (370 km; 230 miles) from the baseline. Within this area, the coastal nation has sole exploitation rights over all natural resources. The EEZs were introduced to halt the clashes over fishing rights, although oil was also becoming important.

The success of an offshore oil platform in the Gulf of Mexico in 1947 was soon repeated elsewhere in the world, and by 1970 it was technically feasible to operate in waters 4,000 metres (13,000 ft) deep. Foreign nations have the freedom of navigation and overflight, subject to the regulation of the coastal states. Foreign states may also lay submarine pipes and cables.

Continental shelf

14.25 The continental shelf is defined as the natural prolongation of the land territory to the continental margin's outer edge, or 200 nautical miles (370 km) from the coastal state's baseline, whichever is greater. A state's continental shelf may exceed 200 nautical miles (370 km) until the natural prolongation ends. However, it may never exceed 350 nautical miles (650 km; 400 miles) from the baseline or exceed 100 nautical miles (190 km; 120 miles) beyond the 2,500 metres (8,200 ft) of the line connecting the depth of 2,500 m. Coastal states have the right to harvest mineral and non-living material in the subsoil of their continental shelf, to the exclusion of others. Coastal states also have exclusive control over living resources 'attached' to the continental shelf, but not to creatures living in the water column beyond the EEZ.

Advisory Opinion – detailed response

14.26 In its Advisory Opinion, the Tribunal decided unanimously that it had jurisdiction to give the Advisory Opinion requested by the Commission and unanimously decided to respond to the request by the Commission.

In response to:

> 'What are the specific obligations of State Parties to the United Nations Convention on the Law of the Sea ('UNCLOS'), including under Part XII: (a) to prevent, reduce and control pollution of the marine environment in relation to the deleterious effects that result or are likely to result from climate change, including through ocean warming and sea level rise, and ocean acidification, which are caused by anthropogenic greenhouse gas emissions into the atmosphere?'

the ITLOS answered:

> '(a) Anthropogenic GHG emissions into the atmosphere constitute pollution of the marine environment within the meaning of article 1, paragraph 1, subparagraph 4, of the Convention
>
> (b) Under article 194, paragraph 1, of the Convention, States Parties to the Convention have the specific obligations to take all necessary measures to prevent, reduce and control marine pollution from anthropogenic GHG emissions and to endeavour to harmonize their policies in this connection. Such measures should be determined objectively, considering, *inter alia*,

the best available science and relevant international rules and standards contained in climate change treaties such as the UNFCCC and the Paris Agreement, in particular the global temperature goal of limiting the temperature increase to 1.5°C above pre-industrial levels and the timeline for emission pathways to achieve that goal. The scope and content of necessary measures may vary in accordance with the means available to States Parties and their capabilities. The necessary measures include, in particular, those to reduce GHG emissions.

(c) The obligation under article 194, paragraph 1, of the Convention to take all necessary measures to prevent, reduce and control marine pollution from anthropogenic GHG emissions is one of due diligence. The standard of due diligence is stringent, given the high risks of serious and irreversible harm to the marine environment from such emissions. However, the implementation of the obligation of due diligence may vary according to States' capabilities and available resources.

(d) Under article 194, paragraph 2, of the Convention, States Parties have the specific obligation to take all measures necessary to ensure that anthropogenic GHG emissions under their jurisdiction or control do not cause damage by pollution to other States and their environment, and that pollution from such emissions under their jurisdiction or control does not spread beyond the areas where they exercise sovereign rights. This obligation applies to a transboundary setting and is a particular obligation in addition to the obligation under article 194, paragraph 1. It is also an obligation of due diligence. The standard of due diligence under article 194, paragraph 2, can be even more stringent than that under article 194, paragraph 1, because of the nature of transboundary pollution.

(e) In terms of specific sources of pollution, marine pollution from anthropogenic GHG emissions can be characterized as pollution from land-based sources, pollution from vessels, or pollution from or through the atmosphere.

(f) Under articles 207 and 212 of the Convention, States Parties have the specific obligation to adopt laws and regulations to prevent, reduce and control marine pollution from GHG emissions from land-based sources and from or through the atmosphere, respectively, considering internationally agreed rules, standards and recommended practices and procedures contained, *inter alia*, in climate change treaties such as the UNFCCC and the Paris Agreement. To this effect, States Parties have the specific obligations to take other necessary measures and, acting especially through competent international organisations or diplomatic conference, to endeavour to establish global and regional rules, standards and recommended practices and procedures.

(g) Under article 211 of the Convention, States Parties have the specific obligation to adopt laws and regulations to prevent, reduce and control marine pollution from GHG emissions from vessels flying their flag or of their registry, which must at least have the same effect as that of generally accepted international rules and standards established through the competent international organisation or general diplomatic conference.

(h) Under articles 213 and 222 of the Convention, States Parties have the specific obligation to enforce their national laws and regulations and to adopt laws and regulations and take other measures necessary to implement applicable international rules and standards established through competent international organisations or diplomatic conference to prevent, reduce and control pollution of the marine environment from anthropogenic GHG emissions from land-based sources and from or through the atmosphere, respectively.

(i) Under article 217 of the Convention, States Parties have the specific obligation to ensure compliance by vessels flying their flag or of their registry with applicable international rules and standards established through the competent international organisation or general diplomatic conference and with their laws and regulations for the prevention, reduction and control of marine pollution from GHG emissions from vessels. To this end, they shall adopt laws and regulations and take other measures necessary for their implementation.

(j) Articles 197, 200 and 201, read together with articles 194 and 192 of the Convention, impose specific obligations on States Parties to cooperate, directly or through competent international organisations, continuously, meaningfully and in good faith, in order to prevent, reduce and control marine pollution from anthropogenic GHG emissions. Under article 197, States Parties have the specific obligation to cooperate in formulating and elaborating rules, standards and recommended practices and procedures, consistent with the Convention and based on available scientific knowledge, to counter marine pollution from anthropogenic GHG emissions. Under article 200, States Parties have the specific obligations to cooperate to promote studies, undertake scientific research and encourage the exchange of information and data on marine pollution from anthropogenic GHG emissions, its pathways, risks and remedies, including mitigation and adaptation measures. Under article 201, States Parties have the specific obligation to establish appropriate scientific criteria on the basis of which rules, standards and recommended practices and procedures are to be formulated and elaborated to counter marine pollution from anthropogenic GHG emissions.

(k) Under article 202 of the Convention, States Parties have the specific obligation to assist developing States, in particular vulnerable developing States, in their efforts to address marine pollution from anthropogenic GHG emissions. This article provides for the obligation of appropriate assistance, directly or through competent international organizations, in terms of capacity-building, scientific expertise, technology transfer and other matters. Article 203 reinforces the support to developing States, in particular those vulnerable to the adverse effects of climate change, by granting them preferential treatment in funding, technical assistance and pertinent specialized services from international organizations.

(l) Articles 204, 205 and 206 of the Convention impose on States Parties specific obligations of monitoring, publishing the reports thereof and conducting environment impact assessments as a means to address marine pollution from anthropogenic GHG emissions. Under article 204, paragraph 1, States Parties have the specific obligation to endeavour to observe, measure, evaluate and analyse the risks or effects of pollution of the marine environment from anthropogenic GHG emissions. Under article 204, paragraph 2, States Parties have the specific obligation to keep under continuing surveillance the effects of activities they have permitted, or in which they are engaged, in order to determine whether such activities are likely to pollute the marine environment through anthropogenic GHG emissions. Under article 205, States Parties have the specific obligation to publish the results obtained from monitoring the risks or effects of pollution from such emissions or to communicate them to the competent international organisations for their dissemination. Under article 206, States Parties have the specific obligation to conduct environmental impact assessments. Any planned activity, either public or private, which may cause substantial pollution to the marine environment or significant and harmful changes thereto through anthropogenic GHG emissions, including cumulative effects, shall be subjected to an environmental impact assessment. Such assessment shall be conducted by the State Party under whose jurisdiction or control the planned activity will be undertaken with a view to mitigating and adapting to the adverse effects of such emissions on the marine environment. The result of such assessment shall be reported in accordance with article 205 of the Convention.'

In response to:

> 'What are the specific obligations of State Parties to the United Nations Convention on the Law of the Sea ('UNCLOS'), including under Part XII ... (b) to protect and preserve the marine environment in relation to climate change impacts, including ocean warming and sea level rise, and ocean acidification?'

the ITLOS answered:

'(a) The Tribunal's response to Question (a) is relevant to its response to Question (b). Subparagraphs (j), (k) and (l) of operative paragraph (3) are of particular relevance in this regard.

(b) The obligation under article 192 of the Convention to protect and preserve the marine environment has a broad scope, encompassing any type of harm or threat to the marine environment. Under this provision, States Parties have the specific obligation to protect and preserve the marine environment from climate change impacts and ocean acidification. Where the marine environment has been degraded, this obligation may call for measures to restore marine habitats and ecosystems. Article 192 of the Convention requires States Parties to anticipate risks relating to climate change impacts and ocean acidification, depending on the circumstances.

(c) This obligation is one of due diligence. The standard of due diligence is stringent, given the high risks of serious and irreversible harm to the marine environment from climate change impacts and ocean acidification.

(d) Under article 194, paragraph 5, of the Convention, States Parties have the specific obligation to protect and preserve rare or fragile ecosystems as well as the habitat of depleted, threatened or endangered species and other forms of marine life from climate change impacts and ocean acidification.

(e) Under articles 61 and 119 of the Convention, States Parties have the specific obligations to take measures necessary to conserve the living marine resources threatened by climate change impacts and ocean acidification. In taking such measures, States Parties shall consider, *inter alia*, the best available science and relevant environmental and economic factors. This obligation requires the application of the precautionary approach and an ecosystem approach.

(f) The obligation to seek to agree under article 63, paragraph 1, and the obligation to cooperate under article 64, paragraph 1, of the Convention, require States Parties, *inter alia*, to consult with one another in good faith with a view to adopting effective measures necessary to coordinate and ensure the conservation and development of shared stocks. The necessary measures on which consultations are required must consider the impacts of climate change and ocean acidification on living marine resources. Under article 118 of the Convention, States Parties have the specific obligation to cooperate in taking measures necessary for the conservation of living marine resources in the high seas that are threatened by climate change impacts and ocean acidification.

(g) Under article 196 of the Convention, States Parties have the specific obligation to take appropriate measures to prevent, reduce and control

> pollution from the introduction of non-indigenous species due to the effects of climate change and ocean acidification which may cause significant and harmful changes to the marine environment. This obligation requires the application of the precautionary approach.'

Key findings of the Opinion – summary

14.27

- GHG emissions are a marine pollution under the UNCLOS, as GHGs:
  - are considered to be a substance or energy;
  - are being introduced by humans, directly or indirectly into the marine environment; and
  - have caused or are likely to result in deleterious effects to the marine environment.
- States must take all necessary steps to prevent, control and reduce, man-made GHG emissions, including ocean-based emissions from vessels, and land- and air-based emissions. States are required to act with strict 'due diligence'.
- States' obligations go beyond existing climate change commitments: compliance with the Paris Agreement alone may not be sufficient to discharge states' obligations.
- Developed countries must take the lead in emissions reduction measures and must aid developing nations.
- States have a duty to prevent 'transboundary harm'. The Tribunal clarified that the UNCLOS imposes strict and specific obligations on states to adopt all measures to ensure that anthropogenic GHG emissions within their jurisdiction or control do not cause damage to other states and their environment, and that any marine pollution from such emissions does not spread beyond their national jurisdiction.
- States are required to monitor the risks and effects of marine pollution, conduct environmental impact assessments for any activity which 'may cause substantial pollution to the environment or significant and harmful changes thereto through anthropogenic GHG emissions', and publish reports on the findings.
- States are legally obliged to protect and preserve the marine environment, which includes restoring degraded habitats and ecosystems.
- Finally, the Tribunal found that states are required to cooperate directly, continuously, meaningfully, and in good faith to meet these obligations.

Status of the Opinion

14.28 Advisory Opinions are legal clarifications of existing obligations, rather than decisions in contentious proceedings, and, as such, they are not legally binding on any state. However, the 169 signatory states are obliged by the UNCLOS to adopt national laws, regulations, and other necessary legal instruments, to comply with their obligations under the UNCLOS and to cooperate with other states in establishing international rules, standards, practices and procedures. This means states will need to enact or update existing domestic legislation targeting GHG emissions from all sources.

However, enacting legislation to comply with the UNCLOS alone is insufficient. States are also required by the UNCLOS to enforce them, as well as any laws and regulations that have been implemented to comply with applicable international rules and standards addressing marine pollution, which includes binding obligations under other treaties.

States will therefore be expected to implement legislation and enforcement measures to ensure compliance with their obligations to prevent marine pollution caused by GHG emissions and protect and preserve marine ecosystems.

While the ITLOS does not address the question of responsibility and liability for climate change and does not mention the legal consequences for states that breach the clarified obligations, it sets a clear precedent on states' existing obligations to act on climate change.

Implications for the marine industry

14.29 GHG emissions are marine pollution under the UNCLOS – Article 194 of the UNCLOS requires states to take 'all measures ... necessary to prevent, reduce and control pollution of the marine environment from any source'.

'Pollution of the marine environment' is defined in Article 1(1)(4) of the UNCLOS as:

> 'the introduction by man, directly or indirectly, of substances or energy into the marine environment, including estuaries, which results or is likely to result in such deleterious effects as harm to living resources and marine life, hazards to human health, hindrance to marine activities, including fishing and other legitimate uses of the sea, impairment of quality for use of sea water and reduction of amenities.'

For a substance to be considered marine pollution, it must

- be a substance or energy;
- be introduced by humans, directly or indirectly into the marine environment; and
- have caused or be likely to result in deleterious effects to the marine environment.

In particular, the Tribunal confirmed that, 'through the introduction of carbon dioxide and heat (energy) into the marine environment, anthropogenic GHG emissions cause climate change and ocean acidification', which result in effects such as sea level rise, harm to living resources and marine life, hazards to human health, hindrance to marine activities, including fishing and other legitimate uses of the sea, impairment of quality for use of sea water and reduction of amenities. This is a significant finding.

States must take all necessary steps to prevent, control and reduce anthropogenic GHG emissions

14.30 Since GHG emissions are a form of marine pollution, the Opinion found that states, therefore, have an obligation under Article 194(1) of the UNCLOS to take all 'necessary measures' to prevent, control, and reduce them.

State obligations go beyond existing climate change commitments: compliance with the Paris Agreement alone may not be sufficient to discharge state obligations

14.31 The clarified obligation to mitigate GHG emissions under Article 194 of the UNCLOS complements (and overlaps) with states' existing obligations to set and adopt measures to implement nationally determined emissions reduction targets (known as Nationally Determined Contributions (NDCs)) under Article 4(2) of the Paris Agreement.

Developed countries must take the lead in emissions reduction measures, and must provide assistance to developing nations

14.32 The Tribunal recognised that the scope and content of these measures will differ depending on states' scientific, technical, economic and financial capabilities, countries with greater means and capabilities must do more to reduce GHG emissions than those with less-developed economies.

States must make specific efforts to avoid transboundary harm

14.33 Just because it is difficult to establish factual and legal causation between GHGs emitted in one state's jurisdiction and marine pollution experienced in another, due to the cumulative nature of GHG emissions in the atmosphere this does not mean states have no obligation to prevent transboundary pollution.

States are obliged to monitor and publicise the environmental risks of pollution

14.34 The Tribunal found that states are required by Articles 204–206 of the UNCLOS to monitor the risks and effects of marine pollution, conduct environmental impact assessments for any activity which 'may cause substantial pollution to the environment or significant and harmful changes thereto through anthropogenic GHG emissions', and publish reports on the findings.

States are legally obliged to protect and preserve the marine environment

14.35 States have an obligation under Article 192 of the UNCLOS to protect and preserve the marine environment and this extends to 'any form of degradation of the marine environment, including climate change impacts, such as ocean warming and sea level rise'. This obligation means maintaining a healthy and balanced marine ecosystem and is an obligation of 'dual significance' in that it promotes the conservation and resilience of marine ecosystems while also mitigating climate change.

Global and regional cooperation

14.36 States must cooperate to formulate rules, standards and recommended practices and procedures, based on the best available science, to mitigate marine pollution from GHG emissions and establish scientific criteria, promote studies, undertake research and exchange information, including data on marine pollution.

INTER AMERICAN COURT OF HUMAN RIGHTS (IACTHR) – ADVISORY OPINION

14.37 An Advisory Opinion from the IACtHR is expected in 2025.

IACtHR formation

14.38 The Organisation of American States[13] established the Court in 1979 to enforce and interpret the provisions of the American Convention on Human Rights.[14] It has two functions – to be both advisory and adjudicatory. In its advisory capacity it issues opinions on matters of legal interpretation which are brought to its attention by OAS bodies or member states.

Membership

14.39 In 1969 the American Convention on Human Rights was adopted and came into force in 1978. By August 1997 it had been ratified by 25 countries: Argentina, Barbados, Brazil, Bolivia, Chile, Colombia, Costa Rica, Dominica, Dominican Republic, Ecuador, El Salvador, Grenada, Guatemala, Haiti, Honduras, Jamaica, Mexico, Nicaragua, Panama, Paraguay, Peru, Suriname, Trinidad and Tobago, Uruguay and Venezuela.

Request for an Opinion

14.40 In January 2023, the Republic of Colombia and the Republic of Chile made a request[15] to clarify the scope of state obligations, in their individual and collective dimension, in order to respond to the climate emergency within the framework of international human rights law, paying special attention to the differentiated impacts of this emergency on individuals from diverse regions

13 Organisation of American States, https://www.oas.org/en/

14 American Convention on Human Rights, https://www.oas.org/dil/treaties_b-32_american_convention_on_human_rights.pdf

15 Request for an advisory opinion on the Climate Emergency and Human Rights submitted to the Inter-American Court of Human Rights by the Republic of Colombia and the Republic of Chile, https://www.corteidh.or.cr/docs/opiniones/soc_1_2023_en.pdf

and population groups, as well as on nature and on human survival on our planet.

The request acknowledged the human rights effects of the climate emergency, especially highlighting the vulnerability of communities and ecosystems in Latin America. Colombia and Chile emphasised the need for regional standards to accelerate action to confront climate change. The applicants mentioned the Advisory Opinion OC-23/17[16] requested by Colombia, where the IACtHR recognised the right to a healthy environment and the relationship between environment and human rights. The request identifies the IACtHR as the suitable body to determine guidelines for creating and implementing climate policies based on a human rights approach.

They asked:

- about the state obligations derived from preventing and guaranteeing human rights to confront climate emergencies;
- about the scope of the states' prevention duty regarding extreme and slow onset climate effects in the light of the Paris Agreement and the scientific consensus not to trespass the 1.5°C global temperature increase;
- about which actions states should take against damages provoked by climate impacts and which differentiated measures should be taken to protect vulnerable communities. Specifically, Colombia and Chile requested the Court to refer to actions regarding regulation, monitoring, environmental impact assessment, contingency plans and mitigation of activities that can worsen the climate emergency. The applicants also asked the Court about the principles that should 'inspire' these actions, especially regarding adaptation, mitigation, and loss and damage;
- about the state's obligation to preserve the right to life balanced against the climate emergency in the light of human rights and science standards. The applicants requested an opinion regarding the scope of substantive and procedural obligations concerning human rights and the environment and specifically asked the Court about the importance of protecting the right to access information to guarantee other human rights, such as the right to life, property, health and participation;
- for an opinion to clarify the differentiated obligations of the states to protect the rights of children and future generations from climate change. Colombia and Chile mentioned American Convention on Human Rights, Articles 1, 4, 5, 11 and 19 and asked about the nature and scope of the right of children to access justice to present judicial actions for preventing the potentially damaging effects of climate change;
- the Court to, following the clarification of the scope of procedural obligations, clarify the nature of the obligations of the states to provide for judicial actions for adequate protection and reparation of the rights affected by the climate emergency. In the same sense, the applicants asked about the necessity to implement the obligation to consult on the climate consequences of certain activities;
- about environmental defenders' protection, referring to the American Convention on Human Rights and the Escazú Agreement. Here, the applicants focused on the obligations that states should comply with for

16 Advisory Opinion OC-23/17, https://www.corteidh.or.cr/docs/opiniones/seriea_23_ing.pdf

protecting environmental defenders, especially Indigenous people and women, for protecting ecosystems in the context of the climate emergency; and

- about the cooperation between states to confront climate change in the region, especially seeking to clarify the shared and differentiated obligations amongst the region's nations. This highlights the need for guidelines to clarify states' role in guaranteeing reparation measures by considering equity and climate justice principles. The applicants also enquired about actions required to confront the migration triggered and exacerbated by climate effects in the region.

Opinion status

14.41 All evidence has been submitted and the Advisory Opinion is currently being drafted.

INTERNATIONAL COURT OF JUSTICE (ICJ) OPINION

14.42 The Court sat in December 2024 and an Opinion is expected in 2025.

ICJ history

The Hague Peace Conferences and the Permanent Court of Arbitration (PCA)

14.43 In 1899 the Hague Peace Conference convened on the initiative of the Russian Czar Nicholas II and marked the beginning of a third phase in the modern history of international arbitration. The objective was to discuss peace and disarmament. It resulted in the adoption of a Convention on the Pacific Settlement of International Disputes, which dealt not only with arbitration but also with other methods of pacific settlement, such as good offices and mediation. The 1899 Convention provided for the creation of permanent process that would enable arbitral tribunals to be set up and would facilitate their work. This institution, known as the Permanent Court of Arbitration, consisted of a panel of jurists designated by each country acceding to the Convention from among whom the members of each arbitral tribunal might be chosen. The Convention also created a permanent Bureau, located in The Hague, with functions corresponding to those of a court registry or secretariat, and laid down a set of rules of procedure to govern the conduct of arbitrations. The Permanent Court of Arbitration was established in 1900 and began operating in 1902.

In 1907, a second Hague Peace Conference, to which the states of Central and South America were also invited, revised the Convention and improved the rules governing arbitral proceedings. Some participants would have preferred the Conference not to confine itself to improving the machinery created in 1899. The United States Secretary of State, Elihu Root, had instructed the US delegation to work towards the creation of a permanent tribunal composed of judges who were full-time judicial officers, with no other occupation, who would devote their time wholly to the trial and decision of international cases by judicial methods. 'These judges,' wrote Secretary Root, 'should be so selected from the different countries that the different systems of law and procedure and the principal languages shall be fairly represented.' The US, the UK and Germany submitted a joint proposal for a permanent court, but the Conference was unable to reach agreement upon it. It became apparent, in the course of the discussions, that one of the major difficulties was finding an acceptable way of choosing the judges, since none of the proposals tabled had garnered widespread support. The Conference confined itself to recommending that states should adopt a draft convention for the creation of a court of arbitral justice as soon as agreement was reached 'respecting the selection of the judges and the constitution of the court'.

The Permanent Court of International Justice (PCIJ)

14.44 Article 14 of the Covenant of the League of Nations gave the Council of the League responsibility for formulating plans for the establishment of a Permanent Court of International Justice (PCIJ), which would be able not only to hear and determine any dispute of an international character submitted to it by the parties to the dispute, but also to give an advisory opinion upon any dispute or question referred to it by the Council or Assembly of the League of Nations. All that remained was for the League Council to take the necessary action to give effect to Article 14. At its second session early in 1920, the Council appointed an Advisory Committee of Jurists to submit a report on the establishment of the PCIJ.

In August 1920, a report containing a draft scheme was submitted to the Council, which, after examining it and making certain amendments, presented it to the First Assembly of the League of Nations, which opened in Geneva in November of that year. The Assembly instructed its Third Committee to examine the question of the Court's constitution. In December 1920, after an exhaustive study by a subcommittee, the Committee submitted a revised draft to the Assembly, which unanimously adopted it. This was the Statute of the PCIJ.

The International Court of Justice (ICJ)

14.45 The outbreak of war in September 1939 had serious consequences for the PCIJ, which had for some years been experiencing a decline in its level of activity. After its last public sitting on 4 December 1939 and its last order on 26 February 1940, the PCIJ in fact dealt with no further judicial business and no elections of judges were held. In 1940 the Court relocated to Geneva, leaving one judge in The Hague together with a few registry officials of Dutch nationality. Despite the war, consideration needed to be given to the future of the Court and to the creation of a new international political order.

In 1942 the US Secretary of State and the Foreign Secretary of the UK declared themselves in favour of the establishment or re-establishment of an international court after the war, and the Inter-American Juridical Committee recommended that the Permanent Court of International Justice (PCIJ) jurisdiction should be extended.

Meanwhile, on 30 October 1943, following a conference, China, the USSR, the UK and the US issued a joint declaration recognising the necessity 'of establishing at the earliest practicable date a general international organisation, based on the principle of the sovereign equality of all peace-loving States, and open to membership by all such States, large and small, for the maintenance of international peace and security'.

Article 33 of the United Nations Charter lists the following methods for the pacific settlement of disputes between states:

- Negotiation
- Enquiry
- Mediation
- Conciliation
- Arbitration
- Judicial settlement
- Resort to regional agencies or arrangements.

Some of these methods involve the services of third parties, such as mediation which places the parties to a dispute in a position in which they can themselves resolve their dispute thanks to the intervention of a third party. Arbitration goes further as the dispute is submitted to the decision or award of an impartial third party, so that a binding settlement can be achieved. The same is true of judicial settlement (the method applied by the ICJ), except that a court is subject to stricter rules than an arbitral tribunal, particularly in procedural matters. Historically, mediation and arbitration preceded judicial settlement.

ICJ membership

14.46 The ICJ is composed of 15 judges elected to nine-year terms of office by the UN General Assembly and the Security Council. These organs vote simultaneously but separately. In order to be elected, a candidate must receive an absolute majority of the votes in both bodies. This sometimes makes it necessary for a number of rounds of voting to be held.

In order to ensure a degree of continuity, one-third of the Court is elected every three years. Judges are eligible for re-election. Should a judge die or resign during their term of office, a special election is held as soon as possible to choose a judge to fill the unexpired part of the term.

Advisory Opinion history

14.47 The small pacific island of Vanuatu led a global campaign to request an Advisory Opinion from the ICJ. The initiative was started by law students from the University of the South Pacific who formed the Pacific Island Students fighting Climate Change.[17]

The UNGA adopted resolution A/RES/77/276[18] on 14 December 2022, requesting the ICJ's Advisory Opinion. The resolution was adopted by consensus after gaining overwhelming support.

On 17 April the UN Secretary-General António Guterres sent the request for an Advisory Opinion to the ICJ. He has stated that such an opinion will help the UNGA, the UN and Member States to 'take the bolder and stronger climate action that our world so desperately needs'.

The UNGA posed the following questions:

- What are the obligations of states under international law to ensure the protection of the climate system and other parts of the environment from anthropogenic emissions of GHGs for states and for present and future generations?
- What are the legal consequences for states under these obligations where they, by their acts and omissions, have caused significant harm to the climate system and other parts of the environment, with respect to:
  - — states, including, in particular, small island developing states, which, due to their geographical circumstances and level of development, are injured or specially affected by or are particularly vulnerable to the adverse effects of climate change?
  - — peoples and individuals of the present and future generations affected by the adverse effects of climate change?

Supporting documents

14.48

- Multilateral treaties relating to climate change, biodiversity, desertification, protection of the ozone layer, the law of the sea, and human rights.
- Scientific reports by the Intergovernmental Panel on Climate Change (IPCC) and other selected institutions.
- Documentation of the development of international law in the areas of state responsibility for internationally wrongful acts, protection of the atmosphere, protection of persons in the event of disasters, protection of the environment in relation to armed conflict, transboundary harm from hazardous activities, and sea level rise in relation to international law.
- Documents relating to the protection of the climate system and other parts of the environment, including UNGA resolutions on protection of the climate for present and future generations, the Rio Conventions, and other select documents on the environment.
- Outcomes of UN conferences and follow-up processes and related documents, including the Millennium Summit and Sustainable Development Conferences and other conferences and processes.

17 Pacific Island Students fighting Climate Change, https://www.pisfcc.org

18 UNGA Resolution A/RES/77/276 Request for an advisory opinion of the International Court of Justice on the obligations of States in respect of climate change (29 March 2023), https://documents.un.org/doc/undoc/ltd/n23/094/52/pdf/n2309452.pdf

- Resolutions by the UNGA and reports on the law of the sea.
- Documents on human rights and climate change, including:
  — UNGA resolutions;
  — Human Rights Council resolutions;
  — reports submitted to the Human Rights Council;
  — general comments, recommendations, and statements by UN human rights treaty bodies; and
  — reports and statements by the special procedures mechanisms of the Human Rights Council.

Public hearing Monday 2 December to Friday 13 December 2024[19]

14.49 Ninety-eight states and 12 international organisations expressed their intention to participate in the oral hearing before the court.

There is an urgent and pressing need for clarity on these questions posed. The *First Global Stocktake* under the Paris Agreement found:

> 'Despite overall progress made; Parties are not collectively on track towards achieving the purpose and long-term goals of the Paris Agreement.
>
> States' nominally determined contribution, if implemented to the full will only reduce the anticipated global temperature increase from 4°C to between 2.1 and 2.8°C and there are gaps between the commitments made in States' NDCs and the policies required to deliver them'.[20]

WHAT THE FUTURE HOLDS

14.50 Although the Advisory Opinions of the ICJ and IACtHR have yet to be published it is expected that they will follow that of the ITLOS, finding that states have a responsibility under international law to take actions to mitigate the effects of climate change. Although these look at state obligations under international law they are likely to have an effect in both public and private sectors. There will be pressure on states to ensure that their domestic arrangements are in line with their obligations under international law. This could result will more rules to ensure that companies are incentivised to reduce their GHG emissions. This could be both a challenge and an opportunity for states and businesses.

As was mentioned earlier (8.05) there has been domestic litigation against states regarding their Paris Agreement obligations and, in the case of *Urgenda* (8.08),[21] the Netherlands was found to have a duty of care under ECHR, Articles 2 and 8 to reduce GHG emissions. Switzerland was also found to be in

19 ICJ Advisory Opinion Obligations of States in respect of Climate Change, https://www.icj-cij.org/case/187
20 United Nations Climate Change, 'Global Stocktake', https://unfccc.int/topics/global-stocktake
21 *Urgenda Foundation v State of the Netherlands* (19/00135) NL:HR:2019:2007.

breach of the ECHR and to have taken insufficient action on climate change. When they arrive, the ICJ and IACtHR opinions are expected to look at the obligations of states to protect against the adverse impacts on human rights related to climate change and will be relevant to all businesses carrying out human rights due diligence.

Appendix I

Abbreviations

ABA ROLI	American Bar Association, Rule of Law Initiative
AFIR	Alternative Fuels Infrastructure Regulations
AFOLU	Agriculture Forestry and Other Land Use
IAR	International Assessment and Review
ANPS	Airports National Policy Statement
AOSIS	Alliance of Small Island States
ARENA	Australian Renewable Energy Agency
ASX	Australian Securities Exchange
BAL	Bristol Airport Ltd
BECCS	Bioenergy and Carbon Capture and Storage
BEIS	Department for Business, Energy and Industrial Strategy
BRT	Bus Rapid Transit
BTR	Biennial Transparency Reports
BSER	Best System of Emission reduction (US)
CBAM	Carbon Border Adjustment Mechanism
CBDP	Carbon Budget Delivery Plan
CBios	CBIO (Decarbonization Credit) – an environmental asset issued by plants (biofuel producers), created for the purpose of reducing the emission of carbon. into the atmosphere. The plants' annual targets for reducing emissions must be. met by purchasing CBios – each one is equivalent to one metric ton of carbon.
CCA	Climate Change Act
CCAC	Climate and Clean Air Coalition
CCAs	Climate Change Agreements
CCEG	Commission Expert Group on Climate Change Policy
CCC	Climate Change Committee
CCL	Climate Change Levy
CCS	Carbon Capture and Storage
CCOI	Creative Community Outreach Initiative (United Nations)
CDM	Clean Development Mechanism
CDR	carbon dioxide removal

CEFC	Clean Energy Finance Corporation
CEQ	Council on Environmental Quality (US)
CMA	Crown Minerals Act 1991 (New Zealand)
CNY	Chinese Yuan Renminbi
COSIS	Coalition Of Small Island States
CSIRO	Commonwealth Scientific Industrial Research Organisation
COP	Conference of Parties
CSRD	Corporate Sustainability Reporting Directive
CWA	Clean Water Act (US)
DAERA	Department of Agriculture, Environment and Rural Affairs (NI)
DCC	Dutch Civil Code
DETEC	Department of Environment, Transport, Energy and Communications (Switzerland)
ECBC	Energy Conservation and Building Code (India)
EED	Energy Efficiency Directive
EEZ	Exclusive Economic Zone
EHCR	European Court of Human Rights
EIA	Environmental Impact Assessment
ELC	Environment Land Court (Kenya)
EMR	electricity market reform
ENSO	El Niño Southern Oscillation
EPBC	Environment Protection and Biodiscovery Conservation Act 1999 (Australia)
WRF	Emission Reduction Fund
ES	Environmental Statement
ESA	Endangered Species Act (US)
ESG	environment, social and governance
ESR	Effort Sharing Regulation
ETI-CGC	Energy Transitions Initiative – Center for Global Commons
eTB	Exchange-traded Treasury Bonds (Australia)
eTIB	Exchange-traded Treasury Indexed Bonds (Australia)
ETF	Enhanced Transparency Framework
ETFs	Exchange Trade Funds
ETS	Emissions Trading System
FoE	Friends of the Earth
FAO	Food and Agriculture Organization

FCA	Financial Conduct Authority
F-gases	F-gases are potent greenhouse gases used mainly for refrigeration, aerosols and heat-resistant coating.
fiat currency	Fiat money is a currency that lacks intrinsic value and is established as a legal tender by government regulation. Traditionally, currencies were backed by physical commodities such as silver and gold, but fiat money is based on the creditworthiness of the issuing government.
FON	Friends of Nature Institute
GCF	Green Climate Facility
GDP	Gross Domestic Product
GHG	greenhouse gas
GEF	Global Environment Facility
GIB	Great Indian Bustard
GIM	National Mission for a Green India
GPA	Global Programme of Action
GPNM	Global Partnership on Nutrition Management
GPSS	Government Pipeline Storage System
$GtCO_2e$	Carbon dioxide equivalent, abbreviated to CO_2e is a metric measure used to compare the emissions from various greenhouse gases on the basis of their global warming potential by converting amounts of other gases to the equivalent amount of carbon dioxide with the same global warming potential.
GWWI	Global Wastewater initiative
GX	Green Transformation
HEAL	Health and Environmental Alliance
HFCs	hydrofluorocarbons
HFC-23	Hydrofluorocarbon (HFC) 23 potent greenhouse gas
IAR	International Assessment and Review
IBAMA	Instituto Basileiro do Meio Ambiante e Recursos
IB	Insulate Britain
ICA	International Consultation and Analysis
ICELA	Indian Council for Enviro-Legal Action
ICJ	International Court of Justice
IEA	International Energy Agency
IETC	International Environmental Technology Centre
INC	Intergovernmental Negotiating Committee
IPCC	Intergovernmental Panel on Climate Change

IPEN	International Pollutants Elimination Network
ITLOS	International Tribunal for the Laws of the Sea
IURC	International Urban and Regional Cooperation
JETPs	Just Energy Transition Partnerships
JI	Joint Implementation
JSO	Just Stop Oil
KSG	German Federal Climate Change Act 2019 – Bundes-Klimaschutzgesetz
LCANZI	Lawyers for Climate Change Action New Zealand Incorporated
LULUCF	land use, land use change and forestry
MBU	Making Best Use
MCD	Municipal Corporation of Delhi
MEPA	Massachusetts Environmental Policy Act (US)
MGP	Methane Guiding Principles
MNRE	Ministry of New and Renewable Energy (India)
MRV	Measurement, Reporting and Verification
MSA	Magnuson-Stevens Fishery Conservation and Management Act (US)
$MtCO_2e$	Million tons of carbon dioxide equivalent – 1 ton is 1,000 kilograms.
Mtoe	Million tons of oil equivalent
NAPCC	National Action Plan on Climate Change
NASA	National Aeronautics and Space Administration
NCQG	New Collective Quantified Goal on Climate Finance
NDC	Nationally Determined Contributions
NECP	National Energy Climate Plans
NEDC	New European Driving Cycle
NEPA	National Environment Policy Act (US)
NGER	National Greenhouse Energy Reporting (Australia)
NGT	National Green Tribunal (India)
NGO	Non-Governmental Organisation
NMEEE	National Mission for Enhanced Energy Efficiency (India)
NMSA	National Mission for Sustainable Agriculture (India)
NMSH	National Mission on Sustainable Habitat (India)
NMSHE	National Mission for Sustaining the Himalayan Ecosystem (India)

NMSKCC	National Mission on Strategic Knowledge for Climate Change (India)
NOAA	National Oceanic and Atmospheric Administration (US)
NOPSEMA	National Offshore Petroleum Safety and Environmental Management Authority
NPCC	Nigerian National Petroleum Corporation
NPDES	National Pollutant Discharge Elimination System
NRDC	Natural Resources Defense Council (US)
NRDC	National Development and Reform Commission (People's Republic of China)
NSM	National Solar Mission (India)
NWM	National Water Mission (India)
OECD	Organisation for Economic Co-operation and Development
OEJ	Office of Environmental Justice
OESEA4	Offshore Energy Strategy Environment Assessment 4
ONR	Office of Nuclear Regulation (UK)
OPP	Office of Pesticide Programs (US)
PCAPS	Priority Climate Action Plans (US)
PCIJ	Permanent Court of International Justice
PHMSA	Pipelines and Hazardous Materials Safety Administration (US)
PTD	Public Trust Doctrine (US)
PSAC	Presidents Science Advisory Committee (US)
RED II	European Renewable Energy Directive
Rest	Retail Employees Superannuation Trust
RET	Renewable Energy Target
RGGI	Regional Greenhouse Gas Initiatives
RMD	Renminbi (Chinese currency)
SCF	Social Climate Fund
SDG	Sustainable Development Goals
SEC	US Securities and Exchange Commission
SICA	Central American Integration System
SIDS	small island developing states
SLACC	South Lakeland Action Climate Change
SLCPs	short-lived climate pollutants
SPS	Strategy and Policy Statement
SRN	Strategic Road Network

SSH	Social Sciences and Humanities
TfL	Transport for London
UNCLOS	United Nations Convention on the Law of the Sea
UNEP	United Nations Environment Programme
UNFCCC	United Nations Framework Convention on Climate Change
UNGA	United Nations General Assembly
UNGPs	United Nations Guiding Principles
UNHCR	United Nations Human Rights Council
UNWTO	United Nations World Tourism Organization
US $	United States Dollar
UTM	Urban Transition Mission
WCC	World Coating Council (formerly International Paint and Printing Ink Council (IPPIC))
WCM	West Cumbria Mining
WMO	World Metrological Organization
WOTUS	Waters of the United States
WWF	World Wild Fund for Nature
ZLEV	zero and low-emissions vehicle

Appendix II

Climate Change Terms

adaptation	Adjustment or preparation of natural or human systems to a new or changing environment which moderates harm or exploits beneficial opportunities.
albedo	Fraction of light that a surface reflects.
anthropogenic	Made by people or resulting from human activities. Usually used in the context of emissions that are produced as a result of human activities.
biofuels	Gas or liquid fuel made from plant material. Includes wood, wood waste, wood liquors, peat, wood sludge, agricultural waste, straw, fish oils, sludge waste, waste alcohol, municipal solid waste, landfill gases and other waste.
carbon sequestration	Terrestrial or biologic, carbon sequestration – the process by which trees and plants absorb carbon dioxide, release the oxygen, and store the carbon.
climate neutral	Climate neutrality refers to the idea of achieving net zero greenhouse gas emissions by balancing those emissions so they equal (or are less than) the emissions that get removed through the planet's natural absorption; reducing emission through climate action.
evapotranspiration	Evapotranspiration (ET) is the combination of evaporation and transpiration.

Appendix III

COP Timeline

TABLE OF COP SUMMITS AND DATES

Dubai, United Arab Emirates	COP28	UN Climate Change Conference – United Arab Emirates, November 2023
Sharm el-Sheikh, Egypt	COP27	Sharm el-Sheikh Climate Change Conference – November 2022
Glasgow, United Kingdom of Great Britain and Northern Ireland	COP26	Glasgow Climate Change Conference – October–November 2021
Madrid, Spain	COP25	UN Climate Change Conference – December 2019
Katowice, Poland	COP24	Katowice Climate Change Conference – December 2018
Bonn, Germany	COP23	UN Climate Change Conference – November 2017
Marrakech, Morocco	COP22	Marrakech Climate Change Conference – November 2016
Paris, France	COP21	Paris Climate Change Conference – November 2015
Lima, Peru	COP20	Lima Climate Change Conference – December 2014
Warsaw, Poland	COP19	Warsaw Climate Change Conference – November 2013
Doha, Qatar	COP18	Doha Climate Change Conference – November 2012
Durban, South Africa	COP17	Durban Climate Change Conference – November 2011
Cancun, Mexico	COP16	Cancún Climate Change Conference – November 2010
Copenhagen, Denmark	COP15	Copenhagen Climate Change Conference – December 2009
Poznan, Poland	COP14	Poznan Climate Change Conference – December 2008

Bali, Indonesia	COP13	Bali Climate Change Conference – December 2007
Nairobi, Kenya	COP12	Nairobi Climate Change Conference – November 2006
Montreal, Canada	COP11	Montreal Climate Change Conference – December 2005
Buenos Aires, Argentina	COP10	Buenos Aires Climate Change Conference – December 2004
Milan, Italy	COP9	Milan Climate Change Conference – December 2003
New Delhi, India	COP8	New Delhi Climate Change Conference – October 2002
Marrakech, Morocco	COP7	Marrakech Climate Change Conference – October 2001
Bonn, Germany	COP6-2	Bonn Climate Change Conference – July 2001
The Hague, Netherlands	COP6	The Hague Climate Change Conference – November 2000
Bonn, Germany	COP5	Bonn Climate Change Conference – October 1999
Buenos Aires, Argentina	COP4	Buenos Aires Climate Change Conference – November 1998
Kyoto, Japan	COP3	Kyoto Climate Change Conference – December 1997
Geneva, Switzerland	COP2	Geneva Climate Change Conference – July 1996
Berlin, Germany	COP	Berlin Climate Change Conference – March 1995

Appendix IV

Climate Change Litigation

AUSTRALIA

Case name:

O'Donnell v Commonwealth of Australia (Federal Court of Australia, Proceeding No. VID482/2020) [2021] FCA 1223

Summary:

On 22 July 2020, the applicant initiated proceedings in the Federal Court of Australia (FCA)[1] against the Commonwealth, the Secretary to the Treasury, and the Chief Executive of the Australian Office of Financial Management (AOFM). The proceedings alleged failures in fiduciary duties, duties of care, and breaches of the Australian Securities and Investments Commission Act 2001 (ASIC Act) due to the non-disclosure of climate change risks in retail investor product disclosure documents for Australian Government Bonds. The applicant lodged the pleadings as a class action, seeking injunctive relief only.

Following strike-out applications by the Commonwealth, the FCA struck out the applicant's pleadings concerning breaches of fiduciary duty and duty of care. However, the FCA allowed the pleading regarding false and deceptive conduct in financial product disclosure documents under the ASIC Act to proceed, permitting the continuation of the class action.

The applicant's claim centred on the assertion that the Commonwealth had failed to disclose material climate change price risk information to investors who acquired certain exchange-traded Australian Government Bonds. The applicant argued that this omission in the Commonwealth's information statements constituted misleading or deceptive conduct in relation to financial services under the ASIC Act. It was contended that climate change risks could impact the future trading price of the exchange-traded Australian Government Bonds in question.

On 8 May 2023, the Commonwealth and the applicant engaged in mediation before an FCA registrar. Subsequently, on 14 August 2023, the applicant filed an application with the FCA to settle and discontinue the proceedings. On 11 October 2023, the parties agreed to discontinue the proceedings with no order as to costs. As part of the non-monetary settlement, the parties agreed to issue a public statement on the matter, which was published on the Treasury

1 See https://www.transparency.gov.au/publications/treasury/australian-office-of-financial-management-aofm/australian-office-of-financial-management-annual-report-2023-24/part-4%3A-annual-financial-statements/litigation---kathleen-o'donnell-v-commonwealth-of-australia-and-others

website on 16 October 2023 and on the website of the applicant's lawyers, Equity Generation Lawyers.[2]

Case name:

McVeigh v Retail Employees Superannuation Pty Ltd (Federal Court of Australia, Proceeding No. NSD1333/2018) [2019] FCA 14

Summary:

In this case[3], the parties reached a settlement where the Australian pension fund agreed to incorporate climate change financial risks in its investments and implement a net-zero by 2050 carbon footprint goal. The case involved Mr McVeigh's action against the Retail Employees Superannuation Trust (Rest), one of Australia's largest superannuation funds, regarding climate change risk assessment and disclosure obligations. Mr McVeigh, a member and beneficiary of the Rest fund, claimed that Rest had breached its obligations under the Superannuation Guarantee (Administration) Act 1992 and the Corporations Act 2001 in managing and disclosing climate change-related business risks. He had requested information from Rest in August 2017 concerning its knowledge and opinion of climate change business risks and the actions taken to respond to such risks. Although some information was provided, McVeigh alleged it was insufficient for him to make an informed judgement about Rest's management and financial condition. Under the Corporations Act 2001, super fund beneficiaries are entitled to request information needed to make informed decisions about the fund's management and financial condition. The plaintiff sought declaratory relief and an injunction requiring Rest to disclose the requested information, alleging that Rest had violated the Corporations Act by failing to provide adequate information.

The matter did not proceed to trial, but Rest made significant acknowledgements in its public statement on 2 November 2020.[4] Rest agreed to settle the litigation brought by Mr McVeigh and acknowledged that climate change poses material financial risks across various categories, including investment, market, reputation, strategy, governance, and third-party risk. Rest committed to actively identifying and managing these issues and developing systems, policies, and processes to mitigate and manage the financial risks of climate change. Rest agreed to implement a long-term objective to achieve a net-zero carbon footprint by 2050, measure and report on climate-related progress, encourage investee companies to disclose in line with the Task Force on Climate-related Financial Disclosures (TCFD) recommendations, publicly disclose the fund's portfolio holdings, and enhance its consideration of climate change risks in its investment strategy. Rest also committed to conducting due diligence and monitoring of investment managers' approaches to climate risk and continuing to develop its management processes and climate change policy. Other Australian superannuation funds and managed funds globally are likely to follow suit or

2 See further, https://climatecasechart.com/wp-content/uploads/non-us-case-documents/2021/20211008_Case-number-VID4822020-Judgment-citation-2021-FCA-1223_judgment-1.pdf

3 *McVeigh v Retail Employees Superannuation Pty Ltd* (Federal Court of Australia, Proceeding No. NSD1333/2018) [2019] FCA 14, https://climatecasechart.com/wp-content/uploads/non-us-case-documents/2019/20190117_NSD13332018_judgment.pdf

4 Rest, public statement, 'Rest reaches settlement with Mark McVeigh' (2 November 2020), https://rest.com.au/why-rest/about-rest/news/rest-reaches-settlement-with-mark-mcveigh

risk facing similar actions by their members or stakeholders. The settlement details can be found on the Equity Generation Lawyers website.[5]

Case name:

Minister for Environment v Sharma (Federal Court of Australia, Proceeding No. VID389/2021) [2022] FCAFC 65

Summary:

In September 2020, eight young people filed a class action in Australia's Federal Court[6] to block the extension of the Whitehaven Vickery coal mine. They argued that Federal Minister Sussan Ley had a common law duty of care to young people and that the project would exacerbate climate change, harming future generations. The primary judge initially declared that the Minister had a duty of care to avoid causing harm to people under 18 from the emissions of carbon dioxide resulting from the coal combustion.

However, the Full Court unanimously decided that this duty should not be imposed. The Chief Justice and other judges argued that the duty, which would require re-evaluating public policy, was inconsistent with the Environment Protection and Biodiversity Conservation Act 1999's (EPBC Act's) decision-making process, and posed issues of indeterminate liability. The plaintiffs announced they would not appeal the decision and requested the Court to discontinue the representative proceeding.[7]

Case name:

Cooper v National Offshore Petroleum Safety and Environmental Management Authority (NOPSEMA) (Federal Court of Australia, Proceeding No. VID647/2023) [2023] FCA 1158

Summary:

In this case[8] Mardudhunera Traditional Custodian, Raelene Cooper, represented by the Environmental Defenders' Office, filed a case in the Federal Court of Australia seeking judicial review of the NOPSEMA's decision to approve Woodside's application to carry out seismic blasting for the Scarborough Gas Project. Woodside said that they were ready to begin seismic blasting, this was despite objections from Traditional Custodians that they had not been consulted.

Despite finding that Woodside's consultation with First Nations stakeholders was inadequate, NOPSEMA gave approval for the testing on 31 July:

5 Rest Settlement https://equitygenerationlawyers.com/wp/wp-content/uploads/2020/11/Statement-from-Rest-2-November-2020.pdf

6 *Minister of the Environment v Sharma* (Federal Court of Australia, Proceeding No. VID389/2021) [2022] FCAFC 65, https://www.fedcourt.gov.au/services/access-to-files-and-transcripts/online-files/minister-for-the-environment-v-sharma

7 See further, https://climatecasechart.com/wp-content/uploads/non-us-case-documents/2022/20220422_VID-389-of-2021-2021-FCA-560-2021-FCA-774-2022-FCAFC-35-2022-FCAFC-65_judgment.pdf

8 *Cooper v National Offshore Petroleum Safety and Environmental Management Authority (No 2)* (Federal Court of Australia, Proceeding No. VID647/2023) [2023] FCA 1158, https://www.judgments.fedcourt.gov.au/judgments/Judgments/fca/single/2023/2023fca1158

> 'Conditions were attached to the approval that further consultation needed to be carried out before commencement of the blasting. Ms Cooper argues that NOPSEMA cannot grant the approval until she has been properly consulted; and alternatively that Woodside cannot begin seismic testing until Woodside has consulted with her, as required under the conditions of Woodside's approval from NOPSEMA.'

On 14 September, an interim injunction was granted until 28 September and the hearing of the matter was brought forward to later in September.

Issue for determination:

- whether the first respondent had statutory power to make the decision where the first respondent was not reasonably satisfied that the Seismic Survey EP demonstrated that the consultation required by Offshore Petroleum and Greenhouse Gas Storage (Environment) Regulations 2009, reg 11A had been carried out, and so was not reasonably satisfied of the criteria in reg 10A(g)(i) and (ii); the first respondent did not have statutory power to make the decision.
- whether, if Ground 1 was established, it would be open, as a matter of law, to refuse the relief sought on any discretionary basis identified by the second and third respondents; no.
- whether the applicant had standing to seek relief in relation to Ground 2 of the Amended Originating Application; not necessary to answer.

On 28 September the Court held as follows:

> 'For reasons which follow, NOPSEMA did not have statutory power to make the decision to accept the environment plan on the stated conditions in circumstances where it was not reasonably satisfied that the consultation required by reg 11A(g) of the Regulations had not been undertaken. Further, the basis identified by Woodside for refusal of the relief in the exercise of the Court's discretion has not been demonstrated to be a basis upon which the Court, acting in accordance with law, should refuse relief. It follows that Ms Cooper is entitled to the relief that she seeks based upon ground 1. It is not necessary to determine the question of standing in relation to ground 2.'

Reasons for the judgment:

> 'Two subsidiaries of Woodside Energy Group Ltd plan to undertake a seismic survey in waters off the coast of the Pilbara region in Western Australia. To do this they must have obtained approval from the National Offshore Petroleum Safety and Environmental Management Authority of an environment plan. On 31 July 2023, they obtained approval for a plan subject to conditions. The conditions require Woodside to undertake further consultation with representatives of Aboriginal and Torres Strait Islander bodies prior to the commencement of the seismic survey.
>
> Ms Raelene Cooper is a Mardudhunera lore woman, elder and a traditional custodian of Murujuga. Ms Cooper was a person who, under the terms of the conditions, was required to be consulted. Ms Cooper has commenced proceedings in this Court seeking judicial review on the basis that NOPSEMA did not have statutory power to make the decision to approve the environment plan for the proposed seismic survey (Ground 1). In the alternative, Ms Cooper claims that Woodside has not complied with the conditions requiring Woodside to consult with her and others and that she has standing to seek a permanent injunction restraining Woodside from undertaking the seismic survey (Ground 2).

The Court has granted an interlocutory injunction restraining Woodside from undertaking any activity described in the environment plan pending the urgent determination of three preliminary issues, namely:

- whether NOPSEMA had statutory power to make the decision to accept the environment plan where it was not reasonably satisfied that the consultation required by reg 11A of the *Offshore Petroleum and Greenhouse Gas Storage (Environment) Regulations 2009* had been carried out, and so was not reasonably satisfied of the criteria in reg 10A(g)(i) and reg 10A(g)(ii);
- whether, if (1) is established, it would be open, as a matter of law, to refuse the relief sought on any discretionary basis identified by Woodside; and
- whether Ms Cooper has standing to seek relief in relation to Ground 2 of her application.'

Case name:

Munkara v Santos NA Barossa Pty Ltd (No 5) (Federal Court of Australia, Proceeding No. VID907/2023) [2024] FCA 717[9]

Summary:

On 30 October, Simon Munkara, a member of the Jikilaruwu clan, filed proceedings and applied for an urgent injunction to prevent Santos commencing pipeline work on the Barossa gas project. The Tiwi Traditional Owner argued Santos had not properly assessed submerged cultural heritage along the route of its Barossa export pipeline. On 15 January 2024, the judge dismissed the case.

In this case the Federal Court has set the standard of proof required to support an assertion as to whether a particular project is likely to cause a significant risk to Aboriginal cultural heritage. A number of significant findings were made about the evidence that will be required to establish the existence of intangible Aboriginal cultural heritage such as Dreaming stories and songlines, and the extent to which that intangible heritage is likely to be harmed by a proposed development.

The decision also considered the issues of identifying which First Nations people possess the appropriate cultural authority to speak for their country, establishing the bounds of spiritual connection with land and sea and how a court might reconcile inconsistent accounts of particular beliefs.

The application was dismissed and lifted the injunction previously imposed on Santos, clearing the way for construction of the Barossa Project pipeline to proceed.

The applicants, Mr Munkara, Ms Puruntatameri and Ms Purtaninga Tipuamantumirri (applicants), who are respectively Jikilaruwu, Munupi and Malawu people from the Tiwi Islands, relied upon their cultural and spiritual connections to sea country to bring the proceedings.

The respondent was Santos NA Barossa Pty Ltd (Santos), which ran an offshore gas project, the Barossa Project. Santos proposed to construct a gas pipeline that passed within 7 km west of the Tiwi Islands for the Barossa Project.

9 *Munkara v Santos NA Barossa Pty Ltd (No 5)* (Federal Court of Australia, Proceeding No. VID907/2023) [2024] FCA 717, https://www.judgments.fedcourt.gov.au/judgments/Judgments/fca/single/2024/2024fca0717

The regulator, the National Offshore Petroleum Safety and Environmental Management Authority (NOPSEMA), accepted an environmental plan in respect of Santos' proposed construction of the pipeline on 9 March 2020.

The applicants had previously obtained an urgent interim injunction to prevent construction of the pipeline on the basis of their allegations that it would significantly impact both 'intangible cultural heritage' and 'tangible cultural heritage', and that construction of the pipeline would constitute an offence because the risk to cultural heritage was not provided for in the approved environmental plan.

In determining whether the pipeline posed a 'significant' risk to 'cultural heritage', it was necessary to look at the degree of chance of impact to the cultural heritage and the nature or the gravity of that impact. Therefore, the 'test for a significant risk is one about sufficiency' requiring the injunction applicant to demonstrate a risk of significant adverse impact upon the cultural heritage. The burden of proof falls on the party seeking to assert the risk, the Tiwi Islanders had to establish on the balance of probabilities that the pipeline posed a risk to cultural heritage, being an impact that was both significant and new, which may be one involving mathematical chance of less than 50 per cent. The judge said that it was not sufficient to prove that the cultural features 'may exist' or that the Tiwi Islanders 'might have' a spiritual connection to sea country, or beliefs in song lines and Dreamings. The Federal Court held that the existence of such burial grounds was found to have no more than a negligible chance of existing, and therefore they were incapable of forming a cultural heritage risk. There was also insufficient evidence to prove that the Tiwi Islanders, as a people, held a communal belief that extended to two spirits into the vicinity of the pipeline route. Therefore, as there was no proof that the cultural features existed, there was no cultural heritage risk posed by the pipeline.

Case name:

Daniel Billy and Others v Australia (Torres Strait Islanders Petition) (CCPR/C/135/D/3624/2019)

Summary:

The Indigenous peoples of the Torres Strait Islands petitioned[10] Australia for violating the International Covenant on Civil and Political Rights (ICCPR). They claimed that Australia's insufficient climate action violated their rights under ICCPR Articles 6, 17, 24(1), and 27. The eight Torres Strait Islanders argued that these violations stemmed from inadequate climate mitigation targets and the state's failure to adopt adaptation measures despite numerous requests. The United Nations Human Rights Council (UNHRC) found it appropriate to consider violations of the Paris Agreement and other international treaties under the ICCPR, providing an avenue for redress of human rights violations related to climate change.

The Committee determined that Australia's failure to protect the Indigenous Torres Islanders from adverse climate change impacts violated their rights to

10 Billy and others v Australia (Torres Strait Islanders Petition) (CCPR/C/135/D/3624/2019), https://juris.ohchr.org/casedetails/3855/en-US

enjoy their culture and be free from arbitrary interferences with their private life, family and home. The right to a life with dignity requires states to protect citizens from threats, including climate change impacts. Additionally, the state's failure to adopt adaptation measures to protect the Islanders' traditional way of life violated their right to enjoy their minority culture. The Committee asked Australia to compensate the Islanders, engage in meaningful consultations, and take measures to secure the communities' safe existence on their islands.[11]

Case name:

Australasian Centre for Corporate Responsibility v Santos Ltd (Federal Court of Australia, Proceeding No. NSD858/2021)

Summary:

In this case[12] the Australasian Centre for Corporate Responsibility (ACCR) made greenwashing claims against Santos Ltd.

In August 2021, ACCR[13] commenced proceedings in the Federal Court alleging Santos Ltd breached the Corporations Act 2001 and the Australian Consumer Law by engaging in misleading or deceptive conduct relating to representations contained in its *2020 Annual Report.*

In August 2022, ACCR amended its case to include alleged greenwashing in Santos' *2020 Investor Day Briefing* and *2021 Climate Change Report*,[14] following additional information produced by Santos in the litigation discovery process.

In February 2023, the Federal Court ordered a court-supervised conferral between the parties' respective lawyers, to clarify and reduce the issues in dispute. Following this ACCR sought and obtained leave of the Court to further amend its case to reduce as far as possible the issues that needed to be heard and determined by the court, and to clarify ACCR's claims in light of information that had arisen in the conferral process.

The representations concerned three major areas:

- representations that Santos had a clear and credible pathway to:
    - reduce its Scope 1 and 2 greenhouse gas emissions by 26–30 per cent by 2030 (from its 2019–20 baseline); and
    - achieve 'net zero' Scope 1 and 2 greenhouse gas emissions by 2040;
- representations that Santos was a producer of 'clean energy', and that natural gas is a 'clean fuel';
- representations that hydrogen produced from natural gas with carbon capture and storage (blue hydrogen) is 'clean' and 'zero emissions'.

11 See further, https://climatecasechart.com/wp-content/uploads/non-us-case-documents/2019/20190513_CCPRC135D36242019_complaint.pdf

12 *Australasian Centre for Corporate Responsibility v Santos Ltd* (Federal Court of Australia, Proceeding No. NSD858/2021).

13 ACCR, media release 'Greenwashing Proceedings in Federal Court' (24 October 2024), https://www.accr.org.au/news/greenwashing-proceedings-in-federal-court/

14 Santos' *2020 Investor Day Briefing* and *2021 Climate Change Report*, https://www.santos.com/wp-content/uploads/2020/12/2020-Investor-Day-FINAL.pdf

In the *2020 Annual Report*, *2021 Climate Change Report* and *2020 Investor Day Briefing*, Santos made a number of statements that it had a clear and credible pathway to achieve 'net-zero' emissions by 2040. A large amount of this reduction was anticipated to come from future carbon capture and storage (CCS) processes and blue hydrogen.

However, ACCR alleged that Santos failed to disclose that it had firm plans to increase its greenhouse gas emissions through expected oil and gas growth and exploration opportunities beyond 2025.

ACCR also alleged that Santos failed to disclose that its net-zero plans depend upon a range of undisclosed and/or unreasonable qualifications and assumptions to reduce or offset Santos' Scope 1 and 2 emissions, calling into question whether Santos had reasonable grounds to assert it had a 'clear and credible' plan to reach net-zero emissions by 2040.

Santos made a number of statements in its *2020 Annual Report* that the natural gas it produces is 'clean fuel' and provides 'clean energy'.

In the *2020 Annual Report*, *2021 Climate Change Report* and *2020 Investor Day Briefing*, Santos made a number of statements that the blue hydrogen it intends to produce is 'clean' and 'zero emissions'. The ACCR said that these representations convey that any emissions generated by the production of blue hydrogen would be captured by CCS, such that there would be zero emissions from blue hydrogen production.

The ACCR claimed that Santos failed to disclose that blue hydrogen production would increase its Scope 1 and 2 emissions.

The ACCR asked the Federal Court to:

1. make declarations that Santos had engaged in misleading or deceptive conduct, or conduct that was likely to mislead or deceive;
2. grant an injunction prohibiting Santos from engaging in the same misleading or deceptive conduct in the future; and
3. grant an injunction requiring Santos to issue a corrective statement regarding the environmental impacts of its operations.

The case is still pending.

Case name:

ASIC v LGSS Pty Ltd [2024] FCA 587

Summary:

In this case[15] the Federal Court found LGSS Pty Ltd, as trustee of the superannuation fund Active Super, contravened the law in connection with various misleading representations concerning its environmental, social and governance (ESG) credentials.

Active Super had claimed in its marketing that it eliminated investments that posed too great a risk to the environment and the community, including

15 *Australian Securities and Investments Commission v LGSS Pty Ltd* [2024] FCA 587, https://download.asic.gov.au/media/ticl0q1b/24-121mr-asic-v-lgss-pty-ltd-2024-fca-587.pdf

gambling, coal mining and oil tar sands. Following the invasion of Ukraine, Active Super also made representations that Russian investments were 'out'.

The Federal Court found that from 1 February 2021 to 30 June 2023, Active Super invested in various securities that it had claimed were eliminated or restricted by ESG investment screens. These securities were held by Active Super both directly and indirectly (via managed funds or Exchange Traded Funds (ETFs)).

The judge rejected Active Super's claims that an ordinary or reasonable consumer would draw a distinction between holding shares in a company and indirect exposures through a pooled fund and stated that:

> 'I am unable to accept LGSS's contention that an ordinary and reasonable member of the relevant class would draw a distinction between holding shares in a company and indirect exposures through pooled funds. It seems to me that such a consumer would not draw that distinction, including in particular because there is nothing in the Impact Reports or on the LGSS website that suggests that the claims that there was, for example, 'No way' Active Super would invest members funds in gambling, tobacco and so on, was to be read subject to a proviso that there was a way in which it would do exactly that, by investing indirectly, not directly. In my view, that distinction is one which no ordinary reasonable consumer would draw.'

The Court also found that Active Super did not engage in misleading representations in relation to its holdings in companies involved in the production of packaging used for tobacco products, and that specific representations in its Sustainable and Responsible Investment Policy were not misleading with respect to Russian or oil tar sands investments (although the remaining representations alleged by ASIC were upheld).

The judge found that on 5 June 2024, Active Super had published representations which were misleading and deceptive in relation to exclusions applied to gambling, coal mining, Russian entities and oil tar sands investments on its website, reports and disclosure documents.

The judge found that the use of the terms such as such as 'not invest', 'No Way' and 'eliminate' were unequivocal and not the subject of any potential qualifications by LGSS's 'Sustainable and Responsible Investment Policy'.

At the time of publishing these representations, Active Super held direct and indirect investments in companies such as:

- SkyCity Entertainment Group Ltd and Pointsbet Holdings Ltd (Gambling)
- Gazprom PJSC and Sberbank of Russia (Russian entities)
- ConocoPhillips and Shell Plc (Oil tar sands)
- Whitehaven Coal Ltd (see **6.17**) and Coronado Global Resources (Coal mining)

The matter has been listed for a further hearing to consider the appropriate form of declaratory relief and will consider the pecuniary penalty to impose for the conduct at a later date.

BRAZIL

Case name:

Instituto Arayara v ANP and Others (unreported) (auction of oil exploration blocks in the Amazon Basin)

Summary:

Following the COP 28 climate summit in Dubai, where Brazil's President stressed the need to reduce greenhouse gas (GHG) emissions, the National Oil, Gas and Biofuels Agency (ANP) auctioned 602 oil and gas exploration blocks, including 21 in the Amazon River Basin. These blocks, according to the Arayara International Institute, violated state environmental guidelines and overlapped with protected areas and Indigenous and Quilombola territories. On 6 December 2023, the Instituto Arayara de Educação e Cultura para a Sustentabilidade filed a public civil action against the ANP, Brazil's Federal Environmental Agency (IBAMA), and the Federal Government, challenging the 4th Bid Cycle for oil exploration blocks in the Amazon Basin. The plaintiff argued that the blocks' inclusion was illegal due to overlaps with Conservation Units, buffer zones, environmental protection areas and areas with endangered species. It contended that the climate emergency necessitates a transition to clean energy and a reduction in GHG emissions which is incompatible with expanding oil exploration. The plaintiff requested the suspension of the auction in Sector AM-T-82 until a technical analysis demonstrating socioenvironmental viability was conducted, particularly with reasoned opinions from bodies such as IBAMA. Ultimately, they sought the exclusion of the contested blocks from the Bid Cycle.

In March 2024, IBAMA and ANP defended the auction, stating that the alleged overlap with Conservation Units did not warrant exclusion from the bidding phase under current regulations, as sensitive areas were considered in the procedure. They highlighted the economic benefits of oil exploration for Brazilian society and noted that the International Energy Agency's NetZero 2050 scenario still relies on oil and natural gas as primary energy sources. They argued that the impacts of GHG emissions could be assessed during the environmental licensing phase at the entrepreneur's expense. The ANP emphasised that social participation is promoted before bidding for exploration rights and that the auction process itself posed no environmental risk. On 1 March 2024, the Federal Government filed its defence, addressing licensing issues and asserting that the contested blocks' offer was technically supported by competent bodies' rules. In March 2024, Atem Participações SA also filed a defence, stressing that the bidding process did not pose an environmental risk and that project impacts would be assessed during the environmental licensing phase.[16]

16 See further, https://climatecasechart.com/non-us-case/instituto-arayara-vs-anp-and-others-on-auction-of-oil-exploration-blocks-in-the-amazon-bazin/

Case name:

Public Defender's Office of the State of Pará v Associação dos Ribeirinhos e Moradores and Others (Public Civil Action (ACP) 0806505-59.2023.8.14.0015) (Project 2620 carbon credits and 'forest carbon grabbing')

Summary:

On 19 July 2023, the Public Defender's Office of the State of Pará (DPE-PA) filed a Public Civil Action (ACP) against Associação dos Ribeirinhos e Moradores, Sindicato dos Produtores Rurais de Portel, Amigos dos Ribeirinhos Assessoria Ambiental Eireli, Brazil Agfor LLC, and the Municipality of Portel. The ACP concerns a project that generated illegal carbon credits sold on the voluntary market. The Ribeirinho REDD+ Project (Project 2620) overlaps with five State Agro-Extractivist Settlement Projects (PEAEX) in Portel, Pará, public lands granted to traditional communities that did not participate in the project. Presented to an international certifying company in 2017, Project 2620 has not yet been registered to generate REDD+ assets for 30 years.

The defendants are accused of irregular property registrations and lacking state authorisation, constituting public land grabbing. The mayor of Portel issued a Public Utility Decree authorising the project, which the DPE-PA argues is unconstitutional. The DPE-PA claims the defendants violated traditional territory rights, failed to comply with federal climate change legislation, and did not benefit the affected communities. The DPE-PA seeks recognition of traditional land possession, suspension of Project 2620, and prevention of the defendants from entering the PEAEX. Additionally, the plaintiff requests annulment of Project 2620 and related transactions, prohibition of the defendants from entering the territories, nullification of the Public Utility Decree, and collective moral damages of R$ 5,000,000.00 to be paid into the Eastern Amazon Fund for the benefit of Portel's extractivist communities.[17]

Case name:

Flexpetro Distribuidora de Derivados de Petróleo Ltda v ANP and Federal Union (Acquisition of CBios) (ProcedCom 5057055-20.2020.4.04.7000)

Summary:

Flexpetro Distribuidora de Derivados de Petróleo Ltda filed a lawsuit against the ANP and the Federal Union, challenging the requirement to acquire Decarbonization Credits (CBios) under the National Biofuels Policy (RenovaBio). The policy, established by Federal Law 13.576/2017, aims to meet Brazil's commitments under the Paris Agreement by promoting biofuels and reducing greenhouse gas emissions. The plaintiff argued that the ANP set decarbonisation targets for 2019 and the decade 2020–29 without ensuring the availability of CBios or regulating the certification process, making it impossible to meet the 2020 target. They requested the suspension of their compulsory target and related fines. An initial injunction was granted but later revoked on appeal, with the court affirming the legitimacy of the targets and the absence of illegality in the ANP's actions.

17 See further, https://climatecasechart.com/non-us-case/public-defenders-office-of-the-state-of-para-vs-associacao-dos-ribeirinhos-e-moradores-and-others-project-2620-carbon-credits-and-forest-carbon-grabbing/

The appeal decision noted that the targets were known since 2018, the 2020 target was reduced for distributors' benefit, and the judiciary should not reassess the public administration's criteria. The final decision dismissed Flexpetro's request, upholding the mandatory targets as legitimate and reasonable. Flexpetro appealed this decision.[18]

CHINA

Case name:

Beijing Grassland Alliance Environmental Protection Center v Xingyi Shangcheng Power Generation Co Ltd (unreported)

Summary:

The Beijing Grassland Alliance Environmental Protection Center, along with three other NGOs, sued Xingyi Shangcheng Power Generation Co Ltd. This coalition of activists successfully compelled the coal-fired power company to address its outstanding emissions obligations under China's national compliance carbon market. Schangcheng Power, a small company in Xingyi, Guizhou province, faced accusations of emitting pollutants above standard levels, tampering with pollution data and failing to maintain monitoring equipment. Additionally, it was alleged that the company exceeded permissible carbon dioxide emissions and failed to pay for 821,596 tons of carbon quotas. The court was asked to order the company to pay for 818,148 tons of carbon credits and implement energy-saving measures.

On 7 June 2024, the court found that the defendant's emissions of sulphur dioxide and dust constituted an environmental tort. However, it ruled that the company had not exceeded standards for waste gas or nitrogen oxides, except during equipment malfunctions, and that the plaintiff failed to prove environmental damage from non-payment of carbon quotas. Shangcheng Power claimed financial difficulties prevented timely purchase of emission allowances, which eventually cost them Yuan 73.18 million by December 2023. The court concluded that the company's repeated failure to fulfil carbon trading obligations was unlawful and contrary to climate change mitigation goals. Despite Chinese law not classifying carbon dioxide as a pollutant, its emissions are subject to stringent controls.[19]

18 See further, https://climatecasechart.com/wp-content/uploads/non-us-case-documents/2022/20220101_ProcedCom-5057055-20.2020.4.04.7000_decision.pdf

19 See further, https://climatecasechart.com/non-us-case/beijing-grassland-alliance-environmental-protection-center-v-xingyi-shangcheng-power-generation-company-limited/

Case name:

Friends of Nature Institute v Ningxia State Grid (unreported)

Summary:

This case involved whether Ningxia State Grid had violated the Renewable Energy Law by not purchasing all electricity from renewable sources, thus failing to protect the environment. On 24 January 2018, the Friends of Nature Institute (FON) sued Ningxia State Grid for abandoning wind and solar power, violating Articles 2 and 14 of the Renewable Energy Law. FON demanded that the defendant purchase all renewable electricity within its grid's coverage, invest 5 per cent of its annual revenue in renewable energy development for five years, disclose clean energy consumption information, offer a public apology and cover the plaintiff's litigation costs. Ningxia State Grid denied all allegations.

On 4 April 2023, the court ruled that Ningxia State Grid did not violate Article 14 and dismissed most of FON's claims. The court found that the defendant met its obligation to purchase wind and solar power, as grid companies are required to purchase all electricity under Article 14 only if consumption is safe. The court emphasised the State Grid's social responsibility to facilitate renewable use and implement low-carbon plans. It also recognised FON's role in environmental litigation and ordered Ningxia State Grid to cover 350,000 RMB (US $49,000) of the plaintiff's litigation costs. FON has appealed the decision.[20]

Case name:

Friends of Nature Institute v Gansu State Grid (unreported)

Summary:

On 6 June 2017, the Friends of Nature Institute (FON) sued Gansu State Grid for violating Articles 2 and 14 of the Renewable Energy Law by not connecting purchased wind and solar power to the grid. FON argued that this failure led to increased GHG emissions and that Gansu State Grid should be held accountable for the environmental damage caused by its reliance on coal-fired power.

The Lanzhou Intermediate People's Court dismissed the case on procedural grounds, but FON appealed. On 28 December 2018, the High Court of Gansu Province overruled the lower court's decision and ordered the Gansu Mining Area Intermediate Court to hear the case. On 5 June 2019, the court accepted the case and a mediation agreement was reached on 10 April 2023. Gansu State Grid agreed to invest in connecting renewable electricity to the grid and to submit annual progress reports and disclose clean energy consumption information for public supervision.[21]

20 See further, https://climatecasechart.com/non-us-case/the-friends-of-nature-institute-v-ningxia-state-grid/

21 See further, https://climatecasechart.com/non-us-case/the-friends-of-nature-institute-v-gansu-state-grid/

Case name:

Beijing Fengfujiuxin Marketing and Technology Co Ltd v Zhongyan Zhichuang Blockchain Co Ltd (unreported)

Summary:

In May 2019, Beijing Fengfujiuxin Marketing and Technology Co Ltd (the plaintiff) and Zhongyan Zhichuang Blockchain Co Ltd (the defendant) signed three contracts for bitcoin mining, with the plaintiff purchasing 1,542 micro data storage servers and receiving 93 per cent of the profits. The plaintiff paid RMB 100 million, but the defendant stopped sharing profits after transferring 18.3463 BTC. The plaintiff sued for 278.1655 BTC or US $95.5 million. On 14 December 2021, the District Court of Chaoyang in Beijing dismissed the claims, citing Article 52(4) of the Contract Law, which voids contracts harming public interests. The court referenced governmental notices on cryptocurrency risks, deeming the contracts invalid. The plaintiff's appeal was dismissed by the Beijing Third Intermediate People's Court on 7 July 2022.[22]

EU

Case name:

Carême v France (*Carême*) (App no 7189/21) CE:ECHR:2024:0409 DEC000718921 (2024) 79 EHRR SE1

Summary:

In the case of *Carême v France* (relinquishment),[23] Mr Carême was mayor of Grande-Synthe, France from 2001 to 2019. Grande-Synthe is a town in Northern France that is particularly exposed to climate-related risks. On 19 November 2018, Mr Carême, acting on his own behalf and in his capacity as mayor, asked the French Government to:

- take all useful measures to curb national GHG emissions;
- adopt all necessary legislative and regulatory initiatives to 'make climate priority mandatory';
- prohibit all policies likely to increase GHG emissions; and
- implement immediate measures to adapt to climate change in France.

When the national authorities failed to respond, Mr Carême appealed to the Conseil d'Etat (French Supreme Administrative Court) on grounds of excess of power.

The petition highlighted the future risks associated with climate change, and the need for immediate and ambitious measures to progressively limit GHG emissions. The first petition claimed a violation of ECHR, Articles 2 and 8.

22 See further, https://climatecasechart.com/non-us-case/beijing-fengfujiuxin-marketing-and-technology-co-ltd-v-zhongyan-zhichuang-blockchain-co-ltd/

23 *Carême v France* (relinquishment) (App no 7189/21) CE:ECHR:2024:0409DEC000718921 (2024) 79 EHRR SE1, https://hudoc.echr.coe.int/eng#{%22itemid%22:[%22002-13678%22]}

In the decision of 19 November 2020, the Conseil d'Etat ruled that the claims were subject to judicial review. The Conseil drew a distinction between the case of the town and that of Mr Carême. For the judges, the municipality had an interest, while the mayor did not. Two further decisions by the same court followed (1 July 2021 and 10 May 2023), in which the Conseil ruled that, whilst the government had adopted additional measures to address climate change, the available evidence did not provide a sufficiently credible guarantee that the GHG emissions reduction plan would be achieved. The Council asked the government to take additional measures before 30 June 2024.

Mr Carême appealed to the ECtHR in 2022, alleging that the measures were insufficient, thereby violating his rights under Convention, Articles 2 and 8. On 31 May 2022, the Chamber in charge of the case relinquished jurisdiction in favour of the Grand Chamber. Two years later, the Court declared the application inadmissible for lack of interest on the part of the applicant.

The French Government argued that the Conseil d'Etat's decision of July 2021 had already deprived the claimant of victim status. The government explained that the decision had satisfied the claims by the claimant before the domestic courts by admitting the admissibility of the application lodged by the town. The ECtHR agreed, once again denying Mr Carême the status of victim.

Having moved to Brussels in May 2019, Mr Carême no longer owned nor rented property in Grande-Synthe. The only link was the fact that his brother lived there. According to its established case law, adult siblings cannot rely on the family life component of Article 8, unless they can demonstrate the existence of additional elements of dependence, which was not the case here.

Mr Carême had also submitted his application in his capacity as former mayor of Grande-Synthe. The Court rejected this ground too, referring to established case law (*Assanidzé v Georgia (*2004);[24] *Slovenia v Croatia (*2020)[25]). In its view, decentralised authorities exercising 'public functions', irrespective of their degree of autonomy from central bodies are regarded, as 'governmental organisations' not entitled to apply to the Court under Article 34 of the Convention. Consequently, the Court concluded that the applicant was not entitled to lodge an application with the Court, or submit a complaint to it, on behalf of this town.

Case name:

Duarte Agostinho and Others v Portugal and Others (App no 39371/20) (2024) 78 EHRR SE9

Summary:

This case[26] was brought by a group of six children and young adults who argued that Portugal and 32 other signatory states had breached the ECHR by failing to cut GHG emissions in line with their Paris Agreement commitments.

24 *Assanidzé v Georgia* (App no 71503/01) CE:ECHR:2004:0408JUD007150301, https://hudoc.echr.coe.int/fre#{%22itemid%22:[%22001-61875%22]}

25 *Slovenia v Croatia* 2020 https://hudoc.echr.coe.int/fre#{%22itemid%22:[%22002-13063%22]}

26 *Duarte Agostinho and Others v Portugal and Others* (App no 39371/20) (2024) 78 EHRR SE9, https://hudoc.echr.coe.int/eng/#{%22itemid%22:[%22002-14303%22]}

It was alleged that the respondent states collectively had contributed to global warming and heatwaves and wildfires that have affected their lives, well-being, mental health and the amenities of their home. It was argued that the respondent states were under a positive obligation to take adequate measures to regulate their contributions to climate change. They relied on ECHR, Articles 2, 3, 8, First Protocol, Article 1 and ECHR, Article 14 (taken with Articles 2 and 8).

The Grand Chamber dismissed the claim for procedural reasons without considering the substantive ECHR arguments. The Court held that the ECHR, Article 1 obligation to 'secure rights and freedoms' only extended to Portugal as this was the state in which all the applicants resided. It was the only state with territorial jurisdiction over them within the meaning of ECHR, Article 1. The ECHR can apply extraterritorially in limited circumstances, the Court has 'consistently rejected' the notion that extraterritorial jurisdiction can apply merely because a state takes a decision 'which has an impact on the situation of a person abroad'.

A key question in the case was, accordingly, whether the respondent states, other than Portugal, could be held responsible for the climate-related impacts that their emissions contributed to, but that were felt overseas. Here, the Court drew parallels to its migration-related case law (*M.N. and Others v Belgium,*[27] on visa applications submitted at embassies abroad). In doing so, it agreed with the applicants that this case did not fit the Court's established models of extraterritorial jurisdiction under ECHR, Article 1 (which is primarily territorial), except when

- a state exercises 'effective control' outside its borders;
- its agents have power and control over a person abroad; or
- more rarely, there are specific procedural elements to a case).

Case name:

Verein Klimaseniorinnen Schweiz and Others v Switzerland (App no 53600/20) CE:ECHR:2024:0409JUD005360020 (2024) 79 EHRR 1

Summary:

In this case[28] the European Court of Human Rights (ECtHR or the Court) ruled that Switzerland had breached the ECHR by not taking sufficient action against climate change. In particular, it found a breach of the right to respect for private and family life contained in Convention, Article 8, based on Switzerland's failure to mitigate the impact of climate change on the lives, health, well-being and quality of life of its citizens. It also ruled that Switzerland had breached the right to a fair trial in terms of Article 6, in that the domestic courts failed to examine the merits of the applicants' complaints, including the scientific evidence.

27 *M.N. and Others v Belgium* (App no 3599/18) CE:ECHR:2020:0505DEC000359918, https://hudoc.echr.coe.int/fre#%7B%22fulltext%22:[%22m.n%20and%20others%20belgium%22],%22documentcollectionid2%22:[%22DECISIONS%22],%22itemid%22:[%22001-202468%22]%7D

28 *Verein Klimaseniorinnen Schweiz and Others v Switzerland* (App no 53600/20) CE:ECHR:2024:0409JUD005360020 (2024) 79 EHRR 1, https://hudoc.echr.coe.int/eng#{%22itemid%22:[%22001-233206%22]}

The application was brought by four individuals and an association of 2,500 women, KlimaSeniorinnen, all of whom were concerned about the impacts which climate change was having on their health, well-being and quality of life. In particular the applicants, whose average age was 73, cited evidence on the disproportionately adverse effects which climate change has on older women.

In November 2016, the applicants submitted a request to the Swiss Federal Department of the Environment, Transport, Energy and Communications (DETEC) to try and compel the Swiss authorities to take all necessary measures required by the Swiss Constitution and the Convention to prevent the increase of global temperatures. DETEC rejected their request based on a lack of standing, indicating that the applicants were pursuing general public interests which did not provide them with victim status under the Convention.

Both appeals to the Federal Administrative Court and the Federal Supreme Court were dismissed. This was on the basis that they hadn't shown that the that the applicants' rights had been sufficiently and directly affected by climate change in a way that was different to the rest of the population.

Their next application was to the ECtHR, claiming that the Swiss Authorities had breached Convention, Article 8 by failing to ensure respect for their private and family life, including their home. They said that their rights under Article 6 had been breached because the Swiss courts had not responded to their requests for effective mitigating measures to be implemented against climate change.

On the 9 April 2024, the ECtHR handed down its judgment in three cases: *Duarte Agostinho* and *Carême* were dismissed, however, in the cases *KlimaSeniorinnen*, the Court made a number of important rulings.

Standing and victim status

Convention, Article 34 allows the Court to receive applications from:

> 'any person, non-governmental organisation or group of individuals claiming to be the victim of a violation by one of the High Contracting Parties of the rights set forth in the Convention of the Protocols thereto.'

The Court held that the individual applicants were not victims for the purpose of Article 34 because they failed to demonstrate the existence of a sufficient link between the harm they had allegedly suffered (or would suffer in the future) and climate change. So the individual applicants' complaints under Convention, Articles 2 and 8 were dismissed. However, the Court held that the applicant association did have *locus standi* and proceeded to determine its Article 8 complaint.

On the question of standing and victim status, the Court had to balance upholding the longstanding principle against admitting so called *actio popularis*-type[29] claims while recognising that, in a climate change context, everyone may be affected or be at risk of being affected. For the first time, the Court accepted a claim brought by an environmental NGO. In doing so, it restated that the Convention does not provide for *actio popularis* but that victim status is not to be applied in a 'rigid, mechanical and inflexible way'. The Court recognised at that:

29 *actio popularis* – the established action of a third party in order to protect the rights of others, or protection of the principle of equality.

'the special feature of climate change as a common concern of humankind and the necessity of promoting intergenerational burden-sharing in this context ... speak in favour of recognising the standing of associations before the Court in climate-change cases.'

Positive obligations of states

Another issue before the Court was the extent to which states have positive obligations under the Convention regarding climate change mitigation. The Court deemed it appropriate to examine the applicant association's complaint from the angle of Article 8 alone.

The Association argued that Article 8 was engaged by Switzerland's failure to take the necessary steps to reduce emissions and combat the immediate risk posed to its vulnerable elderly female members by the climate crisis. The Swiss Government's response was that climate change is a global problem and therefore the applicants could not attribute causation specifically to Switzerland. The government also stated that, given the technical and complex nature of climate change, states should be given a wide margin of appreciation. The living-instrument doctrine[30] did not allow for the Convention to be interpreted in a way that undermined the principle of subsidiarity.[31]

The Court acknowledged that this kind of claim is a new departure for the Court's environmental case law which has dealt with situations involving specific sources of environmental harm as opposed to the wider problem of climate change for which there is no single or specific source of harm. However 'failure by the Court to maintain a dynamic and evolutive approach would risk rendering it a bar to reform or improvement'. The Court's environmental jurisprudence means that the Court recognised the 'intergenerational burden' of the climate crisis and the rights of future generations.

However, applying the principle of subsidiarity, the Court reiterated that states have freedom to decide the specific steps they will take to comply with their positive obligations.

The Court held that Switzerland had failed to comply with its positive obligations under Article 8 to put in place relevant legislative and administrative frameworks to quantify, through a carbon budget or otherwise, national GHG emissions limitations.

Dissenting Opinion – the British Judge, Judge Eicke said the case raised crucial, existential questions about the role of the ECtHR and courts in general faced with the challenges of the climate crisis. Judge Eicke accepted that, in principle, the standing test under Article 34 could be expanded since that is implicit in the principle of effectiveness, but he took the view that the Court should only do so where that was necessary because no individual could bring a case. He made the point that the individual applicants only failed to prove their standing on the evidence, there was nothing intrinsically impossible about individuals being able to bring a climate change human rights claim before the Court. He therefore

30 The living-instrument doctrine is a judicial interpretation method used by the European Court of Human Rights (ECtHR) to interpret the European Convention on Human Rights (ECHR).

31 The principle of subsidiarity is a principle that aims to ensure that decisions are made at the level of government closest to the people, unless EU-level action is demonstrably more effective.

considered that expanding the standing provisions to allow an association to bring a claim was unnecessary and should have been left for 'an appropriate future case'.

Following the case the Swiss authorities will now be supervised by the Committee of Ministers to adopt measures aimed at ensuring compliance with its Convention obligations. The Swiss State was ordered to pay KlimaSeniorinnen €80,000 towards costs.

Case name:

Milieudefensie and Others v Royal Dutch Shell plc (C/09/571932/HA ZA 19-379) NL:RBDHA:2021:5339

Summary:

In April 2019, six environmental associations and NGOs, including Milieudefensie[32] (Greenpeace Netherlands Foundation) and the Environmental Defense Association (Amsterdam), along with 17,319 individual co-claimants, brought a case against Shell. They claimed that Shell's contributions to climate change violated its duty of care under Dutch law and human rights law. The Court was asked to decide if Shell should amend its corporate policy to reduce carbon dioxide emissions across its entire energy portfolio by 2030, relative to 2019 levels. In May 2021, the Court ruled that Shell was subject to a duty of care under Dutch law regarding the harmful effects of climate change and required it to reduce its carbon emissions. This decision was based on the Dutch Civil Code, scientific evidence on climate change, and human rights instruments such as the ECHR and UN Guiding Principles on Business and Human Rights (UNGPs). The Court concluded that Shell had an obligation to protect the claimants' human rights by complying with the implied standard of care in Dutch Civil Code, Article 6:162.

The Court ordered Shell to reduce its net carbon dioxide emissions for the entire Shell Group's global activities by 45 per cent by 2030, compared to 2019 levels, through its corporate policy. These emissions reductions were necessary to align Shell Group's corporate policies with the Paris Agreement and apply across Shell's entire energy portfolio, including Scope 1, 2, and 3 emissions. While the Court imposed an absolute obligation on Shell to reduce Scope 1 emissions, the reduction obligation for Scope 2 and Scope 3 emissions was expressed on a 'best efforts' basis. Shell appealed the 2021 ruling, arguing that corporate emissions reductions were a matter for legislators, not the courts. The Court of Appeal upheld Shell's appeal regarding the specific percentage reduction imposed by the Court in 2021 but made several significant findings, including acknowledging the state's role in setting policy while concluding that businesses have parallel obligations. The Court found that the reduction obligation falls on Royal Dutch Shell, the parent company establishing the Shell group's climate change policies and strategies. Shell's reduction obligation was established under the general tort provision of Dutch Civil Code (DCC), Article 6:162, which contains a duty of care for natural persons and legal entities. Breaching this duty results in liability for damages suffered due to the

32 *Milieudefensie and others v Royal Dutch Shell plc* (C/09/571932/HA ZA 19-379) NL:RBDHA:2021:5339, https://en.milieudefensie.nl/news/verdict-climate-case-milieudefensie-shell-26-may-2021-1.pdf

breach. The Court used several sources to interpret and determine Shell's duty of care, including the ECHR, the Paris Agreement, scientific evidence from the IPCC, the UNGPs, and OECD Guidelines for Multinational Enterprises. [33]

Case name:

Marlene Lemme and Others v State of Bavaria

Summary:

In this case,[34] ten people brought a complaint against the State of Bavaria, Germany, claiming that the state's failure to set adequate climate protection goals and emission reduction paths was in violation of domestic environmental law and constitutional law. They alleged that this failure to mitigate would have an effect on the plaintiffs' human rights and health, as well as damaging animals and nature.

Following the decision in *Neubauer and Others v Germany* (see **8.09**) and the Federal Climate Protection Act (Bundes-Klimaschutzgesetz (KSG)), the State of Bayern could have been in breach of its duty to protect the fundamental rights of the claimants under the Basic Law of the Federal Republic of Germany (Germany's Constitution) and by failing to stipulate a GHG reduction pathway that is adequate and complies with the targets set out in the KSG.

In the 2021 case *Neubauer and Others*, the Federal Court of Germany unanimously declared that the federal government was in breach of its international and European obligations to reduce GHG emissions by failing to set emission reduction goals from 2031 onwards, subsequently violating the rights of citizens.

Following this decision, on 30 June 2021, ten people, supported by the NGO Deutsche Umwelthilfe, drafted a complaint against the State of Bayern. Their claim was that the state legislation for climate protection (Bayerische KSG) was inadequate as it failed to set climate protection goals that complied with the federal KSG and therefore created a higher risk for the rights and freedoms of the claimants.

The plaintiffs claimed that their constitutional rights were being violated on two counts:

- due to the inadequacy of the existing climate protection laws; and
- because of the failure of some state legislatures to create a uniform reduction path for GHG emissions.

They also raised the issue that some of the federal states in Germany (State of Brandenburg, State of Hesse) had not specified any reduction paths at all, or that the chosen pathways were insufficient.

The claimants alleged that Bayerische KSG, Articles 2(1) and (2), 5(1)(1) and 7 were unconstitutional as they lead to two violations of their fundamental constitutional rights:

33 See further, https://climatecasechart.com/wp-content/uploads/non-us-case-documents/2024/20241112_8918_judgment.pdf

34 *Marlene Lemme and Others v State of Bavaria* (German Bundesverfassungsgericht, constitutional complaint of 30 June 2021), https://judicialportal.informea.org/node/9701

- Art 2(1) which grants every person the right to freedom of development, in conjunction with Art 20a, which places a duty upon the state to ensure that the natural foundations of life and animals are protected for future generations;
- partial violation of the duty to protect that the state has under Art 2(2), which establishes the right to life and physical integrity, and Art 14(1), which guarantees the right to property and inheritance.

To ensure that the plaintiffs' losses of freedom are reasonable and that the burden of dealing with GHG emissions is not placed solely upon future generations, the legislature is obliged to implement the necessary reductions in CO_2 emissions and changes in lifestyle, as required by the Constitution and the provisions in the KSG.

As the constitutional petition was not admitted for adjudication no arguments of the respondents were presented.

On 18 January 2022, the First Senate of the Federal Constitutional Court did not admit the complaints for adjudication. The judges, in line with the decision in *Neubauer and Others*, recognised that the obligation to protect against the consequences of climate change cannot be postponed and, if adequate precautions are not taken, there could be a violation on the constitutional rights of future generations. However this complaint was only directed against certain acts or omissions by the state (rather than all emissions) so that these actions alone cannot lead to a disproportionate shift in the reduction burdens. The court confirmed that the state legislature retains some leeway on how to regulate the amount of permissible emissions.

The court also recognised that under German Constitution, Article 20a, states share the burden and the responsibility of ensuring that steps are taken towards climate protection; this does not fall solely upon the federal government. The court stated that the targets set out at the federal level cannot be achieved if there are no implementation measures and legislation at the state level.

The court also emphasised how states have a limited amount of influence in the area of climate protection, which is managed by the federal government. Therefore it is difficult to determine state-specific reduction requirements, especially taking into consideration that emission reduction coordination is currently being approached horizontally through individual emission sectors.

On this basis the court rejected the claims, finding that it is not possible to determine the extent to which the state legislature had the necessary powers to reduce or prevent any future violations of the rights contained in Constitution, Articles 2, 14 and 20a.

Case name:

Urgenda Foundation v State of the Netherlands (19/00135) NL:HR:2019:2007

Summary:

In this case[35] Urgenda set out the facts of climate change in their summons and explained why emissions need to be radically reduced to avert catastrophic

35 *Urgenda Foundation v State of the Netherlands* (19/00135) NL:HR:2019:2007, https://uitspraken.rechtspraak.nl/details?id=ECLI:NL:HR:2019:2007

harm. It provided the grounds upon which it claimed the Dutch State was legally obliged to take action to reduce Dutch GHG emissions.

In its defence, the state acknowledged all of the facts of climate change, including the potentially devastating consequences if no action is taken. The state implicitly acknowledged that it was not doing its share to avoid dangerous climate change. The state rejected the idea that it could be legally obliged to act and argued that there was no legal obligation on the basis of which it was legally bound to reduce GHG emissions. The state also argued that, whether, and to what extent, emissions should be reduced is a political question in which the courts should not intervene.

The Urgenda Foundation, in its reply, strengthened the legal argument that was in the summons. After the statement of reply was filed, the state submitted one final written rebuttal before the hearing.

On 14 April 2015, oral arguments were presented at the District Court in The Hague.

The District Court of The Hague issued its judgment on the 24 June 2015, ordering the Dutch State to lower its emissions by at least 25 per cent before 2020 compared to 1990 levels.

In September 2015, despite calls from leading scientists, lawyers, citizens, companies and the 886 co-plaintiffs for it to accept the decision, the Dutch Government decided to appeal the judgment. It made this decision even though it was taking steps to meet the target set by the Court. The appeal at the Hague Court of Appeal took place on 28 May 2018.

The judgment was delivered on 9 October 2018: the Hague Court of Appeal decided to uphold the 2015 decision.

On 8 January 2019, the state filed its grounds of appeal to the Supreme Court. Despite its initial announcement it was filing the appeal because of its disagreement with the Court of Appeal's approach to the question of 'separation of powers', the state challenged a wide range of findings that were made by the Court of Appeal. This included the finding that the state had a human rights-based obligation to reduce emissions and the necessity to reduce Dutch emissions by at least 25 per cent by 2020 compared to 1990 levels in order to prevent global warming from exceeding 2°C.

On 12 April 2019, Urgenda filed its written defence to the Supreme Court. The case was heard at the Supreme Court on 24 May 2019. On 21 June 2019 Urgenda filed its rejoinder in which it responded to the pleadings and the written submissions of the state.

On 13 September 2019, two chief advisers to the Supreme Court, the Procurator General and Advocate General, published an Advisory Opinion. The Advisory Opinion assessed every argument that had been put forward by the state and concluded than none of them were persuasive. They therefore concluded that the judgment of the Court of Appeal should be upheld.

On 20 December 2019 the Supreme Court, the highest in the country, stated that the Dutch Government must reduce emissions immediately in line with its human rights obligation.

Case name:

Neubauer and Others v Germany (BvR 2656/18)

Summary:

In the case brought by Luisa Neubauer and nine youth climate activists[36] against the German Federal Government, the plaintiffs argued that the 2019 German Federal Climate Change Act (Bundes-Klimaschutzgesetz (KSG)) failed to meet Germany's responsibilities under the Paris Agreement and violated their fundamental rights under the German Constitution. They contended that the KSG lacked a detailed plan for reducing greenhouse gas (GHG) emissions, thereby shifting the burden of combating climate change onto future generations. The plaintiffs sought declaratory relief, asserting that the law's inadequate emissions reduction targets were unconstitutional and that the government must set new targets for reducing GHG emissions. They also claimed that the KSG violated their rights to freedom, a future consistent with human dignity and an ecological minimum standard of living.

The court considered whether the post-2030 burdens on freedom inherent in the KSG could be justified under constitutional law or whether the KSG had offloaded reduction burdens onto future generations. The court recognised climate protection as a human right within the fundamental rights to life, health and physical integrity, obligating the state to protect against the risk of climate change. The court found that the Constitution must be interpreted fairly for all generations, establishing a duty to protect future generations, especially where irreversible processes are at stake. The court unanimously ruled that the KSG was partially unconstitutional for failing to protect future generations from future infringements of their rights and ordered the legislature to amend the KSG by the end of 2022. The German Government complied, enhancing the climate protection policy and raising its GHG emissions reduction targets to a 64 per cent reduction by 2030, an 88 per cent reduction by 2040 and climate neutrality by 2045.[37]

Case name:

Kaiser and Others v Volkswagen AG (Braunschweig Regional Court, 14 February 2023)

Summary:

In a judgment on 14 February 2023, the court dismissed the action by climate activists, supported by Greenpeace, seeking to prohibit the distribution of Volkswagen (VW) vehicles with combustion engines from 2030 and to reduce VW's CO_2 emissions by 65 per cent, compared to 2018 levels, by 2030. The claimants cited the 'Climate-Decision' by the German Constitutional Court (BVerfG, 24 March 2021, 1 BvR 2656/18), alleging VW violated constitutional property, health and freedom rights due to its contribution to climate change. The court referred to a decision by the German Constitutional Court on 18 January 2022, which found that the German legislature had complied with

36 Bundesverfassungsgericht (Federal Constitutional Court, 'Constitutional complaints against the Federal Climate Change Act partially successful', Press Release No. 31/2021, 29 April 2021, https://www.bundesverfassungsgericht.de/SharedDocs/Pressemitteilungen/EN/2021/bvg21-031.html

37 See further, https://climatecasechart.com/non-us-case/neubauer-et-al-v-germany/

its climate-related constitutional obligations by enacting the German Climate Protection Act on 31 August 2021. The court in Braunschweig concluded that VW's climate-related obligations do not exceed those of the legislature and deemed the plaintiffs' demands unreasonable. The court left open the issues of whether the claimants' rights had been breached, whether VW qualifies as an infringer, and whether VW's operations are causal for the alleged breach.[38]

Case name:

Schaefer Kalk GmbH & Co KG v Germany (Case C-460/15) EU:C:2017:29

Summary:

In this case[39] Schaefer Kalk operated a facility covered by the EU carbon emissions trading system (EU ETS) and argued that CO_2 that is transferred to a non-covered facility and becomes chemically bound and is therefore not released into the atmosphere should not be considered 'emitted'.

During the lime calcination process carbon dioxide is emitted, which Schaefer Kalk transferred to an installation that was not covered by the EU ETS for the production of precipitated calcium carbonate (PCC). As Schaefer Kalk needed to get their monitoring plan approved, they applied for authorisation to subtract the CO_2 transferred for PCC production from the amount of GHG emissions in the company's emissions report. They argued that the transferred carbon dioxide is chemically bound in the PCC and cannot be emitted into the atmosphere and therefore cannot be regarded as 'emissions' as defined in Directive 2003/87/EC, Article 3(b).

The German Emissions Trading Authority at the Federal Environment Agency had approved the monitoring plan without looking at the issues of subtracting transferred CO_2. Schaefer Kalk brought a complaint which was rejected. They then brough the matter before the Berlin Administrative Court, the Berlin Administrative Court transferred the matter to the European Court of Justice. The Court of Justice gave a preliminary ruling deciding that the second sentence of Commission Regulation (EU) No 601/2012on the monitoring and reporting of greenhouse gas emissions pursuant to Directive (EC) 2003/87, Article 49(1) and point 10(B) of Annex IV to that regulation were invalid as it systematically included the CO_2 transferred to another installation for the production of precipitated calcium carbonate in the emissions of the lime combustion installation, regardless of whether or not that CO_2 was released into the atmosphere.

The framework encompasses a comprehensive scope, categorising the eligible carbon removal activities into four main areas:

- permanent carbon removal (storing atmospheric or biogenic carbon for several centuries),
- temporary carbon storage in long-lasting products (such as wood-based construction products) of a duration of at least 35 years and that can be monitored on-site during the entire monitoring period, and
- temporary carbon storage from carbon farming.

38 See further, https://climatecasechart.com/non-us-case/kaiser-et-al-v-volkswagen-ag/
39 *Schaefer Kalk GmbH & Co KG v Germany* (Case C-460/15) EU:C:2017:29, https://eur-lex.europa.eu/legal-content/EN/TXT/?uri=CELEX%3A62015CJ0460

The legal issues surrounding carbon capture and utilisation (CCU) within the EU are moving rapidly to align with the goal of achieving carbon neutrality by 2050. Under the EU ETS, recent amendments and court rulings have expanded the scope of accepted CCU applications, particularly looking at the importance of permanent chemical binding of CO_2 in products. However, there is still the definitional issue of what 'permanently chemically bound' means and the criteria for assessing the duration of carbon storage in products.

Case name:

Vegetarian Society of Denmark v Danish Crown 2021 BS-472/2022-VLR; 1009/23[40]

Summary:

In May 2021, Danish NGOs, including the Danish Vegetarian Association and the Climate Movement in Denmark, sued Danish Crown, a leading pork producer in the EU, for misleading marketing claims. The company asserted that its pork was 'more climate-friendly than you would think' and 'climate controlled'. In March 2024, the court ruled that the first claim was not misleading but found the second violated the Danish Marketing Practices Act by misrepresenting the environmental impact of the company's products. Danish Crown had used labels claiming pigs were 'climate-controlled' without independent verification, limiting consumers' ability to make informed decisions. Although the company stopped using the label in 2021, the court acknowledged that its Climate Road Programme justified the label. This case, the first greenwashing trial in Denmark, has been highlighted by industry campaigners as a significant statement on the legal stance against greenwashing in the food sector. Activists hope it will lead to broader changes in the industry.[41]

Case name:

FossielVrij NL v KLM (C/13/71948/HA ZA 22-524) NL:RBAMS:2024:1512

Summary:

In *FossielVrij NL v KLM*[42] on 24 May 2022, FossielVrij NL issued a summons to KLM at an AirFrance-KLM shareholder meeting, alleging that KLM's 'Fly Responsibly' campaign made misleading claims about the sustainability of flying. The Dutch court ruled that KLM had violated consumer law by making misleading environmental claims.

FossielVrij argued that KLM's advertisements misled consumers about the environmental benefits of their products, violating the Dutch Unfair Commercial Practices Act. The Court of Amsterdam found that 15 of the 19 statements made by KLM were misleading, including claims that flying

40 See Steen, 'Denmark – The Vegetarian Society and the Danish Climate Movement vs. the Cooperative Danish Crown – Rulings of the Western High Court and the Supreme Court: New trends in climate litigation' (2024) 5 Diritto Processuale Amministrativo Law Journal 1021–1024,

41 See further, https://climatecasechart.com/non-us-case/vegetarian-society-et-al-of-denmark-v-danish-crown/#:~:text=At%20the%20end%20of%20May,think.'%20Danish%20Crown%20is%20a

42 *FossielVrij NL v KLM* (C/13/71948/HA ZA 22-524) NL:RBAMS:2024:1512, https://www.clientearth.org/media/cx4po41h/klm-judgment-20-march-2024.pdf

could become environmentally sustainable and that purchasing KLM products reduced the impact of flying on climate change. The court declared these statements unlawful but did not award the requested penalty, ordering KLM to pay Fossielvrij's costs.[43]

Case name:

In Re Tax Benefits for Aviation [2022] G 106-107/2022-10, V 140/2022-10 [2022] G 106-107/2022-10, V 140/2022-10[44]

Summary:

The applicant, a consumer utilising both rail and air services, applied for relief, citing a diagnosis of multiple sclerosis and health issues exacerbated by the climate crisis. She argued that existing Austrian tax laws favouring aviation over rail travel contributed to environmental problems and violated her constitutional rights, including:

- the right to equality before the law;
- the right to life; and
- the right to private and family life.

The applicant contended that tax benefits for aviation companies created an unjustified disparity in treatment between equivalent means of transport, negatively impacting consumers who choose rail travel. The tax advantages granted to aviation companies, in contrast to railway companies, violated her fundamental rights. These rights included the right to equality before the law, where the applicant asserted that the tax benefits led to unequal treatment of equivalent means of transport in direct competition. She argued a violation of her right to life, saying that climate change, exacerbated by tax benefits to aviation, posed a threat to human life, and that the state had failed in its positive obligation to adopt measures to prevent such threats. The applicant also alleged a violation of her right to private and family life, as the state's encouragement of climate-damaging behaviour through tax benefits violated its positive obligations to protect health, well-being, and bodily integrity from environmental hazards.

On 27 June 2023, the Constitutional Court of Austria dismissed the application as inadmissible. The court cited the amendment to the Value-Added Tax Act as of 1 January 2023, which extended value-added tax (VAT) exemptions from aviation and maritime shipping to cross-border rail transport. The court determined that the contested provision was no longer in force, leading to a lack of standing for the applicants. Additionally, the court held that the obligation to pay VAT was directed at businesses, excluding consumers from challenging relevant provisions.

43 See further, https://climatecasechart.com/non-us-case/fossielvrij-nl-v-klm/

44 *Re Tax Benefits for Aviation* [2022] G 106-107/2022-10, V 140/2022-10 (Constitutional Court of Austria), https://climaterightsdatabase.com/2024/01/09/in-re-tax-benefits-for-aviation/

Case name:

Luciano Lliuya v RWE (Case No. 2 O 285/15)

Summary:

Saúl Luciano Lliuya, an Andean farmer and mountain guide from Peru, along with over 50,000 residents of Huaraz, faces the threat of a flood wave due to glacial melt. In November 2015, he sued the energy company RWE in a German court, claiming that RWE's CO_2 emissions contributed to the climate crisis and the flood risk. Saúl is concerned about the urgent need for protection for himself, his family and the people of Huaraz.

In 2016, the court dismissed the claim, citing a lack of a 'linear causal chain'. Evidence included studies linking flood risk to global warming and a study finding no significant glacial instability. In May 2022, judges and experts visited the Palcacocha Lake area to assess the risk. RWE maintains that a single company cannot be held responsible for climate change.

The case is still ongoing.[45]

Case name:

Asmania and Others v Holcim (Cantonal Court of Zug (Kantonsgericht Zug))

Summary:

In July 2022, four residents of the Indonesian island of Pari initiated legal proceedings against the Swiss-based company Holcim (formerly Lafarge Holcim). They filed a request for conciliation before the Justice of the Peace of the Canton of Zug, Switzerland, as required by the Swiss Civil Procedure Code. Supported by three NGOs—HEKS/EPER (Switzerland), the European Center for Constitutional and European Rights (ECCHR), and WALHI (Indonesia)—the plaintiffs seek compensation for climate change-related damages on Pari, a reduction of CO_2 emissions and financial contributions to adaptation measures.[46]

After a failed conciliation hearing in October 2022, the plaintiffs lodged a lawsuit against Holcim with the Cantonal Court of Zug in February 2023. This case is part of a global movement and represents only the second climate litigation brought by individuals from the Global South. The plaintiffs aim to hold Holcim accountable for both historical and future emissions, seeking not only compensation but also the preservation of livelihoods threatened by climate change.[47]

45 See further, https://climatecasechart.com/non-us-case/lliuya-v-rwe-ag/

46 See Reyes and Burri, 'Transnational corporate liability in the era of loss and damages: the case of Asmania Et Al. V Holcim', European Center for Constitutional and Human Rights, https://www.ecchr.eu/fileadmin/Publikationen/Duartes_Burri_Transnational_corporate_liability_in_the_era_of_loss_and_damage_2024.pdf

47 See further, https://climatecasechart.com/non-us-case/four-islanders-of-pari-v-holcim/

Case name:

Hugues Falys, FIAN, Greenpeace, Ligue des Droits Humains v TotalEnergies (The Farmer Case)[48]

Summary:

Hugues Falys, a farmer from the Hainaut province in Belgium is taking legal action before the Tournai Commercial Court, on the border with France, against TotalEnergies for its responsibility for climate change.

Falys' legal action is the first climate case ever brought in Belgium against a multinational company. Three Belgian NGOs, FIAN, Greenpeace, and the Ligue des Droits Humains (LDH), are have joined forces to intervene in the case, with support from the Belgian Climate Coalition. The case seeks recognition for the damages suffered by Hugues Falys, but also to ensure TotalEnergies's compliance with the targets of the Paris Agreement. The case asks the court to request TotalEnergies to implement a credible transition plan, which includes a halt to new investments in fossil fuel projects, a 47 per cent reduction in gas and oil production by 2030, and a more stringent 75 per cent reduction by 2040.

The first hearing took place on 16 April 2024 in the Commercial Court of Tournai. During the hearing, the five parties agreed on a schedule for the exchange of pleadings, which will take place on 19 and 26 November 2025.

INDIA

Case name:

Nuggehalli Jayasimbha v Government of NCT of Delhi (unreported, 20 May 2020)

Summary:

The case[49] dealt with property rights, government authority, and fairness in a land dispute in Delhi.

The petitioner challenged the Delhi government's actions regarding a disputed property, focusing on land ownership and land use regulation. The main legal issues were whether the government's actions were legal and if proper procedures were followed.

The court emphasised the need for the government to follow lawful processes and protect the petitioner's rights. The decision highlighted the importance of fair hearings and proper notice to affected parties.

48 *Hugues Falys, FIAN, Greenpeace, Ligue des Droits Humains v TotalEnergies (The Farmer Case)* (Commercial Court of Tournai), https://climatecasechart.com/non-us-case/hugues-falys-fian-greenpeace-ligue-des-droits-humains-v-totalenergies-the-farmer-case/

49 *Nuggehalli Jayasimbha v Government of NCT of Delhi* (unreported, 20 May 2020), https://indiankanoon.org/doc/159137499/?ref=the-wave.net

This case sets a precedent for property rights in Delhi, balancing government authority and individual rights. In conclusion, the case underscores the importance of procedural fairness and adherence to legal frameworks in administrative decisions.

Case name:

MK Ranjitsinh and Others v Union of India and Others (unreported, 21 March 2024)[50]

Summary:

This case was brought to look at balancing the need to safeguard biodiversity in the preservation of the Great Indian Bustard[51] and mitigating the impacts of climate change through interpretation of Indian Constitutional provisions and other legal framework in India and international commitments.

A writ petition was filed with the Supreme Court of India asking it to invoke its jurisdiction to issue an order to protect two endangered birds, the Great Indian Bustard (GIB) and the Lesser Florican. The number of Great Indian Bustards is at around 200 individuals and the loss is mainly due to the degradation of its habitat as well as hunting for sport and food. It is also at risk from the construction of infrastructure, such as roads, wind turbines, solar energy projects and electricity pylons.

The original case was brought by MK Ranjitsinh a well-known conservationist who was concerned with the plight of the GIB and its smaller cousin the Lesser Florian. He succeeded in gaining a judgment of the Supreme Court on 19 April 2021 when the Supreme Court blocked the installation of overhead transmission lines over a wide area and mandated that they should be buried underground instead. The Indian Government viewed this order as impractical and appealed. The Ministry of Environment, Forests, and Climate Change, the Ministry of Power, and the Ministry of New and Renewable Energy (MNRE) requested that the judgment dated 19 April 2021, should be reversed because if it were to be implemented this would cause adverse implications for the power sector, India's international commitment for energy transition and fulfilment of its promise under the Paris Agreement signed by India in 2015 under the United Nations Framework Convention on Climate Change (UNFCCC). In this case the court had to decide two major issues:

- whether to modify of the directions issued under the earlier judgment dated 19 April 2019; and
- how to balance the preservation of GIB and India's commitment to control climate change through just transition (moving fossil fuels to renewable energy).

The court reviewed the factors causing threats to GIBs, the actions taken by the Government of India, specifically the programme 'Habitat improvement and

50 *MK Ranjitsinh and Others v Union of India and Others* (unreported, 21 March 2024), https://indiankanoon.org/doc/128036238/

51 WWF, 'Great Indian Bustard', https://www.wwfindia.org/about_wwf/priority_species/threatened_species/great_indian_bustard/

conservation breeding of great Indian bustard'[52] launched in 2016 and other measures. The court also discussed the impacts of climate change and India's commitments and efforts to control it. An observation was that the promotion of renewable energy sources is crucial for promoting social equity by ensuring access to clean and affordable energy for all segments of society therefore fostering inclusive growth and development across the country. The court emphasised the duty of the state under Article 48[53] and fundamental duty of citizens under Article 51A of the Constitution of India[54] as Constitutional commitments to ensure protection of the natural world and compassion for living creatures. The court related these articles to Articles 21 and 14 of the Indian Constitution and declared that the right to a clean environment and the right against the adverse effects of climate change has its source in Article 21 which recognises the right to life and personal liberty and Article 14 which indicates equality before law and equal protection of law. This justified the actions of the state. The court dealt with intersection between climate change and human rights as well as a novel issue of the intricate interface between the conservation of an endangered species, such as the GIB and the need to protect against the climate change. Powerlines now need to be underground in areas where the GIB lives.

Case name:

M/S Singh Timber Traders and Others v State of UP and Others, Allahabad High Court (unreported, 8 July 2020)

Summary:

In 2020, the Supreme Court delivered a judgment regarding the Uttar Pradesh Tax on Entry of Goods Act, 2007.[55] The petitioners, M/S Singh Timber Traders, argued that the tax on timber entering the local area was unconstitutional and unfairly burdened their business.

The issues were whether the tax violated the petitioners' right to trade under Indian Constitution, Article 19(1)(g) and hether the tax on timber was legally valid.

The petitioners claimed the tax was discriminatory and not applied uniformly, affecting their market competitiveness and imposing financial strain. The respondents defended the tax, stating it was within the state's legislative powers and aimed at generating local revenue.

52 Wildlife Institute of India, 'Habitat improvement and conservation breeding of great Indian bustard', https://wii.gov.in/campa_gib

53 Indian Constitution, Article 48 Invocation of Responsibility for a Breach of an Obligation to the International Community as a Whole. Article 48 provides:

'1. Any State other than an injured State is entitled to invoke the responsibility of another State in accordance with paragraph 2 if:
   (a) the obligation breached is owed to a group of States including that State, and is established for the protection of a collective interest of the group; or
   (b) the obligation breached is owed to the international community as a whole.'

54 Indian Constitution, Article 51A, https://indiankanoon.org/doc/867010/

55 *M/S Singh Timber Traders and Others v State of UP and Others,* Allahabad High Court (unreported, 8 July 2020) , https://indiankanoon.org/doc/159982119/. See also AIR 2015 (NOC) 882 (23 December 2014), https://indiankanoon.org/doc/112794368/?ref=the-wave.net

Judgment:

The Supreme Court ruled that:

1. The tax was within the state's legislative powers but must be applied uniformly without discrimination.
2. The tax should not unreasonably restrict the right to trade.
3. Any discriminatory or disproportionate aspects of the tax would be invalidated.

The judgment clarified the balance between state revenue generation and traders' rights, significantly impacting the timber trade in Uttar Pradesh. This case highlights the court's role in evaluating economic legislation and protecting traders' rights under the Indian Constitution.

For detailed legal analysis, refer to the full judgment or legal databases.

Case name:

Sukhdev Vihar Welfare Residents Association v State of NCT of Delhi 22 (THC) of 2013 (MA No 19 of 2014)[56]

Summary:

Operating a waste-to-energy plant in a densely populated area leads to GHG emissions.

In 2013, the applicants, a welfare residents association, challenged the construction and operation of a waste-to-energy plant by the Municipal Corporation of Delhi (MCD).[57] The plant was to be built in a densely populated residential area and would affect the lives of the residents. The incineration of unsegregated municipal solid waste emits large quantities of GHGs, including CO_2 and nitrogen oxides which contribute to global climate change. There are also large amounts of indirect GHGs, including carbon monoxide, non-methane volatile organic compounds and sulphur dioxide. The incinerator also emits more CO_2 per MW/hour than any fossil fuel-based power source including coal/fuel power plants. MCD argued that the plant was a state-of-the-art facility and offered a clean, efficient and effective alternative to dumping of municipal solid waste in landfill sites. It was in the public interest that the plant operated.

On 2 February 2017, the National Green Tribunal (NGT)[58] allowed the operation of the plant. The need was to ensure processing of municipal waste with least residue by developed and tested technologies. Examining public health and interest in conjunction with environmental protection, the balance tilted in favour of permitting the plant to continue its operation for the processing of municipal solid waste from waste to energy. Applying the precautionary

56 *Sukhdev Vihar Welfare Residents Association v State of NCT of Delhi* 22 (THC) of 2013 (MA No 19 of 2014)https://www.casemine.com/judgement/in/5c060d44b338d16e11efe632
57 Municipal Corporation of Delhi (MCD), https://mcdonline.nic.in/portal
58 National Green Tribunal (NGT), https://www.greentribunal.gov.in

principle[59] through monitoring and adhering to standards would ensure that there were no adverse impacts on public health and environment.

The NGT observed that the plant has been developed as a Clean Development Mechanism (CDM) project. CDM projects, as registered with the UNFCCC, are projects that adopt precision in technology that takes care of environmental issues as per the international standards including stoppage of generation of GHG emissions. They are considered to be environment friendly and are thus eligible for carbon credit.

According to the Tribunal, the project adopted anti-pollution measures, improved technology, introduced new mechanisms for segregation and brought emissions not only within the prescribed limits but even stricter standards imposed by the regulatory authorities. Based on the scientific evidence and inspection reports, the waste-to-energy plant was permitted to operate.

Case name:

Society for Protection of Environment & Biodiversity v Union of India (No 490/2016 (Principal Bench))[60]

Summary:

Quashing those parts of environmental impact assessment (EIA) regulation that exempt the construction sector from environmental clearance.

In 2016, the applicant, an environmental society, filed a case before the NGT raising objections to the 2016 draft notification that exempted building and construction projects from the environmental clearance requirement. According to the applicant, the unregulated building and construction activities would cause irreversible damage to the environment, having serious repercussions on climate change. This exemption was also in derogation of India's international commitments to the Rio Declaration 1992 and Paris Agreement 2015, especially when read in the light of the precautionary principle.

The respondent, Ministry of Environment and Forests, contended that the draft notification was a policy decision taken by the Government of India to provide affordable housing to the weaker section of the society under the 'Housing for All by 2022'[61] scheme. The NGT, exercising its jurisdiction, upheld the applicant's application. The 2016 draft notification diluted the regime of environmental clearance in building and construction activities, leading to severe environmental impacts. The principle of non-regression,[62] an accepted norm in international environmental law, mandates that environmental law should not be modified to the detriment of environmental protection.

59 Precautionary principle: the precautionary principle is an approach to risk management, where, if it is possible that a given policy or action might cause harm to the public or the environment and if there is still no scientific agreement on the issue, the policy or action in question should not be carried out. However, the policy or action may be reviewed when more scientific information becomes available.

60 *Society for Protection of Environment & Biodiversity v Union of India* (No 490/2016 (Principle Bench)), https://www.casemine.com/judgement/in/5b17d5604a9326780100622a

61 *Housing for All by 2022*, https://www.swaniti.com/wp-content/uploads/2022/10/Housing_For_all.pdf

62 Principle of non-regression it can be defined as a prohibition on state conduct that results in environmental degradation or in the weakening of environmental laws.

The NGT declared illegal those parts of a government draft notification that exempted specific building and construction projects from the environmental clearance requirement. Domestically, the construction sector emits 22 per cent of India's total annual CO_2 emission with a significant energy footprint. In the name of 'ease of doing responsible business', the government ignored environmental impacts that had a direct bearing on environmental protection, climate change and sustainable development. Environmental clearances, as a part of the precautionary approach, require the drafting of an EIA report.

The EIA report evaluates carbon emissions associated with the construction project, its adverse impact on the environment, and best practice strategies to reduce these emissions. This helps in achieving the ambitious targets and is directly linked to the climate change and Sustainable Development Goals (SDGs).

Case name:

Indian Council for Enviro-Legal Action (ICELA) v Ministry of Environment, Forest and Climate Change (MoEF) (App no 170/2014)[63]

Summary:

In 2014, ICELA, an environmental NGO, filed an application against the Ministry of Environment, Forest and Climate Change, and companies producing HCFC-2 to stop emitting HFC-23. The emission of this by-product has 14,800 times more global warming potential (being a GHG) compared to CO_2 thereby leading to ozone depletion. The petitioner relied on constitutional mandates – Articles 48A[64] (duty of the state to protect the environment) and 51A(g)[65] (fundamental duty of the citizen to protect and improve the environment) of the Constitution and Environment Protection Act 1986, s 3 – that give powers to Central Government to take such measures as deemed necessary or expedient for the purpose of protecting and improving quality of the environment and preventing, controlling and abating environmental pollution.

However, the respondent, the Ministry of Environment, Forest and Climate Change raised an objection stating that the petition was unmaintainable as it fell outside the jurisdiction of the NGT. The by-product HFC-23 does not fall within the Acts specified in Schedule-I of the NGT Act and therefore the Tribunal could not entertain the petition.

On 10 December 2015, the NGT held it had the jurisdiction to hear the case as the GHG had been a matter of concern at the national and international level as part of the environment. The NGT Act 2010[66] is social welfare legislation and intended to provide justice in civil environmental cases. However, the Tribunal found that the regulation of HFC-23 related to a matter of global policy which must be regulated under international law. As such the court understood that

63 *Indian Council for Enviro-Legal Action (ICELA) v Ministry of Environment, Forest and Climate Change (MoEF)* (App no 170/2014), https://www.casemine.com/judgement/in/5c06107cb338d16e11efe67f

64 Indian Constitution, Article 48A, https://indiankanoon.org/doc/871328/

65 Indian Constitution, 51A(g), https://indiankanoon.org/doc/1644544/

66 NGT Act 2010, https://www.indiacode.nic.in/handle/123456789/2025?view_type=browse#:~:text=An%20Act%20to%20provide%20for,giving%20relief%20and%20compensation%20for

'there would be a very little role for the statutory authorities within the country to take appropriate measures.'

The Tribunal acknowledged that HFC-23 has an effect on global warming being part of GHGs, and that, at present, there is a gap in scientific understanding of HFC-23's toxic impact on the air and its categorisation as a pollutant. The Tribunal further observed 'the international conventions and treaties have to provide a path for domestic legislation and in any case, it has failed and be regulated without further delay'. Accordingly, the NGT directed the regulatory authorities and expert bodies to conduct a comprehensive database study on HFC-23, being a pollutant and the extent of its impact on global warming, being part of GHGs. On 27 September 2021, India ratified the Kigali Amendment of the Montreal Protocol, to reduce and phase out the use of hydrofluorocarbons by 80 per cent by 2050.

Case name:

In re Court on its own motion v State of Himachal Pradesh and Others (CWPIL No. 23/2019)[67]

Summary:

In February 2014, India's NGT issued a ruling on its own motion imposing a number of restrictions on activities around the Rohtang Pass,[68] an environmentally sensitive area in the Himalayan state of Himachal Pradesh.

The NGT has jurisdiction in a 2010 statute 'over all civil cases where a substantial question relating to environment … is involved and such question arises out of [one or more of seven environmental protection statutes enacted between 1974 and 2002]'.

The Tribunal may initiate cases and impose remedies. In February 2014, on its own motion, the Tribunal found that Black Carbon, which can be produced through vehicle use, is a major causative factor for rapid melting of glaciers in the Himalayan region. The Tribunal cited a study suggesting that 40 per cent of the glacial retreat could be attributed to the impact of Black Carbon and concluded that Black Carbon emission reduction could address glacial melting. The Tribunal concluded that Indian citizens have the right to a wholesome, clean and decent environment, derived from Articles 48A (which requires the state to protect and improve the environment), 51A (requiring a citizen to protect and improve the natural environment) and 1 (protecting the right to life as a fundamental right) of the Constitution.

Although the Tribunal described how GHG can cause global warming and affirmed the applicability of the 'polluter pays' principle to the respondents in this case, it did not assign Himachal Pradesh responsibility for mitigating global warming. It did, however, order the government of Himachal Pradesh to undertake sweeping measures to reduce pollution, including random pollution checks, restricting transport in certain areas to compressed natural gas and electric buses, and implementing a reforestation programme. These measures

67 *In re court on its own motion v State of Himachal Pradesh and Others* (CWPIL No. 23/2019), https://indiankanoon.org/doc/112188932/

68 Himalayan Wonders, 'Rohtang Pass', https://www.himalayanwonders.com/content/attractions/rohtang-pass.html?selocation=UK

must be overseen by a Monitoring Committee that makes quarterly reports to the Tribunal.

Case name:

Ridhima Pandey v Union of India (Original Application No. 187/2017; Civil Appeal No. 388/2021)[69]

Summary:

Ridhima Pandey, a nine-year-old from the Uttarakhand region, was the plaintiff in a climate change case filed in March 2017 with the NGT. The plaintiff's petition argued that the Public Trust Doctrine,[70] India's commitments under the Paris Agreement, and India's existing environmental laws and climate-related policies require action to mitigate climate change. It also argued that the term 'environment', as used in the Environment (Protection) Act 1986, necessarily encompasses the climate.

The case was brought under NGT Act 2010, s 2(m), which authorises claims that raise 'a substantial question relating to the environment'. The petition cited the principles of sustainable development, precaution, and intergenerational equity, as well as judicial decisions based on similar legal principles in the Netherlands (*Urgenda Foundation v State of the Netherlands*), Pakistan (*Leghari v Pakistan*), and the US (*Juliana v US*).

Pandey argued that she, along with all children and future generations, had the right to a healthy environment under the principle of intergenerational equity. Pandey also argued that climate change affects children disproportionately. Children were more vulnerable to impacts like heatwaves, displacement, diseases, and malnutrition. As climate was an inherent part of the environment, she asserted that safeguarding the environment and protecting forests was critical to addressing climate change.

The petition noted that India is the third-largest national emitter of GHGs (behind China and the US) and among those countries that are most susceptible to adverse climate change impacts. It identifies 1° C or 350 ppm of atmospheric CO_2 as the critical pair of thresholds for India (and the world) to avoid exceeding for the sake of avoiding severe climatic changes, facts described in the petition as rooted in '[t]he best climate science'.

To remedy the alleged injury to the present and future climate, the petition asked the court to order the national government to undertake a variety of measures, including but not limited to inclusion of climate change in the issues considered by EIAs, preparation of a national GHG emissions inventory, and preparation of a national carbon budget against which particular projects' emissions impacts could be assessed.

On 15 January 2019, the NGT dismissed the case, reasoning that the climate change is already covered in the process of impact assessments under the

69 *Ridhima Pandey v Union of India* (Original Application No. 187/2017; Civil Appeal No. 388/2021), https://www.casemine.com/judgement/in/5de5cb7146571b2fd68a3f39

70 Public Trust Doctrine: public trust doctrine is a foundational principle under environmental jurisprudence. According to our principle, aspects of our natural heritage are not mere possessions but are instead held in a sacred trust by the government for the collective welfare.

Environment Protection Act of 1986, and therefore, 'There is no reason to presume that Paris Agreement and other international protocols are not reflected in the policies of the Government of India or are not taken into consideration in granting environment clearances'.

KENYA

Case name:

Legal Advice Centre T/A Kituo cha Sheria and Anor v Attorney General and Others[71] (Iten ELC Petition No. 007 of 2022) [2024] KEELC 1521 (KLR)

Summary:

A climate change petition by the Illchamus and Tugen Communities in Kenya essentially suing the Government for the impacts of climate change flooding in Lake Baringo

Members of Ilchamus and Tugen communities living on the shores of Lake Baringo in Kenya together with Kituo cha Sheria (a Kenyan Human Rights NGO) filed a climate change petition – Iten ELC Petition No. 007 of 2022 – before the Environment and Land Court (ELC) in Iten.

The petitioners alleged the violation of several rights under the Constitution of the Republic of Kenya 2010.[72] They sought to enforce the climate change duties of public officials under the Climate Change Act[73] and other related constitutional rights under the Constitution of the Republic of Kenya 2010.[74]

The petitioners said that they are victims of climate change-related flooding which has caused displacement and loss of life and property.

The petitioners said that the flooding has been caused by hydro-meteorological variables due to climate change. The ELC in Iten allowed an application by the petitioners requesting the Chief Justice and the President of the Supreme Court of Kenya to set up a panel of three judges, an ELC bench, to hear their case on the failure, neglect and or refusal by several government officials to discharge their obligations under the Climate Change Act 2016.

The petitioners sought 12 substantive orders, among them:

- a declaration that relevant government officials, failed, refused and or neglected to take precautionary measures to anticipate, prevent or minimise the causes of climate change and mitigate its adverse impacts;

71 *Legal Advice Centre T/A Kituo cha Sheria and Another v Attorney General and Others* (Iten ELC Petition No. 007 of 2022) [2024] KEELC 1521 (KLR), https://kenyalaw.org/caselaw/cases/view/284073/

72 Constitution of the Republic of Kenya 2010 http://www.parliament.go.ke/sites/default/files/2023-03/The_Constitution_of_Kenya_2010.pdf

73 Climate Change Act No. 11 of 2016 Laws of Kenya http://kenyalaw.org:8181/exist/rest/db/kenyalex/Kenya/Legislation/English/Acts%20and%20Regulations/C/Climate%20Change%20Act%20-%20No.%2011%20of%202016/docs/ClimateChangeAct11of2016.pdf

74 Constitution of the Republic of Kenya 2010, http://www.parliament.go.ke/sites/default/files/2023-03/The_Constitution_of_Kenya_2010.pdf

- a declaration that relevant government officials failed, refused and or neglected to avert, minimise and address effects of climate change suffered by petitioners;
- an order to compel relevant government officials to rehabilitate, relocate, and restore damaged infrastructure;
- an order for compensation for climate change damage; and
- an order for resettlement of flood victims.

Case name:

Save Lamu and Others v National Environmental Management Authority and Amu Power Co Ltd [2019] KEELC 4739 (KLR)[75]

Summary:

Whether the National Environmental Management Authority violated public participation requirements in issuing a license to construct a coal-fired power plant and whether a coal company's EIA adequately considered climate change and other factors.

Kenya's National Environmental Tribunal set aside the issuance of a license by the National Environmental Management Authority (NEMA) to Amu Power Co for the construction of the Lamu Coal-fired Power Plant ('Lamu Plant'). The Lamu Plant would be the first coal-fired power plant in Kenya.

The Tribunal found that the NEMA had violated the Environmental Impact Assessment & Audit Regulations (EIA Regulations) by granting an EIA License without proper and meaningful public participation in the process.

The Tribunal also found that Amu Power Co's Environmental & Social Impact Assessment was incomplete and scientifically insufficient in violation of the EIA Regulations.

Applying the precautionary principle, the Tribunal found one of the insufficiencies of the assessment was the inadequate consideration of climate change and the Climate Change Act of 2016. The Tribunal ordered that, if the Amu Power Co wanted to carry on with the project, it should choose to pursue the project, to conduct a new EIA study in compliance with the EIA Regulations. The Tribunal instructed the Amu Power Co that the new EIA study must include:

> 'all approved and legible detailed architectural and engineering plans for the plant and its ancillary facilities (such as the coal storage and handling facility and the ash pit with its location in relation to the sea shore), consideration of the Climate Change Act 2016, the Energy Act 2019 and the Natural Resources (Classes of Transactions subject to Ratification) Act 2016 in so far as the project will utilise sea water for the plant and/ or if applicable.'

75 *Save Lamu and Others v National Environmental Management Authority and Amu Power Co Ltd* [2019] KEELC 4739 (KLR), http://kenyalaw.org/caselaw/cases/view/176697/

NEW ZEALAND

Case name:

Lawyers for Climate Action NZ Inc v Climate Change Commission [2022] NZHC 3064

Summary:

In this case involving the Climate Change Response Act 2002 (amended in 2019), which targets net-zero emissions by 2050 and establishes a Climate Change Commission, a legal challenge was initiated on 1 July 2021. Hundreds of New Zealand lawyers (LCANZI) sued the Climate Change Commission and the Minister for Climate Change, James Shaw, alleging that the Commission's advice on emissions budgets and Nationally Determined Contributions (NDCs) under the Paris Agreement violated New Zealand administrative law. They claimed the Commission made errors in calculating reductions, prioritising certain considerations, adopting carbon accounting methods and allowing offshore mitigation. The Commission's reliance on the Intergovernmental Panel on Climate Change's (IPCC's) 2018 report led to figures inconsistent with the 1.5°C target.

The Minister initially supported the Commission's advice but revised his stance following Cabinet directives due to concerns over fuel and energy costs. During litigation, the Minister acknowledged errors and accepted that the Amended Regulations did not align with New Zealand's 2050 target, emissions budgets and NDC. The court ordered the reconsideration of the Amendment Regulations to ensure compliance with the Principal Act, with the Minister required to reassess the settings by 30 September 2023.[76]

Case name:

Smith v Fonterra Cooperative Group Ltd and Others [2024] NZSC 5

Summary:

In this case[77] Michael Smith brought tort claims against New Zealand's seven largest GHG emitters, collectively responsible for one-third of all New Zealand's GHGs. He argued their activities amounted to torts of public nuisance, negligence, and a novel climate duty. Smith further argued that these emissions affected him personally. As a Māori leader with an interest in customary land, Smith argued that the defendants' actions would harm him through impacts related to rising sea levels, loss of sites of cultural and spiritual significance, damage to fisheries, and adverse health impacts. Smith asked the Court to issue declarations against the defendants, and to require them to reduce emissions. Notably, Smith did not seek damages. His case was against: Fonterra Cooperative Group Ltd, Genesis Energy Ltd, Dairy Holdings Ltd, New Zealand Steel Ltd, Z Energy Ltd, Channel Infrastructure NZ Ltd and BT Mining.

76 See further, https://climatecasechart.com/wp-content/uploads/non-us-case-documents/2022/20221123_2022-NZHC-3064_judgment.pdf

77 *Smith v Fonterra Cooperative Group Ltd and Others* [2024] NZSC 5, https://www.courtsofnz.govt.nz/assets/cases/2024/2024-NZSC-5.pdf

The claimant in brought claims in:

- public nuisance;
- negligence; and
- a new climate change duty.

The claimant brought the claim both as an individual who was impacted by climate change and in his capacity as a community elder who was representing vulnerable Māori living in coastal areas of New Zealand. The defendants were seven significant GHG emitters across a range of sectors although, as the claimant acknowledged, there was no principled basis for singling out the seven defendants in particular.

The New Zealand High Court declined to strike the claim out on the basis that the defendants may have breached an 'inchoate' climate change duty of care. The New Zealand Court of Appeal struck out the claim on the basis that it was inconsistent with fundamental principles of New Zealand (and English) common law.

However, the Supreme Court allowed Mr Smith's claims in these three areas to proceed to trial.

The Supreme Court was only considering whether the claims should be struck out and emphasised that 'a refusal to strike out a cause of action is not a commentary on whether or not the claim ultimately will succeed'.

The Supreme Court only addressed Mr Smith's claim in nuisance (being that the defendant companies were substantially and unreasonably interfering with rights to public health, safety, comfort, convenience and peace). Having found that the nuisance claim was tenable, the Court allowed the remaining two causes of action to proceed on the basis that they would not materially add to costs, hearing time or other court resources that would be used in any event.

The Supreme Court noted that, whilst the common law had not previously faced climate change, in the 19th and early 20th centuries it had to deal with another crisis, although of a lesser scale, when the industrial revolution enlarged the risk of accidents through the mechanisation of factories, transportation and mining. Consequently with the global industrial revolution, the common law had to deal with new, widespread risk and damage caused by air and water pollution and the escape of biohazards. Climate change engages comparable complexities, albeit at a 'quantum leap scale enlargement'.

The Supreme Court emphasised that the principles governing public nuisance ought not to stand still in the face of enormous environmental challenges attributable to human economic activity. The common law, where it is not clearly excluded, responds to challenge and change in a considered way, through trials involving the testing of evidence.

The Supreme Court concluded that it is not the case that all defendants causing or contributing to a nuisance need to be before the court (or are capable of being so). It is arguable that in the case of public nuisance, a defendant must take responsibility for their contribution to a common interference with public right. Their responsibility should not be contingent on the absence of co-contribution or be in effect discharged by the equivalent acts of others.

The Supreme Court identified that even an extensive scheme of regulation might leave gaps and problems for other legal processes to address. The Court said that engaging with climate claims does not need extensive supervisory remedies, or the construction of a rival scheme of regulation. The Court acknowledged that Mr Smith was hoping the claim would catalyse further private and regulatory action, rather than inserting the Court as an ongoing regulator itself. The Supreme Court suggested that even purely declaratory relief might have this effect.

Case name:

Students for Climate Solutions Inc v Minister of Energy and Resources [2024] NZCA 152

Summary:

In 2021, Students for Climate Solutions sued the Minister of Energy and Resources,[78] claiming that the Minister failed to consider climate change impacts when granting petroleum exploration permits under the Crown Minerals Act 1991 (CMA). They argued that this omission made the decision unreasonable and disregarded the Treaty of Waitangi. However, the Court of Appeal rejected their challenge, stating that climate change obligations cannot be imposed if they strain the legislation beyond Parliament's intention. The Court also noted that, while climate change impacts on Māori are relevant, the Minister can address this by focusing on local issues and engaging with affected iwi and hapū.

On 7 May 2024, the Court unanimously dismissed the challenge, noting that climate change is not an explicit consideration under CMA, s 29A. The Court found that the CMA's purpose was to support mineral exploration for New Zealand's economic benefit and allow petroleum exploration in Taranaki for a 'just transition'. The Court acknowledged the seriousness of climate change but concluded it was not a mandatory relevant consideration under the CMA, emphasising that legislation should not be strained beyond Parliament's intention.[79]

NIGERIA

Case name:

Oronto Douglas v Shell Petroleum Development Co Ltd and Others (1999) 2 NWLR (Pt.591) 466[80]

Summary:

Whether there is evidence that the right of the appellant was affected, or direct injury done to him.

78 *Students for Climate Change Inc v Minister of Energy and Resources* [2024] NZCA 152, https://www.justice.govt.nz/jdo_documents/workspace___SpacesStore_76a83d0f_0889_4f83_81a0_e9b020199911.pdf

79 See further, https://climatecasechart.com/wp-content/uploads/non-us-case-documents/2024/20240507_2022-NZHC-2116_decision.pdf

80 *Oronto Douglas v Shell Petroleum Development Co Ltd and Others* (1999) 2 NWLR (Pt.591) 466, https://www.lawglobalhub.com/oronto-douglas-v-shell-petroleum-development-company-ltd-ors-1988-lljr-ca/

The appellant was an environmental activist who filed a claim against the respondents and the Federal Environmental Protection Agency. The claim was for a declaration and injunction to stop the respondents from continuing with a liquefied natural gas project until an EIA was conducted.

The respondents filed a preliminary objection and argued that the appellant lacked the necessary standing and that the procedure of the claim was defective. The trial judge ruled in favour of the respondents, stating that the appellant had no legal standing and that the procedure was confused.

The appellant filed an appeal, arguing that they had sufficient personal interest, the activities of the respondents posed environmental danger, and they had a statutory interest in the subject matter. The appellant also argued that there was no mix-up in the originating process and that the ruling was against the weight of evidence. The court found that the respondents were premature in moving to dismiss the action and that there were not enough materials for the trial judge to make a valid decision. The court emphasised the importance of filing a statement of claim and an affidavit in support of a motion to dismiss for want of legal competence.

The appeal was allowed as the Court of Appeal concluded that the trial judge misdirected himself and set aside his decision, remitting the matter back to the Federal High Court for a retrial before another judge.

The Court of Appeal held:

- That where a defendant filed a motion on notice of preliminary objection, he also needed to accompany the motion with an affidavit. (*Nwabueze v Okoye* (1988) 4 NWLR (pt.91) 664;[81] *Bello v NBN Ltd* (1992) 6 NWLR (pt.246) 206[82]; *Fawehinmi v Abacha* (1996) 9 NWLR (pt.475) 710[83]).
- That on the issue of the filing or non-filing of a supportive affidavit to demurrer proceedings this court in clear and unequivocal terms declared in *Free Enterprises (Nig.) Ltd v GTOSA* (1998) 1 NWLR (Pt.532) page I that it is mandatory under Federal High Court (Civil Procedure) Rules, Orders 27 and 33 to accompany demurrer proceedings with a supportive affidavit.
- That a court is duty-bound to make a pronouncement on the issue of the competency of the suit raised before it at the earliest opportunity. Even if the issue of objection is technical it cannot be ignored but it must be raised with sufficient facts to enable the court to deal fairly with the case of both parties. The court cannot speculate on the facts.
- That in ascertaining the locus standi[84] of a person to prosecute any action, it is usually the statement of claim that should be examined to see whether there is vested a justiciable right capable of being enforced. *Olagbegi v Ogunneye II* (1996) 5 NWLR (pt. 448) 332:[85] the issue of locus standi involves the issue of the court's jurisdiction to entertain the matter brought to it. It has been held that such issue cannot ordinarily be considered solely

81 *Nwabueze v. Okoye* (1988) 4 NWLR (pt.91) 664, https://ng.vlex.com/vid/nwabueze-anor-v-obi-915375209

82 *Bello v NBN Ltd* (1992) 6 NWLR (pt.246) 206, https://edojudiciary.gov.ng/wp-content/uploads/2020/06/PDP-Preliminary-Objection.pdf

83 *Fawehinmi v Abacha* (1996) 9 NWLR (pt.475) 710, https://nigerialii.org/akn/ng/judgment/ngsc/2000/2/eng@2000-04-27

84 'locus standi' – the right or capacity to bring an action to court.

85 *Olagbegi v Ogunneye II* (1996) 5 NWLR (pt.448) 332.

on the face of the writ of summons without a statement of claim filed: *Multi-Purpose Ventures Ltd v A.-G. River State* (1997) 9 NWLR (pt.522) 642[86] and *Elendu v Ekwoaba* (1995) 3 NWLR (pt.386) 704.[87] In the case of *A.G. Enugu State v Avop plc* (1995) 6 NWLR (pt.399) 90[88] at 113 Tobi. I.CA. said: 'In deciding the issue of locus standi at the trial Court, only the Statement of Claim should be looked into.'

- For a plaintiff to establish their locus standi in an action for declaratory order they must prove that their legal right or interest which they seek to protect is not a right common to the community at large, unless they can show that they suffered damages more than any person.

Case name:

Centre for Oil Pollution Watch (COPW) v Nigerian National Petroleum Corp'n (NNPC) (2018) (unreported)

Summary:

The Supreme Court of Nigeria (SCN) has broadened the rule of standing by recognising the appellant NGO's right to sue the respondent. This decision allows public-spirited individuals and organisations to initiate legal actions against public authorities and private entities to ensure compliance with laws protecting the environment. The Court emphasised that anyone, including NGOs, seeking the enforcement of statutory provisions or public laws designed to protect human lives, public health and the environment should be considered as having legal standing. This recognition of public interest litigation is crucial for addressing barriers to justice, especially for impoverished communities disproportionately affected by environmental and climate change problems. The Court's stance reflects a growing concern about climate change and the need for stronger measures to safeguard the environment for present and future generations.

The SCN has also affirmed the enforceability of environmental human rights in Nigeria. It held that Section 20 of the Nigerian Constitution, which mandates the state to protect the environment, is justiciable when read with Section 4(2), which grants the power to make laws to effectuate Section 20. Additionally, the Court recognised that Section 33, which guarantees the right to life, implicitly includes the right to a clean and healthy environment. The enforceability of the environmental right under Article 24 of the African Charter on Human and Peoples' Rights, as domesticated by the African Charter Act, Cap. A9 LFN 2004, was also affirmed. This decision aligns with the constitutional human rights approach to environmental and climate protection previously adopted by the Federal High Court in *Jonah Gbemre v Shell and Others*, marking a positive shift in the SCN's attitude towards environmental and climate change-related claims. It provides additional human rights and constitutional tools for potential climate litigation in Nigeria.[89]

86 *Multi-Purpose Ventures Ltd v A.G. River State* (1997) 9 NWLR (pt.522) 642.

87 *Elendu v Ekwoaba* (1995) 3 NWLR (pt.386) 704.

88 *A.G. Enugu State v Avop plc* (1995) 6 NWLR (pt.399) 90.

89 See further, https://climatecasechart.com/non-us-case/centre-for-oil-pollution-watch-copw-vs-nnpc-2018-supreme-court-of-nigeria/

Case name:

Gbemre v Shell Petroleum Development Co of Nigeria Ltd and Others (Suit No FHC/B/CS/53/05) (2005) 6 AHRLR 152

Summary:

In this case concerning gas flaring in the Niger Delta, the applicant, Gbemre, representing the community, sued the Nigerian Government for failing to stop Shell's gas flaring and Shell for its continuous flaring during exploration and production. The applicant argued that Shell's activities harmed the community's environment and contributed to climate change, violating their rights to life and human dignity under the 1999 Nigerian Constitution and the African Charter on Human and Peoples Rights. The Federal High Court ruled that these rights include a clean, poison-free, and pollution-free environment, and found Shell's failure to conduct an Environmental Impact Assessment (EIA) violated the EIA Act and the community's rights. The court ordered the cessation of gas flaring and mandated the Attorney General to amend the Associated Gas Re-injection Act to align with human rights obligations, without awarding damages, costs or compensation.[90]

Case name:

Alame and Others, Chief Minapakama and Others, Okpabi and Others, Okochi Nwoko Ododo and Others v Shell Plc (formerly known as Royal Dutch Shell plc) and Shell Petroleum Development Co of Nigeria Ltd [2024] EWCA Civ 1500[91]

Summary:

In 2015, the Ogale and Bille Nigerian communities filed claims against the UK company Royal Dutch Shell plc and its Nigerian subsidiary Shell Petroleum Development Co (SPDC) in the UK High Court. Both claims sought a remedy for extensive oil pollution which considerably affected their livelihoods and the environment.

The plaintiffs consisted of 42,500 residents of Nigeria who sought a remedy for extensive oil pollution which affected their livelihoods and the environment.

The claimants argued that Shell had failed to adequately prevent oil spills and subsequently to adequately clean up these spills in order to avoid serious contamination of agricultural lands and waterways.

The timeline of the case is as follows:

- March 2016: the Technology and Construction Court gave permission to the claimants to sue Shell in England and ruled that formal legal proceedings could proceed to the next stage in the London High Court. The company challenged both communities' lawsuits, arguing that

90 See further, https://climatecasechart.com/non-us-case/gbemre-v-shell-petroleum-development-company-of-nigeria-ltd-et-al/

91 *Alame and Others, Chief Minapakama and Others, Okpabi and Others, Okochi Nwoko Ododo and Others v Shell plc (formerly known as Royal Dutch Shell plc) and Shell Petroleum Development Co of Nigeria Ltd* [2024] EWCA Civ 1500, https://www.judiciary.uk/wp-content/uploads/2024/12/Alame-v-Shell.pdf

pipeline sabotage and illegal refining had been the main sources of pollution across the Niger Delta, and that the cases should be heard in Nigeria instead of the UK.

- January 2017: the High Court held that the communities could not seek redress against Shell in UK courts. The judge concluded that there was not sufficient evidence that Shell exercised a high degree of oversight, control or direction over SPDC, and, therefore, that the parent company had no legal responsibility for pollution by its Nigerian subsidiary.
  The claimants appealed this decision, arguing that the judge reached this conclusion before disclosure of relevant documents or hearing witnesses regarding the relationship between Shell and SPDC.
- February 2018: the Court of Appeal upheld the High Court's ruling, with a majority of judges holding that the parent company did not hold a duty of care towards affected communities. Following the dismissal, the claimants announced their intention to bring the case to the UK Supreme Court.
- April 2018: over 40 UK and international human rights, development and environmental NGOs submitted a letter to the Supreme Court supporting the claimants' application to appeal. They said that the Appeal Court's judgment could greatly limit access to justice for people harmed by UK companies' international operations.
- July 2018: the Supreme Court announced that the Appeal Panel had decided to defer consideration of the claimants' application to appeal until judgment was given in a similar parent company liability case being examined at the Supreme Court, *Vedanta Resources plc and Another (Appellants) v Lungowe and Others (Respondents)*.
- May 2019: civil society organisations asked the UK Supreme Court to allow the fishing communities to appeal against the 2017 ruling saying that Shell did not hold a duty of care towards affected communities.
- July 2019: the UK Supreme Court granted permission to appeal.
- May 2020: claimants filed an appeal with the UK Supreme Court. They argued that Royal Dutch Shell owed them a common law duty of care in respect to the extensive environmental harm caused by their business operations in Nigeria.
- February 2021: the Supreme Court allowed the appeal and ruled that the case against Royal Dutch Shell and its Nigerian subsidiary could proceed in the UK courts. Notably, the Court's decision determined that there was an arguable case that Shell is legally responsible for the systemic pollution affecting the Ogale and Bille communities.
- July 2021: it was revealed that Shell did not contest the UK courts' jurisdiction, and that its Nigerian subsidiary, SPDC would be joined to the claims.
- January 2023: over 11,000 people and 17 institutions from Ogale, Nigeria joined over 2,000 people from the Bille community in their individual claims that sought compensation for individual loss of livelihoods due to the ongoing water pollution and health impact.
- November 2023: the High Court ruled that the individuals' claims of human rights abuses could proceed in the UK justice system. The judge found it was arguable that oil pollution violated the individuals' legally protected rights to a clean and healthy environment. Shell claimed it had no legal responsibility for the pollution, asserting that the blame fell on its subsidiary, SPDC.

- March 2024: the High Court ruled that the claims should be treated as a 'global claim'.
- October 2024, the Court of Appeal granted a landmark appeal for the Ogale and Bille communities, allowing their claims to proceed to a full trial. This decision overturned a previous ruling that would have severely limited the communities' ability to seek justice for the alleged extensive pollution caused by Shell's operations.

PAKISTAN

Case name:

Leghari v Pakistan ((2015) WP No. 25501/201)

Summary:

In the case of Asghar Leghari, a Pakistani farmer, the plaintiff contended that the government's failure to implement the National Climate Change Policy of 2012 and the Framework for Implementation of Climate Change Policy (2014–2030) had adversely affected Pakistan's water, food and energy security, thereby infringing upon his fundamental right to life. Leghari and his neighbours experienced threats to their crops due to water scarcity and intensified storms, which he attributed to climate change. He argued that the government's inaction, delay and lack of seriousness in addressing climate change challenges jeopardised the nation's food, water and energy security. A study by Lahore University of Management Sciences and the WWF revealed that no provinces had established a climate change policy, as the responsibility had previously been left to individual provinces. In its final order, the court introduced the concept of 'climate justice' as a successor to 'environmental justice', emphasising a human-centred approach that linked human rights with development. The court aimed to protect the rights of vulnerable populations and ensure equitable distribution of the burdens and benefits of climate change. It acknowledged the challenges of climate justice, particularly in identifying polluters beyond national borders, and articulated a vision for water justice as a human right to access clean water, as a sub-concept of climate justice.[92]

92 See further, https://climatecasechart.com/non-us-case/ashgar-leghari-v-federation-of-pakistan/

SOUTH AFRICA

Case name:

EarthLife Africa Johannesburg v Minister of Environmental Affairs and Others (65662/16) [2017] ZAGPPHC 58; [2017] 2 All SA 519 (GP) (8 March 2017)[93]

Summary:

Challenge to environmental review of coal-fired power plant development for failure to adequately consider climate change-related impacts

In this case South Africa's High Court was asked to determine whether, under the National Environmental Management Act 107 of 1998,[94] 'relevant' considerations for environmental review of plans for a new 1,200 MW coal-fired Thabametsi Power Project[95] included the project's impacts on global climate change. The project would operate until about 2060.

The court noted that the statute does not expressly consider climate change but said that such considerations are relevant and that the absence of any environmental review of the project made its approval unlawful. This issue came before the court as a result of EarthLife Africa[96] Johannesburg's appeals.

The first appeal was submitted to the Minister of Environmental Affairs challenging the adequacy of the project's environmental review. EarthLife argued that the review was invalid because it largely ignored climate change. The second, in the High Court in Pretoria, challenged the Minister's determination that the review was legally valid even though it would have to be supplemented by a climate change analysis because issues related to climate mitigation and adaptation had not been 'comprehensively assessed and/or considered'.

The court cited several reasons, including South Africa's commitments under the Paris Agreement, that climate change was a relevant consideration for the environmental review of the Thabametsi Project. As the review, which was approved by the Minister, effectively ignored climate change, the court held it to be legally invalid.

After this decision, the Minister of Environmental Affairs reconsidered the permit application in the light of a newly finalised climate change impact assessment and again approved the environmental authorisation for the plant on 30 January 2018. The Minister reasoned that, while the power plant would have significant GHG emissions and therefore cause climate change impacts, the power generation benefits of the project outweighed the harm caused.

On 26 March 2018, EarthLife Africa and the Trustees for the Time Being of the Groundwork Trust challenged the Minister's decision, asking the court to set aside the decision as unlawful for failing to consider site-specific climate change impacts associated with the project.

93 *EarthLife Africa Johannesburg v Minister of Environmental Affairs and Others* (65662/16) [2017] ZAGPPHC 58; [2017] 2 All SA 519 (GP) (8 March 2017), https://www.saflii.org/za/cases/ZAGPPHC/2017/58.pdf

94 National Environmental Management Act 107 of 1998, https://www.gov.za/documents/national-environmental-management-act#main-content

95 Thabametsi Coal Power Plant, Limpopo Province, https://www.power-technology.com/projects/thabametsi-coal-power-plant-limpopo-province/

96 EarthLife Africa, https://earthlife.org.za

On 19 November 2020, the High Court issued an order setting aside all governmental authorisations for the coal-fired power plant. The court also ordered the defendants to pay court costs.

Case name:

Trustees for the Time Being of GroundWork Trust and Another v Minister of Environmental Affairs, ACWA Power Khanyisa Thermal Power Station RF (Pty) Ltd, and Others (61561/17) (27 May 2021, unreported)

Summary:

This case[97] revolved around environmental law and the duty of the state to protect the environment.

The environmental organisation GroundWork filed a motion requesting that South Africa's High Court review and set aside the Department of Environmental Affairs' authorisation to develop a 600 MW coal-fired power plant, the 'Khanyisa Project', without first considering the climate change impacts of the plant. They also challenged the Minister of Environmental Affairs' rejection of Groundwork's application to appeal the authorisation.

They argued that this dismissal directly contradicted the court's decision in *EarthLife Africa Johannesburg v. Minister of Environmental Affairs and Others* handed down on 8 March 2017. This case considered similar authorisation for a 1,200 MW coal-fired plant called the Thabametsi Project. In *EarthLife Africa Johannesburg*, the court held that the climate change impacts of a proposed coal-fired power station are required to be assessed and comprehensively considered as part of an environmental impact assessment under the National Environmental Management Act 107 of 1998 before an authorisation decision is reached. National Environmental Management Act, Section 24O(1)(b) further requires consideration of impacts, mitigation measures, and domestic as well as international policy commitments before granting an environmental authorisation. In *EarthLife Africa Johannesburg*, the Court recognised South Africa's commitments under the Paris Agreement as one of the reasons that climate change is a relevant consideration for the environmental review of a coal-fired power plant. This is one of two court applications filed by GroundWork in September 2017 to oppose new coal-fired power plants in the Mpumalanga Highveld –an air quality priority area.

As the litigation unfolded, it emerged that the Khanyisa Project had breached the conditions of its environmental authorisation and that its authorisation had expired. The Department of Forestry, Fisheries and Environment (DFFE) agreed that the authorisation was no longer valid. The Khanyisa Project's developer, ACWA, did not file answering papers and the matter proceeded on an unopposed basis.

On 27 May 2021, the High Court declared that the environmental approval for the planned 600 MW Khanyisa coal-fired power station had expired. It ordered ACWA to pay the costs of the litigation.

97 *Trustees for the time being of Groundwork Trust and Another v Minister of Environmental Affairs, ACWA Power Khanyisa Thermal Power Station RF (Pty) Ltd and Others* (61561/17) (27 May 2021, unreported) https://www.saflii.org/za/cases/ZAGPPHC/2022/208.pdf

UGANDA

Case name:

Tsama William and Others v Uganda's Attorney General and Others (024 of 2020)

Summary:

The applicants alleged that the Environment Management Authority and the Bududa Local Government Council had failed to implement effective measures to prevent landslides in Bududa District, leading to the violation of their fundamental rights, including the right to life, a clean and healthy environment, property and physical and mental health. The applicants argued that the respondents were aware of the landslide risks, exacerbated by climate change, and had positive obligations under national and international law to address these risks.

The applicants claimed that the respondents' failure to fulfil their obligations resulted in multiple landslides on 3 December 2019, which displaced them, killed 20 of their relatives, and caused significant property and environmental damage. They sought declarations that their fundamental rights had been infringed and that the respondents were responsible for these violations. Additionally, the applicants sought UGX 6,800,000,000 in damages and compensation for the loss of life, property and other fundamental rights, as well as the costs of resettlement to safer areas.[98]

Case name:

Mbabazi and Others v Attorney General and National Environmental Management Authority (Civil Suit No. 283 of 2012)

Summary:

In 2012, the plaintiffs sought relief on behalf of four Ugandan minors, arguing that Articles 237 and 39 of the Ugandan Constitution make the government a trustee of natural resources, including the atmosphere, and that imposes a duty to preserve these for future generations. They cited extreme weather events as evidence of the government's failure to meet its constitutional duty. The plaintiffs requested the court declare the government's inaction on climate change a violation of its public trust duty and sought orders for accurate greenhouse gas accounting and a mitigation plan. The High Court ordered a 90-day mediation process, with no further action taken as of October 2017.[99]

98 See further, https://climatecasechart.com/wp-content/uploads/non-us-case-documents/2021/20210503_Miscellaneous-Cause-No.-024-of-2020_application-1.pdf

99 See further, https://climatecasechart.com/wp-content/uploads/non-us-case-documents/2012/20120920_Civil-Suit-No.-283-of-2012_complaint.pdf

UK

Case name:

R (on the application of Friends of the Earth Ltd) v Secretary of State for International Trade/UK Export Finance (UKEF) [2023] EWCA Civ 14[100]

Summary:

In this case the Court of Appeal rejected Friends of the Earth's application for a judicial review of the UK Government's decision to provide $1.15 billion in export finance for a liquified natural gas project in Mozambique. This continued a trend for the UK courts in declining to find that emissions-intensive projects are unlawful (see Supreme Court's rejection of Friends of the Earth's challenge to the Heathrow Airport expansion in 2020).

The Court found that the Government was only required to reach a 'tenable' view that funding the project was aligned with the UK's obligations under the Paris Agreement, and that it was not irrational for the government to conclude that the investment decision was compatible with the Paris Agreement. The Court also considered that the government was not required to obtain a quantification of the indirect emissions (besides purchased energy) occurring in the project's value chain (Scope 3 emissions) before making its investment decision.

The Administrative Court was split and the judges could not agree on the outcome of the case. The Administrative Court dismissed Friends of the Earth's application for judicial review.[101]

Friends of the Earth appealed:

- the Government was required to adopt a view that its decision was aligned with the UK's obligations under the Paris Agreement and that there was no rational basis on which the respondents could conclude that the investment decision was compatible with the Paris Agreement (the Paris Agreement challenge); and
- the respondents failed in their duty of enquiry to obtain a quantification of the project's Scope 3 emissions (the Scope 3 challenge).

Paris Agreement challenge

The Court noted that the Paris Agreement is an unincorporated international treaty that does not give rise to domestic legal obligations. Paris Agreement, Article 2, which provides that the Paris Agreement aims to:

> 'strengthen the global response to the threat of climate change, in the context of sustainable development and efforts to eradicate poverty, including by: ... (c) making finance flows consistent with a pathway towards low greenhouse gas emissions and climate-resilient development'

100 *R (on the application of Friends of the Earth Ltd) v Secretary of State for International Trade/UK Export Finance (UKEF)* [2023] EWCA Civ 14, https://caselaw.nationalarchives.gov.uk/ewca/civ/2023/14/data.pdf

101 *R (on the application of Friends of the Earth Ltd) v Secretary of State for International Trade/UK Export Finance (UKEF)* [2023] EWCA Civ 14 https://www.judiciary.uk/wp-content/uploads/2023/01/R-on-the-application-of-Friends-of-the-Earth-Limited-v-Secretary-of-State-for-International-Trade-and-others2.pdf

is a declaration of the Treaty's purposes. Article 2 did not create an obligation on the government to demonstrate that its investment decisions were consistent with a pathway towards limiting global warming to well below 2°C and efforts limit it to 1.5°C.

At the time the investment decision was made the government considered that the project was aligned with the UK's obligations under the Paris Agreement because it would help Mozambique transition away from more damaging fossil fuels in line with its NDC and Paris Agreement commitments. The gas from the project would replace more polluting fuels and there would be some net reduction in emissions.

Although the Court was not prepared to give a definitive interpretation of the provisions of the Paris Agreement or their legal effect, it did find that the government's view that its decision was in alignment with the UK's obligations under the Paris Agreement was tenable, and that was sufficient.

The reasons the court gave were:

- the Government chose to consider the UK's obligations under the Paris Agreement when making its investment decision but was not obligated to do so by domestic law. Further, there was a lack of clear guidance as to how unincorporated treaties such as the Paris Agreement should be construed as a matter of domestic law;
- the Paris Agreement was one of the factors which the government considered when reaching the investment decision. The Court considered that courts should not allocate weight as between competing factors;
- the question of whether it was an error of law for the government to have concluded that funding the project was aligned with the UK's obligations under the Paris Agreement must be judged by considering whether it had adopted a tenable view of that question; and
- the fact that the government said that it had concluded that its decision was compliant with the UK's obligations under the Paris Agreement did not affect this conclusion. The Court said that:

  > 'it must be open to the executive to say that it wants to comply with an unincorporated treaty, even though there may be different views as to what precisely it means. It must also be able to say, without successful challenge, that it thinks on balance and in good faith that a particular decision is compliant, even if it later changes its policy or is shown to have been wrong in the view that it took.'

The Court did not accept Friends of the Earth's argument that the investment decision was irrational because the government later acknowledged that the financing of the project did not align with the UK's obligations under the Paris Agreement.

The uncertainty and complexity of project meant that the government could not predict a precise outcome of the project's emissions. The government had to decide, considering all relevant and material factors, including the UK's obligations under the Paris Agreement.

The correct standard was whether the government's view that the decision aligned with the UK's obligations was tenable when it was taken. There was no domestic law requirement for it to be certain that the decision complied with those obligations.

Scope 3 challenge

The Court decided that the government was not required to quantify of the project's Scope 3 emissions:

- the question for the Court was whether it was irrational for the government to have made its investment decision without quantifying the Scope 3 emissions;
- the Court noted that, despite the Scope 3 emissions not being quantified, it was always understood that they would be significantly larger than the Scope 1 and 2 emissions. Additionally, quantifying the Scope 3 emissions would not answer the question of whether, and to what extent, gas from the project would replace more polluting fossil fuels and over what timescale;
- the Court concluded that the government's decisions about quantifying the Scope 3 emissions and the adequacy of the project's climate change report were 'well within the substantial margin of appreciation allowed to the decision-makers'. A failure to make an estimate of the Scope 3 emissions as part of the decision-making process did not itself render the decision irrational.

Case name:

R (on the application of Finch on behalf of the Weald Action Group and Others) v Surrey CC and Others [2022] EWCA Civ 187[102]

Summary:

Whether the UK regulations require EIAs for fossil fuel production to assess the Scope 3/end-use GHG emissions arising from these developments.

In December 2018, Horse Hill Developments Ltd, sought planning permission from Surrey CC to retain and expand an existing onshore oil well site (comprising two wells) and to drill for four new wells, enabling the production of hydrocarbons from six wells over a period of 25 years. Planning permission was granted. Sarah Finch applied for judicial review of the Council's decision, acting on behalf of the Weald Action Group. Her claim was unsuccessful before the High Court and the Court of Appeal. The appellant then appealed to the Supreme Court. The Supreme Court allowed Ms Finch's appeal.[103]

Finch related to the requirements for EIAs in the Town and Country Planning (Environmental Impact Assessment) Regulations 2017.[104] These Regulations, which originally implemented EU Directive 92/11/EU (as amended)[105] require

102 *R (on the application of Finch on behalf of the Weald Action Group and Others) v Surrey CC* [2022] EWCA Civ 187, https://www.judiciary.uk/wp-content/uploads/2023/01/R-on-the-application-of-Friends-of-the-Earth-Limited-v-Secretary-of-State-for-International-Trade-and-others2.pdf

103 *R (on the application of Finch on behalf of the Weald Action Group and Others) (Appellant) v Surrey CC (Respondent)* [2022] UKSC 64, https://www.supremecourt.uk/cases/uksc-2022-0064.html

104 Town and Country Planning (Environmental Impact Assessment) Regulations 2017 (SI 2017/571), https://www.legislation.gov.uk/uksi/2017/571/contents

105 Council Directive 92/11/EEC of 3 March 1992 amending Directive 89/396/EEC on indications or marks identifying the lot to which a foodstuff belongs (as amended) [1992] OJ L65/32, https://eur-lex.europa.eu/legal-content/en/ALL/?uri=CELEX:31992L0011

categories of project to prepare EIAs and submit them in Environmental Statements alongside planning applications. The EIA process is designed to ensure that authorities cover environmental issues in discretionary assessments of the acceptability of relevant projects. An EIA does not impose restrictions on which projects can or cannot be approved.

The substantive parts of the Regulations are replicated in EIA instruments binding other (non-planning) project authorities, such as the North Sea Transition Authority for offshore oil and gas and the Marine Management Organisation for marine works, so the principle in *Finch* has impacts beyond planning. Regulations require EIAs to 'identify, describe and assess' the 'direct and indirect significant effects' of a project on, among other things, the air, climate and landscape (reg 4(2)).

Surrey CC had initially considered that the EIA for the project should include an assessment of the combustion emissions from the oil to be produced. But the Council later changed its mind. It accepted as sufficient an Environmental Statement which assessed only direct releases of GHGs at the project site over the lifetime of the project and contained no assessment of the impact on climate of the combustion of the oil. In consequence, no information about the combustion emissions was made available to the public or considered by the council before it granted development consent for the project.

Supreme Court's decision

The Supreme Court reversed the decisions of the lower courts and allowed the appeal by a 3-2 majority, finding that the Council's decision was unlawful as it relied on an insufficient EIA. The Supreme Court's issues were whether it was unlawful for the council not to require the EIA to include an assessment of the impacts of downstream GHG emissions resulting from the eventual use of the refined products of the extracted oil. Not always the way in litigation, but in this case, there was in fact a large degree of factual agreement between the parties. It was agreed that the project involved the extraction of oil for commercial purposes for a period estimated at 20 years, in quantities sufficient to make an EIA mandatory and that it was not just likely but inevitable, that the oil extracted would be sent to refineries and that the refined oil would eventually undergo combustion, which would produce GHG emissions. It was also not disputed that these emissions, which could easily be quantified, would have a significant impact on climate. The only issue, therefore, was whether the combustion emissions were effects of the project at all.

As a result of *Finch*, the government withdrew its defence of the proposed coal mine in Cumbria, but the developer, West Cumbria Mining, continued to defend the decision to approve planning permission for the mine. In *(1) Friends of the Earth (2) South Lakeland Action on Climate Change v (1) Secretary of State for Levelling Up, Housing and Communities (2) West Cumbria Mining and (3) Cumbria CC (Whitehaven coalmine)* [2024] EWHC 2349 (Admin)the judge quashed the Secretary of State's decision to grant planning permission for a new coal mine in Cumbria. See **6.17**.

Case name:

R (on the application of ClientEarth) v Financial Conduct Authority [2023] EWHC 3301 (Admin)[106]

Summary:

ClientEarth's request for judicial review of the Financial Conduct Authority's (FCA's) decision to approve the prospectus of Ithaca Energy plc was refused permission after a renewed application. The judge also held that the challenge was not an Aarhus Convention claim.

Aarhus Convention claim: The Aarhus Convention grants the public rights regarding access to information, public participation and access to justice, in governmental decision-making processes on matters concerning the local, national and transboundary environment. It focuses on interactions between the public and public authorities

ClientEarth said it was essential for the protection of investors that, when fossil fuel companies seek to list on the London Stock Exchange, the prospectus should include full and transparent disclosure of climate-related risks. ClientEarth said this would allow investors to make informed decisions and encourage finance flows to shift to support net zero. ClientEarth said that otherwise there were risks that investors would be left with unviable stranded assets and investments losing value in the face of net zero.

Ithaca is an oil and gas operator in the North Sea, with interests in oil and gas fields including Cambo and Rosebank. ClientEarth argued that the risks disclosed in the prospectus for Ithaca were too general and that there was no explanation of how the risks would affect Ithaca's business or how significant they were.

The prospectus had to comply with the EU Prospectus Regulation,[107] as retained EU law. The FCA could only approve the prospectus if it met the requirements of the Prospectus Regulation.

ClientEarth said that the FCA had erred in law by approving Ithaca's prospectus in circumstances where the prospectus failed:

- to disclose adequately the climate-related risks associated with Ithaca's securities; and
- to include Ithaca's assessment of the materiality of its climate-related financial risks,

both in breach of Prospectus Regulation, Article 16 which provides that a prospectus must include risk factors material for taking an informed investment decision, with each risk factor being adequately described, explaining how it affects the issuer or the securities being offered. It states that when drawing up the prospectus, the issuer must assess the materiality of the risk factors based

106 *R (on the application of ClientEarth) v Financial Conduct Authority* [2023] EWHC 3301 (Admin), https://www.judiciary.uk/wp-content/uploads/2023/01/R-on-the-application-of-Friends-of-the-Earth-Limited-v-Secretary-of-State-for-International-Trade-and-others2.pdf

107 Regulation (EU) 2017/1129 of the European Parliament and of the Council of 14 June 2017 on the prospectus to be published when securities are offered to the public or admitted to trading on a regulated market, and repealing Directive 2003/71/EC, https://www.legislation.gov.uk/eur/2017/1129/contents

on the probability of their occurrence and the expected magnitude of their negative impact, but it does not make disclosure of this assessment mandatory.

ClientEarth argued that the prospectus only referred to climate change, the Paris Agreement and the net-zero commitment in broad generic terms. ClientEarth said that references to the possibility of climate activism negatively affected the process of obtaining approval for further development, and the effects on the hydrocarbon industry, were not specific enough, and did not describe Ithaca's particular situation, as opposed to the situation of the industry in general.

ClientEarth argued that the question of whether an issuer has complied with its obligation to disclose its assessment of the materiality of a risk factor is a question of law for the court, and not a matter of discretion or rationality. On this, the judge held that previous case law established that the requirements of Article 16 were not hard-edged questions for the court, but that they required an evaluative judgement which could admit more than one view, such as that the FCA's decision to approve Ithaca's prospectus could only be challenged on normal public law grounds.

The judge concluded that Ithaca's prospectus did address risks to Ithaca's business and securities arising out of climate change factors, associated regulatory measures and changes in consumer use. The result was that the FCA's judgement that the Article 16 requirements were met was not arguably unlawful. The judge also held that there was no obligation in Article 16 to disclose Ithaca's risk assessment.

ClientEarth also argued that the FCA's conclusion that the prospectus contained the necessary information, as required by Prospectus Regulation, Article 6, was irrational as Article 6 required a prospectus to contain the information which was material to an investor for making an informed assessment of the assets, liabilities and prospects of the company. The judge found this ground unarguable because the prospectus did identify the Paris Agreement as a material risk for the business and did address risks arising out of climate-related factors.

Case name:

R (on the application of (1) Friends of the Earth Ltd (2) ClientEarth and (3) Good Law Project) v Secretary of State for Energy Security and Net Zero [2024] EWHC 995 (Admin)[108]

Summary:

In May 2024, the High Court held that the government's Carbon Budget Delivery Plan (CBDP), which the Secretary of State for the Department for Business, Energy and Industrial Strategy (BEIS) had devised under Climate Change Act 2008 (CCA 2008), s 13 (and which was now under the purview of the Secretary of State for Energy Security and Net Zero), was unlawful.

108 *R (on the application of (1) Friends of the Earth Ltd (2) ClientEarth and (3) Good Law Project) v Secretary of State for Energy Security and Net Zero* [2024] EWHC 995 (Admin), https://www.judiciary.uk/wp-content/uploads/2024/05/Friends-of-the-Earth-v-Secretary-of-State-for-Energy-Security-and-Net-Zero-003.pdf

The CBDP was a revised version of the Net Zero Strategy, which had been quashed by a judge two years earlier and aimed to remedy its legal flaws (*R (on the application of Friends of the Earth Ltd) v SSBEIS* [2023] 1 WLR 225. In the judgment, the Secretary of State had still not lawfully demonstrated the government could meet the targets of their sixth carbon budget.

Five grounds of challenge were given:

- ground 1 – the Secretary of State failed to consider mandatory material considerations when purporting to comply with CCA 2008, s 13;
- ground 2 – the Secretary of State proceeded on the basis of an assumption that all of the quantified proposals and policies would be delivered in full, and this assumption was not supported by the information as to risk to delivery with which the Secretary of State was provided;
- ground 3 – the Secretary of State's conclusion that the proposals and policies would enable the carbon budgets to be met was irrational;
- ground 4 – the Secretary of State applied the wrong legal test to CCA 2008, s 13(3) (sustainable development); and
- ground 5 – the Secretary of State failed to include in the CBDP information that he was required to include.

The judge disposed of grounds 1 to 3 together because were about the Secretary of State having inadequate evidence concerning the delivery risk to policies to the effect that he could not rationally conclude the policies would achieve their projected emissions reductions. Ground 4 was a self-contained issue of statutory interpretation concerning s 13(3). Ground 5 concerned the Secretary of State's duty to publish a consultation document under s 14.

The judge found that grounds 1–4 had all been made out.

Grounds 1, 2 and 3: A cautious approach to delivery risk

The argument against the CBDP centred on the claim that there was insufficient evidence to demonstrate the likelihood of the policies achieving their intended emissions cuts, violating CCA 2008, s 13(1), which requires the Secretary of State to adopt policies it 'consider[s] will enable the carbon budgets' to be met.

Many policies come with 'delivery risk', uncertainty as to the quantity of emissions that may be reduced. The judge quoted from the request made by the Secretary of State to officials to provide their delivery risk information. The request explained that it was 'clear', from the judgment in (*R (on the application of Friends of the Earth Ltd) v SSBEIS* [2023] 1 WLR 225) that the Secretary of State 'needs sufficient information on delivery risks to make an informed judgment about whether carbon budgets can be met. This must include qualitative explanation of risks and planned mitigations…'.

The judge disposed of grounds 1, 2 and 3 on primary and alternative bases. The primary basis was that the Secretary of State had wrongly assumed all policies would be delivered in full. It was a question of fact whether the Secretary of State had made such an assumption, and it was conceded that the legal point of such an assumption would be irrational. The alternative basis, assuming that the Secretary of State had made no such assumption, was then that whether information provided to the Secretary of State was a lawful basis for making a rational decision.

The judge thought not: the legal standard applied was whether the Secretary of State had enough information to 'work out for himself whether the proposal or policy was likely to miss the target by a small or large amount and if so by how much'.

Ground 4: Sustainable development

Ground 4 concerned the question of statutory interpretation, whether the Secretary of State misconstrued CCA 2008, s 13(3), which required them to certify that the policy plan 'taken as a whole, must be such as to contribute to sustainable development'.

The Secretary of State confirmed that, in his view, the 'overall contribution' of the proposals was 'likely' to contribute to sustainable development. The claimants argued this was an error as the standard was certainty, denoted by 'must', not likelihood. The judge agreed, given the phrasing 'connotes a degree of certainty that a particular outcome will eventuate'. He concluded that in 'no reasonable view, could it be said that "likely" means "must"'.

Ground 5: Section 14

Under ground 5, the claimants argued that the Secretary of State's duty under CCA 2008, s 14, to publish a report for public consultation setting out his proposals and policies, needed to include delivery risk analysis for each policy. The court rejected this as the sector-level delivery risk analyses were sufficient.

Case name:

R (on the application of Friends of the Earth Ltd and Others) v Heathrow Airport Ltd [2020] UKSC 52[109]

Summary:

The Supreme Court unanimously allowed an appeal concerning whether the Secretary of State for Transport's failure to take account of the UK's climate change commitments under the Paris Agreement rendered the designation of the Airports National Policy Statement[110] (ANPS), favouring the development of a third runway at Heathrow Airport, unlawful.

On 26 June 2018, the Secretary of State designated the ANPS under Planning Act 2008 (PA 2008), s 5(1).[111] The ANPS supports the development of a third runway at Heathrow Airport to deliver additional hub airport capacity in the Southeast of England.

On 12 December 2015 the UK Government adopted the Paris Agreement on Climate Change, which enshrines an aspiration to achieve net-zero GHG

109 *R (on the application of Friends of the Earth Ltd and Others) v Heathrow Airport Ltd* [2020] UKSC 52 https://www.supremecourt.uk/cases/uksc-2020-0042.html

110 HM Government, Department for Transport, *Airports National Policy Statement: new runway capacity and infrastructure at airports in the South East of England* (2018), https://www.gov.uk/government/publications/airports-national-policy-statement

111 Planning Act 2008, https://www.legislation.gov.uk/ukpga/2008/29/contents

emissions during the latter half of the 21st century. The UK ratified the Paris Agreement on 17 November 2016.

The respondents (and others) challenged the ANPS on the basis that it failed to take account of the Paris Agreement. The High Court[112] dismissed their application for judicial review, but the Court of Appeal[113] allowed the appeal and held that the ANPS was unlawful.

The Secretary of State designated the ANPS under PA 2008, s 5(1). PA 2008, s 5(7) provides that national policy frameworks such as the ANPS must give reasons for the policy adopted. Section 5(8) states that these reasons must include an explanation of how that policy takes account of existing 'Government policy' relating to the mitigation of and adaptation to climate change.

The Supreme Court rejected the respondents' argument that the reasons in the ANPS needed to refer to the Paris Agreement targets in order to comply with s 5(8). The March 2016 statements of Andrea Leadsom MP and Amber Rudd MP and the formal ratification of the Paris Agreement did not mean that the government's commitment to the Paris Agreement constituted 'government policy' in the sense in which that term is used in the statute. Climate Change Act 2008 (CCA 2008), s 1 sets a national carbon target.

Section 4 obliges the government to establish carbon budgets for the UK. These are more demanding than the limits which the UK is currently obliged to have in place under the Paris Agreement. The Court said that, at the point the ANPS was designated, in June 2018, there was no established 'government policy' on climate change beyond that already reflected in the CCA 2008.

PA 2008, s 10(2) and (3) requires the Secretary of State to designate national policy frameworks which contribute to the achievement of sustainable development. He has to consider the environmental, economic and social objectives that make up sustainable development and, in particular, have regard to the desirability of mitigating and adapting to climate change.

The Court dismissed the respondents' argument that the Secretary of State breached this duty on the ground that he failed to have proper regard to the Paris Agreement when designating the ANPS. The evidence showed that the Secretary of State took the Paris Agreement into account and, to the extent that its obligations were already covered by the measures in the CCA 2008, ensured that these were incorporated into the ANPS framework.

The Court also dismissed the respondents' argument that the Secretary of State separately breached his s 10 duty by failing to have regard to, firstly, the effect of GHG emissions created by the North West Runway scheme after 2050 and, secondly, the effect of non-CO_2 emissions.

The UK's policy on the Paris Agreement's global goals, including the post-2050 goal for GHG emissions to reach net zero, was in development in June 2018. The Secretary of State did not act irrationally in deciding not to assess post-

112 High Court decision: [2019] EWHC 1070 (Admin), https://www.bailii.org/ew/cases/EWHC/Admin/2019/1070.html

113 Court of Appeal decision: [2020] EWCA Civ 214, https://www.bailii.org/ew/cases/EWCA/Civ/2020/214.html

2050 emissions by reference to future policies which had yet to be formulated. The Secretary of State's department was also still considering how to address the effect of non-CO_2 emissions in June 2018.

PA 2008, s 5(3) requires the Secretary of State to produce an appraisal of sustainability in respect of frameworks such as the ANPS. This is also required by EU law. The Court dismissed the respondents' complaint that the appraisal of sustainability accompanying the ANPS was defective because it did not refer to the Paris Agreement and emphasised that the purpose of these reports is to provide the basis for informed public consultation, it holds that an unduly legalistic approach should not be taken when assessing their adequacy. Whether a report provides a sound and sufficient basis for public consultation is a matter that falls within the Secretary of State's discretion and the exercise of this discretion will only be found unlawful if it is one that no reasonable decision-maker would have made. In this instance, the targets set out in the CCA 2008, which were referred to in the appraisal of sustainability, took the UK's obligations under the Paris Agreement sufficiently into account. The Court therefore upheld this ground of appeal as well.

Case name:

Bristol Airport Action Network Co-ordinating Committee v Secretary of State for Levelling Up, Housing and Communities [2023] EWHC 171 (Admin)[114]

Summary:

Here, the High Court dismissed a challenge, brought primarily on climate change grounds by various local environmental groups and residents, to the grant of planning permission for the expansion of Bristol Airport.

- Planning authorities are entitled to consider, in a generalised way, whether emissions from a proposed development would materially affect the UK's ability to meet its carbon budgets and targets.
- Local decision makers may assume that separate pollution control regimes will operate effectively in respect of the emissions from a proposed development.
- Aviation carbon emissions are primarily to be considered at a national, rather than local, level in accordance with government policy.

The first interested party, Bristol Airport Ltd (BAL), applied to North Somerset Council for planning permission to increase the airport's capacity by about two million passengers per year. The application was refused by the Council, but BAL's appeal against that refusal was allowed, following an inquiry by a panel of planning inspectors.

The claimant alleged that, in relation to climate change issues, the panel erred in:

- its interpretation that the Council's development plan policies did not directly address aviation emissions;

114 *Bristol Airport Action Network Co-ordinating Committee v Secretary of State for Levelling Up, Housing and Communities* [2023] EWHC 171 (Admin), https://www.bailii.org/ew/cases/EWHC/Admin/2023/171.html

- its interpretation of the national policy 'Making Best – Use of Existing Runways' (MBU);
- finding that it was required to 'assume' that the Secretary of State would comply with his duty under the Climate Change Act 2008 (CCA 2008), as per paragraph 188 of the National Planning Policy Framework (NPPF);
- failing to consider the impact on the local carbon budget for the Council; and
- its conclusion that the impact of non-CO_2 emissions could be excluded from the EIA prepared by BAL and should not weigh in the balance against the proposed expansion.

The claimant submitted that the panel failed to give adequate reasons.

The judge dismissed each of the grounds raised by the claimant, including the reasons challenge. The key question underpinning the inquiry (to which there was no substantial dissent) was whether emissions from the proposal would be so significant that they would materially affect the ability of the UK to meet its carbon budgets and the target of net zero by 2050.

Ground 1 – the court noted the principle in *Tesco Stores Ltd v Dundee CC* [2012] UKSC 13,[115] that planning policy statements are not to be construed as statutory or contractual provisions.

Although the relevant policies here were broad enough to cover the issue of aviation emissions, they did not seek to show how the Council should address that issue as a planning authority. Aviation emissions, which can occur at any point during an aircraft's journey to and from the airport, are clearly different from other forms of emissions that can be reduced in the Council's own area. The panel was entitled to conclude that aviation emissions should be addressed 'indirectly', meaning they would only become relevant if they were likely to have a material impact on the Secretary of State's ability to meet his climate targets and budgets (which the panel did not consider to be the case here). Aviation emissions were not, therefore, a material consideration against BAL.

Ground 2 – the court found that the panel considered carbon emissions from all sources, including aviation, in detail. The court noted that planning authorities are entitled to make judgements of a generalised nature about the likelihood of a proposal harming the achievement of a national target. The MBU, also showed that the admitted increase in CO_2 emissions was a matter for national, not local, decision-making.

Ground 3 – the claimant's main argument was that the panel erred in law in treating the CCA 2008 and the various duties placed on the Secretary of State under it as a 'separate pollution control regime' that would operate effectively, relying on the different approach taken in relation to air quality in *Gladman Developments Ltd v Secretary of State for Communities and Local Government and Others* [2019] EWCA Civ 1543.[116]

115 *Tesco Stores Ltd v Dundee CC* [2012] UKSC 13, https://www.supremecourt.uk/cases/uksc-2011-0079.html

116 *Gladman Developments Ltd v Secretary of State for Communities and Local Government and Others* [2019] EWCA Civ 1543, https://www.judiciary.uk/live-hearings/gladman-development-ltd-v-the-secretary-of-state-for-communities-and-local-government-others/

The judge explained that the relationships between local and national decision-making in the areas of air quality and emissions from aviation are significantly different, with the latter controlled at the national level pursuant to the CCA 2008, including through trading schemes, in contrast to air quality issues which have a significant and discrete local element. Disapplying the assumption in paragraph 188 of the NPPF, that other regimes would operate effectively, would lead local decision makers into an area of national policy with which they are not directly concerned.

Ground 4 – the court found that the impact of the proposal on the Council's local carbon budget was only a consideration 'to which the decision-maker may have regard if, in their judgment and discretion, they think it is right to do', (the third category of 'relevant considerations' summarised in *R (on the application of Friends of the Earth Ltd) v Heathrow Airport Ltd* [2020] UKSC 52[117]).

Given the decision letter demonstrated that the panel engaged with the issue before concluding that it had no basis in law or policy, and therefore giving it no weight, the claimant failed to overcome the high threshold of irrationality. Lane J reiterated the court's concern not to adopt a stance which may result in it wrongly substituting its own view on weight for that of the decision maker.

Ground 5 – The claimant submitted that the impact of non-CO_2 emissions was a matter of critical importance to determining the impact of the airport's expansion on climate change and should have been in the environmental statement. The judge referred to the 'well-established' position that EIA compliance is a matter of planning judgement, challengeable only on a *Wednesbury* basis.[118] The EIA did not ignore the non-CO_2 emissions but noted the uncertain state of scientific knowledge regarding their assessment, and their present exclusion from domestic and international legislation and targets. Accordingly, the EIA did not disclose a 'patent defect' that the panel unlawfully failed to recognise. Applying *Friends of the Earth*, leaving a matter about which there is scientific uncertainty for further consideration within the development process did not breach the precautionary principle.

117 *R (on the application of Friends of the Earth Ltd) v Heathrow Airport Ltd* [2020] UKSC 52, https://www.supremecourt.uk/cases/uksc-2020-0042.html

118 *Wednesbury* basis: the *Wednesbury* principle also known as the principle of reasonableness and originates from the decision in *Associated Provincial Picture Houses Ltd v Wednesbury Corp'n* (1948) 1 KB 223, https://www.bailii.org/cgi-bin/format.cgi?doc=/ew/cases/EWCA/Civ/1947/1.html&query=(Associated)+AND+(Provincial)+AND+(Picture)+AND+(Houses)+AND+(Ltd)+AND+(v)+AND+(Wednesbury)+AND+(Corporation)+AND+((1948))+AND+(1)+AND+(KB)+AND+(223), a case before the UK Court of Appeal. It was held 'that if the decision of competent matter is so unreasonable that no reasonable authority could ever come to it, then the courts can interfere'. The *Wednesbury* principle refers to a standard of unreasonableness used in assessing the application for judicial review of a public authority's decision.

Case name:

R (on the application of Packham) v Secretary of State for Energy Security and Net Zero and Secretary of State for Transport (challenge to the 'new approach to Net Zero')[119]

Summary:

Mr Packham wrote to the Prime Minister, the Energy Secretary and the Transport Secretary to challenge the policy U-turn, saying that the Prime Minister did not have the legal right to change at will the timeline to help the UK meet net zero because the actioning of policies in the Carbon Budget Delivery Plan (CBDP) is governed by statute. If those policies were delivered in full, the country would make all the carbon savings needed to meet previous budgets and 97 per cent of the carbon savings needed to fulfil carbon budget six. Any changes had to be made according to a process in Climate Change Act 2008 (CCA 2008), s 6.

In the absence of a satisfactory response to his pre-action protocol letter, Mr Packham filed his legal claim at the High Court. He said the response to his letter made it clear that the policies on vehicles and boilers were abandoned without any public consultation, without informing the Climate Change Committee, without informing Parliament and without providing any reasons for the delays. He said that if the government was right that it could abandon, revise or delay key policies published in a report required by CCA 2008, s 14, then such a report was effectively worthless. It would be a mere snapshot; accurate and meaningful for just one day every five years.

Mr Packham's grounds for judicial review were:

- The obligation under CCA 2008, s 13 to have proposals and policies to meet carbon budgets is continuing and the proposals and policies must be current. If they are altered, there must always be plans in place to meet the budgets. The Secretaries of State breached this obligation.
- There was a failure to consider considerations listed under CCA 2008, s 10, such as the risk to delivery of proposals and policies and achievement of the carbon budgets and the 2050 net zero target.
- There was a failure to consult on the changes, particularly a failure to consider ongoing consultations about off-grid heating and minimum energy efficiency in rental properties.
- The decisions were based on misinformation, for instance that the UK's 'over-delivery' on previous GHG reduction targets meant that some measures were no longer needed or that carbon budgets 'impose unacceptable costs on hard-pressed British families … . that no-one was ever told about' and the understanding that 'the last Carbon Budget process was … voted through with barely any consideration given the hard choices needed to fulfil it'. All of that messaging was wrong, because under CCA 2008, s 10, the financing and social impact of the policies were considered when setting the sixth carbon budget

119 *R (on the application of Packham) v Secretary of State for Energy Security and Net Zero and Secretary of State for Transport* (challenge to the 'new approach to Net Zero'), unreported as settled out of court.

- There was a breach of the duty to inform the public of the reasons for the decisions to change the policies

In October 2024 Christopher Packham agreed a settlement with the government over two legal challenges against a decision to remove or delay some environmental policies.

Case name:

R (on the application of (1) Greenpeace Ltd (2) Uplift) v (1) Secretary of State for Business, Energy and Industrial Strategy and (2) the Oil and Gas Authority [2023] EWHC 2608 (Admin) (North Sea oil and gas licensing)[120]

Summary:

The UK High Court dismissed two judicial review claims brought by environmental NGOs Greenpeace and Uplift against government decisions relating to new oil and gas exploration and production in the North Sea.

The challenges were brought due to concerns over the compatibility of a further licensing round with the UK's climate objectives. The High Court dismissed the claims, holding that the issues in dispute were 'plainly a matter of judgment and not law'.

The claims primarily concerned decisions taken by the Secretary of State for Business, Energy and Industrial Strategy (now the Secretary of State for Energy Security and Net Zero) and the Oil and Gas Authority (OGA).

Petroleum Act 1998, s 3[121] permits the OGA to grant licences to search and bore for petroleum. A licence holder must also obtain the OGA's consent before starting a project, and that cannot be given without the Secretary of State's agreement, usually following an EIA.

The Secretary of State's policy for further licensing for offshore oil and gas exploration and production was contained in the *Offshore Energy Plan*. Under the Environmental Assessment of Plans and Programmes Regulations 2004[122] the Secretary of State was required to carry out a strategic environmental assessment of the Plan. This assessment was referred to as OESEA4 and was announced in March 2021, along with the development of a Climate Compatibility Checkpoint to ensure that the compatibility of any future licensing rounds would be assessed against the UK's climate objectives.

An issue for the court was whether the Secretary of State acted unlawfully by not considering, as part of OESEA4 or the Checkpoint, downstream emissions of GHGs from the end use by consumers of oil and gas as a fuel ('Scope 3' emissions). For the Checkpoint, a consultation on its design considered

120 *R (on the application of (1) Greenpeace Ltd (2) Uplift)* v *(1) Secretary of State for Business, Energy and Industrial Strategy and (2) the Oil and Gas Authority* [2023] EWHC 2608 (Admin) (North Sea oil and gas licensing), https://www.judiciary.uk/wp-content/uploads/2023/10/CO4583-Greenpeace_CO4830_Uplift_-v-SSESNZ_-Summary-19-10-2023-final.pdf

121 Petroleum Act 1998, s 3, https://www.legislation.gov.uk/ukpga/1998/17/section/3#:~:text=3%20Licences%20to%20search%20and,to%20which%20this%20section%20applies.

122 Environmental Assessment of Plans and Programmes Regulations 2004 (SI 2004/1633), https://www.legislation.gov.uk/uksi/2004/1633/contents

whether a further test should be added to assess whether Scope 3 emissions from the combustion of UK oil would be expected to fall in line with UK climate objectives if further licensing rounds were approved (known as 'test 5'). However, the consultation document identified several issues with adding test 5, including that:

- methodologies for tracking Scope 3 emissions were 'in their infancy' and that there was no 'universally agreed approach' to measuring them; and
- there was a risk of double counting because Scope 3 emissions from exported oil and gas produced in the UK would be covered by the destination country's emissions accounting and targets.

Following the consultation, the Department's Oil and Gas Exploration and Production unit informed the Secretary of State that it would advise against the inclusion of test 5.

On 7 September 2022, the Secretary of State adopted the Plan as assessed in OESEA4, approved the final design of the Checkpoint (omitting test 5) on the following day, and agreed that the Checkpoint should be applied ahead of the next licensing round. The Secretary of State also decided that a further licensing round would be compatible with the UK's climate objectives.

The challenges brought by Greenpeace and Uplift failed on all seven grounds raised:

- Issue 1 – The Secretary of State's decision not to assess Scope 3 emissions from further oil and gas licensing rounds in OESEA4 was irrational and/or in breach of the 2004 Regulations: The court relied on the case of *R (on the application of Finch on behalf of the Weald Action Group and Others) v Surrey CC* [2022] EWCA Civ 187. In this case, the Department acknowledged that the processes and products associated with end use would result in GHG emissions, it was not considered that they were sufficiently connected to implementation of the Plan to be considered in OESEA4 and therefore did not constitute a likely significant effect of implementing the Plan itself. On this basis, the court found that it was lawful for the government to decline to assess Scope 3 emissions.
- Issue 2 – In breach of the 2004 Regulations, the Secretary of State failed to properly assess 'reasonable alternatives' by not assessing the option of not proceeding with further licensing rounds: the claimants said that the Secretary of State was not entitled to assume, under Alternative 1a, as he did, that UK demand would not reduce more quickly than had been projected for the Plan and the Secretary of State was not entitled to assume that a greater proportion of oil and gas consumed in the UK would need to be imported. The judge found that this was a 'matter of judgment' for the Secretary of State and that he was entitled to assume that *some* of the additional hydrocarbons produced in accordance with the Plan would be consumed in the UK, thereby reducing the need for imports.
- Issue 3 – The Secretary of State unlawfully failed to publish any reasons for deciding that a further licensing round would be compatible with the Checkpoint and the UK's climate objectives. The judge reminded the claimants that there is no general common law duty to give reasons for administrative decisions and that 'whether such an obligation may arise is highly sensitive to the specific context'. In this case, the court found

that there was nothing to support the imposition on the Secretary of State of a common law obligation to give reasons for the application of the Checkpoint, particularly in circumstances where there was no obligation to produce or apply the Checkpoint given that it was only indicative and non-statutory in nature.

- Issue 4 – The Secretary of State's decision to approve the design of the Checkpoint was unlawful because it excluded test 5 for reasons which were unlawful and irrational. The court found that it was a matter of judgement for the Secretary of State as to whether there was an appropriate test for taking Scope 3 emissions into account and concluded that there was no basis upon which to find that the reasons given by him for not including test 5 in the Checkpoint were irrational or tainted by any error of law.
- Issues 6 and 7 – The OGA's decision to carry out a further licensing round was unlawful because OESEA4 was unlawful, and the decision was irrational because it relied upon the Secretary of State's adoption of the Checkpoint without test 5. As a result of the claimants being unsuccessful on the above grounds, the challenges under Issues 6 and 7 also failed.

Case name:

(1) Friends of the Earth and (2) South Lakeland Action on Climate Change v (1) Secretary of State for Levelling Up, Housing and Communities (2) West Cumbria Mining and(3) Cumbria CC [2024] EWHC 2349 (Admin) (Whitehaven coalmine)[123]

Summary:

In 2022 the Secretary of State for Levelling Up, Housing and Communities granted planning permission to West Cumbria Mining Limited (WCM) for the first deep coal mine in the UK for 30 years at Whitehaven, Cumbria. WCM had described the project as a 'net zero mine' on the basis that it would compensate for emissions generated from the mine by carbon offsetting.

Friends of the Earth and South Lakeland Action on Climate Change – Towards Transition (SLACC) brought statutory review proceedings seeking to have the planning permission quashed. The central focus of the challenge was on the way the Secretary of State addressed GHG emissions resulting from the proposed extraction of coal and their effects on climate change.

A number of issues were considered by the court.

- Whether the Secretary of State's decision that GHG emissions from the burning of Whitehaven coal were not a 'significant likely effect' of the project that they did not require assessment under the EIA regime, was unlawful (ie the same main issue addressed in *Finch*, see **6.07**).
- Whether the conclusion that the project would have a neutral or beneficial effect on global GHG emissions as a result of substitution was unlawful. WCM had argued that emissions from the burning of

123 *(1) Friends of the Earth and (2) South Lakeland Action on Climate Change v (1) Secretary of State for Levelling Up, Housing and Communities (2) West Cumbria Mining and(3) Cumbria* CC (Whitehaven coalmine) [2024] EWHC 2349 (Admin) https://www.judiciary.uk/judgments/friends-of-the-earth-and-another-v-secretary-of-state-for-levelling-up-housing-and-communities-and-others/

Whitehaven coal would not give rise to any material additional emissions, because this would replace coal being supplied from US coal mines to the UK and European steel-making market. In essence WCM submitted that if coal was extracted at Whitehaven, then a broadly equivalent amount of coal would remain in the ground in US mines.

Part of FoE and SLACC's case was that the extraction of coal at Whitehaven would increase the supply of that type of coal in the market so that its price would decrease, and likewise the price of steel, leading to an increase in demand.

The judge started by clarifying that WCM had to establish that there would be no net increase in GHG emissions as a result of the US coal substitution effect upon which it relied. It needed to produce full information on how that balanced out or offset the GHG emissions in a way that would allow the public to respond to that information via the EIA process. WCM would have had to show a high degree of substitution and, if that was shown, also that there would be no other demand for US coal substituted by the Whitehaven coal. Neither of these were addressed by WCM's environmental material, nor was it suggested that these were matters incapable of assessment.

- Whether the Secretary of State failed to look at the evidence and submissions on the impact of a decision to grant planning permission for the coal mine on the ability of the UK to perform its leadership role in promoting international action to address climate change.

  The claimants' arguments were:
  - that the mine would result in a substantial net increase in GHG emissions and would therefore set a bad precedent internationally for the development of coal mines elsewhere in the world; and
  - that, even if the Secretary of State were to accept that the project would operate as a net-zero mine, that would still be a harmful precedent, because any further mining projects of the same nature would depend upon the offsetting of GHG emissions, in circumstances where offsets are a finite global resource.

  The judge accepted that these were principal controversial issues on which the Secretary of State had a legal duty to give reasons explaining how they had been resolved.
- Whether the Secretary of State erred in law in the treatment of WCM's proposed scheme for offsetting GHG residual, mitigated emissions from the coal mine itself.

  The Secretary of State accepted the offsetting arrangements entered into by WCM, involving the purchase of credits in the voluntary carbon market, as reducing the net change in GHG emissions from the operation of the mine to zero. WCM claimed that the emissions, once offset, would represent 0 per cent of the UK's national carbon budgets.

  FoE submitted that the domestic legislation relating to carbon accounting did not allow offsets from outside the UK to be considered and relied on a number of policy documents advising that UK emissions must be tackled without reliance on offsets from outside the UK. However, this submission was not addressed during the decision-making process.

Case name:

R (on the application of Coal Action Network) v (1) Welsh Ministers (2) Coal Authority and (3) Energybuild Mining Ltd [2024] EWCA Civ 168[124]

Summary:

Whether the Coal Authority, when granting an application to deconditionalise a coal licence, had misunderstood its powers, and whether the Welsh Ministers had any powers, under devolution legislation, in respect of that application.

On 19 May 2023, the judge handed down judgment, dismissing the Coal Action Network's challenge to the authorisation of coal-mining operations at Aberpergwm, an underground drift mine, in the Vale of Neath.

The claimant unsuccessfully challenged the decision of the Welsh Ministers dated 10 January 2022 in saying that it did not have the power under Coal Industry Act 1994, s 26A[125] to approve or refuse the authorisation of coal-mining operations granted in a licence that was issued in 1996 and subsequently varied by the Coal Authority, most recently in 2013. The claimant also unsuccessfully challenged the decision of the Coal Authority dated 25 January 2022 to grant the operator, Energybuild Mining Ltd's, application that it had discharged the conditions precedent contained in the licence.

The licence authorising coal mining operations was granted in 1996. Authorisation was suspended on terms – the discharge of general conditions precedent and planning conditions precedent – which were to be satisfied by 1996 and 1998 respectively. Under the licence, coal mining operations could not take effect until the conditions precedent had been discharged.

The licence was varied in 2000, 2005, 2011 and 2013, with the latest variation amending the conditions to require the operator to secure planning permissions and all other rights and permissions necessary by 31 December 2020. In 2014, and in compliance with the 2013 variation, the operator made an application for planning permission, which was subsequently determined by the Local Planning Authority in 2018. On 16 September 2020, the operator applied to the Coal Authority for a notice to the effect that the conditions relating to the conditional areas of the licence (as defined in the 2013 Variation Agreement) had been fulfilled.

In the decision of 25 January 2022, the Coal Authority granted the operator's 2020 application. As 1994 Act, s 26A allowing the Welsh Ministers to approve or refuse coal-mining operations, did not enter into force until 1 April 2018, the Welsh Ministers did not decide on the operator's application.

The claim gave rise to two points of statutory interpretation under the 1994 Act:

- whether the Welsh Ministers erred in law in deciding that s 26A was inapplicable to applications relating to a licence granted in 1996 and varied in 2013; and
- whether the Coal Authority unlawfully fettered its discretion and/or failed to consider material considerations in approving the operator's application.

124 *R (on the application of Coal Action Network) v (1) Welsh Ministers (2) Coal Authority and (3) Energybuild Mining Ltd* [2024] EWCA Civ 168, https://www.judiciary.uk/wp-content/uploads/2024/02/Coal-Action-Network-v-Welsh-Ministers.pdf

125 Coal Industry Act 1994, https://www.legislation.gov.uk/ukpga/1994/21/contents

The judge dismissed the challenge to the Welsh Ministers' decision. In particular the judge held that the claimant's interpretation of s 26A 'gives the provision a degree of retrospective force'. The judge also agreed with the Welsh Ministers' submission that if a licence is granted subject to conditions precedent, 'ordinarily, the recipient of the licence is entitled to expect that if they satisfy those conditions, the authorisation contained in the licence will take effect'.

On the second ground, the judge held that, as the Coal Authority had issued an authorisation subject to the satisfaction of conditions, it was confined to determining whether, in its reasonable opinion, the conditions precedent had been fulfilled. Ultimately, it would be inconsistent with the provisions of the 1994 Act for the Coal Authority 'to treat an application for a determination that conditions imposed in a licence have been satisfied as a fresh opportunity to determine whether, or on what conditions, coal-mining operations should be authorised'.

Case name:

Trump International Golf Club Scotland Ltd and The Trump Organization LLC v Scottish Ministers [2015] UKSC 74[126]

Summary:

Trump International Golf Club Scotland Ltd (TIGC) had developed a golf resort at Menie Estate and Menie Links, Balmedie, Aberdeenshire. In 2011, Aberdeen Offshore Wind Farm Ltd applied for consent under Electricity Act 1989 (the 1989 Act), s 36 to construct and operate the European Offshore Wind Deployment Centre in Aberdeen Bay. The application concerned the construction of up to 11 wind turbines, which might be of different sizes, with a maximum power generation of 100 MW. The proposed windfarm would be located about 3.5 km from the golf resort and would be seen by people at the resort. TIGC opposed the application. In March 2013, the Scottish Ministers granted consent (the Consent) for the development and operation of the windfarm subject to conditions.

TIGC challenged the Consent on various grounds in the Scottish courts without success.

TIGC then appealed to the Supreme Court on two remaining grounds, arguing that the Consent should be quashed:

- because the Scottish Ministers had no power under the 1989 Act to grant consent to the windfarm application as only the holder of a licence to generate, transmit, or supply electricity granted under s 6, or a person exempted under s 5 from holding such a licence may apply under s 36 ('the Section 36 Challenge'); and
- because condition 14 of the Consent, which required the submission and approval of a design statement, was void for uncertainty ('the Condition 14 Challenge').

The Supreme Court unanimously dismissed the appeal by TIGC.

126 *Trump International Golf Club Scotland Ltd and The Trump Organization LLC v Scottish Ministers* [2015] UKSC 74, https://www.supremecourt.uk/cases/uksc-2015-0160

Section 36 challenge

TIGC's Section 36 Challenge was rejected. It was not supported by the structure and language of the 1989 Act. Further, there was nothing in the policy background to the 1989 Act which required the Court to take a different view of the statutory provisions. There were several reasons for this:

- the 1989 Act aimed to liberalise the British electricity market by privatisation;
- the policy did not address who would construct generating stations, and it was not a necessary part of the policy that the persons who built generating stations would also be the persons generating the electricity;
- the 1989 Act contains two separate regulatory regimes:
  - — one for the construction of generation stations and overhead lines, and
  - — one for the licensing of electricity supply, including generation. Since devolution, there have been separate regulators for those activities in Scotland;
- the Scottish Ministers have a duty when considering a s 36 application to have regard to environmental matters, and wide powers to impose conditions to protect the environment ([17]).

There is no need to require a s 36 applicant to hold, in advance, a generating licence or exemption, as the Scottish Ministers may (pursuant to s 36(5)) include appropriate conditions in a consent.

It is established practice in both British jurisdictions for commercial organisations to apply for and obtain s 36 consents before they seek a licence to generate electricity, or an exemption.

Condition 14 challenge

The short answer to this challenge was that, even if Condition 14 were unenforceable, the Consent would not be invalidated. Condition 7 required that the development be constructed in accordance with the supplemental environmental information statement (SEIS) which covered important elements of the benefits promoted by Condition 14, and the Scottish Ministers could insist on compliance with the SEIS. Further, the scope of the development was defined by Annex 1 of the Consent and the SEIS specified the maximum size and location of the turbines. Condition 14 was not therefore a fundamental condition determining the scope and nature of the development which, if invalid, would invalidate the Consent

Even if Condition 14 could not be enforced, a planning condition is only void for uncertainty if it can be given no sensible or ascertainable meaning. This cannot be said for Condition 14, which provides that the Scottish Ministers must approve the design statement before the development can begin. Further, Condition 14 was not invalid owing to any uncertainty as to what amounted to compliance with its terms. Construing the Conditions as a whole (in particular Conditions 13 and 24), it was clear that the Consent contained a mechanism enabling the Scottish Ministers to use both the construction method statement and the design statement to regulate the design of the windfarm in the interests of environmental protection, and to require compliance with those statements.

Given those conclusions, it was unnecessary to consider whether terms could be implied into the Consent. Had it been necessary, however, an inference would have been drawn that the Consent read as a whole required the developer to conform to the design statement.

There is not a complete bar on implying terms into planning permissions, and the planning legislation cases relied on by TIGC which suggest otherwise were not directly applicable to conditions under the 1989 Act given the different statutory language. Whether words are implied into a document depends on the interpretation of the express words and, while restraint is required when implying terms into public documents with criminal sanctions, there is no reason for excluding implication altogether.

Finally, the flexibility conferred on the Scottish Ministers in Conditions 7 and 13 to modify the way in which the windfarm was constructed and operated does not invalidate those conditions, as the Scottish Ministers were not able to alter the nature of the approved development.

Cases against corporations: activist company law claims

Case name:

ClientEarth v Shell plc and Others [2023] EWHC 2182 (Ch)

Summary:

This case[127] involved ClientEarth's derivative action against Shell's board of directors under the UK Companies Act 2006 (CA 2006), s 260. ClientEarth, a minority shareholder, alleged that the directors breached their duties under CA 2006, s 170, by failing to adopt and implement a strategy to manage climate risk and to comply with an order issued by the Hague District Court. The High Court of Justice dismissed the application for permission to continue the claim, finding that ClientEarth's allegations did not establish a prima facie case and that the directors' decisions were within the range of reasonable decisions available to them at the time.

The court also noted that ClientEarth's primary purpose for bringing the claim was to advance its own policy agenda rather than to promote the success of Shell for the benefit of its members. This landmark case raised important questions about the role and responsibility of corporations and their directors in addressing climate change risks and the potential limits of legal action to hold directors accountable. Ultimately, the court concluded that the directors had not breached their statutory duties and ordered ClientEarth to pay the costs of the proceedings.[128]

127 *ClientEarth v Shell plc and Others* [2023] EWHC 2182 (Ch), https://www.judiciary.uk/wp-content/uploads/2023/07/ClientEarth-v-Shell-judgment-240723.pdf

128 See further, https://climatecasechart.com/wp-content/uploads/non-us-case-documents/2023/20230512_2023-EWHC-1137-Ch-2023-EWHC-1897-Ch-2023-EWHC-2182-Ch-_judgment.pdf

Case name:

(1) McGaughey and (2) Davies v Universities Superannuation Scheme Ltd and Others [2023] EWCA Civ 873[129]

Summary:

This is a UK company law, climate litigation and pension law case, seeking permission for a derivative claim to enforce duties of the directors of the UK university pension fund, USS Ltd. This case was the first to sue directors of a major UK corporation to divest fossil fuels and is the first case of beneficiaries of a pension corporation bringing a derivative claim for breaches of directors' statutory duties.

The High Court accepted that the claimants had standing to bring a derivative claim, but refused permission based on *Foss v Harbottle*.[130] The claimants secured permission to appeal to the Court of Appeal with a hearing in June 2023, but were unsuccessful, as the judge held that the appropriate procedure was a 'beneficiary derivative claim' where directors' duties may be held on trust. The fossil fuel risk claim was not addressed in substance but 'well suited' for being brought as an action for breach of trust.

The claimants alleged that directors of the USS Ltd had breached their statutory duties to act for proper purposes, act in good faith and avoid conflicts of interest, and applied to bring a derivative claim in the company's name against the directors.

From 2018, major strikes took place in UK universities after the CEO Bill Galvin attempted to remove the guaranteed pension from university staff: this was halted after sector-wide strikes, and Oxford University staff threatened to remove the Vice Chancellor unless the pension cuts were opposed. Subsequently, the planned pension cuts were halted. In 2019, the board of USS Ltd voted to pass a special resolution to ensure that they could not be removed except by the existing board (rather than by university employers and the University and College Union).

At a board meeting, the CEO Bill Galvin stated 'DB pensions in the UK have failed. That is not controversial.' In March 2020, USS Ltd conducted a valuation of pension assets when the stock market had crashed due to the Covid-19 pandemic. This predicted that there would be a £17.9 billion deficit in the pension fund, on the assumption that assets would grow at 0.0 per cent for 30 years (later changed to a 0.29 per cent assumption). In November 2020, USS Ltd conducted an Ethical Investment Survey, which showed that a majority of university staff wished to divest from fossil fuels, but it did not act on or publish the survey results. As a result of the deficit predictions in the March 2020 valuation, USS Ltd and university employers proposed cutting pension benefits in April 2022. The claimants, Prof Neil Davies and Dr Ewan McGaughey, then filed their action, after crowd-funding money for the claims, that:

129 *(1) McGaughey and (2) Davies v Universities Superannuation Scheme Ltd and Others* [2023] EWCA Civ 873, https://www.bailii.org/ew/cases/EWCA/Civ/2023/873.html

130 *Foss v Harbottle* (1843) 67 ER 189, https://lawprof.co/company/derivative-action-cases/foss-v-harbottle-1843-67-e-r-189/

- conducting a valuation of assets with an assumption of 0.29 per cent growth over the next 30 years and predicting deficits breached the duty to act for proper purposes under Companies Act 2006, s 171(b),
- the resulting benefit cuts had a discriminatory impact on women, young people and on grounds of race, contrary to the duties in Equality Act 2010, ss 19 and 61, and the duty to act for proper purposes,
- the directors wasted beneficiaries' money by inflating operating costs, contrary to the duty to avoid any possibility of a conflict of interest under Companies Act 2006, s 175, and
- the directors unlawfully failed to divest or have any plan for divesting fossil fuels, which posed a 'significant risk of financial detriment', in light of the right to life under Companies Act 2006, s 171 and Human Rights Act 1998, s 3, and in light of the beneficiaries' expressed preferences.

In March 2022, after the Russian invasion of Ukraine, USS Ltd announced £450 million of losses in Russian investments, including fossil fuels. In April 2022 it pressed ahead with cuts to the pension, reducing the defined benefit pension threshold from £60,000 to £40,000, reducing accrual rates from 1/75th of salary per year to 1/85th, and reducing the inflation cap, estimated to be a 30 per cent cut to an average pension.

After the High Court hearing, and following the UK mini-budget, the CEO Bill Galvin announced his resignation.

The judge in the High Court held that, while beneficiaries of a pension fund corporation could bring derivative claims, the Court of Appeal decision in *Harris v Microfusion* and the rule in *Foss v Harbottle* meant that the claimants had to show they suffered loss reflected by a loss to the company, and that the directors 'benefited themselves from the breach of duty'. It followed that the claimants' claims for breach of duty to act for proper purposes could not be brought, including the claims alleging misconduct in the valuation and discrimination, and claims alleging a significant risk of financial detriment in the failure to divest fossil fuels or have a plan. The judge added that the claimants had failed to state sufficiently what the losses from fossil fuels were.

Court of Appeal

The claimants applied for permission to appeal to the Court of Appeal and received permission for a hearing in 2023. The claimants alleged that the High Court applied the wrong legal tests, that all duties under the Companies Act 2006 must be capable of enforcement, and that key parts of their evidence on the imprudent valuation assumptions, and the risk of significant financial detriment from fossil fuels were missed.

The Court of Appeal held, the claimants ought to have pursued a 'beneficiary derivative claim' rather than a common law company derivative claim. The judge held it was 'not unarguable' that certain directors' duties that the claimants alleged were breached were capable of being held on trust by the trust fund (USS) for the benefit of the beneficiaries and were therefore capable of enforcement by the claimants. However, this was separate from the company (USS Ltd) that was the corporate trustee where the directors sat, and the rules of procedure differed, in particular with more requirements to gather the views of other beneficiaries. The Court of Appeal did not analyse the substantive claims including on the risks associated with fossil fuel investment but held that this was particularly apt for a beneficiary claim.

The case was the first in the UK to bring actions against directors personally for their failure to divest fossil fuels in light of climate risk. Solicitors at Ince stated that despite the High Court's rejection, the case showed 'there is an increasing momentum by activists, shareholders and others to hold them accountable for climate change'.

On appeal to the Court of Appeal the case was described as having 'immense significance' for the future of fossil fuels.

Case name:

Foss v Harbottle (1843) 67 ER 189[131]

Summary:

In general, only the company is entitled to sue for wrongs committed against *the company* and shareholders are not entitled to sue. Two shareholders in a real estate company brought a claim against the directors for breach of their duties through misapplication of capital. The Court of Chancery held that the shareholders were not entitled to bring the claim.

The judge said:

> 'Whilst the Court may be declaring the acts complained of to be void at the suit of the present Plaintiffs, who in fact may be the only proprietors who disapprove of them, the governing body of proprietors may defeat the decree by lawfully resolving upon the confirmation of the very acts which are the subject of the suit. The very fact that the governing body of proprietors assembled at the special general meeting may so bind even a reluctant minority is decisive to shew that the frame of this suit cannot be sustained whilst that body retains its functions. In order then that this suit may be sustained it must be shewn either that there is no such power as I have supposed remaining in the proprietors, or, at least, that all means have been resorted to and found ineffectual to set that body in motion.' (p 204)

The reasoning was basically that, since the majority shareholders could ratify the acts of the directors that were allegedly in breach of their duties, the shareholder should not be entitled to sue.

Note that the rule here is subject to common law and statutory exceptions.

Case name:

National Highways Ltd v Person Unknown and Others [2023] EWCA Civ 182[132]

Summary:

The Court of Appeal overturned a High Court judge's refusal to grant summary judgment in claims for final injunctions where the defendants had

131 *Foss v Harbottle* (1843) 67 ER 189, https://lawprof.co/company/derivative-action-cases/foss-v-harbottle-1843-67-e-r-189/

132 *National Highways Ltd v Person unknown and Others* [2023] EWCA Civ 182, https://nationalhighways.co.uk/media/le5ncp3o/nhl-review-hearing-final-skeleton.pdf

failed to engage with the proceedings by either filing defences or any evidence in opposition to the claims. The Court of Appeal criticised the first instance judge's approach as impermissible speculation as to what defences might be advanced at trial.

This case is of interest in the context of the Civil Procedure Rules and the extent to which a court could and should assess evidential disputes before entering summary judgment; particularly where there has been a wholesale failure by defendants to engage in proceedings.

The appeal is also another example of the Court of Appeal being prepared to grant an injunction on anticipatory basis against unnamed defendants.

Interestingly, the Court of Appeal noted (at [23]) that the network operated by the claimant was distinct from the notion of the highway at common law because there was a statutory restriction on any pedestrian use other than for accident or emergencies (which does not cover protest): see the Motorways Traffic (England and Wales) Regulations 1982 (SI 1982/1163), reg 15. In fact, as the Court noted, this made the national highway network distinct from other private or even public land and it might be thought to accord with commonsense.

The practical effect of this statutory provision might have been that the defendants could not rely on a lawful excuse defence, whether framed in human rights principles or otherwise. However, the provision was not relied upon by the claimant either at first instance or in argument before the Court of Appeal.

The claimant, National Highways Ltd is the highways authority for the Strategic Road Network (SRN) under Highways Act 1980, s 1A.[133] The litigation concerned claims by National Highways Ltd for interim and final injunctions to prevent 'Insulate Britain' protesters from shutting the M25 and associated road network (including feeder roads). The claimant sought the interim and final injunctions to protect the highway network, relying on underlying claims in the torts of trespass and nuisance (whether private or public).

The judge at first instance had been required to consider whether to continue interim injunctions at a return date, pending a full trial or accede to the claimant's application to enter summary judgment making the injunctions final. The judge also considered the claimant's claim for a declaration of its rights as owner of the M25 and associated road network. However, the judge found that such a declaration served no useful purpose and may cause confusion given the more elaborate and balanced terms of the injunction orders.

The claimant was asking the court to make the injunctions final by entering summary judgment against 138 defendants. The lower court, noting that an injunction is not a cause of action, required the claimant to evidence, on the balance of probabilities, that each defendant was responsible for actionable nuisance. Of the named defendants, 29 had been successfully pursued for contempt due to breach of the terms of interim injunctions and there were judgments made in the contempt proceedings against each of them. A further 109 were arrested by police and named, the evidence was general and did not establish that each individual was responsible in the tort of nuisance.

133 Highways Act 1980, https://www.legislation.gov.uk

Only three named defendants had provided a defence or any other formal response to the claims and these tended to deal with facts supporting the specific defendant not being present or part of the protests as alleged and two defendants were released from the claim on that basis. The named defendants did not engage with the proceedings formally including failing to respond to the application for summary judgment or filing any evidence.

In respect of the 29 defendants who had been found to be in contempt, the judge was prepared to accept the judgments on contempt as being dispositive of breach and thus established nuisance such that this claim was made out. Thus, the court made final injunctions against these defendants.

In respect of the further 109 named defendants, who were arrested by police, the judge decided that the evidence from the claimant was general and did not establish that each individual was responsible in the tort of nuisance. Therefore the judge decided that these were matters that would have to be subject to a trial. In this case the judge continued the interim injunction pending trial.

The claimant appealed the refusal to grant summary judgment in circumstances where no defence or formal evidence was submitted by the named defendants to the Court of Appeal.

The Court of Appeal characterised the judge's error in these terms:

> '… the judge did correctly identify the test for the grant of an anticipatory injunction in [38] of his judgment, unfortunately he fell into error in considering the question whether the injunction granted should be final or interim. His error was in making the assumption that, before summary judgment for a final anticipatory injunction could be granted, [the claimant] had to demonstrate in relation to each defendant that that defendant had committed the tort of trespass or nuisance and that there was no defence to a claim that such a tort had been committed. That error infected both his approach as to whether a final anticipatory injunction should be granted and as to whether summary judgment should be granted.'

The difficulty for the judge in respect of the anticipatory injunction was that the whole nature of an anticipatory breach is that the anticipatory nature of the breach means that there '… is certainly no requirement for the grant of a final injunction that the claimant prove that the relevant tort has already been committed'.

Vastint Leeds BV v Persons Unknown [2018] EWHC 2456 (Ch); [2019] 4 WLR 2[134] is authority for the proposition that, in a claim for an anticipatory injunction, it is no obstacle that 'the claimant's cause of action is not complete'.

The judge at first instance had decided between those found guilty of contempt as providing evidence of prior breach and thus granted a final injunction, and those who had not been found to have breached and whose breach thus was solely anticipatory.

134 *Vastint Leeds BV v Persons Unknown* [2018] EWHC 2456 (Ch); [2019] 4 WLR 2, https://www.judiciary.uk/wp-content/uploads/2022/07/Birmingham-CC-v-Afsar-No-4-2020-EWHC-864-QB-1.pdf

The judge had also applied the wrong test in asking whether there was any potential defence to the claim for the defendants. The defendants had failed to enter a defence or to provide any formal evidence in support of their position.

The claimants relied on the dicta of Cockerill J in *King v Stiefel* [2021] EWHC 1045:[135]

> '21. The authorities therefore make clear that in the context of summary judgment the court is by no means barred from evaluating the evidence and concluding that on the evidence there is no real (as opposed to fanciful) prospect of success. It will of course be cautious in doing so. It will bear in mind the clarity of the evidence available and the potential for other evidence to be available at trial which is likely to bear on the issues. It will avoid conducting a mini-trial. But there will be cases where the Court will be entitled to draw a line and say that -even bearing well in mind all of those points – it would be contrary to principle for a case to proceed to trial.
>
> 22. So, when faced with a summary judgment application it is not enough to say, with Mr Micawber, that something may turn up…' (at [21]–[22] of that decision)

Thus, in respect of the 109 named, the Court of Appeal concluded:

> '41. It is no answer to the failure to serve a defence or any evidence that, as the judge seems to have thought (see [35(5)] of the judgment), the defendants' general attitude was of disinterest in Court proceedings. Whatever the motive for the silence before the judge, it was indicative of the absence of any arguable defence to the claim for a final injunction. Certainly it was not for the judge to speculate as to what defence might be available. That is an example of impermissible 'Micawberism' which is deprecated in the authorities, most recently in *King v Stiefel*. If the judge had applied the right test under CPR 24.2 and had had proper regard to CPR 24.5, he would and should have concluded that none of the 109 named defendants had any realistic prospect of successfully defending the claim at trial and that accordingly, [the claimant] was entitled to a final injunction against those defendants.'

The Court of Appeal also granted a final injunction against 'persons unknown' consistent with the claimant's submission that:

> '… whilst the law had been in a state of flux, the decision of the Court of Appeal in *London Borough of Barking and Dagenham v Persons Unknown* [2022] EWCA Civ 13; [2022] 2 WLR 946[136] represents the law as it currently stands. In that case, this Court held that there was power under section 37 of the Senior Courts Act 1981 to grant a final injunction against persons who were unknown and unidentified, so-called "newcomers". This Court held there was no jurisdictional obstacle to such an injunction, rejecting the reasoning of the earlier Court of Appeal decision in Canada Goose.'

The Court noted that there was an appeal to the Supreme Court pending in respect of the *Barking* case in the Court of Appeal but left it to the lower court to discharge the injunction against persons unknown if the approach in *Barking* was overturned by the Supreme Court.

135 Cockerill J in *King v Stiefel* [2021] EWHC 1045 (Comm), https://www.casemine.com/judgement/uk/6400ef86831a7b3248444155

136 *London Borough of Barking and Dagenham v Persons Unknown* [2022] EWCA Civ 13; [2022] 2 WLR 946 https://www.bailii.org/ew/cases/EWCA/Civ/2022/13.html

Case name:

Transport for London v Persons Unknown and Others [2023] EWHC 1038 (KB)[137]

Summary:

Transport for London brought a claim under the Highways Act 1980 to protect the rights of the public to the 'use and enjoyment' of the highways. Transport for London was successful, and the judge found the defendants' acts had constituted trespass and both private and public nuisance. The environmental activist group, Insulate Britain (IB), carried out London protests designed to cause serious disruption. These protest tactics included activists deliberately blocking highways by sitting down in the road, and many gluing themselves to the road's surface and/or locking themselves to each other to make their removal more time-consuming. IB has repeatedly stated that these protests will continue until its demands are met.

These demands are:

- first, that the government immediately promises full funding and assumption of government responsibility for the insulation of all social housing in Britain by 2025; and
- that the government immediately promises to produce, within four months, a legally binding and fully funded national government plan for a full low-energy and low-carbon whole-house retrofit of all homes in Britain by 2030.

Transport for London (TfL) sought a final injunction against 129 of 138 named defendants and certain defined persons unknown. The injunction sought an order preventing protesters from blocking specified roads and areas in a significant part of the TfL strategic road network. The locations in question include bridges or 'junctions of great importance' and surrounding access roads, as well as certain longer protected stretches of road such as the A4 and the North Circular. The case came before Morris J on 29–30 March and on 3 May he gave judgment.

TfL made its injunction claim pursuant to its duty under Highways Act 1980, s 130 (protection of public rights) 'to assert and protect the rights of the public to the use and enjoyment of any highway for which [it is] the highway authority' and on the basis that the conduct of the defendants in participating in the IB protests constituted:

- trespass;
- private nuisance; and/or
- public nuisance.

The claimant's evidence was that the protests of IB and Just Stop Oil (a similar group):

> 'have been very dangerous and disruptive, creating an immediate threat to life, putting at risk the lives of those protesting, those driving on the roads and those

137 *Transport for London v Persons Unknown and Others* [2023] EWHC 1038 (KB), https://content.tfl.gov.uk/1-sealed-judgment-order-in-tfl-insulate-britain-case-aa.pdf

policing the protests' also 'At times, the protests have also caused a risk of violence between protesters and ordinary users of the highways.'

The judge said that he was satisfied on the evidence before him that, subject to material considerations arising under the European Convention on Human Rights, Articles 10[138] (freedom of expression) and [139] (freedom of assembly and association), the conduct, both in the past and threatened in the future, of the defendants in protesting on the relevant roads by deliberately blocking and obstructing those roads, prima facie constituted the torts of trespass, private nuisance and public nuisance. Regarding trespass, the protesters directly entered on to the claimant's land other than for the purpose of exercising a public right of way.

For private nuisance, 'the protests cause a substantial and unreasonable interference with the enjoyment and exercise of the rights of way of other road users'.

For the public nuisance, the protests prevent the public from freely, safely and conveniently passing along the relevant highways, the actions deliberately causing a physical obstacle on the roads, rendering them impassable or more difficult to pass along.

The court was also satisfied that there was a real and imminent risk of further protests on the part of the defendants. IB had repeatedly stated that it would continue to protest and would not be discouraged by injunctions. One of the named defendants sought to engage with the proceedings suggested that there was no arguable defence to the claimant's claim. The final injunction was not restricted to IB protests but to those under any other banner. Damages would also not be an adequate remedy.

For the 'persons unknown', in the light of the guidelines specified in *Canada Goose UK Retail Ltd v Persons Unknown* [2020] EWCA Civ 303,[140] the court was also 'satisfied that it is just and convenient to grant the final injunction against the persons unknown'.

A protest which obstructs the highway may be lawful under Articles 10 and 11 unless (among other things) the interference with these rights is in pursuit of a legitimate aim and is 'necessary in a democratic society' so that a fair balance is struck between the legitimate aim and the requirements of freedom of expression and freedom of assembly. A consideration is whether there is a fair balance between the rights of the individual and the general interest of the community including the rights of others.

The judge considered (among other things) that the aims of preventing obstruction of the public on the relevant highways and preventing violence and danger which occur when this is jeopardised are sufficiently important to justify interference with the defendants' rights. There was also no less restrictive or alternative means to achieve the prevention of obstructive and

138 ECHR, Article 10, https://fra.europa.eu/en/law-reference/european-convention-human-rights-article-10#:~:text=Article%2010%201.,authority%20and%20regardless%20of%20frontiers

139 ECHR, Article 11, https://fra.europa.eu/en/law-reference/european-convention-human-rights-article-11-0#:~:text=Everyone%20has%20the%20right%20to,the%20protection%20of%20his%20interests.

140 *Canada Goose UK Retail Ltd v Persons Unknown and Another* [2020] EWCA Civ 303.

disruptive protests other than a final injunction. The court gave judgment for the claimant for a final injunction in the terms of the draft order before the court. To protect the public and the claimant's rights, the final injunction would last for five years, with the court reviewing yearly 'for supervisory purposes'.

Case name:

Canada Goose UK Retail Ltd v Persons Unknown and Another [2020] EWCA Civ 303[141]

Summary:

On 5 March 2020 the Court of Appeal handed down judgment in this case. There had been protests at the claimant's Regent Street shop against the brand's use of animal fur and down. The Court of Appeal gave wide and authoritative guidance in relation to claims for injunctions against unnamed defendants ('persons unknown').

The claimant obtained an interim injunction, and then applied for a summary judgment. The application failed, both because the claim form had not actually been served on any defendant and on the merits. The interim injunctions were also discharged, following the principles set out by the Supreme Court in *Cameron v Liverpool Insurance Co Ltd* [2019] UKSC 6[142] and the Court of Appeal in *Ineos Upstream Ltd v Persons Unknown* [2019] EWCA Civ 515.[143] The claimant's appeal to the Court of Appeal failed.

The judgment looked at the situation of when claims can be brought against persons unknown, as opposed to proceedings brought against named parties. For example, claims cannot be brought against defendants who are both anonymous and not identifiable, such as hit and run drivers, as serving a claim against anonymous, unidentifiable defendants is conceptually impossible.

The first exception is for anonymous, identifiable defendants, such as squatters. These must be described in 'a way that makes it possible in principle to locate or communicate with him and to know without further enquiry whether he is the same as the person described in the form' ([60]). The second exception is for 'people who will or are highly likely in the future to commit an unlawful civil wrong, against whom an action is threatened but has not yet occurred, injunction is sought'. These people might be said to be unidentifiable unless and until they become identifiable through their future actions, although they may still be anonymous. The Court of Appeal termed these defendants 'newcomers'.

Canada Goose sought to invoke the civil jurisdiction of the courts as a means of permanently controlling ongoing public demonstrations by a continually fluctuating body of protesters and use remedies in private litigation to prevent what it saw as public disorder. Private law remedies are not well suited to such a task.

141 *Canada Goose UK Retail Ltd v Persons Unknown and Another* [2020] EWCA Civ 303, https://vlex.co.uk/vid/canada-goose-uk-retail-852914500

142 *Cameron v Liverpool Insurance Co Ltd* [2019] UKSC 6, https://www.bailii.org/uk/cases/UKSC/2019/6.html

143 *Ineos Upstream Ltd v Persons Unknown* [2019] EWCA Civ 515, https://www.bailii.org/ew/cases/EWCA/Civ/2019/515.html

Case name:

(1) Shell UK Ltd (2) Shell International Petroleum Ltd and (3) Shell UK Oil Products Ltd v Persons Unknown [2023] EWHC 1229 (KB)[144]

Summary:

In this case, Shell's UK entity brought a against 'Persons Unknown' to restrict protesting at their petrol stations. They were successful and subsequently an order was produced, restricting anyone 'in connection with protest campaigns' from 'disrupting the sale or supply of fuel' at Shell petrol stations in England and Wales.

The claimants, Shell UK Oil Products Ltd and two others, sought interim injunctions against Persons Unknown to restrain unlawful protests by environmental activists at petrol stations known as the Haven and the Tower. The claimants objected to the third claimant, Shell UK Oil Products Ltd, being heard at the hearing due to late documentation. Despite submissions inviting the court to uphold the judge's reasoning, no transcript of his judgment was obtained by the claimants.

Evidence showed peaceful protests by environmental activists with no violence reported. Protests on 28 April 2022 included photographing and filming activities on forecourts.

Just Stop Oil's campaign aimed to continue until the government halted new oil and gas projects in the UK. Injunctions prohibited specified acts at Shell Petrol Stations by the defendants.

The Tower injunction had a deterrent effect on unlawful activities. Ms Branch from Extinction Rebellion sought to set aside or vary the May 2022 injunctions, citing potential adverse effects on her civil rights. The claimant sought to amend the description of 'Persons Unknown' as a defendant in the petrol stations claim.

The claimant relied on the tort of conspiracy to injure due to not owning all petrol stations and equipment. A cross-undertaking in damages was proposed as a remedy for the defendants. The court found that injunctions were necessary to prevent harm to the claimants' rights. The balance of convenience favoured continuing the relief. The petrol stations injunction applied specifically to Shell-branded stations' forecourts.

The injunctions interfered with the defendants' rights under Articles 10 and 11 but were deemed necessary and proportionate. Section 12(3) applied to communication restraints falling under Article 10. Alternative methods of service were deemed appropriate for the injunctions. The court considered granting a third-party disclosure order against the Commissioner for information on arrested individuals.

A number of issues were considered:

144 *(1) Shell UK Ltd (2) Shell International Petroleum Ltd and (3) Shell UK Oil Products Ltd v Persons Unknown* [2023] EWHC 1229 (KB), https://www.bailii.org/ew/cases/EWHC/KB/2023/1229.html

- the validity of interim injunctions against Persons Unknown for unlawful protests;
- the rights of defendants under Articles 10 and 11 in light of the injunctions;
- the application of the tort of conspiracy to injure by unlawful means;
- consideration of balancing rights of assembly and expression with business interests;
- compliance with s 12(3) regarding communication restraints;
- the propriety of alternative service methods for the injunctions; and
- granting a third-party disclosure order against the Commissioner.

The court granted interim injunctions against Persons Unknown to restrain unlawful protests at Shell Petrol Stations, finding them necessary and proportionate to protect the claimants' rights. The court also considered the application of the tort of conspiracy to injure and compliance with communication restraints under Article 10. Additionally, alternative service methods were approved, and a third-party disclosure order against the Commissioner was considered.

US

Case name:

BP plc and Others v Mayor and City Council of Baltimore, 593 US _ (2021)

Summary:

In this case,[145] starting in July 2017, state and local governments started to file lawsuits against oil and gas companies alleging that their exploration, production and marketing of fossil fuels was contributing to the plaintiff's climate related injuries. For many years the decision was about whether the case should be heard in the federal courts or not.

In 2018, the Mayor and City Council of Baltimore (City) filed suit against 26 oil and gas companies in the Circuit Court for Baltimore City. They alleged that the defendants' conduct in promoting and selling fossil fuels, despite their awareness of the associated hazards, and their campaign against regulations, was based on deception and misinformation and that their failure to develop less dangerous alternatives had contributed to the City's climate change-related injuries. The City's complaint asserted eight causes of action, seven based on state tort law and one based on the Maryland Consumer Protection Act.

The complaint sought monetary damages, civil penalties, and equitable relief. Two of the defendants removed the case to federal court, asserting eight grounds for removal. Baltimore then moved to remand the case back to state court. The district court rejected all eight grounds for removal and granted Baltimore's motion for remand back to state court.

145 *BP plc and Others v Mayor and City Council of Baltimore*, 593 US _ (2021), https://www.supremecourt.gov/opinions/20pdf/19-1189_p86b.pdf

The defendants appealed the remand order, and the US Court of Appeals for the Fourth Circuit affirmed the lower court, finding that 28 U.S.C. § 1442 does not provide a proper basis for removal of the suit.

The City challenged the removal by citing the lack of subject-matter jurisdiction that the federal court had over state laws. As the standard for removal puts the onus on the party seeking removal, the judge rejected the reasons given by the oil companies for keeping the case at the federal level. The defendants appealed to the Fourth Circuit on judge's order, but the Fourth Circuit upheld it, ruling that the federal-officer exemption did not apply to the companies despite their close-workings with the federal government.

The Fourth Circuit's decision was shared by seven other circuits in which the appellate court can only look at the circumstances on the removal jurisdiction, while the Seventh Circuit had recently joined the opinion of the Fourth and Fifth Circuit's view in which appellate courts can review other relevant matters to the case to make their determination.

The oil companies argued that if their case was handled under the Seventh Circuit, they would have been able to maintain the federal jurisdiction based on the argument that federal laws supersede state laws.

The oil companies petitioned the Supreme Court to resolve the circuit split with the federal-officer removal statute.

The Court issued its decision on 17 May 2021. In a 7-1 ruling, the Court vacated the Fourth Circuit's decision and remanded the case for further review. The majority agreed with BP and others that the Fourth Circuit erred in considering all factors for review to deny the change of jurisdiction requested by the City, therefore vacating their decision and not ruling on the merits of Baltimore's complaints related to the petitioners.

In May 2021, the Court granted review of three other similar cases in which a city or state had successfully changed jurisdiction in an environmental lawsuit, vacating the Circuit court rulings that allowed these changes to proceed on the basis of the *BP* opinion, and remanding these cases for further review.

Case name:

Suncor Energy (USA) Inc and Others v Board of County Commissioners of Boulder County and Others (No 21-1550)[146]

Summary:

Action by Colorado local governments seeking damages and other relief from fossil fuel companies for climate change harms. Colorado Supreme Court issued an Order to Show Cause Requiring Response to Issue of Whether Boulder County and City of Boulder's Climate State Law Claims Could Proceed. On 29 July, the Colorado Supreme Court ordered the Board, the City, and the district court to address why the Supreme Court should not grant the issue raised in the defendants' petition regarding '[w]hether the district

146 *Suncor Energy (USA) Inc and Others v Board of County Commissioners of Boulder County and Others* (No. 21-1550), https://www.supremecourt.gov/search.aspx?filename=/docket/docketfiles/html/public/20-783.html

court erroneously concluded that respondents' claims could proceed under state law'. The Supreme Court denied the petition with respect to the issue of '[w]hether a Colorado tribunal may exercise personal jurisdiction over an out-of-state defendant for its alleged contributions to interstate and international GHG emissions that are not traceable to conduct in Colorado'.

Case name:

Held v State of Montana (DA 23-0575)

Summary:

This case[147] was brought by 16 youth plaintiffs and was the first in the US to be brought on the basis of a constitutional right to a healthy environment. The youths specifically argued that Montana had pursued an energy policy that 'permits' and 'encourages' the promotion and extraction of fossil fuels, without having regard for the negative impacts that rising GHG emissions have on climate change. Additionally. They also argued that a provision within Montana Government Environmental Policy Act (MEPA) that prevents state agencies from considering GHG emissions or the potential impacts on the climate when conducting environmental reviews interferes with their constitutional rights.

When the first Montana state constitution was ratified in 1889, Montana was a 'sparsely populated frontier state'; by the 1960s, a growing population was matched by growing calls for greater protection of the environment and for civil rights. This led to the establishment of a constitutional convention with 100 'ordinary' Montanans elected to be involved in the process. Motivated by the environmental movements and the fact that Montana's natural resources would be exploited if not protected by law, the delegates actively sought to include the right to a clean and healthful environment within the new constitution. The Montana constitution has the right to a clean and healthful environment included within its declaration of rights (the equivalent of the Bill of Rights within the federal US constitution). This puts the right to a clean and healthful environment on the same level as other fundamental rights, such as the rights to freedom of expression and freedom of religion. Recent case law has confirmed that the right to a clean and healthful environment is fundamental, and the state is obligated to protect environmental rights.

The plaintiffs challenged the provision within MEPA that forbids the state and state agencies from considering the impacts of climate change or GHG emissions in their environmental reviews.

After considering the scientific evidence that GHG emissions are a significant contributor to human-made climate change, and the extent to which state agencies have been aware of the risks posed by GHG emissions, the judge concluded that the plaintiffs are being harmed by climate change, and these harms can be directly attributed to Montana's energy policies and the state's failure to consider GHG emissions in its environmental reviews. Because the MEPA limitation affects the fundamental right to a clean and healthful

147 *Held v State of Montana* (DA 23-0575).

environment, the strict scrutiny standard[148] is applied. In US courts, this is the highest level of judicial review, which means that Montana would have had to prove a compelling state interest to justify the interference with the plaintiffs' fundamental rights to a clean and healthful environment. By preventing consideration of the impact of GHG emissions on climate change, the court held that the strict scrutiny standard was not met, and the MEPA limitation was struck down as unconstitutional. The judgment has the effect of invalidating any state statutes that prohibit consideration of GHG emissions and their impacts.

Counsel for the state of Montana deemed the case a 'publicity stunt' and promptly filed a notice of appeal. In January 2024, the Montana Supreme Court declined a motion to stay judgment, finding that the district court had not abused its discretion.

Case name:

Chevron USA Inc v NRDC, 467 U.S. 837 (1984)

Summary:

In this case[149] it was decided that a government agency must conform to any clear legislative statements when interpreting and applying a law, but courts will give the agency deference in ambiguous situations as long as its interpretation is reasonable.

The decision articulated the doctrine known as the '*Chevron* defence'. This is a two-part test:

- whether Congress has spoken directly to the precise issue at question; and
- whether the agency's answer is based on a permissible construction of the statute'.

This was a challenge to the government's interpretation of the word 'source' in the Clean Air Act 1963 which did not define what the source of pollution was. Initially the Environmental Protection Agency (EPA) defined 'source' to cover any significant change or addition to a plant or factory. This was changed in 1981 to mean only an entire plant or factory which allowed the building of new projects without going through the EPA's review process.

The Natural Resources Defense Council (NRDC) challenged the legality of the EPA's definition. The NRDC won the case in the Federal court but the Supreme Court overruled the decision. (However, 40 years later in June 2024 the Supreme Court overruled *Chevron* in *Loper Bright Enterprises v Raimondo* on the grounds that it conflicted with administrative procedure.)

148 Strict scrutiny standard: a form of judicial review that courts in the US use to determine the constitutionality of government action that burdens a fundamental right or involves a suspect classification (including race, religion, national origin, and alienage).

149 *Chevron USA Inc v NRDC,* 467 U.S. 837 (1984), https://supreme.justia.com/cases/federal/us/467/837/

Case name:

City of Baltimore v Philip Morris (1:23-cv-00303-JRR)[150]

Summary:

Since 1998, the Master Settlement Agreement (MSA)[151] has required tobacco companies to pay most states, including Maryland, in perpetuity because of the harmful effects of cigarettes on human health. The MSA does not address the harm that cigarettes impose on non-human life, environments and ecosystems.

Although cigarette manufacturers had designed biodegradable filters they found that their customers preferred non-biodegradable plastic filters and so stayed with those. This resulted in better sales and they knew that people would litter the non-biodegradable products.

In November 2022 the City of Baltimore filed a complaint to the Circuit Court of Baltimore City. The complaint included 11 counts:

- one violation of Maryland's Illegal Dumping and Litter Control Law;
- four violations of the Baltimore City Code;
- trespass;
- strict liability for a design defect;
- negligent design defect;
- public nuisance;
- strict liability for a failure to warn; and
- negligent failure to warn.

In February 2023 the defendant filed a notice to move the case from the circuit court in Baltimore City to the district court for the District of Maryland. In January 2024 the District Court rejected the defendants' arguments and granted the plaintiffs' request for the case to be to moved back to the Circuit Court of Baltimore City.

On 19 March 2024, the defendants filed a motion to dismiss for failure to state a claim. On 10 May the plaintiff filed a memorandum of law in opposition to the defendants' motion to dismiss. On 24 June the defendants filed a reply in support of their motion to dismiss.

Case name:

City of New York v Chevron Corp'n, 993 F.3d 81 (2d Cir. 2021)[152]

Summary:

The City filed suit against five multinational oil companies under New York tort law, seeking to recover damages for the harms caused by global warming. In this case, the City said that its taxpayers should not have to shoulder the burden of financing the City's preparations to mitigate the effects of global

150 *City of Baltimore v Philip Morris* (1:23-cv-00303-JRR), https://www.publichealthlawcenter.org/litigation-tracker/baltimore-v-philip-morris-2022

151 Master Settlement Agreement, https://www.publichealthlawcenter.org/topics/commercial-tobacco-control/master-settlement-agreement

152 *City of New York v Chevron Corp'n*, 993 F.3d 81 (2d Cir. 2021).

warming. Rather, the City suggested that a group of large fossil fuel producers were primarily responsible for global warming and should bear the brunt of these costs.

The Second Circuit held that municipalities may not utilise state tort law to hold multinational oil companies liable for the damages caused by global GHG emissions. The court said that global warming is a uniquely international concern that touches upon issues of federalism and foreign policy. Therefore, it calls for the application of federal common law, not state law. The court also held that the Clean Air Act grants the EPA – not federal courts – the authority to regulate domestic GHG emissions. Therefore, federal common law actions concerning such emissions are displaced.

Finally, the court held that while the Clean Air Act has nothing to say about regulating foreign emissions, judicial caution and foreign policy concerns counsel against permitting such claims to proceed under federal common law absent congressional direction. Because no such permission exists, the court concluded that each of the City's claims was barred and the complaint must be dismissed.

Case name:

Dwyer v Allbirds, Inc (7.21-cv-05238), 598 F. Supp. 3d 137 (S.D.N.Y. 2022)

Summary:

This case[153] is a significant example of a greenwashing class-action lawsuit that was dismissed by the court. Allbirds, a shoe company, markets its products with sustainability claims such as 'Sustainability Meets Style' and 'Low Carbon Footprint'. The plaintiff alleged that these claims were misleading, focusing on the carbon footprint calculations and the environmental impact of materials using the Higg Material Sustainability Index (Higg MSI). Additionally, the plaintiff challenged Allbirds' claims about the welfare of sheep from which it sources wool.

In April 2022, the Southern District of New York dismissed the case, ruling that the criticisms of the Life Cycle Assessment (LCA) and Higg MSI were merely that – criticisms – and that Allbirds' statements about sheep welfare were non-actionable puffery. The court emphasised the importance of transparency and public substantiation in environmental claims, noting that Allbirds clearly outlined its carbon footprint calculations and LCA methodology on its website. The ruling also highlighted that companies have some leeway in using 'puffery' in advertising, as Allbirds' statements about sheep living 'the Good Life' were deemed subjective and not something a reasonable consumer would rely on as a factual claim.[154]

153 *Dwyer v Allbirds, Inc* (7.21-cv-05238) , 598 F. Supp. 3d 137 (S.D.N.Y. 2022), https://www.classaction.org/media/dwyer-v-allbirds-inc.pdf

154 See further, https://climatecasechart.com/wp-content/uploads/case-documents/2022/20220418_docket-721-cv-05238_opinion-and-order.pdf

Case name:

Juliana v US (6:15-cv-01517-TC) (unreported)

Summary:

In 2015, 21 youth plaintiffs filed a climate-related lawsuit[155] against the US and several executive branch officials, representing the non-profit organisation Our Children's Trust. The case, filed in the US District Court of Oregon, alleged that the government had knowingly violated their due process rights to life, liberty and property, and its sovereign duty to protect public grounds by encouraging and permitting the combustion of fossil fuels. The plaintiffs sought both declaratory and injunctive relief, including a declaration of the federal government's fiduciary role in preserving the atmosphere and an injunction against actions contravening that role. This case exemplifies 'atmospheric trust litigation', a concept rooted in the public trust doctrine and international responsibility related to natural resources. The Ninth Circuit dismissed the suit in January 2020 for lack of standing, a decision upheld in February 2021. Despite filing an amended complaint to address standing, the Ninth Circuit dismissed the amended suit in May 2024, and the Supreme Court declined to hear the case by March 2025.[156]

Case name:

Loper Bright Enterprises v Raimondo, 603 U.S. 369 (2024)[157]

Summary:

In June 2024 the Supreme Court issued a judgment overruling the doctrine of the *Chevron* defence and stating that courts 'must exercise their independent judgement in deciding whether the agency has acted within its statutory authority'.

The case arose out of a dispute under the Magnuson-Stevens Fishery Conservation and Management Act (MSA),[158] which authorises regional councils to set standards for fishing off the coast of the US. To ensure that those standards are followed, vessels may be required to carry an 'observer' who monitors their fishing activity. The statute states three groups may be required to cover the costs of the observers, but it does not address whether Atlantic herring fishermen may be required to bear them. The National Marine Fisheries Service, the federal agency that administers the MSA, adopted a rule that required Atlantic herring fishermen to pay the fees for the observers as well.

Businesses that operate in the Atlantic herring fishery challenged the rule in two federal district courts. They argued that because the statute expressly listed three

155 *Juliana v US* (6:15-cv-01517-TC) https://static1.squarespace.com/static/571d109b04426270152febe0/t/57a35ac5ebbd1ac03847eece/1470323398409/YouthAmendedComplaintAgainstUS.pdf

156 See further, https://climatecasechart.com/case/juliana-v-united-states/

157 *Loper Bright Enterprises v Raimondo*, 603 U.S. 369 (2024), https://law.justia.com/cases/federal/appellate-courts/cadc/21-5166/21-5166-2022-08-12.html

158 Magnuson-Stevens Fishery Conservation and Management Act, https://www.fisheries.noaa.gov/resource/document/magnuson-stevens-fishery-conservation-and-management-act

categories of vessels that must pay for the observers, the federal agency did not have statutory authority to add another to the list. Both district courts upheld the rule as a permissible reading of the MSA. The Court of Appeal for the First and DC Circuits each affirmed, both in reliance on the *Chevron* doctrine. (See *Chevron USA Inc v NRDC.*[159])

The Supreme Court granted certiorari[160] and overruled the *Chevron* doctrine. The Court found that the Administrative Procedure Act, which was not addressed in *Chevron*, 'incorporates the traditional understanding of the judicial function, under which courts must exercise independent judgment in determining the meaning of statutory provisions'. The Court rejected the 'presumption' of agency expertise, reasoning that resolving statutory ambiguity is within a court's, not an agency's, competency, and to the extent there are facts within an agency's expertise, the agency can inform, but not bind, a court. The Court also rejected the rationale that *Chevron* promotes uniformity, given the unevenness of its application. Finally, it found that *stare decisis* did not require adherence to the decision in *Chevron*, which had proven unworkable in practice. The Court vacated and remanded.

Case name:

Minnesota v American Petroleum Institute, 63 F.4th 703 (8th Cir. 2023)[161]

Summary:

Action brought by Minnesota against members of the fossil fuel industry for allegedly causing climate change harms by misleading the public by downplaying the threat of climate change and the role of their products in causing climate change. On 24 January 2024 (15 days after the US Supreme Court declined to review the Eighth Circuit's affirmance of the remand order in Minnesota's case), the federal district court for the District of Minnesota lifted the stay on the case and remanded it to state court.

Case name:

Rhode Island v Shell Oil Products Co, 35 F.4th 44 (1st Cir. 2022)

Summary:

The State of Rhode Island filed a lawsuit against fossil fuel companies, including Chevron and Exxon, seeking to hold them accountable for the adverse impacts of climate change on state-owned or -operated facilities, real property and other assets. Superior Court Justice William Carnes, presiding over the case, has addressed claims of bias from the defendants. In a short order,[162] Justice Carnes stated that he will not accept as true the viewpoints he previously cited from a United Nations Climate Change Conference and two Associated Press

159 *Chevron USA Inc v NRDC*, 467 U.S. 837 (1984).

160 Certiorari: a writ or order by which a higher court reviews a case tried in a lower court.

161 *Minnesota v American Petroleum Institute*, 63 F.4th 703 (8th Cir. 2023), https://law.justia.com/cases/federal/appellate-courts/ca8/21-8005/21-8005-2023-03-23.html

162 *Rhode Island v Shell Oil Products Co*, https://www.courts.ri.gov/Decisions/Superior-PC-2018-4716.pdf

news articles, responding to calls from Exxon, Chevron and Shell to strike these references from an April decision.[163]

Case name:

City of Hoboken v Chevron Corp'n, 45 F.4th 699 (3d Cir. 2022)[164]

Summary:

Lawsuit seeking to recover climate change-related damages allegedly resulting from the defendant energy companies' production of fossil fuels and concealment of fossil fuels' harms. A New Jersey Superior Court rejected fossil fuel industry defendants' argument that it should dismiss the City of Hoboken's climate change case against them because it was 'nearly identical' to the State of New Jersey's suit. The court denied the defendants' motion to dismiss on this ground. The defendants' motion, which asserted multiple other grounds for dismissal, remains pending.

Case name:

Mayor and City Council of Baltimore v BP plc, 31 F.4th 178 (4th Cir. 2022)[165]

Summary:

City of Baltimore lawsuit seeking to hold fossil fuel companies liable for climate change impacts. A Maryland Circuit Court granted fossil fuel companies' motion to dismiss the Mayor and City Council of Baltimore's claims seeking to hold the companies liable for climate change-related injuries resulting from the companies' alleged 'sophisticated campaign of deception to misrepresent and conceal their products' risks'. Aligning itself with the reasoning of decisions that held that New York City's and Delaware's claims against fossil fuel companies were pre-empted or largely pre-empted, the Maryland court rejected Baltimore's contention that its lawsuit did not seek to regulate or impose liability for GHG emissions. The court found 'that Baltimore's complaint is entirely about addressing the injuries of global climate change and seeking damages for such alleged injuries' and that Baltimore's explanation 'that it only seeks to address and hold Defendants accountable for a deceptive misinformation campaign is simply a way to get in the back door what they cannot get in the front door'. The Maryland court concluded that federal common law applied because the case involved global emissions, that the Clean Air Act displaced federal common law related to domestic emissions, and that the Clean Air Act pre-empted Baltimore's state law claims based on domestic emissions. The Maryland court further concluded that state law could not provide a remedy for claims arising from foreign emissions. The court distinguished the Fourth Circuit's decision that the companies' pre-emption defence did not create federal jurisdiction over Baltimore's claims, citing 'the heightened standard unique to the removability inquiry'. Although

163 See further, https://climatecasechart.com/wp-content/uploads/case-documents/2023/20230428_docket-PC-2018-4716_decision.pdf

164 *City of Hoboken v Chevron Corp*'n, 45 F.4th 699 (3d Cir. 2022), https://casetext.com/case/city-of-hoboken-v-chevron-corp

165 *Mayor and City Council of Baltimore v BP plc*, 31 F.4th 178 (4th Cir. 2022), https://climateintegrity.org/uploads/media/Baltimore_Order.pdf

the Maryland court dismissed Baltimore's claims on pre-emption grounds, the court also concluded – 'to make the record complete' – that Baltimore failed to state claims of public and private nuisance, failure to warn, design defect, and trespass. The court also ruled that Baltimore's Maryland Consumer Protection Act claim was time-barred.

Case name:

City and County of Honolulu v Sunoco LP, 39 F.4th 1101 (9th Cir. 2022)[166]

Summary:

Lawsuit seeking damages and other relief from fossil fuel companies for alleged conduct that the City and County of Honolulu contends actually and proximately caused climate change impact. On 13 January 2025, the US Supreme Court denied two petitions for writ of certiorari in which fossil fuel companies sought review of the Hawai'i Supreme Court's decision allowing the City and County of Honolulu to proceed with its climate change-based claims against the defendants. Justice Alito did not participate in the consideration or decision of the petitions.

Case name:

County of San Mateo v Chevron Corp'n, 32 F.4th 733 (9th Cir. 2022)

Summary:

This case[167] was an action by California counties and cities seeking damages and other relief from fossil fuel companies for sea level rise. The action was against 32 fossil fuel companies to hold them accountable for climate deception and make them pay for damages they knowingly caused, including increased flooding, sea level rise and coastal erosion.

The allegations were:

- global warming – observed effects and known cause;
- that the defendants went to great lengths to understand, and either knew or should have known the dangers associated with their fossil fuel products;
- that despite their early knowledge that global warming was real and posed grave threats, the defendants did not disclose known harms associated with the extraction, promotion and consumption of their fossil fuel products and instead affirmatively acted to obscure those harms and engaged in a campaign to deceptively protect and expand the use of their fossil fuel products when they could have chosen to facilitate and be part of, a lower-carbon future, but instead chose corporate profits and continued deception;
- that, in contrast to their denial and downplaying of the risks of climate change in public, the defendants' internal actions demonstrated their

166 *City and County of Honolulu v Sunoco LP*, 39 F.4th 1101 (9th Cir. 2022), https://casetext.com/case/city-of-honolulu-v-sunoco-lp-2

167 *County of San Mateo v Chevron Corp'n*, 32 F.4th 733 (9th Cir. 2022), https://www.govinfo.gov/app/details/USCOURTS-ca9-18-15499

awareness of, and intent to profit from, uses of fossil fuel products they knew were hazardous;

- that the defendants' actions have slowed the development of alternative energy sources and exacerbated the costs of adapting to and mitigating the adverse impacts of the climate crisis;
- that the defendants intended for consumers to use their fossil fuel products in a way the defendants knew was harmful; and
- that the defendants' deceit only recently came to light, and their misconduct was ongoing.

As result San Mateo County has suffered, is suffering and will suffer injuries from defendants' tortious conduct:

- sea level rise-related conditions and injuries;
- extreme precipitation and landslide-related conditions and injuries;
- extreme wildfire;
- drought-related conditions and injuries; and
- public health conditions and injuries.

The briefing was completed in February 2023 for fossil fuel companies' petition for writ of certiorari seeking review of the Ninth Circuit's affirmance of remand orders in cases brought by the County of San Mateo and other California local governments. The case originally was distributed for the justices' conference on 3 March but was rescheduled on 27 February – a new date was not noted on the docket.

In April 2023, the US Supreme Court denied fossil fuel industry defendants' petitions for writ of certiorari seeking review of decisions affirming remand orders that sent climate change cases brought by state and local governments back to state courts. The fossil fuel companies had asked the Court to consider whether there was federal jurisdiction over state-law claims seeking redress for injuries allegedly caused by the effects of interstate or transboundary GHG emissions on the global climate because federal common law necessarily governs such claims.

Case name:

City of Oakland v BP plc, 969 F.3d 895 (9th Cir. 2020)

Summary:

In this case, the City of Oakland and the City of San Francisco filed public nuisance actions against fossil fuel companies. The companies sought review of the Ninth Circuit's decision to remand the cases to California state court. The key issues involved the removability of state-law tort claims under federal law and the waiver of rights to appeal post-removal amendments. The cities argued that their claims were governed by California state law and not federal common law. Ultimately, the US Supreme Court denied the petition, and the cities' motion for remand remains pending in the district court. [168]

168 See further, https://climatecasechart.com/wp-content/uploads/case-documents/2023/20231127_docket-22-16810-22-16812_memorandum.pdf

Case name:

Board of County Commissioners of Boulder County v Suncor Energy (USA) Inc, 25 F.4th 1238 (10th Cir. 2022)

Summary:

Colorado local governments sued fossil fuel companies for climate change damages. On 29 July, the Colorado Supreme Court asked the Board, the City and the district court to explain why the it should not consider the defendants' question regarding whether the district court was wrong to allow the case under state law. The Supreme Court decided not to consider the question concerning whether a Colorado court could have authority over an out-of-state company for its alleged contributions to greenhouse gas emissions that are not linked to actions in Colorado.[169]

Case name:

Sierra Club v California Department of Water Resources (24WM000008) (a 2024 filing)

Summary:

The Sierra Club and other organisations filed a lawsuit in the California Superior Court against the California Department of Water Resources (DWR) for approving the Delta Conveyance Project. The project involves diverting large quantities of fresh water from the San Francisco Bay-Delta estuary through a 45-mile-long tunnel from the Sacramento River in the North Delta to pumping plants in the South Delta. The DWR aims to address rising sea levels and other foreseeable consequences of climate change and extreme weather events through this project. The organisations claim that the project approval violated the California Environmental Quality Act (CEQA), the Delta Reform Act, and Fish and Game Code § 3511, which protects fully protected birds. The organisations allege that the DWR did not consider feasible alternatives that would comply with the Delta Reform Act, climate change adaptation laws and the California Endangered Species Act and that the CEQA review did not adequately address the cumulative impacts on the Bay Delta watershed, particularly concerning water supplies in the context of sea level rise, changes in storm patterns and watershed run-off. The organisations contend that the EIR failed to disclose and evaluate the effects of worsening climate change and project operations on surface water, water supply, listed fish species, water quality, and public health, including the exacerbation of harmful algal blooms. Additional allegations include that the environmental impact report failed to adequately discuss the implications of climate change for future water deliveries associated with the project.[170]

169 See further, https://climatecasechart.com/wp-content/uploads/case-documents/2025/20250211_docket-2024SA206_notice.pdf

170 See further, https://climatecasechart.com/wp-content/uploads/case-documents/2024/20240119_docket-24WM000008_petition-for-writ-of-mandate.pdf

Case name:

Smith v Keurig Green Mountain, Inc (4:18-cv-06690-HSG)

Summary:

This class action lawsuit alleged that defendant misrepresented the recyclability of single-use 'coffee pods', which, the complaint alleged, have numerous negative effects, including contributing to methane emissions.

Keurig was unsuccessful in its attempt to get the complaint dismissed, arguing that a reasonable consumer would not have been misled and that they would have known the K-Cup pods could not be recycled everywhere.

In 2020, Keurig agreed to pay $31 million to resolve separate claims that it had created a monopoly in the market for single-serve coffee pods. In that case, consumers claimed Keurig had suppressed its competition in order to stay in control of the market, allowing the company to charge higher prices.

A federal judge in California approved a $10 million settlement between Keurig and consumers who argued they were misled into believing the company's single-serving K-Cups were more recyclable than they actually are.

The judge overseeing the case called the settlement agreement 'fair, reasonable and adequate'. Eligible class members will receive between $5 and $36 per the settlement agreement.

Case name:

Neighbours for a True Oasis v Village of Port Washington North (609509/2024) (a 2024 filing challenging a plan to sell a forested area for development)

Summary:

In this case, the petitioners contested a New York village's proposal to sell a 7.45-acre forested area for the development of 44 town homes. The petitioners claimed that this land had been designated as permanent open space in connection with a prior development project. They argued that the village's actions contravened New York State Constitution's Environmental Rights Amendment, the State Environmental Quality Review Act (SEQRA) and the public trust doctrine.

The SEQRA cause of action included allegations that the village planning board failed to consider the adverse impacts of greenhouse gas (GHG) emissions and the creation of 'heat islands' due to extensive paving of the site. Additionally, the petitioners sought the imposition of a constructive trust over the area.[171]

171 See further, https://climatecasechart.com/wp-content/uploads/case-documents/2024/20240531_docket-6095092024_petition-1.pdf

Case name:

In re Hawai'i Electric Light Co (SCOT-22-0000418) (a 2023 filing that rejected a power purchase agreement for a biomass facility)

Summary:

In a legal challenge[172] to the Hawai'i Public Utilities Commission's (PUC's) approval of an amended power purchase agreement (PPA) with a company planning to construct and operate a biomass-fuelled energy production facility, the Hawai'i Supreme Court found that the PUC had erred. The Court ruled that the PUC failed to explicitly consider the reduction of greenhouse gas (GHG) emissions, as required by the state's utilities law, before approving the amended PPA. Additionally, the Court determined that the PUC had denied due process to Life of the Land, an environmental non-profit organisation, by limiting its opportunity to be heard regarding the impacts of the biomass facility. Consequently, the Court vacated the decision and order approving the amended PPA and remanded the case to the PUC for a hearing that complied with procedural due process.[173]

Case name:

Protect the Public's Trust v US Department of State (1:22-cv-02231) (an FOIA lawsuit seeking documents related to the Special Presidential Envoy for Climate)

Summary:

The Freedom of Information Act (FOIA) lawsuit seeks the release of communications and meeting requests involving a senior adviser to the Special Presidential Envoy for Climate. The plaintiff argues that disclosing these documents is in the public interest, providing insight into the federal government's energy and climate priorities amid high energy prices and inflation.

Additionally, the plaintiff claims that the release will enhance public understanding of the Special Envoy for Climate Change's role and how high-ranking officials comply with laws, rules, and regulations regarding foreign policy, disclosures of work for foreign entities and potential conflicts of interest.[174]

172 *In re Hawai'i Electric Light Co* (SCOT-22-0000418), https://www.courts.state.hi.us/wp-content/uploads/2023/03/SCOT-22-0000418con.pdf

173 See further, https://climatecasechart.com/wp-content/uploads/case-documents/2019/20190510_docket-SCOT-17-0000630_opinion.pdf

174 See further, https://climatecasechart.com/wp-content/uploads/case-documents/2022/20220323_docket-122-cv-00799_complaint.pdf

Case name:

Friends of the Earth v Council on Environmental Quality (1:22-cv-01128)

Summary:

Friends of the Earth (FOE) filed a Freedom of Information Act (FOIA) lawsuit against the Council on Environmental Quality (CEQ) to obtain information related to the preparation of a US Department of the Interior report on federal oil and gas leasing and its climate impacts. FOE claimed the report, directed by President Biden and released in November 2021, was inadequate and possibly altered due to political pressure. The FOIA request sought records, including communications between the CEQ, the White House and other agencies. After receiving the records, FOE agreed to dismiss the lawsuit in November 2023, following a settlement on the merits and attorneys' fees.[175]

Case name:

Massachusetts v Environmental Protection Agency, 549 U.S. 497 (2007)

Summary:

The 2007 Supreme Court decision in *Massachusetts v EPA*[176] established that greenhouse gases (GHGs) qualify as air pollutants under the Clean Air Act, allowing the EPA to regulate these emissions. This decision was welcomed by climate change advocates as it confirmed the importance of addressing global climate change. However, the regulation of GHGs following this decision faced numerous challenges. The EPA's efforts have often been delayed or struck down in courts, and international progress has also stopped. The decision has played a significant role in the US response to climate change, but it has not been entirely successful in achieving its goals.

Despite this, the EPA has managed to reduce some GHG emissions, and *Massachusetts v EPA* has left the regulatory system better than before. However, the decision has also closed other routes to abating GHG emissions under federal and state common law. The doctrines of displacement and pre-emption have limited the ability of private parties to challenge GHG emissions using common law. This has left few viable legal routes for addressing these emissions, and the lacklustre progress on climate change since the decision highlights the need for more effective solutions.

175 See further, https://climatecasechart.com/wp-content/uploads/case-documents/2023/20231130_docket-122-cv-001128_stipulation.pdf

176 See https://www.epa.gov/climate-change/endangerment-and-cause-or-contribute-findings-greenhouse-gases-under-section-202a

Case name:

Sackett v Environmental Protection Agency, 598 U.S. 651 (2023)[177]

Summary:

Micheal and Chantell Sackett ran an excavation company that wanted to develop a property several hundred feet from Priest Lake, a popular vacation site in the Idaho Panhandle. Sackett began backfilling an Idaho lot with gravel to build a home. The Environmental Protection Agency (EPA), in response to a neighbour's complaint, halted the work and informed Sackett that the property contained federally protected wetlands and that the backfilling violated the Clean Water Act (CWA), which prohibits discharging pollutants into 'the waters of the United States,' 33 U.S.C. § 1362(7).

The EPA ordered Sackett remove the gravel and stop any further construction without a permit. The EPA threatened penalties of over $40,000 per day.

The EPA classified the Sackett wetlands as 'waters of the United States' because they were near a ditch that fed into a creek, which fed into Priest Lake, a navigable, intrastate lake.

The Sacketts sued in 2008 and the case made its way through the federal courts system for the next 14 years. The lawyers argued that the wetland the Sacketts had filled was not a protected 'water of the united States' merely because there was a dry land between it and other bodies of water and so wasn't subject to EPA regulation.

The CWA has, since 1972, had an essential role in protecting the country's diverse array of aquatic environments from pollution and keeping them safe for fishing, swimming, wildlife and drinking. The Act has also been the target of polluters and developers who would like to limit its regulatory scope. One area focused on is the phrase 'waters of the United States' (WOTUS). The phrase refers to the many different bodies of water to be found within the geographical borders of the nation.

The Ninth Circuit affirmed summary judgment in favour of the EPA. However, the Supreme Court reversed this decision. CWA jurisdiction over an adjacent wetland requires that the adjacent body of water constitutes waters of the US (a relatively permanent body of water connected to traditional interstate navigable waters) and a continuous surface connection between the wetland and that water, making it difficult to determine where the 'water' ends and the 'wetland' begins.

The Court reviewed the history of judicial interpretation of 'the waters of the United States' and enforcement by federal agencies, which argued that the significant-nexus test was sufficient to establish jurisdiction over 'adjacent' wetlands. Under that test, nearly all waters and wetlands are potentially susceptible to regulation, 'putting a staggering array of landowners at risk of criminal prosecution for such mundane activities as moving dirt'. The CWA's use

177 *Sackett v EPA*, 598 U.S. 651 (2023), https://www.supremecourt.gov/opinions/22pdf/21-454_4g15.pdf

of 'waters' encompasses only relatively permanent, standing, or continuously flowing bodies, ordinarily called streams, oceans, rivers, and lakes. Wetlands qualify as 'waters of the United States' only if 'indistinguishable from waters of the United States,' having a continuous surface connection to bodies that are waters of the United States in their own right, with no clear demarcation between waters and wetlands.

Index

[all references are to paragraph number]

www.ingramcontent.com/pod-product-compliance
Ingram Content Group UK Ltd.
Pitfield, Milton Keynes, MK11 3LW, UK
UKHW051449290926
15471UKWH00008B/1095

9 781526 531452